The Pirates Reader

THE
PIRATES
READER

EDITED BY

RICHARD PETERSON

University of Pittsburgh Press

Published by the University of Pittsburgh Press, Pittsburgh, Pa., 15260

Manufactured in the United States of America
Printed on acid-free paper
10 9 8 7 6 5 4 3 2 1
ISBN 0-8229-4199-6

Permissions and source information for each article appear at the bottom of the page
on which the article begins.

CONTENTS

The Greatest World Series Ever and the Damn Yankees

From Depression Baseball to Depressing Baseball

A Miracle Season and the End of an Era

The Pirates Reader

INTRODUCTION

So many of my memories of Pittsburgh in the late 1940s and early 1950s are of playing ball on grassless city fields and hitchhiking out to Forbes Field to watch the Pirates. The seasons of my youth on the South Side flowed by to the rhythm of games played with baseballs and bats held together with masking tape and nails and the sound of batting practice as I walked toward Forbes Field's towering white clay facade on a knothole Saturday afternoon. In the spring and summer I lived to play softball and baseball at Ormsby playground and Quarry Field and died watching the rinky-dink Pirates lose game after game. In the autumn I reluctantly turned to school yard football and followed the same old Steelers, then even more reluctantly followed minor-league hockey and college basketball, all the while yearning for the start of spring training and the beginning of another Pirate season.

Like the poet Donald Hall and countless other baseball Peter Pans, I also have strong memories of playing catch with my father, when we had time for each other, and going out to major-league games together. But I can't recall some perfect field-of-dreams moment of playing catch or summon from my past some Forbes Field epiphany when I suddenly realized if I didn't become a Pirate some day I'd end up a wino roaming the back alleys and river banks of Pittsburgh's South Side in search of my lost youth and bottles of deposit. Playing catch with my father or going out to Pirate games in the late 1940s gave me a chance to spend some time with a man who seldom had anything to say. Rather than cherished moments of magical exchanges and discoveries, my baseball memories of my father stand out because they were the times he was willing to talk about the few things that mattered to him.

On those occasions when my father offered to play catch, he'd gradually open up about his own boy's life on the South Side. As we tossed the ball back and forth, he'd talk about his good old days when, as the Bluetail Kid, he pitched for a Lithuanian team that went up and down the South Side playing against rival "Polacks, Hunkies, and Serbs." He told stories about his younger brother Tony, who was called Mustard Face because he loved mustard sandwiches as much as he loved baseball, and his older

Adapted from "Rinky Dinks and the Single Wing," by Richard Peterson, in *Pittsburgh Sports: Stories from the Steel City*, edited by Randy Roberts (Pittsburgh: University of Pittsburgh Press, 2000).

brother Joe, who was called Joky because he loved cards and dice more than playing ball. My father told me not to worry about being so damn short and skinny because he was puny looking in his own day. If I paid attention, I might learn a few things about throwing drops and in-shoots and maybe turn out some day to be a damn good pitcher like Rip Sewell or Murry Dickson or like Frankie Petrauskas was a long time ago.

On the occasions when my father took me out to Forbes Field in the late 1940s, he enjoyed talking about the great Pirate teams of the past because there wasn't much to cheer about when watching the Pirates of the present, except for a brief early run at the pennant in 1948. The Pirates were rapidly becoming my bumbling boys of summer, but at least for a while I had my father's stories of great Pittsburgh teams as proof that there was a time—maybe long ago, but a time—when ballplayers in a Pirate uniform could actually play baseball. There were stories about Fred Clarke's Pirates, who lost the first modern World Series in 1903 to Cy Young and the Boston Red Sox, though they were called the Pilgrims in those days. There were even better stories about the 1909 Pirates, who beat out Frank Chance, Mordecai "Three Finger" Brown, and the great Chicago Cubs for the National League pennant and won the World Series against the Detroit Tigers. It was fun hearing my father talk about Honus Wagner, who ran circles around Ty Cobb, and about a rookie pitcher named Babe Adams, who won all three of his starts, including a shutout in the seventh game, to give Pittsburgh its first World Series championship in the very first year the Pirates played baseball at Forbes Field.

All that was before my father's time, but not the Pirates of 1925, of Pie Traynor, Max Carey, and Glenn Wright. This was my father's team, the team that played its way past John McGraw's New York Giants into the World Series against the defending champion Washington Senators. Branded cowards by fans and the press after losing three of the first four games, my father's Pirates made baseball history by coming back and beating the great Walter Johnson in the seventh and deciding game of the World Series on Kiki Cuyler's bases-loaded, ground-rule double in the cold, rain, and fog at Forbes Field. Two years later, even with Paul and Lloyd Waner in the outfield, the Pirates lost the World Series in four straight games, but that was against the New York Yankees and Murderer's Row.

Though Forbes Field went the way of the wrecking ball after Bill Mazeroski recorded the last out of the last game on June 28, 1970, I can still see the mammoth, aging ballpark and still hear my father urging me to take it all in, as if it were the eighth wonder of the world. In his eyes it was the biggest, best damn looking ballpark in baseball. To get a sense of its beauty, he'd tell me to look out at the Pitt Cathedral looming majestically behind the left-field bleachers or at the trees in Schenley Park surrounding the red-bricked outfield wall. To get a feel for its size, he'd point at the towering scoreboard topped by the Gruen clock, at the deep recesses in center field, and at the iron gates in right-center field where fans could walk out of the ballpark at the end of the game. He'd tell me to look around at the massive steel and concrete grandstands, double-decked in right field and triple-decked behind home plate where the crow's nest still sat as a sad reminder of the year Gabby Hartnett hit the home run that cost the Pirates the 1938 pennant and broke my father's heart.

Forbes Field wasn't some bandbox like Ebbets Field with cheap signs all over the place or the Polo Grounds with its ridiculous cigar shape and "Chinese" home runs down the lines. My father wasn't happy when they put in the Greenberg Gardens and shortened left field by thirty feet, but Forbes Field still had plenty of room for Rosey Rowswell's doozie-marooneys, for doubles down the lines and triples in the alleys. Center field was still so deep that the ground crew rolled the batting cage out to the 457 mark and it rarely interfered with a game. And even when Barney Dreyfuss, the Pirate owner who built Forbes Field, had to shorten right field for a new grandstand, he put up a high screen down the right-field line to prevent cheap home runs. Forbes Field wasn't built for home-run hitters—that's why they put the Greenberg Gardens out there in 1947 for Hank Greenberg and Ralph Kiner—but the ballpark was a line-drive hitter's paradise with all its open space. No pitcher, not Babe Adams or Wilbur Cooper, not Dizzy Dean or Carl Hubbell, had ever pitched a no-hitter at Forbes Field and, as far as my father was concerned, no pitcher ever would.

I'm glad my father had his proud memories of Pirates past, because, when I looked down with him from the bleachers or the grandstands at Forbes Field, we saw a Pirate team on its way to becoming one of the worst in baseball. It was a good thing that my father quit going to games with me after I was old enough to get out to Oakland by myself because by the 1950s, the Pirates were the joke of the National League. After finishing last in 1950, the Pirates, like Stalin's Soviet Union, embarked on a five-year plan that doomed Pittsburgh fans to an emotional Siberia. With the fabled and controversial Branch Rickey as the baseball mastermind, the Pirates came in next to last in 1951, Rickey's first year in Pittsburgh, then finished dead last for the next four years. Desperate for success after being forced out of Brooklyn, Rickey was ready to trade anyone to any team willing to deal with him. He got rid of popular players like pitcher Cliff Chambers, infielder George Strickland, and outfielders Wally Westlake and Gus Bell for the likes of bespectacled Dick Cole, who should have worn his glove on his shin, prematurely bald Joe Garagiola, who discovered in last-place Pittsburgh that "baseball is a funny game," and banjo-hitting Johnny Berardino, who parlayed a trip to the Pirates minor-league Hollywood Stars into a successful acting career in television soap operas.

In 1952 I was a die-hard, thirteen-year-old, knothole-gang witness to a Pirate team that was so awful it became the stuff of legend. One of baseball's all-time disasters, the 1952 Pirates, Rickey's infamous rinky dinks, ended the season a whopping 22½ games out of seventh place with a record of 42-112. My poor idol Murry Dickson lost twenty-one games as the leader of a staff that used up twenty pitchers, fourteen of them, including minor-league strikeout phenom Ron Necciai, finishing a collective 5-38 for the year. The twenty-six position players included two nineteen-year-old rookies fresh out of Pittsburgh high schools. First baseman Tony Bartirome, destined to become a Pirate trainer after lasting one year in the major leagues, and center fielder Bobby Del Greco, whom I played softball against in the Greater Pittsburgh League a decade later, combined for one home run and hit .217 and .200 respectively for a team so terrible Joe Garagiola described them as a ninth-place ball club in an eight-team league.

The only bright spot for the Pirates in 1952 was a sore spot for Branch Rickey, who had a much-deserved reputation for being a tightwad when it came to paying veteran players. Ralph Kiner's home runs may have been the reason a handful of sorrowful Pirates fans still came out to Forbes Field, but Rickey didn't see it that way. The Pirates finished last in 1952 with Kiner and his $90,000 salary and they could damn well finish last in 1953 without him. Rickey's solution was to offer Kiner to Chicago in a ten-player deal that included Garagiola and two other Pirates for six Cubs—five were ex-Dodger farm hands—and $150,000.

On June 4, 1953, when Rosey Rowswell sent word of the Kiner trade out over the radio just before the Pirates and the Cubs were scheduled to play a Ladies' Day matinee, I felt betrayed by Rickey. Growing up in a working-class neighborhood, I saw Kiner as a baseball god. Short and skinny, I dreamed that someday I might become a Murry Dickson, but Ruth-like Kiner was beyond my baseball fantasies. Like my baseball buddies, I cocked my right elbow at the plate and swung with an uppercut, but we knew that Kiner's towering home runs were the stuff of the Mighty Casey and Ozark Ike. Playing in a shot-and-a-beer, steel-mill town, Kiner was strictly Hollywood. Saying Fords were for singles hitters, he drove Cadillacs, dated starlets, including Elizabeth Taylor, and eventually married tennis professional Nancy Chaffee, who paraded around decaying Forbes Field with her leashed Afghan hounds.

If baseball in the 1950s had a Shakespeare looking to write about a star-crossed team, he could have turned to the Pirates and found plenty of material. Before and after the Kiner trade, the Pirates were the stuff of theater, though mostly low comedy. They even became the subject of a 1951 Hollywood movie called *Angels in the Outfield* in which a hapless Pirate team, led by a foul-mouthed, brawling manager played by Paul Douglas, becomes a pennant winner when the angelic spirits of baseball greats descend upon Forbes Field to help win games as long as the manager keeps his temper.

With no angels in the outfield or anywhere else, my most vivid memories of Rickey's Pirates, as they finished last in 1953 without Kiner and last again in 1954 and 1955, are of inept players and ridiculous plays. There were all those bonus babies and rookie phenoms who should have been arrested for indecent exposure after putting on big-league uniforms. The Pirates signed the basketball All-American O'Brien twins, who flopped badly, and acquired the brothers Freese, who also failed to double the pleasure of Pirate fans. When not signing teenagers, Rickey picked up aging veterans better suited for an old-timers game, like ex-Yankee slugger Johnny Lindell, who was trying to hang on, without much success, as a knuckleball pitcher, and ex-Yankee World Series hero Joe Page, who had a 11.17 earned run average in his one hazy season with the Pirates. Even when the Pirates finally crossed baseball's color line and signed African Americans, the players turned out mediocre at best. While other teams had future Hall of Famers like Jackie Robinson, Larry Doby, and Willie Mays, we had Curt Roberts.

While my father grew up watching Hall of Famers Pie Traynor, Max Carey, and the Waner brothers, I'm stuck with vivid nightmares of Gene Freese doing his best impression of Fred Merkle by failing to run down and touch second base on what should have been a game-winning hit against the Phillies; of Tommy Saffell, in an opening-day game against the Dodgers, turning to play a ball off the outfield wall as the ball landed beside him; and of Danny Kravitz, who couldn't catch a foul pop up behind home plate without a catcher's mitt glued to the top of his head. I listened to Rosey Rowswell re-create Pirate road losses from ticker-tape accounts of the games, and, on one unforgettable occasion, after high-school baseball practice, heard Bob Prince describe, in a voice of disbelief, the last inning of a game from Wrigley Field in which Sad Sam Jones completed a no-hitter against the Pirates by walking the first three batters, then striking out Dick Groat, Roberto Clemente, and Frank Thomas to end the game.

After graduating from high school in 1956, I spent the next few years playing sandlot baseball and bumming my way through temporary jobs and unemployment lines. The Pirates, when I needed it the most, finally gave me something to cheer about. In the late 1950s, with Roberto Clemente, drafted by Rickey out of the Dodger farm system, and Dick Groat, another of Rickey's basketball All-Americans, emerging as stars, and young pitchers like Vernon Law, Bob Friend, and Roy Face surviving earlier beatings, the Pirates became a good team. When they added nineteen-year-old rookie Bill Mazeroski, traded Dick Littlefield and Bobby Del Greco for Rookie of the Year Bill Virdon, and gave up hometown hero Frank Thomas for Don Hoak, Harvey Haddix, and Smoky Burgess, they had the nucleus for a championship team.

With a residue of the few decent players to survive the Rickey years, supplemented by the good trades made by Rickey's successor, Joe L. Brown (appropriately enough for the Pirates, the son of the famous comedian Joe E. Brown), the Pirates, after nearly a decade of finishing last or next to last, made a run for the National League pennant in 1958 before finishing in second place. They fell back to fourth place in 1959, then won the pennant in 1960, their first in thirty-three years, and beat Casey Stengel's heavily favored Yankees on Mazeroski's dramatic home run after an improbable World Series of close Pirate wins and lopsided losses. In the fall of 1960, I snaked and danced my way through Pittsburgh's downtown streets in celebration of the Pirate victory, but by the next fall I was off to Edinboro State College and the Pirates were back in the doldrums.

By the time things finally turned completely around for the Pirates in the 1970s, I'd taken a teaching position at Southern Illinois University and was a Pittsburgh sports fan in exile. I watched the Pirates on WGN out of Chicago, WTBS out of Atlanta, and KPLR out of St. Louis, or tried to listen to a fading and crackling KDKA at night as they played their way to two dramatic World Series victories in 1971 and 1979. The irony, however, of watching the Pirates on television is that the great Pirate teams of the 1970s loom small in my mind's eye, mere reflections of the television screen. But, because I grew up with Pittsburgh sports in the 1950s, those Pirate rinky dinks still seem as large as life, though the memories are often painful. In a way, they even appear larger than life in my memories. They were the closest thing I had to heroes in an otherwise drab blue-collar world. They played out their follies at a magnificent ballpark, at one time a symbol of civic pride, but now just a Pittsburgh sports memory. They gave me pride and hope, no matter how foolish and misguided, because they were my Pirates. No matter how often they disappointed and angered me, they still deserved my loyalty and love because they were all I had. I was thrilled with the World Series wins in the 1970s and the magnificent play of Roberto Clemente and Willie Stargell, but my strongest emotions and memories still belong to those bumbling Pirates.

After thirty years of exile, I relish my trips back to my hometown, but, because of my close identification with the Pirates, emotionally I never left. Thanks to those misfit teams of Branch Rickey, I still feel a deep loyalty and pride in the city of my youth. I hate to lose, but, win or lose, the Pirates were the one certainty I had in a life of working-class uncertainties. No matter how unhappy or confused or inferior I felt, I could always go out to the ballpark. And no matter how many times I watched the Pirates lose, there was always that hope that this time they were going to win. The ballpark in Pittsburgh is different today, but my loyalty is exactly the same.

The Pirates Reader is a tribute to Pirate fans everywhere and to the rich tapestry of Pirate history, where heroes, worthy of statues, have led the Pirates to glorious victories and, at times, endured painful defeats. It is also a celebration of baseball's great storytellers. There are early pioneers of baseball journalism, such as Henry Chadwick, the father of baseball statistics, and Alfred H. Spink, founder of *The Sporting News*. Hall of Fame writer Fred Lieb profiles Honus Wagner, arguably the greatest ball player who ever wore a Pirate uniform, while the legendary Ring Lardner trumpets the Pirates' first World Series championship and later has fun with the 1927 World Series. Later generations of gifted writers have their own Pirate stories to tell—Roger Angell explores the mystery surrounding Steve Blass's sudden inability to throw strikes, Eliot Asinof interviews the incomparable Willie Stargell, and George Will uniquely portrays Pirate relief pitcher Jim Gott. Pittsburgh's own legendary sportswriters are also well represented in *The Pirates Reader*. The contributors range through the decades and include John H. Gruber, the Pirates' first official scorer, Ralph S. Davis, the first dean of Pittsburgh sportswriters, the legendary Myron Cope, who gets inside the miraculous season of 1960, and Les Biederman, who celebrates its remarkable outcome.

The storytelling begins with the poetry and magic of baseball. This prelude is comprised of moments drawn from the 1970s, perhaps the Pirates' most triumphant and tragic decade. After that, *The Pirates Reader* goes back to the modest beginnings of professional baseball in Pittsburgh and the ballplayer who gave the Pirates their team name, and journeys through the many exciting and entertaining events and personalities in Pirates history, arriving finally at the grand opening of a new ballpark and the induction into the Hall of Fame of the Pirate hero who gave Pittsburgh its most dramatic moment in baseball.

After the stories of the Pirates' wonderful history come to an end, *The Pirates Reader* offers the only encore possible, a return to that perfect moment at 3:36 P.M. on October 13, 1960, when Bill Mazeroski, with one swing of the bat, filled a city and its fans with the spirit of joyful celebration and reminded all of us that baseball's playing field is where dreams still come true, if you keep faith in the team of your youthful dreams.

Writing Baseball

Walt Whitman once said of baseball, "It's our game . . . America's game: has the snap, go, fling, of the American atmosphere—belongs as much to our institutions, fits into them as significantly, as our constitutions, laws: is just as important in the sum total of our historic life." Poets have long been fascinated by baseball—Whitman, Robert Frost, Marianne Moore, William Carlos Williams, to name a few. But perhaps no one has expressed a love for the national pastime so extensively and lyrically as has the much-honored poet Donald Hall. In his books and essays, he has created a perfect field where fathers play catch with their sons and the timeless, circular quality of the game unites amateur ballplayers from baseball's earliest history with the present generation of professional millionaires.

Hall's interest in the Pittsburgh Pirates began in 1973, when, to gather material for a book, he and a small group of friends participated in the Pirate spring training camp. Their experiences produced the collection Playing Around, *published in 1974. Hall's own fascination and eventual friendship with Pirate pitcher Dock Ellis, "maverick citizen in the country of baseball," inspired him to write* Dock Ellis in the Country of Baseball, *first published in 1976. This first chapter is one of Hall's most lyrical celebrations of baseball as generative and cyclical, yet somehow transcendental and transformative as well.*

The Country of Baseball

DONALD HALL

Baseball is a country all to itself. It is an old country, like Ruritania, northwest of Bohemia and its seacoast. Steam locomotives puff across trestles and through tunnels. It is a wrong-end-of-the-telescope country, like the landscape people build for model trains, miniature with distance and old age. The citizens wear baggy pinstripes, knickers, and caps. Seasons and teams shift, blur into each other, change radically or appear to change, and restore themselves to old ways again. Citizens retire to farms, in the country of baseball, smoke cigars and reminisce, and all at once they are young players again, lean and intense, running the base paths with filed spikes.

Or they stay in the city, in the capital of the country of baseball. At the mouth of the river, in the city of baseball, young black men wear purple leather maxicoats when they leave the ball park. Slick dressers of the twenties part their hair in the middle and drive roadsters. In old *barrios* everyone speaks Spanish. Kids playing stickball, and kids running away from cops, change into fierce adults rounding third base in front of fifty thousand people, and change again into old men in their undershirts on front stoops.

Though the grass transforms itself into a plastic rug, though the players speak Arkansas or Japanese, though the radio adds itself to the newspaper, and the television to the radio, though salaries grow from workingmen's wages to lawyers' compensations, the country remains the same; everything changes, and everything stays the same.

The players are white and black, Cuban and Welsh and Mississippi farmers. The country of baseball is polyglot. They wear great mustaches and swing bottle-shaped bats, and some of them dress eccentrically. John McGraw's Giants play two World Series wearing black uniforms. Now the citizens' hair shortens, their loose uniforms turn white, their faces turn white also, and the white world cheers—while on the other side of town, black crowds cheer black ballplayers. Now the hair returns—beards, handlebar mustaches, long locks hanging beside the catcher's mask; now brightly colored knickers cling close to thick legs; now bats are scooped out at the thick end; now black and white play together again.

In the country of baseball, the magistrates are austere and plain-spoken. Many of its citizens are decent and law-abiding, obedient to their elders and to the rules of the community.

But there have always been others—the mavericks, the eccentrics, the citizens of independent mind. They thrive in the country of baseball. Some of them display with Lucifer the motto, "I will not serve." Some of them are known as flakes, and unless they are especially talented bounce from club to club, to retire from the active life sooner than the others. Left-handed pitchers are reputed to be craziest of all, followed by pitchers in general, and left-handers in general. Maybe forty percent of the population in the country of baseball is flaky, at least in the opinion of the other sixty percent.

When Al Hrabosky meditates hate, in his public solitude behind the St. Louis mound, he perpetuates a great tradition.

The country of baseball begins to take shape at the age of six. Earlier, sometimes. Dock Ellis's cousin gave him a baseball to hold when Dock was in his crib. But Little League starts at six and stickball and cowpastureball at about the same age. At seven and eight and nine, the players begin to reside wholly in the country of baseball. For the people who will live there forever, the long summers take on form—time and space shaped by the sharp lozenge of the base paths. Then high school, maybe college, maybe rookie league, Class A, Double A, Triple A—the major leagues. In the brief season of maturity, the citizens of this country live in hotels, watch movies, pick up women who lurk for them in lobbies, sign autographs for kids, and climb onto the team bus for the ride to the ball park at five in the afternoon.

In their brief season, they sit for a thousand afternoons in front of their lockers, pull on archaic stockings, set their knickers at the height they affect, and josh and tease their teammates. Tony the trainer measures a tender elbow, tapes an ankle. Then the citizens saunter without urgency onto the field, gloves under arms, and pick up a ball.

Richie Hebner sees Richie Zisk. "Hey," he says, "want to play catch?"

Baseball, they tell us, is part of the entertainment industry.

Well, money changes hands; lawyers make big money; television people and their sponsors make big money. Even the citizens make big money for a while. But like actors and magicians and country singers and poets and ballet dancers, when the citizens claim to be in it for the money, they are only trying to be normal Americans. Nothing is further from the country of baseball than the business life. Although salaries grow and contract clauses multiply, the business of baseball like the business of art is dream.

In the cardboard box business, a boss's expectations rise like a plateau gradually elevated, an infinite ramp leading to retirement on the ghost plains of Arizona. And in the country of cardboard boxes, the manners of Rotary proliferate: the false laughter, the bonhomie of contracts, the golf played with boss's boss. Few flakes survive, in the country of cardboard boxes.

But in the country of baseball, men rise to glory in their twenties and their early thirties—a garland briefer than a girl's, or at least briefer than a young woman's—with an abrupt rise, like scaling a cliff, and then the long meadow slopes downward. Citizens of the country of baseball retire and yet they never retire. At first it may seem that they lose everything—the attention of crowds, the bustle of airplanes and hotels, the kids and the girls—but as they wake from their first shock, they discover that they live in the same place, but that they live in continual twilight, paler and fainter than the noon of games.

Dock visits an old friend, Alvin O'Neal McBean, retired to his home in the Virgin Islands. In the major leagues, McBean was *bad*. The language of Rotary does not flourish in locker rooms or dugouts; the citizens' speech does not resemble the honey-tongued *Reader's Digest*; eccentricity breeds with outrage. "McBean would as soon curse you as look at you," Dock says—even if you were his manager or his general manager; and he could *scream*. He was therefore not long for the major leagues. Now Alvin O'Neal McBean supervises playgrounds, the old ballplayer teaching the kids old tricks, far from reporters, umpires, and Cadillacs. "He's made the Adjustment," says Dock. "He doesn't *like* it, but he's made the Adjustment."

The years on the diamond are fantasy. The citizens *know* they live in fantasy, that the custom cars and the stewardesses and the two-inch-thick steaks belong to the world of glass slippers and golden coaches drawn by unicorns. Their fathers were farmers and one day they will be farmers also. Or their fathers loaded crates on boxcars for a hundred dollars a week and one day they too will load crates on boxcars for a hundred dollars a week. Just now, they are pulling down two thousand.

But for them, the fantasy does not end like waking from a dream or like a transformation on the stroke of midnight. They make the Adjustment, and gradually they understand that even at a hundred dollars a week, or even on top of a tractor, they live in a crepuscular duplicate of their old country.

And most of them, whatever the thought, never do just what their fathers did. When they make the Adjustment, they sell insurance or real estate to their former fans, or they open a bar in the Missouri town they came from. They buy a restaurant next to a bowling alley in their old Oakland neighborhood, and they turn paunchy, and tilt a chair back behind the cash register, remembering—while they compute insurance, while they pull draft beer—the afternoons of August and the cold September nights under the blue lights, the pennant race at the end of the dying season.

The country of baseball never wholly vanishes for anyone once a citizen of that country. On porches in the country of baseball old men are talking. Scouts, coaches, managers; car salesmen, manufactures' representatives, bartenders. No one would let them exile themselves from that country if they wanted to. For the kids with their skateboards, for the men at the Elks, they remain figures of youth and indolent energy, alert at the plate while the pitcher fidgets at the mound—a young body always glimpsed like a shadow within the heavy shape of the old body.

The old first baseman, making the final out of the inning, in the last year he will play, underhands the ball casually toward the mound, as he has done ten thousand times. The ball bounces over the lip of the grass, climbs the crushed red brick of the mound for a foot or two, and then rolls back until it catches in the green verge. The ball has done this ten thousand times.

Basketball is not a country. It's a show, a circus, a miracle continually demonstrating the Newtonian heresy that muscle is lighter than air, bodies suspended like photographs of bodies, the ball turning at right angles. When the game is over, basketball does not continue; basketball waits poised and immobile in the locked equipment room, like the mechanical toy waiting for a hand to wind it.

Football is not a country. It's a psychodrama, brothers beating up on brothers, murderous, bitter, tender, homosexual, ending with the incest of brotherly love, and in the wounds Americans carry all over their bodies. When the game is done, football dragasses itself to a bar and drinks blended whiskey, maybe seven and seven, brooding, its mouth sour, turned down, its belly flowing over its angry belt.

In the country of baseball days are always the same.

The pitchers hit. Bunting, slapping weakly at fat pitches, hitting line drives that collapse in front of the pitching machine, they tease each other. Ken Brett, with the fireplug body, lifts one over the center-field fence, as the big hitters emerge from the dugout for the honest BP. "Did you see *that*?" he asks Wilver Stargell. "Did you see *that*?" he asks Al Oliver.

The pitcher who won the ball game last night lifts fungoes to a crowd in left field—outfielders, utility infielders, even pitchers who pause to shag flies in the midst of running. When they catch a ball, they throw it back to the infield by stages, lazy arcs linking outfielders to young relief pitchers to coaches. Everyone is light and goofy, hitting fungoes or shagging flies or relaying the ball. Everyone is relaxed and slightly self-conscious, repeating the motions that became rote before they were ten. Some of the citizens make catches behind their backs, or throw the ball from between their legs. Behind the mound, where a coach begins to throw BP to the regulars, Paul Popovich and Bob Moose pick up loose baseballs rolled toward the mound, and stack them in the basket where the BP pitcher retrieves three at a time. Now they bounce baseballs on the cement-hard turf, dribbling them like basketballs. Moose dribbles, fakes left, darts right, jumps, and over Popovich's jumping body sinks a baseball in a wire basket for a quick two points.

Coaches slap grounders to infielders, two deep at every position. Third, short, second, first, a bunt for the catcher. The ball snarls around the horn. Third, short, second, first, catcher. At the same time, the rubber arm of the BP pitcher stretches toward the plate, where Bob Robertson takes his turn at bat. Two balls at once bounce toward Rennie Stennett at second. A rookie up from Charleston takes his cuts, and a shortstop jabs at a grounder from Bob Skinner, and Manny Sanguillen leaps to capture a bunt, and the ball hums across the field, and Willie Stargell lofts an immense fly to center field. Behind the cage, Bill Robinson yells at Stargell, "Buggy-whipping, man! Buggy-whipping!"

Stargell looks up while the pitcher loads himself with balls, and sees that Joe Garagiola is watching him. Tonight is Monday night. "Hey, man," he says slowly. "What are the rules of this bubble gum contest?" He whips his bat forward, takes a cut, tops the ball, grimaces. Willie has two fractured ribs from a ball thrown by a forty-one-year-old Philadelphia relief pitcher. Philadelphia is trying to catch Pittsburgh and lead the Eastern Division.

"What rules?" says Garagiola. "I don't have them with me."

Willie whips his bat forward with accelerating force. "How many pieces?" He hits a line drive off the right-field wall.

Garagiola shrugs. "Four or five," he says. "Something like that." He laughs, his laugh a little forced, as if he felt suddenly foolish. "Got to have a little fun in this game."

Nearer to game time, with the pitchers running in the outfield, the screens gone from the infield, five Pirates are playing pepper between the dugout and the first-base line. Dave Giusti holds the bat, and fielding are Ramon Hernandez, John Morlan, and Daryl Patterson. Giusti hits miniature line drives back at the other relief pitchers. Everyone laughs, taunts, teases. Giusti hits one harder than usual at Hernandez. Another. The ambidextrous Puerto Rican—who tried pitching with both arms in the same inning until they stopped him; who pitches from the left side now, and strikes out the left-handed pinch hitter in the ninth inning—Ramon drops his glove, picks up a baseball in each hand, winds up both arms as he faces Giusti head on, and fires two baseballs simultaneously. Giusti swings laughing and misses them both.

In the outfield, big number seventeen lopes with long strides, then idles talking to fans near the bullpen for ten minutes, then fields grounders at second base, says something to make Willie Stargell laugh, and walks toward the dugout. Seeing Manny Sanguillen talk with Dave Conccpcion and Pedro Borbon, soft Spanish fraternization with the enemy, he throws a baseball medium fast to hit Manny in the flesh of his thigh. Manny jumps, looks around, sees who it is, laughs, and runs with gentle menace toward him. But Dock has turned his back, and leans on his folded arms at the top of the dugout, scanning the crowd for friends and for ladies, his high ass angled up like a dragster, his big handsome head solemnly swiveling over the box seats—bad Dock Ellis, black, famous for his big mouth, suspended in 1975 for a month without pay, the suspension rescinded and pay restored, Dock, famous for his Bad Attitude, maverick citizen in the country of baseball.

At Old Timer's Day in Cincinnati, Edd Roush is an honorary captain, who hit .325 in the Federal League in 1914, .352 in the National League in 1921, and played eighteen years. Lou Boudreau plays shortstop. His gut is huge, but he breaks quickly to his left and scoops a grounder from the bat of Pee Wee Reese, and throws to Mickey Vernon at first. I saw Lou Boudreau, player-manager for Cleveland, hit two home runs leading his team at Fenway Park in the one-game American League pennant play off in 1948. I discovered Pee Wee Reese eight years earlier, when I was twelve, and the soft voice of Red Barber on WOR chatted about the new shortstop up from the Louisville Colonels. Joe Nuxhall pitches, who pitched in the major leagues when he was fifteen years old, and still pitches batting practice for the Cincinnati Reds. And Carl Erskine pitches, and Harvey Haddix. Harvey Kuenn comes to the plate, and then Dixie Walker—who played right field for the Brooklyn Dodgers, and confessed to Mr. Rickey in the spring of 1947 that he could not play with a black man. Dixie Walker flies out to a citizen who retired last year, still limber as a squirrel, playing center field again—Willie Mays.

In the country of baseball, time is the air we breathe, and the wind swirls us backward and forward, until we seem so reckoned in time and seasons that all time and all seasons become the same. Ted Williams goes fishing, never to return to the ball park, and falls asleep at night in the Maine summers listening to the Red Sox on radio from Fenway Park; and a ghostly Ted Williams continues to play the left-field wall, and his flat swing meets the ball in 1939, in 1948, in 1960. In the country of baseball the bat swings in its level swoop, the ball arcs upward into the twilight, the center fielder gathers himself beneath it, and *Dixie Walker flies out to Willie Mays.*

◆　◆　◆

ROBERTO CLEMENTE

W. P. Kinsella is best known for his first novel, Shoeless Joe, *published in 1982 and made into the Academy Award–nominated film,* Field of Dreams, *in 1989. Kinsella's baseball novels and short stories create a fabulous kingdom, where the dead and the living perform on the same diamonds, and baseball games are played beyond the boundaries of time and space.*

In "Searching for January," Kinsella turns to one of his favorite themes, the magic return of a tragically lost ballplayer for a brief moment seemingly outside of time. For baseball fans, but especially for Pirate fans who watched and admired the greatness of Roberto Clemente, Kinsella's story is a heartfelt reminder of the hopeless hope in the days following the tragic plane crash and the impossible dream of the return of a hero now regarded as larger than life. Better yet, Kinsella transports readers to a place, like Hall's country of baseball, where baseball heroes play forever on fields of memory and dreams.

Searching for January

W. P. KINSELLA

On December 31, 1972, Pittsburgh's all-star outfielder Roberto Clemente took off on a mercy flight taking clothing and medical supplies to Nicaraguan earthquake victims. Some time that night his plane went down in the ocean. His body was never recovered.

The sand is white as salt but powdery as icing sugar, cool on my bare feet, although if I push my toes down a few inches, yesterday's heat lurks, waiting to surface with the sun.

It is 6:00 A.M. and I am alone on a tropical beach a mile down from our hotel. The calm ocean is a clear, heart-breaking blue. Fifty yards out a few tendrils of sweet, gray fog laze above the water; farther out the mist, water, and pale morning sky merge.

It appears slowly out of the mist, like something from an Arthurian legend, a large, inflatable life raft, the depressing khaki and olive-drab of military camouflage. A man kneeling in the front directs the raft with a paddle. He waves when he sees me, stands up and calls out in an urgent voice, but I can't make it out. As the raft drifts closer I can see that the lone occupant is tall and athletic-looking, dark-skinned, with a long jaw and flashing eyes.

"Clemente!" is the first word I hear clearly. "I am Clemente! The baseball player. My plane went down. Days ago! Everyone must think I am dead."

What he says registers slowly. Clemente! It has been fifteen years. Is this some local fisherman playing a cruel joke on a tourist?

"Yes," I call back, after pausing too long, scanning his features again. There is no question: it is Roberto Clemente. "I believe everyone does think you're dead."

"We crashed on New Year's Eve," he said. "I'm the only one who survived."

He steps lithely into the water, pulls the raft up on the beach, tosses the paddle back into the raft.

"Five days I've been out there," he says. "Give or take a day. I sliced up the other paddle with my pocket knife, made a spear. Caught three fish. Never thought I'd enjoy eating raw fish. But I was so hungry they tasted like they were cooked. By the way, where am I?"

I tell him.

He thinks a minute.

"It's possible. We crashed at night on the way to Managua. The plane was carrying three times the weight it should have, but the need was so great. Supplies for the earthquake victims.

"You look so surprised," he says after a pause. "Have they called off the air search already, given us up for dead?" When I remain silent he continues. "Which way is your hotel? I must call my wife, she'll be so worried."

"I am surprised. More than surprised. You are Roberto Clemente, the baseball player?"

"Of course."

"You were lost at sea?"

"Until now."

"There's something not quite right."

"Like what?" says Clemente.

"Like what year do you think this is?"

"When we took off it was 1972, but New Year's Eve. We crashed in the ocean. It must be January fifth or sixth, maybe even the seventh, 1973. I haven't been gone so long that I'd lose track of the year."

"What if I told you that it was March 1987?"

"I'd laugh. Look at me! I'd be an old man in 1987. I'd be . . ."

"Fifty-two. Fifty-three in August."

"How do you know that?"

"I know a little about baseball. I was a fan of yours."

He smiles in spite of himself.

"Thank you. But 1987? Ha! And I don't like the way you said *was*. *Was* a fan of mine." He touches spread fingers to his chest. "These are the clothes I wore the night we crashed. Do I look like I've been wearing them for fifteen years? Is this fifteen-year growth of beard?" he asks, rubbing a hand across his stubbly chin. "A six-day beard would be my guess."

His eyes study me as if I were an umpire who just called an outside pitch strike three: my pale, tourist's skin, the slight stoop as if the weight of paradise is too much for me.

"Say, what are you doing out here alone at dawn?" Clemente says skeptically. "Are you escaped from somewhere?"

"No. But I think you may be. Believe me, it is 1987."

"Can't be. I can tell. I'm thirty-eight years old. I play baseball. See my World Series ring." He thrusts his hand toward me, the gold and diamonds glitter as the sun blushes above the horizon.

I dig frantically in my wallet. "Look!" I cry. "I'm from Seattle. Here's the 1987 Seattle Mariners schedule." I hold the pocket-sized schedule out for him to look at.

"Seattle doesn't have a team."

"They have a new franchise, since 1977. Toronto came in the same year. Read the schedule."

He studies it for a moment.

"It's crazy, man. I've only been gone a few days."

We sit down on the sand, and I show him everything in my wallet: my credit cards, an uncashed check, my driver's license, coins, and bills.

"Try to remember when your plane went down. Maybe there's a clue there."

We walk slowly in the direction of the hotel, but at the edge of the bay, where we would turn inland, Clemente stops. We retrace our steps.

"It was late in the night. The plane was old. It groaned and creaked like a haunted house. I was sitting back with the cargo—bales of clothes, medical supplies—when the pilot started yelling that we were losing altitude. We must have practically been in the water before he noticed. We hit the ocean a few seconds later, and I was buried under boxes and bales as the cargo shifted. A wooden box bounced off my head, and I was out for . . . a few seconds or a few minutes." He rubs the top of his head.

"See, I still got the lump. And I bled some, too." He bends toward me so I can see the small swelling, the residue of dried blood clinging around the roots of his sleek, black hair.

"When I woke up I was in front of the emergency door, the cargo had rolled over me and I was snug against the exit. The plane must have been more than half submerged. There was this frightening slurping, gurgling sound. Then I realized my clothes were wet. The raft was on the wall right next to the door. I pulled the door open and the ocean flooded in. I set out the raft, inflated it, and took the paddles and the big water canteen off the wall. I yelled for the others but I don't know if they were alive or if they heard me. There was a mountain of cargo between me and the front of the plane.

"I climbed into the raft, paddled a few yards, and when I looked back the plane was gone. I've been drifting for five or six days, and here I am."

"I don't know where you've been, but you went missing New Year's Eve 1972. They elected you to the Baseball Hall of Fame in 1973, waived the five-year waiting period because you'd died a hero."

"Died?" Clemente begins a laugh, then thinks better of it. "What if I go back with you and call in?"

"You'll create one of the greatest sensations of all time."

"But my wife, my family. Will they all be fifteen years older?"

"I'm afraid so."

"My kids grown up?"

"Yes."

"Maybe my wife has remarried?"

"I don't know, but it's certainly a possibility."

"But, look at me, I'm thirty-eight years old, strong as a bull. The Pirates need me in the outfield."

"I know."

"My teammates?"

"All retired."

"No."

"If I remember right, Bruce Kison was the last to go, retired last year."

"Willie Stargell?"

"Retired in 1982. He's still in baseball but not playing."

"Then I suppose everyone that played at the same time, they're gone too? Marichal? Seaver? Bench? McCovey? Brock? McCarver? Carlton?"

"Carlton's won over three hundred games, but he doesn't know when to quit. He's a marginal player in the American League. So is Don Sutton, though he's also won three hundred. Jerry Reuss is still hanging on, maybe one or two others. Hank Aaron broke Babe Ruth's home-run record, then a guy from Japan named Sadaharu Oh broke Hank Aaron's record."

"And my Pirates?"

"Gone to hell in a handbasket. They won the World Series in '79, Willie Stargell's last hurrah. They've been doormats for several seasons, will be again this year. Attendance is down to nothing; there's talk of moving the franchise out of Pittsburgh."

"They need Roberto Clemente."

"Indeed they do."

"And Nicaragua? The earthquake?"

"The earth wills out," I said. "The will of the people to survive is so strong. . . . The earthquake is history now."

"And Puerto Rico? Is my home a state yet?"

"Not yet."

He looks longingly toward the path that leads to the hotel and town. We sit for a long time in that sand white as a bridal gown. He studies the artifacts of my life. Finally he speaks.

"If I walk up that path, and if the world is as you say—and I think I believe you—I will become a curiosity. The media will swarm over me unlike anything I've ever known. Religious fanatics will picnic on my blood. If I see one more person, I'll have no choice but to stay here."

"What are your alternatives?"

"I could try to pass as an ordinary citizen who just happens to look like Roberto Clemente did fifteen years ago. But if I become real to the world I may suddenly find myself white-haired and in rags, fifty-three years old."

"What about baseball?"

"I could never play again. I would give myself away. No one plays the game like Clemente."

"I remember watching you play. When you ran for a fly ball it was like you traveled three feet above the grass, your feet never touching. 'He has invisible pillows of angel hair attached to his feet,' my wife said one night, 'that's how he glides across the outfield.'

"Perhaps you could go to the Mexican Leagues," I suggest. "Remember George Brunet, the pitcher? He's still pitching in the badlands and he's nearly fifty."

"I suffer from greed, my friend, from wanting to claim what is mine: my family, my home, my wealth. My choice is all or nothing."

"The nothing being?"

"To continue the search."

"But how?"

"I've searched a few days and already I've found 1987. Time has tricked me some way. Perhaps if I continue searching for January 1973, I'll find it."

"And if you don't?"

"Something closer then, a time I could accept, that would accept me."

"But what if this is all there is? What if you drift forever? What if you drift until you die?"

"I can't leap ahead in time. It's unnatural. I just can't."

"If you came back to baseball, Three Rivers Stadium would be full every night. You could make Pittsburgh a baseball city again. You'd have to put up with the media, the curious, the fanatics. But perhaps it's what you're destined to do."

"I am destined to be found, maybe even on this beach, but fifteen years in your past. I intend to be found. I'll keep searching for January."

He walked a few steps in the direction of the raft.

"Wait. I'll go and bring you supplies. I can be back in twenty minutes."

"No. I don't want to carry anything away from this time. I have five gallons of water, a bale of blankets to warm me at night, the ingenuity to catch food. Perhaps my footprints in the sand are already too much, who knows?"

He is wading in the clear water, already pushing the raft back into the ocean.

"If you find January . . . if the history I know is suddenly altered, I hope I went to see you play a few times. With you in the line-up the Pirates probably made it into the World Series in '74 and '75. They won their division those years, you know . . . you would have been the difference . . ."

I watch him drift. Trapped. Or am I trapped, here in 1987, while he, through some malfunction of the universe, is borne into timelessness? What if I were to accompany him?

"Wait!" I call. "There's something . . ."

But Clemente has already drifted beyond hearing. I watch as he paddles, his back broad and strong. Just as the mist is about to engulf him, as ocean, fog, and sky merge, he waves his oar once, holding it like a baseball bat, thrusting it at the soft, white sky.

From Backlots to Big Leagues: Pittsburgh's Early Baseball

William E. Benswanger, an insurance executive and patron of the arts, never wanted to be involved with the Pittsburgh baseball club, though he was an avid Pirate fan growing up. Pirate owner Barney Dreyfuss had trained his son Sammy to take over the ownership of the Pirates. But when Sammy died of pneumonia on February 19, 1931, at the age of thirty-six, a grief-stricken Dreyfuss turned to Benswanger, his son-in-law, for help. After Dreyfuss's death in 1932, his widow asked Benswanger to become president of the Pittsburgh Pirates. Despite his earlier reticence, Benswanger became a popular Pirate off-the-field leader and a repository for the history of baseball's earliest days.

The Dreyfuss family owned the Pirates for forty-six years, until, in 1946, it sold the club to a group of owners headed by Bing Crosby, Tom Johnson, Frank McKinney, and John Galbreath. Four months after the sale, Bill Benswanger talked about the early history of baseball in Pittsburgh with clarity and detail at a meeting of the Historical Society of Western Pennsylvania. He is not correct, however, in one detail of how the Pirates got their team name. The Philadelphia Athletics of the American Association had not disbanded after the Brotherhood of Players revolted against the reserve clause and formed the Players League in 1890. They were still alive in 1891 when they fought Pittsburgh for the rights to Louis Bierbauer after the collapse of the Players League.

Professional Baseball in Pittsburgh

WILLIAM E. BENSWANGER

Baseball is an informal game and must be discussed in an informal manner—even in its history. The game originated in 1839 at Cooperstown, New York, and today a baseball shrine stands in that town. Following the Civil War, the leading clubs in Pittsburgh were the Enterprise, Olympic, and Xantha teams. They played at the old Union Park in what was then the city of Allegheny. For a time the city was represented in the International League but for the most part baseball was independent and amateur in those days. In addition to competing with other strong clubs of this region, such as the Nashannicks of New Castle, the Braddocks, the Sewickleys and others, they also met major league opposition from time to time in exhibition games.

The first genuine professional, or salaried, club here made its bow with

"Professional Baseball in Pittsburgh," from *Western Pennsylvania Historical Magazine* 30, nos. 1 and 2 (March–June 1947). Reprinted by permission of the Western Pennsylvania Historical Society.

the organization of the Alleghenys on February 22, 1876, as a member of the International Association; and the Alleghenys defeated the Xanthas 7 to 3 at Union Park on April 15, 1876. The following year, 1877, witnessed the debut of Jimmy Galvin with the Alleghenys. He was the most famous of Pittsburgh's early pitchers and his brilliant career embraced the International League, the American Association, the National League and the Players' League. A high spot of his first professional season, about which the fans of that era grew excited, was his famous eighth-inning home run on May 2, 1878, which defeated pitcher Tommy Bond and the Boston Nationals, 1 to 0.

In 1878 all the old players left and the Alleghenys were reorganized to join the International League, only to disband on June 8 after playing just twenty-six games. For three years thereafter there was little baseball activity in Pittsburgh, except for the East Liberty Stars at their big field on Collins Avenue; the East End Gyms; the colored Keystone club; and a County League team.

In 1882 Pittsburgh made its major league start, beginning a career in top-flight baseball that has continued uninterruptedly through sixty-five consecutive seasons. That year the city became one of the charter members of the American Association then a major league. The league was organized here and the leading spirit was H. Denny McKnight, who was elected president of the league, in addition to being president of the Pittsburgh club. Al Pratt was the local manager in 1882 and for part of 1883, and when he resigned he was succeeded by Denny Mack, whose proper name was McGee. Later Mack was supplanted by Bob Ferguson, and on August 18, 1884, Ferguson gave way to Horace Phillips, who continued as manager until the city entered the National League.

In 1884 E. C. Converse, of the National Tube Company, succeeded McKnight as president of the club, which remained in the American Association for five years, from 1882 to 1886, inclusive, finishing fourth in 1882, seventh in 1883, tenth in 1884, third in 1885, and second in 1886. Prior to the season of 1885 the first big deal was consummated, when Pittsburgh purchased the star players of the Columbus club when that club withdrew from the American Association. The players brought here were pitcher Ed Morris, a mighty lefthander, who continued to reside here after his playing days, until the time of his death in 1937 at the age of seventy-eight; pitcher Frank Mountain; catchers Fred Carroll and Rudolph Kemmler; infielders Jocko Fields, Pop Smith, Billy Kuehne, and John Richmond; and outfielders Tom Brown and Fred Mann. (Incidentally, Morris helped the writer with Ralph Birkofer in training camp at San Bernardino, California, in 1935 and 1936.)

In addition, pitcher Jimmy Galvin came back from the Buffalo club. Other acquisitions were Hank O'Day, then a pitcher and later a leading umpire, from Toledo; and Peter Meegan, also a pitcher, from the Reading and Richmond clubs.

Two of the pitchers of that year had won places in baseball's then mythical Hall of Fame by pitching no-hit major league games. Galvin was one of the few to do it twice. Pitching for Buffalo on August 20, 1880, he won from Worcester, 1 to 0, and on August 4, 1884, he shut Detroit out without a hit and won, 18 to 0, still the most lopsided no-hit game in big league history. Pitching for Columbus on May 29, 1884, Morris shut Pittsburgh out without a hit and won, 5 to 0. Galvin, like Morris, continued to live in Pittsburgh. He died here in 1899. The only old Pittsburgh players retained for 1885 were catcher Doggy Miller and outfielder Charley Ecen. O'Day remained only one season and joined Washington in 1886.

After five years in the American Association, Pittsburgh entered the National League in 1887, obtaining the franchise relinquished by Kansas City. The league was then ten years old. So the season of 1946 was Pittsburgh's sixtieth consecutive year in the National League. Horace Phillips remained in charge of the club as manager, with William A. Nimick as president. The earlier American Association club had removed to Recreation Park in 1884, and it was in that park that Pittsburgh's first National League game was played on April 30, 1887, the locals defeating Chicago, 6 to 2, with Galvin pitching against the great John Clarkson, who shared with King Kelly the distinction of being the first player sold for as much as $10,000—an incredible figure in those days.

Nimick remained as president of the club until 1890. Phillips continued as manager until the 1889 season was under way, when he suffered a breakdown and was placed in a sanitarium, where he died a few years later. Edward Hanlon, then a Pittsburgh outfielder, later to win fame as manager of the three-time pennant winning Baltimore Orioles, Brooklyn Superbas and Cincinnati Reds, was appointed to succeed Phillips.

In 1890 the Brotherhood revolt led to the formation of the Players' League in a war against the National, with a club in Pittsburgh, playing at Exposition Park. The Pittsburgh Nationals were riddled by players jumping to the new league. Only two players remained loyal at the start, those being outfielder Billy Sunday, later a noted evangelist, and pitcher Bill Sowders, though catcher Miller and infielder Fred Dunlap changed their minds after jumping, and returned. Those who jumped were pitchers Galvin, Morris, Harry Staley, and Al Maul; catchers Carroll and Fields; infielders Jake Beckley, Kuehne, Deacon White, and Jack Rowe; and Hanlon.

It was a disastrous season for the riddled Nationals at Recreation Park, and J. Palmer O'Neil, who became president, was often hard pressed to keep the club off the financial rocks. Players were changed so frequently that no fewer than fifty were used during the season. The club won only 23 games while losing 113, a record that stood until Cleveland lost 134 in 1899. On Labor Day, Pittsburgh lost three games—in one day. Guy Hecker, a former Louisville pitcher, was manager of the ill-fated Pittsburgh club that year.

Peace followed the disbandment of the Players' League after the 1890 season, and there was a return to stability in 1891. Hanlon, Maul, Galvin, Staley, Beckley and Carroll returned to the Nationals, the others going elsewhere. A notable addition from another source was Connie Mack, for forty-six years head of the Philadelphia Athletics, but then one of the smartest and trickiest catchers in baseball. He was obtained from Buffalo in the Players' League, to which club he had jumped from Washington. Hanlon was reappointed manager on his return, but was deposed in August, to be succeeded by William H. McGunnigle, who had previously managed Brooklyn.

It was in 1891 that the Pittsburgh club got the nickname that has become a trademark. It was agreed that all players who had jumped to the Players' League should return to their old clubs in the National or American Association. The Philadelphia Athletics, of the American Association, had disbanded in the meantime, but the American Association, as a league, claimed that club's players. Through an oversight, the names of infielder Louis Bierbauer and outfielder Harry Stovey were omitted from the list of players claimed, whereupon Pittsburgh took Bierbauer and Boston signed Stovey. When the Association protested, the matter was referred to a board of arbitration, which upheld the action of the Pittsburgh and Boston clubs as being within legal baseball rights, and ruled that Bierbauer and Stovey had been free agents. The Association refused to accept the ruling, declared war on the National League, and withdrew from the National Agreement. The signing of Bierbauer by Pittsburgh was denounced as "an act of piracy." That led to Pittsburgh's being called the Pirates, a name that has stuck to this day.

With W. C. Temple (famous Temple Cup donor), Al Buckenberger, W. H. Watkins and W. W. Kerr holding the office of president in turn, and with frequent managerial changes in a series of pilots that included Buckenberger, Tom Burns, Connie Mack, Watkins, and Patsy Donovan, the Pittsburgh club continued on its way in the National League with varying fortunes, but with little real success, barring a second-place finish in 1893, until the big uplift resulted from the coming of Barney Dreyfuss and his Louisville stars, to merge with the local club and give Pittsburgh winning baseball in 1900. After the season of 1899, the National League, which had had twelve clubs, eliminated four and became an eight-club league. The same circuit as established in 1900 has existed to this day without change. Louisville was one of the clubs dropped and Mr. Dreyfuss merged his club with Pittsburgh, creating an unusually strong club, which won pennants in 1901, 1902, and 1903. Among the players who came from Louisville were Fred Clarke, Honus Wagner, Tommy Leach, Deacon Phillippe, Claude Ritchey, and Dummy Hoy. Among those already here were Sam Leever, Jack O'Connor, Fred Ely and Rube Waddell, whose home was at Butler.

Spring training became popular and with one or two exceptions Pittsburgh has trained in only three places–Hot Springs, Arkansas, Paso Robles, and San Bernardino, California. Many exciting experiences have seen their lot on these trips, such as the closing of the banks in 1933, with fifty people and three thousand miles from home; the California earthquake in 1933; the tornado in Mississippi in 1936; the floods in California and Nevada in 1938; and numerous mishaps with players through the years.

Such players as Whitey Alperman, Phil Lewis, Lew Moren, Hans Lobert, Frank Smith, and Steve Swetonic have been developed here, to say nothing of the greatest player of all, Honus Wagner, who hails from Carnegie.

Pittsburgh won league pennants, as stated above, in 1901, 1902, and 1903. In the latter year Mr. Dreyfuss challenged the Boston Americans to a post-season series and this became the World Series, now such a popular exhibition. League pennants were won again in 1909, the year in which Forbes Field was opened, 1925, and 1927; and world championships in 1909 and 1925. Sunday baseball made its debut in 1935; ladies' and children's days in 1932. When Forbes Field was built, it was the first of the modern steel and concrete structures and was a wonder to the public. The answer has been given as to whether it was wanted.

In only seven of the past forty-seven years, has Pittsburgh finished in the second division, so it is plain that high-class, winning baseball has been provided. When we review some of the names of the players who have been here, it is evident that Pittsburgh has had better baseball than almost any other city. At random let us mention Clarence Beaumont, Fred Clarke, Honus Wagner, Tommy Leach, Lefty Leifield, Jack Chesbro, Jess Tannehill, Max Carey, Carson Bigbee, Lloyd and Paul Waner, Chief Wilson, Rabbit Maranville, Glenn Wright, Joe Cronin, Dick Bartell, Walter Schmidt, George Gibson, Remy Kremer, Johnny Gooch, Pie Traynor, Hazen Cuyler, Kitty Bransfield, Al Lopez, Earl Smith, Lee Meadows,

Burleigh Grimes, Al Mamaux, Vic Aldridge, Babe Herman, Fred Lind-strom, Vic Willis, Billy Southworth, Deacon Phillippe, and Sam Leever, with a host of others.

Barney Dreyfuss died on February 5, 1932, and was succeeded as president by the writer, Mrs. Dreyfuss being the controlling stockholder until the recent sale of the club. Fred Clarke was manager from 1900 to 1915, inclusive, and was succeeded by Jimmy Callahan for 1916 and part of 1917, Honus Wagner and Hugo Bezdek finishing that year. Bezdek also managed in 1918 and 1919; then George Gibson in 1920, 1921 and part of 1922. Bill McKechnie took the helm in June 1922, and remained until after the season of 1926, when Donie Bush followed for 1927, 1928, and part of 1929. Jewel Ens followed Bush in 1929 and remained through 1931. Gibson returned for 1932, 1933 and part of 1934. In June 1934, Pie Traynor succeeded Gibson and stayed until after the season of 1939. Frank Frisch was manager from 1940 to 1946, inclusive.

During the war the club bent all effort toward building morale and played games at Indiantown Gap and Deshon Hospital, as well as at camps and posts throughout the East—Army, Navy, Coast Guard and Marines. Amateur baseball in this vicinity has been encouraged and the club has worked closely with city authorities and amateur organizations. As the club enters its sixty-first year in the National League, under new owner-ship, the previous owners extend well wishes and Godspeed.

◆　◆　◆

A NATIONAL LEAGUE TEAM

Pittsburgh began its National League tradition on April 30, 1887, at Recreation Park on the city's North Side, when they defeated Cap Anson's defending champion Chi-cago White Stockings by a score of 6-2. The game was a historic event for Pittsburgh, made even more so because the opposing pitchers, John Clarkson for Chicago and James "Pud" Galvin for Pittsburgh, were great nineteenth-century stars and future members of the Baseball Hall of Fame. Despite the excitement of Pittsburgh's debut in the National League, the team finished with a losing record in 1887 and, with the exception of a second-place finish in 1893, would finish no higher than fifth place for the rest of the century, including its disastrous last-place finish in 1890 with a record of 23-113. The Pirate winning tradition in the National League would have to wait for the beginning of the twentieth century and the arrival of Barney Dreyfuss and Honus Wagner.

A Brilliant Victory

STAFF REPORTER

ALLIES DEFEAT THE CHICAGOS WITH EASE
BIG CROWD OF SPECTATORS

It is now a matter of history that the Alleghenies have played their first game in the league championship contest and scored a brilliant victory. Between 9,000 and 10,000 people saw the initial game at Recreation Park on Saturday, and were given an exhibition of ball playing that has not been excelled in this city. The home players even surprised their friends and astounded the Chicagos.

Anson in the early part of the game insisted that Galvin was not in his correct position in the box; the Chicago captain claimed that Jimmy was illegally lifting his right foot. Umpire Quest, however, couldn't see it that way, nor would Galvin get rattled. Clarkson pitched well, and at some points of the game he was irresistible.

Dalrymple was the first man to go to bat, and rapped out a splendid three-bagger to right field; it went hotly along the foul line. Brown followed with a scratch hit, but was retired when trying to steal second. Miller went to base on balls; got to second on a passed ball and a wild throw by Daly enabled him to reach third and Dalrymple scored. Miller scored on Barkley's long fly to centre field. McKinnon scored in the second inning on his own single and Whitney's three-bagger. Two more runs were made in the fourth inning on Coleman being hit with a pitched ball; McKinnon's three-base hit and Whitney's single. An error by Sunday allowed Miller to reach first in the eighth and he stole second. McKinnon's double to right field brought him home.

The visitors did not score until the seventh inning. Anson made a single; got to third on Pfeffer's double and scored on Williamson's long fly to Brown. A three-base hit and a passed ball allowed Sullivan to score in the ninth. Anson and Ryan were both put out at third after making respectively a two-base hit. They tried to reach third, but the brilliant work of the out-field cut them off.

Base Ball Notes

The receipts for Saturday's game were about $4,500.

Chicago people will no longer term the Alleghenies chumps.

Anson is a great kicker, but his noise has no effect on Galvin.

From the *Pittsburgh Post*, May 2, 1887. Copyright/*Pittsburgh Post-Gazette*, 2002. All rights reserved. Reprinted with permission.

The Chicagos now hold the opinion that the Alleghenies can run bases.

The professional gamblers of this city lost heavily on the Chicagos Saturday.

The Cincinnati *Inquirer* thinks that many of the "League blowhards" will strike a snag before they are through with the Smoky City boys.

◆　◆　◆

BECOMING THE PIRATES

Louis Bierbauer played for Pittsburgh from 1891 through 1896. A fan favorite, he was a brilliant second baseman and a clutch hitter. Bierbauer played for the American Association's Philadelphia Athletics from 1886 through 1889, but jumped his contract to join the Players League for the 1890 season. When the Players League went defunct after one season, all its players were supposed to return to their original teams. Philadelphia, however, had accidentally omitted Bierbauer's name from the reserve list. After the Pittsburgh organization signed him to a new contract and Philadelphia protested, an interleague committee ruled on February 14, 1891 that Bierbauer had signed a valid contract with Pittsburgh. Bierbauer's place in Pittsburgh baseball history was secured when the Philadelphia papers called Pittsburgh the "Pirates" for stealing Bierbauer—the tag stuck, and eventually replaced the Alleghenies as the team's official name.

Alfred H. Spink's The National Game, *first published in 1910, was one of the earliest attempts to write an official history of baseball. Spink, who founded* The Sporting News *in 1886, wrote hundreds of biographical sketches for his history, including this entry for Louis Bierbauer. Nearly thirty years after Bierbauer's death, Harry Keck of* The Pittsburgh Sun-Telegraph *observed that his grave remained unmarked. A modest headstone now marks the grave for Bierbauer, a native of Erie, and for his wife.*

Louis Bierbauer

ALFRED H. SPINK

Louis Bierbauer, who led the second basemen of the National League in 1892 and 1893, was with the Pittsburgs those two years.

Bierbauer won his first laurels while covering second for the Athletics of Philadelphia.

From *The National Game* (St. Louis, Mo.: The National Game Publishing Company, 1910).

At the time he was considered the greatest second baseman in the American Association.

And he was a magnificent fielder and a fine batsman.

Bierbauer, one-time king of second basemen and all around player, first blossomed into promise as a player with the old Erie Penn. Malleables, twenty-five years ago. His first engagement away from home was with the Warren, Pa., team, then in a bitter baseball struggle carried on in the oil regions. Shortly after this he jumped over to Hamilton, Ontario in the Primrose League, where Joe Quest, the famous second baseman of the late twenties found him and induced Bierbauer to go to Philadelphia and play with the Athletics.

Bierbauer's position was behind the bat, but Quest gave him a trial at second, and so brilliant did he play that position that shortly afterwards he supplanted Quest and became the leading favorite with the fans of the Quaker City. He remained with the Athletics for six years and when the celebrated war inaugurated by Johnny Ward and others against the contract system was waged Bierbauer joined the Brotherhood and was assigned to Brooklyn, where he played one year, until the brotherhood disrupted, leaving him free to sign elsewhere. Managers at once got busy for his services.

Ned Hanlon, then managing Pittsburg, went to Erie in the depth of the Winter to secure a contract from Bierbauer. He found him on Presque Isle Peninsula, his favorite "hang-out." Hanlon had to cross the ice on the harbor in a bitter storm, but he finally reached Bierbauer's shack and before leaving had secured his signature to a contract to play with Pittsburg.

The announcement made by Hanlon on his return to Pittsburg created a ferment in baseball circles. Philadelphia advanced prior claims, contending that he had been under contract to them when he had jumped to the Brotherhood. The matter was fought out in court and the decision was made in favor of Pittsburg and with the Pirates Bierbauer continued for six seasons.

He was a great favorite there up to the time he came to St. Louis, where he remained two years—his last in the National League, then he played a year with Columbus, and two with Buffalo in the Eastern League. His last appearance as a professional was with Hartford.

Today he works daily as a molder in the Jarecki shops in Erie, Pa. He is the same old Bierbauer, enthused with the great American game, and his son, Louis Jr., is the pride of his heart. Father and son are much alike in demeanor and in stature. The young man played last season in the Erie City League, where he was the star. He is a left-hander and a whirl-wind. Manager Broderick of the Sailors watched him work and last Winter quietly took him in tow and trained him for the opening of this season. Despite the fact that he is but 24 years old and new to professional baseball he has proved himself a real find, and Erie fans will be greatly disappointed if he does not follow the footsteps of his father and make good in "higher company."

The Bierbauer family is a family of ball players. Young Roy J. Bierbauer, 15, brother of Louis, Jr., promises to be a good one. His father says he will be the best of them all. Young Roy is manager of an Erie amateur team and is a wonder for a boy of his years.

"Godfather of Pirates" Lies in Unmarked Grave

HARRY KECK

Louie Bierbauer, who was responsible for the nickname of Pirates for the Pittsburgh club, lies in an unmarked grave in Erie, Pa., and some of his friends are planning to do something about it.

One of these is John G. Carney, who writes feature articles for the *Erie Daily Times*.

"When the Pirates and Detroit Tigers played in the World's Series of 1909, Louie was working for me as a molder," Carney says, "and I kept him informed of the progress of the games as the reports came to me by telephone. Louie loved the Pirates and rooted for them until the day of his death in 1926.

"One day last summer I was passing through Erie Cemetery and decided to visit the grave of Bierbauer, tales of whose prowess as second baseman of the Pirates had thrilled me when I was a youngster. I couldn't locate it and appealed to the caretaker, who took me to an unmarked grave.

"Let me tell you that a feeling came over me similar to that which engulfed the late A. J. McMahon when he visited the weed-covered grave of his old friend Jack Dempsey, the Nonpareil, who a few short years before had been the toast of the sports world as the middleweight boxing champion. The incident inspired McMahon to write one of sports' immortal poems, 'The Nonpareil's Grave.'

"The response to this moving lament was spontaneous. Money came in from all corners of the globe, from pennies to substantial sums, and soon an imposing monument marked the resting place of the great champion.

"I would like to see some such thing happen to mark the grave of my friend, Louie Bierbauer, who was the father of Elsie Janis, the stage star who did so much to buoy the spirits of our soldiers in World War I, and will be happy to account for any donations if sent to me at Post Office Box 812, Erie, Pa."

This is the story of Bierbauer's baseball career: He was born in Erie, September 28, 1865, and played for the Athletics in the old American Association from 1886 to 1889. He jumped to Brooklyn in the Players' League in 1890 and when that organization disbanded was supposed to revert to his former club, but instead signed with Pittsburgh. This so infuriated the Philadelphia newspapermen that they began calling the Pittsburghers "Pirates," and the name stuck.

Louis was a prime favorite with the Pittsburgh fans for six seasons, being a good hitter and a sensational fielder. He moved on to the St. Louis National League club to round out his major league career in 1897 and '98. There must be some of the old-timers around who have fond memories of the "Godfather of the Pirates" and who will be glad to contribute to Mr. Carney's fund to have his grave marked.

Building a Winning Tradition

The two most dominant figures in shaping the history of baseball in Pittsburgh were Barney Dreyfuss, the Pirates' greatest owner and the father of the World Series, and Honus Wagner, the Pirates' greatest ballplayer and one of the Hall of Fame's origi- nal inductees. In Dreyfuss's thirty-two years as owner of the Pirates, his teams won six National League pennants and two World Series championships. Wagner won eight National League batting titles in the eighteen years he played in Pittsburgh and was considered the greatest player in the game by many of his contemporaries. His statue, which now stands on the grounds at PNC Park, was first unveiled at Schenley Park, outside Forbes Field, on April 30, 1951, just months before Wagner's death.

"Barney Dreyfuss Enters the Scene" and "The Mighty Honus" are chapters from Fred Lieb's Pittsburgh Pirates. *Lieb began his distinguished career in 1911 and continued as an active journalist until his death in 1980 at the age of ninety-two. As the author of a Pirate team history, he had the singular advantage of knowing Barney Dreyfuss and of watching Honus Wagner play baseball.*

Barney Dreyfuss Enters the Scene

FREDERICK G. LIEB

After operating eight seasons as a twelve-club league, the National League again voted to cut down to an eight-team circuit in 1900. Andy Freedman, a Tammany politician in New York, who owned the Giants, had long spon- sored a move in the old league "to cut off the deadwood."

His campaign met with eventual success when the National League club owners voted to lop off Louisville and Cleveland in the West and Washington and Baltimore in the East. No piece of legislation passed in baseball ever had more far-reaching effects than this reduction to the present eight National League cities. It made possible the expansion of the American League to the east, as Ban Johnson took up vacated territory in Cleveland, Washington, and Baltimore, brought about the destructive war between the two present big leagues, and was responsible for the golden era in Pittsburgh baseball.

The owner of the Louisville club was a little energetic man of 125 pounds, a 34-year-old German-Jewish immigrant, who was already find- ing America the land of opportunity. Until his death, in 1932, he spoke with a pronounced German accent, but he was destined to become the

From *Pittsburgh Pirates* (New York: G. P. Putnam's Sons, 1947).

power behind Pittsburgh baseball, and one of the game's most successful, able, and forward-looking club owners.

The National League learned early that Barney Dreyfuss was a battler. In the nineties only four major-league clubs played Sunday baseball: Chicago, St. Louis, Louisville, and Cincinnati. Louisville, with one of the smallest populations in the loop, depended largely on its Sunday gate, so some of Dreyfuss' fellow club owners decided to give little Barney the works.

In an early attempt to cut off some of the alleged deadwood, the bigwigs of the National League decided on a schedule that gave Louisville no Sunday games. Fortunately for Barney, Joe Vila, the former enterprising sports writer of the old *New York Morning Sun*, pulled one of his spectacular scoops. While A. H. Soden, president of the Boston club and chairman of the schedule committee, was having a few beers at the old Fifth Avenue Hotel in New York, the enterprising Joe lifted the draft of the schedule from Soden's coat and copied it down while standing in a telephone booth. Vila printed the schedule in full the next morning.

After reading Vila's scoop, Dreyfuss yelled bloody murder during the following day's meeting. His English wasn't good at that early day and his pronunciation even worse, but he raised so much hell at the meeting that Soden's schedule was scrapped and a new one drawn up giving Dreyfuss his full quota of Sunday games.

It looked as though the winter of 1899–1900 would be a tough one for Dreyfuss. His Louisville ball park burned down in the fall. Then he learned from his alert secretary, Harry C. Pulliam, later president of the National League, of the contemplated move to cut down to eight clubs and leave Louisville out in the cold.

"What'll I do?" Barney asked Harry.

"Get hold of some money; get hold of lots of it, and get it in a hurry," advised Pulliam. "Then be ready for anything that may happen. And I'd try to cultivate the friendship of Jim Hart in Chicago, John T. Brush in Cincinnati, and Frank Robison in St. Louis. They like you, and they're for you."

"I can get the money, all right," said Barney.

In the meantime, Dreyfuss had been tipped off by two good publisher friends in Pittsburgh that Captain Kerr and Philip A. Auten, his associate, were tired of losing money on the Pirates and were ready to get out.

Early in 1900 John T. Brush, then the Cincinnati club owner, called up Dreyfuss and asked him whether he could meet him at French Lick, Ind. "It's a business matter of considerable importance, and I think it may mean a lot to you," said Brush. And it was no understatement!

When Barney arrived at the Hoosier resort, Brush quickly talked turkey. "W. H. Watkins [the former Pirate manager] has put up $5,000 on an option to buy the Pittsburgh club," he said. "I was backing Watkins, but for reasons of my own I find I will be unable to go through with the deal. You know what's going to happen in the league. How would you like to pick up the option and stay in the National League?"

"Well, I would have to go back to Louisville and talk to some people and see whether they would go along with me," said Dreyfuss.

His Louisville friends said they would stand behind him, so early on the following Monday morning Barney, accompanied by Watkins, appeared in Kerr's Pittsburgh office. Kerr at first insisted that the option had expired and that Watkins had forfeited his $5,000.

Dreyfuss eventually convinced the Captain that wouldn't be fair, and Kerr asked: "Do you want to take up the option?"

"Well, the reason I'm here is that I'm interested in getting into Pittsburgh baseball," said the Louisville club owner.

Before Barney left he had made an agreement with Kerr that Dreyfuss would get a half interest in the Pittsburgh club providing he would bring the best Louisville players with him. As the league had not yet dropped Louisville officially, the transaction was made in the form of a trade, with Pittsburgh giving up $25,000 and five players, Jack Chesbro, George Fox, John O'Brien, Arthur Madison, and William Gould, for 14 Louisville players, the pick of the Colonels, topped by the fighting manager-left fielder, Fred Clarke, and the great all-round player, Hans Wagner. Others were: Second Baseman Claude Ritchey; Third Baseman Tommy Leach; Catchers Charley Zimmer and Cliff Latimer; Pitchers Charles "Deacon" Phillippe, Pat Flaherty, George Edward "Rube" Waddell, Walter Woods, and Elton Cunningham; and a few lesser athletes, Mike Kelly, later for many years the owner of the Minneapolis club, Tom Massitt, and C. Doyle.

After the National League streamlined itself to eight clubs, Jack Chesbro returned to Pittsburgh, and another pair of Colonels, Fred Ketcham and Louis Deal, joined the exodus to the Pirates.

The Pittsburgh club had a reorganization, and at a stockholders' meeting, Dreyfuss was named president; Phil Auten, vice-president; W. W. Kerr, treasurer; Harry C. Pulliam, secretary, and Fred Clarke, manager.

2

Dreyfuss, the new Pirate president, was born in Freiberg, Baden, February 23, 1865, was educated in his native Germany, and was early employed as a bank clerk in Karlsruhe. Disliking the idea of compulsory military training, young Barney immigrated to the United States when he was seventeen years old. Landing at old Castle Garden at New York's Battery, the young fellow's destination was Paducah, Kentucky, Irvin Cobb's old home town, where Barney had relatives. He had just about enough money to get to his Kentucky destination, but in his German schoolbooks he had read much about Niagara Falls and had been fascinated by pictures of the great cascade. To him, America and Niagara Falls were almost synonymous, so by carefully budgeting his meal money and sitting up several nights in day coaches, he went from New York to Paducah by way of Buffalo and Niagara Falls and saw the great natural wonder he had dreamed about.

Through Paducah relatives, Barney obtained his first American job with the Bernheim distillery. What's more, he really started at the bottom—cleaning whisky barrels for six dollars a week. But Dreyfuss was intelligent, smart at figures, and soon was advanced to an office position in the organization. Eventually he climbed to the head bookkeeper's stool.

If it hadn't been for failing health when Barney was in his late teens, he might never have become interested in baseball. He worked nine hours on his high stool, and then was up until midnight studying English and taking courses to make himself more proficient. He never had robust health and soon suffered from headaches, poor digestion, and a general rundown condition.

A Paducah doctor gave him some sage advice. "You're working too hard, Barney, and not getting any recreation or fun out of life. If you want to live a while in this country, you've got to stop working and cramming all the time. Get into some outdoor activity. Did you ever play baseball?"

"No," said Barney, "I don't know anything about it."

"Well, it's time you learned."

Dreyfuss took the hint and soon was captivated by the red-blooded American national game. He was in the country only a little over a year when he organized a semipro ball club in Paducah, and even played a little second base on it. When the club went to Memphis for a game, Paducah won by a score of 22 to 2. Discussing the contest later, Barney, who had an uncanny memory for names, faces, places and details, remarked: "The score was bigger than the gate receipts, so I fed it to the squirrels in the public square in Memphis." The late George B. Dovey, a former president of the Boston Braves, was a member of Barney's Paducah team.

Though Dreyfuss left Germany so he wouldn't have to goosestep with the former Kaiser's minions, Barney was no pacifist and got some more sunshine, fresh air, and exercise serving with Bullitt's Light Artillery, later absorbed into the Kentucky National Guard. In later years, when Barney was in a particularly good humor, he would take a faded picture out of his desk drawer, showing a determined, mustachioed artilleryman, looking ready to conquer the world. "We marched at Cleveland's inauguration," he would say not unproudly.

Barney was also an early Kentucky colonel, other than being president-owner of the Louisville Colonels. "While I was running the Louisville club there were just two Republicans in Kentucky," Dreyfuss would reminisce. "By some magic or other, one of them managed to get himself elected governor of the state. As I was the other one, he made me a colonel, but I never did get a uniform out of it."

3

When the Bernheim distillery interests moved to Louisville in 1888, Dreyfuss, who by this time was credit man, went along. Louisville then had a team in the old American Association, along with Pittsburgh, the old St. Louis Browns, and early Athletics. It was called a "beer and whisky league," as most of its backers were brewery or distillery people. While the principal Louisville owners were Dr. Stuckey and George Ruckstool, there was whisky money behind the club, and Barney acquired a small block of stock shortly after his arrival in Louisville. He just liked to mess around with baseball.

By 1890, Dreyfuss was elected treasurer of the club. Shortly after Louisville was admitted into the twelve-club National League, Harry Pulliam was elected president of the Colonels, and Barney served under him as secretary-treasurer. When Barney obtained control of the club, he and Pulliam exchanged places, Dreyfuss moving up to the executive position.

The inside operations of a big-league club had an early fascination for him, and by nature he was a man who had little toleration for a team that wasn't a winner. His club need not necessarily be a champion, but if it stayed in the race and finished well in the first division, he was pleased, if not completely satisfied.

In his latter years, his proudest boast was the many years of first-division baseball that he gave to Pittsburgh, his adopted city. "We are a first-division town, and I'm a first-division club owner," he once told the author. "I just couldn't—I wouldn't—stand for a second-division team." In the thirty-two years that he served as president of the Pirates, his clubs finished in the second division only six times, including his last two years on earth. Dreyfuss actually looked at the second division as something akin to a disgrace. If you finished there, you were a failure.

Admitting that four clubs had to finish in the lower four, he merely shrugged his shoulders, and said: "Well, it's not for me." He had a great pride in his own ability and accomplishments. He believed firmly in

Barney Dreyfuss. "Smartness pays off in baseball as well as in any other activity, and I think I'm a pretty smart fellow," he once confessed. "America is, and always has been, a land of opportunity, and if I had put the same time, energy, brains, money into another business, I would have succeeded just as well, and perhaps made more money. But baseball is my business."

He drank little and never touched tobacco. Once he remarked quite philosophically: "When I wanted to smoke, I couldn't afford it. When I could afford it, I didn't want to smoke."

He wasn't too easy to get along with, and at times could be severe, dominating, critical, and stubborn. Many ball players felt he was a hard man to deal with. Yet he befriended many of the men who had worked for him. He had his periodical feuds and brushes with Pittsburgh sports writers. He was also a relentless fighter. In debates in the National League council halls, his fellow club owners often accused him of being arbitrary, unreasonable, and obstinate. "Barney, you're like a bulldog," Charley Ebbets, former Brooklyn president, once told him. "You get hold of something, and you never let go." When Dreyfuss lost the great George Sisler through the adverse vote of chairman Garry Herrmann, of the old National Commission, Barney started a one-man fight to unseat Herrmann from his Commission job. Herrmann was also president of the Cincinnati Reds, and he and Barney were close, early associates in the league. But that counted for naught when Barney went on the warpath; after a four-year campaign, Dreyfuss had his revenge when Herrmann was ousted from his Commission chairmanship.

Pittsburgh wasn't always in agreement with Barney's moves on the Pirates. There were even times when the town was incensed at the little man from Freiberg. But Barney took his own counsel and if he made mistakes, well, he made them, and they were on his own head. He offered no excuses.

Yet when the former Paducah bookkeeper closed his earthly books, his contribution to baseball was large. He was one of the game's greatest and most far-seeing club owners. If, when in a moment of anger or peeve, he occasionally did a small thing, his vision was wide and his heart and keen mind were always on the side of better baseball. He said baseball was his business, so it was his business to keep the game and his club prosperous. Instinctively he recognized that clean baseball—a game above the slightest breath of suspicion—was the only baseball that paid.

The Mighty Honus

FREDERICK G. LIEB

Barney Dreyfuss had no first-division clubs during his sojourn in Louisville. He had to call on all of his native shrewdness to get by, but even though his 1899 Louisville club finished ninth, two positions behind Pittsburgh, he was in the process of building a strong first-division club when the National League voted to streamline down to eight clubs.

Major-league outfits had no full-time paid scouts in the nineties, and Dreyfuss, the Louisville owner, would have had little money for a scouting staff even if the system had then been in vogue. But from the first, Barney always believed he knew ball players and could pick them. From the time he began signing the Louisville club's checks, he kept his so-called "dope book." Barney learned to do his own scouting through the columns of the baseball weeklies, the *Sporting News* and *Sporting Life*, Spalding's and Reach's *Guides*, and the sports pages of the daily newspapers. Whenever he read that a minor-league batter was having a succession of good days, or a pitcher was racking up a string of victories, the player's name went into the dope book. If the price on the player wasn't too high, and anything over $1,000 was almost prohibitive, there was a good chance he would land on Dreyfuss' Colonels. And considering the ninth-place finish of the 1899 Colonels, Barney brought a surprisingly good crop of players to Pittsburgh from his Louisville club, including two of the immortals of baseball history, John Peter (Honus) Wagner and Frederick Clifford Clarke. Without them Pittsburgh's great baseball success in the first decade of this century would not have been possible.

Wagner is not only the greatest all-time Pirate and the foremost National League ball player, but many persons consider him the number-one ball player of all time. In that group is that doughty former American Leaguer, Ed Barrow, former manager of the Tigers and Red Sox and the man who had Babe Ruth in both Boston and New York.

Only recently Barrow revealed to the author that but for a matter of $100 the Pittsburgh club would have had Wagner three years before the Louisville-Pittsburgh merger of 1900. We'll come to that a little later. After Barrow broke away from the Pittsburgh district in 1896, to accept the management of the Paterson, N.J., club, he recruited his players largely from western Pennsylvania. He knew several of Honus' older brothers,

From *Pittsburgh Pirates* (New York: G. P. Putnam's Sons, 1947).

including Al, a railroad engineer, whom Barrow always claims could have been as good a player as Hans.

Barrow received a tip that Hans, after a little early minor leaguing, was a free agent, and that any go-getting young manager who had the enterprise to take a trip to Hans' home town of Mansfield (now Carnegie), Pa., could sign young Wagner for the asking. In fact, Al Wagner told Barrow: "You don't want me, you want to sign my brother John. He's the real ball player of the family." Al directed Barrow to Mansfield.

"Arriving in Mansfield, I asked some fellows loitering around the station where I might find Hans Wagner," related Barrow. "They told me if I'd walk down the railroad track for a mile or so, I'd likely run into him. One of them agreed to accompany me as a guide. It was in the early spring, and there was still some snow around. In some places I had to wade through puddles left by the spring thaw. We walked up the tracks about two miles and came upon a group of boys and young men. A husky, but clumsy-looking chap was throwing pieces of coal against the side of a freight car. I knew at once he was the player I was looking for, and I signed him then and there to a Paterson contract for a little over $100 a month.

Wagner, himself, confirms the story that Ed Barrow signed him on the railroad tracks. "Only Ed doesn't tell it all," said Honus. "He left out the best part. When we saw him come, we all ran like hell, and he had to chase us before he could get me. We thought he and his partner were a couple of railroad bulls who were trying to arrest us for throwing rocks at company property."

"Shortly after I signed Wagner, Captain Kerr, of the Pittsburgh club, sent for me and wanted to buy Honus' contact," continued Barrow. "I refused, but I told the Captain I would give him first chance at the Dutchman, if he developed. Wagner had a good season with Paterson in 1896, and a better one in 1897. By that time I had become president of the Atlantic League, but I still retained my interest in the Paterson club.

"In midseason of 1897, Harry Pulliam, who was secretary of the Colonels for Dreyfuss, offered me $2,000 for Wagner's release. In accordance with my verbal agreement with Captain Kerr, I immediately wired him of Pulliam's offer. He wired back that he would match the $2,000 Louisville offer and buy Wagner. In the meantime, Pulliam asked for a little more time. He called up Barney Dreyfuss in Louisville, and Barney authorized Harry to boost the bid by $100. I then advised Captain Kerr of the new offer. I never heard from Kerr again and don't know to this day whether he received my second wire or felt that I was playing one club against the other, which I wasn't. I really wanted to play fair with him and give him every opportunity to get this great prospect. However, not hearing from the Captain, I let Wagner go to Dreyfuss and Pulliam for $2,100.

"Yet, there seems a certain justice that Wagner should have spent his greatest years in Pittsburgh, because he was headed for the Pirates almost from the time I first signed him."

2

Wagner was born in what was formerly Mansfield, Pa., on February 24, 1874. Oddly enough, the great player's birthday was only a day later than that of the man for whom he worked during his entire major-league career, Barney Dreyfuss. The elder Wagners were born in Germany, and the family's name for John Peter was "Hans" or "Johannes," German terms for John. Hence the Honus, the name by which Wagner was known to millions of fans. Later on, as his infield wizardry made him his league's outstanding ball player, writers and the fans also referred to him as "The Flying Dutchman." To such intimates as Fred Clarke, Tommy Leach, and Kitty Bransfield, he was usually just plain "Dutch."

Honus went to work at the early age of twelve in the coal mines and industrial plants of western Pennsylvania, but he was happy only in the great outdoors. All five of the Wagner brothers played baseball, and used to have a Wagner Brothers ball club.

"That's how I could play all positions," Hans later confessed. "On our family team you had to know how to play everywhere, as we always were shifting."

In naming Wagner as his candidate for baseball's greatest all-time player, Barrow stressed the Dutchman's versatility. "He became baseball's greatest shortstop, because he eventually helped his club most in that position. But had Honus remained at third base, first base, or the outfield, he could have been just as great in those positions."

The late John J. McGraw, of the Giants, who also had Honus on his all-time player list, also stressed Wagner's ability to play anywhere. Tommy Leach lists Wagner first also; for many years he was Wagner's distinguished fellow player in Louisville and Pittsburgh. "I saw Wagner play every position but pitcher and catcher, and it would have made no difference where Honus finally settled," said Tommy. "He was just a standout, towering over any other player of the past or present."

The Wagner brothers also had a family basketball quintet and for twenty years Honus played professional basketball during the winters, much to the distress of Barney Dreyfuss. He used to report for baseball in the spring, his hulking body covered with "wire burns," the result of rubbing his huge frame against the wires of the early basketball cages. Drey-fuss had a great dread his star would suffer a cracked knee, or other last-ing injury.

"Barney used to fret about my basketball playing," recalls Hans. "I would tell him ball players, especially a big fellow like me, needed a lot of winter exercise to keep from getting soft. But he was always afraid I'd damage a knee. He kicked so much that I asked him to come out some night to see me play. Basketball was just a sport for me, and I got a lot of fun out of it. After Barney came to see me, he still objected, but not so strongly, and let me play." But, eventually, late in Wagner's career, Drey-fuss won his point.

While Ed Barrow signed Wagner for Paterson, Honus' big league springboard in 1896, the hefty Dutchman had collected a few hundred dollars for playing ball before that. He played semipro ball around Car-negie and hooked up briefly with Mansfield, Ohio, of the Ohio State League. There John Peter did everything but catch, and frequently took his turn on the mound. However, his first real baseball employer was the late George Moreland, well-known Pittsburgh baseball figure, first as a club owner-manager of teams in the western Pennsylvania-Ohio steel, coal, and oil belt, and later as one of the country's foremost baseball stat-isticians.

Moreland had Al Wagner on his Steubenville club of the Tri-State League in 1895, and things weren't going well. Al suggested to George that he engage his kid brother, Hans, to help out.

"What does he play?" asked George.

"You can play him anywhere," shot back Al.

"Oh, he's that kind of a player," said Moreland, unimpressed. "A Jack-of-all-trades and a master of none. I've seen that kind of ball player be-fore."

"But, you haven't seen Hans," Al insisted.

Steubenville wasn't too far from Mansfield, Pa., so Moreland told Al he could send for his younger brother. The next morning, when Moreland came down for breakfast, there was Hans in the hotel lobby, his uniform wrapped up in a newspaper parcel. He hadn't even waited for a passenger train but came by hopping a freight.

Moreland put Hans in left field that day, saying "because I had to put nine men in the field." Hans had no shoes and played in his stocking feet, but the pitchers on the other side couldn't get him out. He also played shortstop for Moreland at Steubenville and hit .402 in 44 games. Wagner also played 20 games that season for Adrian in the Michigan State League, and after the Steubenville club blew, his last 65 contests for Warren, Pa., in the Iron-Oil League. A teammate on the Warren team was Claude Ritchey, of Emlentown, Pa., who later was to play second base alongside Honus for many years, on the Pirates. The Flying Dutchman played in three leagues in 1895, and then, in the 21 seasons from 1897 to 1917, in only one—the venerable old National.

3

Wagner, perhaps the greatest of right-handed hitters, was eight times National League batting champion, the last time when he was 37 years of age, in 1911. He put almost as many records in the National League book as did Ty Cobb in the American, though that amazing little Giant, Mel Ott, knocked out a number of Wagner records in recent years. Even so, Honus has many of the most important ones left: playing in the most National League games, 2,785; was the most times at bat, 10,427; cracked out the most hits, 3,430; for the most total bases, 4,888, as he led the old league in singles, 2,426, doubles, 651, and triples, 252. His lifetime batting average through 21 National League seasons was .329. And as evidence that he whacked the stars as freely as the bushers, he hit the great Christy Mathewson for .324 in the 327 times he faced him, and .356 in 135 times at bat against Brooklyn's immortal southpaw, Nap Rucker.

Wagner never knew what it was to finish under .300 in his minor- or major-league career until he was 40 years old. Hitting, with him, was a gift and his great proficiency was due to his patience and faithful practice. Yet hitting with him was sheer fun, whether in a league game or in batting practice. He was never happier than when he had a bat in his hand.

It wasn't often that the Pennsylvania Dutchman fell into a batting slump. When one gripped him it was usually of brief duration, and Honus had his cure. "When I'd stop hitting, I'd look down at my feet and see what was wrong," he said. "I'd shift my feet a bit, and then the hits would start coming again."

There are numerous good anecdotes about pitchers trying to find Wagner's weakness. John McGraw, who as Giant manager tried for years to find something that John Peter couldn't hit, told a number of them. And there was no man who had a greater admiration for the Dutchman than McGraw.

A brash young pitcher who had just joined the Giants had been called to the mound in the late innings in a game against the Pirates. Wagner was coming up, and as the kid left the bench he inquired of McGraw, "What shall I pitch to him?"

"Just pitch—and then duck," advised McGraw.

Another McGraw story was of a pitcher named "Crazy" Schmidt, who was briefly with Baltimore in the old twelve-club National League. Wagner at the time was still with Louisville. Having none too good a memory, but wishing to succeed in the majors, Schmidt kept a notebook in which he wrote down the weaknesses of National League batsmen.

As Wagner came to the plate, Schmidt pulled the book from his hip pocket and began thumbing the pages. McGraw, the Oriole third baseman, walked over to the pitcher's box and asked: "Well, have you found the Dutchman's weakness?"

Schmidt put a fat thumb on one of the pages and replied: "It says here, give him a base on balls."

Wagner never hit .400 in the majors; his high was .381 in 1900, when he won his first National League batting crown. While Wagner frequently led his league in doubles and triples, he was never much of a home-run hitter. During his entire career he batted against the old dead ball, and against the trick deliveries permitted prior to 1920. Only twice did he hit as many as ten home runs. Yet there were times when he'd get his near-200-pound chassis behind a swing and really smack that old mushy pellet. Poll Perritt, former Giant pitcher, used to tell of a homer that the mighty John hit against his delivery: "I threw Wagner a fast ball and was still in my follow-through, with my arm extended in front of me, when the ball came back at me like a rifle bullet. I couldn't have ducked if I tried, but fortunately the ball sailed under my arm and then began to rise, and cleared the center-field fence."

After his retirement from active play, Honus expressed the wish that he might have played long enough to get a crack at the Jack-rabbit ball that came in with the Babe Ruth home-run era. "I used to do pretty well," said John, "but I'd like to have had a few cracks at that lively ball. Even so, I don't think I would have had too many home runs. I wasn't that kind of a hitter. I didn't lift a ball the way Babe Ruth did, but was more of a line-drive hitter."

4

Wagner was a bulging, squat giant, with a wide, thick chest, and legs so bowed one could have rolled a barrel through them. Weighing around 190 pounds, he had big awkward-looking feet, and great gangling gorilla-like arms. The arms hung loosely hinged from his wide shoulders and from the ends dangled great hams of hands.

Looking at the man, one got the idea that he possessed great strength but that he was clumsy and awkward. Yet Hans could have taken on his famous fellow star, the graceful Nap Lajoie, in a foot race, and beaten him by yards in a 100-yard-dash, or a sprint around the bases. He moved with the speed of a large bear, and it was something to see those bowlegs move around the bases, a treat present-day fans can only imagine. One had to see it to appreciate Wagner. He led his league in stolen bases almost as often as in hitting, stealing 720 bases, with a high of 61 in 1907, when the big fellow was 34 years old. Only the deer-limbed Ty Cobb, Eddie Collins, and Pittsburgh's own Max Carey excelled Honus in wholesale base larcenies in the last half century.

He wasn't as ruthless a base runner as Ty Cobb and he never deliberately injured a fellow player. But like players of his day, he kept his spikes filed to a razor's edge, and when he was under way, it took a hardy infielder to block his path. Powerful as a gorilla and hard as nails from his winter basketball and summer baseball, when he got into motion he generated the momentum of a runaway locomotive on a downgrade.

Honus was spiked frequently but rarely took time out for an injury. That would have been being a sissy. From 1898, his first complete National League season, to 1916, his last regular season, he fell under the record of 123 games only once, playing 113 in 1914. But as late as 1915, when he was in his nineteenth season in the National League, at the age of 41, he played in every one of his team's 156 games.

After playing all outfield positions, third base, and first base in his seasons in Louisville and early years in Pittsburgh, Wagner finally settled at shortstop in the latter part of the 1902 season, and he then played there for the better part of sixteen seasons. Of all positions, shortstop was the one in which he could use his uncanny skill to the best advantage. With those long arms and great baskets of hands, he seemed to draw balls to him like a magnet. It made no difference whether they were on the ground, or in the air, in back of third base, the outfield grass, or over second base, Honus was there. They still tell a story in Pittsburgh how Wagner slipped in the river mud in old Exposition Park, and while sitting on the ground threw out his man at first base.

Honus recalls some of his early difficulties with rough boys in the league. "I had been in the league only a short while, when we were playing Baltimore," he reminisced. "They used to call them the rowdy Orioles, and they weren't fooling. I hit a long ball deep into the outfield and should have made an easy home run out of it, but when I got to first base, Jack Doyle gave me the hip and Heinie Reitz almost killed me when I rounded second. Hughie Jennings tripped me at short, and when I got to third John McGraw was waiting for me with a shotgun. I did well to get a triple out of it.

"After the game, Fred Clarke, our manager, said to me: 'What the hell kind of a way is that to play baseball? Letting everybody kick you around!

If you can't do any better than that, you won't be with us when we leave Baltimore the day after tomorrow.'

"So the next day I hit a ball down to McGraw, and it was a close play at first. But if Doyle had any idea of giving me the works again, I beat him to it. I banged into him with my shoulder and knocked him into right field. McGraw's throw sailed into the outfield and finally bounded into a stand, and it worked the same as a home run. After I scored and returned to the bench, Fred Clarke smiled his approval: 'That's the way to play the game, Dutch,' he said. 'Make 'em respect you.'

"Around the same time, with a man on base, Fred says: 'Lay one down.'

"Well, I see a fat pitch coming up and I think it's too good to pass up. I line it over the fence for a home run. As I round third, I see Clarke coming out from the bench, and he meets me at the plate as I score. I think he is going to congratulate me, but he bawls me out: 'Hey, you Dutchman, didn't I tell you to bunt? We obey orders on this club, and that hit over the fence will cost you twenty-five dollars.'

"But I said: 'What d'you mean bunt? I don't know what a bunt is. I've been around for only a week.'

"I talked him out of the fine, and about a week later I came up with runners on base. Clarke said: 'Bunt another one for me, Dutch.' Then he gives me the wink, and I know he means for me to give it the business."

5

As a player John Wagner was modest and shy, almost to a fault. As a present-day Pirate coach, he is a more loquacious fellow than when he was the National League's top star. Honus didn't like swell hotels, or restaurants where they served a lot of fancy food. He wanted a place where he could get his teeth into a good steak without a lot of trimmings, corned beef and cabbage, and such dishes as Mama Wagner used to cook in Mansfield.

After Wagner had won six batting championships, the National League wanted to honor John Peter at its annual meeting in New York in 1909, but had a difficult time inducing Honus to come east for the meeting. "I'm a hitter, not a speaker," he protested. While he was at the very apex of his career, a New York newspaper sent one of its ace sports writers to see Wagner and get an interview. It was a hot, sultry summer night, and Honus had his bath tub filled with ice and beer bottles. "Help yourself," said the Flying Dutchman, but he was freer with his beer than his conversation.

He said that in his early days in the league ball players weren't much for conversation, on his own club as well as others. "Why, I was three years in the league before ball players began speaking to me, and then not too nice, either," he reminisced.

"I remember when I was playing third base for Louisville, we had a game with the Giants. Jot Gore, one of the New York outfielders, belted his second home run of the game. As he was passing third, I said to him, 'Nice hit.' He looked around at me and yelled back, 'Go to ——.'

"However, I always considered Barney Dreyfuss my pal. I could talk to him, and frequently he would come to me and discuss young players, asking: 'How do you like that young pitcher?' or 'Do you think our new outfielder has it?'"

Present-day top-ranking players make fortunes in their by-products. Babe Ruth made as much money on the side as he collected in his princely big-league salaries. Bobbie Feller doesn't overlook a bet in capitalizing on his fame as a pitcher, and after he lost his big baseball pay during four wartime years, no one can blame him. Yet Wagner seemed to think it was below his dignity to capitalize on his fame as a ball player.

At a time when vaudeville was in its heyday, and Wagner was champion batsman of the National League, and Ty Cobb and Nap Lajoie the great batting rivals of the American, a theatrical manager tried to build up a postseason act featuring Honus, Ty, and Nap. He made the two American Leaguers flattering offers, provided they could get Wagner. When they wrote to Wagner, he replied, "Not interested," even though it would have meant nearly $1,000 a week for him.

Lajoie then called on Honus and pointed out it would be easy money, picked up with little effort. All they were asking of Wagner was to appear on the stage, say a few words, take three swings, and wallop a phony ball into the wings. "It's no use, Nap," he replied. "I'm a ball player, not an actor."

Likewise he turned down an offer to pose as manager of the men's furnishing department of a Pittsburgh department store during the off season. Honus could have made his own hours, as long as he showed up once a day. But again the answer was a polite but positive No.

Nor would he endorse cigarettes or tobacco. A tobacco company once asked John Gruber, for many years the Pirates' official scorer, whether he could get Wagner's permission to use his picture in connection with some cards inside the package. They offered Gruber ten dollars if he could get Wagner's signature.

Wagner sent Gruber a note: "Dear John: I don't want my picture in cigarettes, but I don't want you to lose the ten dollars, so I am sending you a check for that sum."

Gruber framed the check, and it hung in his den until the day he died.

Wagner remained a bachelor until near the end of his playing career, December 30, 1916, when he married Miss Bessie B. Smith, who has been a fine companion in his latter years. Since returning to the Pirates as a coach, he has lost much of his shyness as a player, and is more of a mixer. He now goes to baseball dinners and has lost his fear of the dais. In fact, he has won new fame as a storyteller and likes to entertain young Pittsburgh players with his tall tales. And John has told them some lollapaloosas.

There is the story of Wagner's minor-league days, when the batter hit a terrific drive over the center-field fence. The center fielder backed helplessly to the boards and sorrowfully saw the ball sail out of the yard. But it seems a railroad train was passing at the time, and the ball dropped into the engine's smokestack. Just around that time, the engineer (maybe it was Honus' brother, Al) gave his locomotive a little more steam. With the first puff of smoke, the ball was coughed up again. The locomotive puffed and huffed, and pretty soon it coughed the ball right back into the baseball orchard, where the outfielder caught it for as pretty a put-out as anyone had ever seen. What's more Honus insists it actually happened.

Even that isn't the craziest thing that Wagner says he saw happen. His version of this battiest incident follows: "I hit a drive to left field, and the left fielder jumped up the screen to get the ball. The ball struck about two inches above his outstretched glove, and bounded back on the field. I looked up as I reached second, thinking the hit was good for a double, but I see that outfielder still on the screen as though he is nailed there. He's cussin' and shoutin' and trying to shake himself loose. Well, before anyone else can recover the ball, I've stretched it into a home run. You wanna know what happed to that outfielder? When he jumped up for the ball, his belt caught on a wire, and there he stayed until someone pried him loose."

When Zack Taylor, the former catcher, joined the Pirates as coach in 1947, Honus, without cracking a smile, said: "It's easy to get to the park nowadays, ain't it? Back in the days when we played in Allegheny, I used to ride to our old Exposition Park on horseback. One day that darn horse wouldn't get on the ferry boat, so I rode him right into the river and made him swim across, with me on top of him."

Then he regaled Zack with a tale of his first automobile: "It was so high I could look into everybody's second-story windows as I drove by. And it had five hundred pounds of tools in it. And whenever we bounced over a trolley track, the tools rattled more'n the car."

Arthur Daley, the *New York Times'* able sports columnist, quotes a Pirate rookie as saying: "Mr. Wagner, I don't think I can believe your stories."

"That may be so, sonny," replied Hans, "but I never told you anything that you can't repeat to your mother."

◆   ◆   ◆

THE FIRST WORLD SERIES GAME

In 1903, twenty-eight-game winner Jack Chesbro and twenty-game winner Jesse Tannehill defected to the newly formed American League. This meant that while the 1903 Pirates hung on to win the National League pennant for the third year in a row, they were not as strong as they had been the past two seasons. Despite an injury-plagued season and the mental collapse of Ed Doheny, a sixteen-game winner in 1902, Barney Dreyfuss still had great confidence in his ball club and challenged the American League pennant-winning Boston team to a championship series. On September 16, 1903, Dreyfuss and Boston owner Henry Killilea signed an agreement to play a postseason series for the "championship of the United States."

The first World Series game in baseball history was played, as scheduled, on October 1, 1903, at the Huntington Avenue Grounds in Boston. The Pirates, after scoring four runs in the first inning, went on to defeat the Boston Americans handily, 7-3. Tommy Leach had the first hit, a triple, and scored the first run in World Series history when Honus Wagner singled him home. Deacon Phillippe, a twenty-four game winner, easily outpitched the legendary Cy Young. Leach had four hits in the game, but twenty-one-year-old Jimmy Sebring, the youngest player on either team, was the batting star with three hits, four runs batted in, and the first World Series home run. As far as Pirate fans were concerned, Pittsburgh had the superior team, and Boston would be lucky to win a game in the nine-game series.

Pirates Wallop the Beaneaters

JOHN H. GRUBER

DEACON PHILLIPPE HAS AMERICAN LEAGUE CHAMPIONS AT HIS MERCY, AND THEY FALL MIDST WILD ENTHUSIASM ON PART OF VISITING ROOTERS

FINAL SCORE 7 TO 3—EASY ALL THE WAY

The Pittsburg champions were victorious today in the first of nine games with the Boston Americans for the world championship. There is gloom in old Boston town tonight, and the gloom is intensified by the knowledge that Pittsburg has a faster team in every respect. The work put up by the National League champions simply made the Boston men look like counterfeit money. This is no gush, but the downright truth, and it is this that makes the gloom so thick here. Local fans cannot see how their team is going to win a game, let alone the series.

A crowd of 16,242 people were in the park. They began gathering long before the hour set for the game to begin. The stands were jammed and a rope was stretched a few feet from the fence, and between this rope and the fence the people were tightly wedged. The top of the fence was lined with spectators who dangled their feet in imminent peril of tumbling upon the mass below. Tin horns and other noise-producing instruments were seen in the crowd, but there was no call for them. Poor Boston was humbled—outplayed at every point.

Dreyfuss Is Enthusiastic

In the grand stand sat the delegation of Pittsburg rooters, among whom was President Pulliam of the National League, who had all he could do to refrain from joining in the lusty shouts and vigorous hat swingings indulged in by the men who at home are the staidest of the staid. Once the president did get to his feet and raise his hat. After the game he declared it was one of the proudest moments in his baseball life.

James J. Corbett, the ex-champion pugilist, was among the Pittsburg crowd, but did not take sides. There was not an American League official present. Probably Ban Johnson had an inkling of the downfall of his champions and remained away to avoid a pain in the region of his heart.

When Pittsburg went upon the field for practice a mighty shout went up, it evidently being taken as an indication that the contest would soon begin. The Pirates had the people applauding continually by their fast and snappy play. A shout mightier than the other went up when the Bostons took the field for practice. At once the difference in the teams was noticeable. It was marked by the crowd, for Boston has probably the most impartial fans in the country.

Beaneaters Lack Snap and Vim

The Bostons lacked the snap and vim displayed by the three-time National League champions.

A roar swept across the field when the gong sounded for the game to begin. The umpires, O'Day and Connolly, and the two captains, Clarke and Collins, met at the plate and held a confab, watched by the great crowd in deep silence.

Connolly unexpectedly arrived in Boston this morning. He stated that he had not been officially notified by the American League club of his selection. He had read of it in the newspapers and had come on. Connolly would do nothing until his terms, which he sent to President Killilea of the Boston club, who lives in Milwaukee, had been accepted. He umpired behind the bat today, while O'Day took the bases. Tomorrow O'Day will be behind the bat and Connolly on the bases.

When the quartet of celebrities parted at the home plate the crowd yelled, and when "Cy" Young walked to the pitcher's position it fairly screamed. It crowed a little more when Beaumont and Clarke were rather rapidly disposed of. That, however, was its last yell. The Pirates began to biff the ball in all directions, scoring four runs and winning the game then and there.

Phillippe the Whole Cheese

The chief cause of Boston's downfall was the work of Deacon Phillippe on the rubber. The deacon was all there, and had everything a champion pitcher should have. Only six hits were made off his delivery, two going into the crowd and counting as three-baggers and two others being of the scratchy order. One was a Texas leaguer into left field, and the other a hard drive to Bransfield. The deacon struck out 10 batsmen, something he did not accomplish in the National League.

The American League champions were absolutely powerless before Phillippe. Of the first seven men who faced him, he struck out five, fanning the entire side in the second inning. Not a man went to base on balls before the steady firing of the deacon. His grand performance was cheered by the spectators and vociferously applauded by the Pittsburg delegation, which soon was the only live thing in the stands.

Phillippe was given splendid support. Behind the bat Eddie Phelps never did better work. The outfield did the bulk of the work, and did it to perfection. Clarke made a sensational catch in the fourth of a long liner by Collins, and Beaumont made two catches, one near the ropes and the other back of second base, which opened the eyes of the Boston fans. The infield did not have much to do but were ready for all emergencies.

Couldn't Reach First Base

For three innings only one Boston man reached first base and he never got one inch farther. In the fourth the Boston people woke up for an instant. After two men were out Freeman fired a hot ball at Bransfield which Kitty was unable to handle. Parent then hit to Leach, who threw the ball past Bransfield. Freeman got to third and Parent to second. Now the local fans began to root, but it was no good, as Lachance rolled the ball to Phillippe and was thrown out at first.

In the next two innings not a Beaneater reached first base. In the seventh Freeman caught one of the Deacon's curves and sent the ball against the right field fence for three bases. Nobody being out the spectators saw a chance of at least sidestepping a white wash and began to yell. Parent followed with a hit along the left field foul line into the crowd. It went for three bases and Freeman scored. Lachance sent a high fly to Clarke and Parent came home. Ferris was hit by a pitched ball, but never left first base, Criger and Young struck out.

It was one, two, three in the eighth, but in the ninth the local fans had another chance to yell a little. Freeman knocked an easy one to Wagner, who fumbled.

Crowd Took on Life

At this the crowd straightened up and looked expectantly. Parent dropped the ball into center field for a single, sending Freeman to second. Lachance sent a fly to Clarke. Freeman got to third, but Parent was held at first. Ferris dropped the ball in center field for a single, scoring Freeman. O'Brien, Boston's utility man, was sent to bat for Criger. He struck out. Then big Charley Farrell, bigger than ever, went to bat for Young. He pushed the ball to Phillippe and was thrown out, ending the game.

The Pittsburg champions found old Cy Young's benders to their liking and had little trouble in getting hits, once the ball was sent rolling. Beaumont, the first man up for Pittsburg, went out to Stahl and Clarke went out on a foul fly to Criger. This made things look a little blue for the Pittsburg rooters. Leach woke them up by sending the ball into the crowd in right field for three bases. Wagner smashed the ball past Collins for a single, sending Leach home with the first run.

Rooters Cut Loose

The Pittsburg rooters cut loose vigorously and renewed the applause when Wagner stole second. Bransfield hit to Parent, who fumbled. Kitty was safe at first and Wagner perched at third. Without loss of time, Bransfield stole second.

Criger threw the ball over Parent's head. Wagner came home and Bransfield reached third base. Ritchey was given his base on balls and promptly stole second. The Pittsburg rooters were on their feet on and off at these stages, but when Sebring hit to left for a single, scoring Bransfield and Ritchey, there was bedlam.

Every mother's son of them was on his feet yelling like mad and sailing his hat in frantic delight. There were Johnny Newell, Charley Black, Al Pratt, Carnegie Orris and the rest of them, including Barney Dreyfuss, forgetting the dignity that becomes old age, indulging in the wildest kind of antics, while all around them was dense silence. Phelps reached first base on a missed third strike, but Phillippe struck out, retiring the side. Every Pirate had taken a turn at bat.

Some More Scoring

In the third inning, after Wagner went out to Collins, Bransfield hit to right for a three-baser and scored on a single by Sebring. In the fourth Beaumont reached first on a fumble by Parent, went to second on a single by Clarke, and came home on a single by Leach.

The seventh and last run was made in the seventh when Sebring hit to deep center for a home run.

Sebring's work at the bat was one of the best features of the great contest. Jim made all three of his hits count. His first brought in two runs, his second brought in one and his last scored himself. Leach was a heady man at bat also. Five times he faced the pitcher, and four times he hit safely. Among his hits were two three-baggers.

It is Manager Clarke's intention to pitch Leever to-morrow. If the Pirates win, Bill Kennedy will be given a chance against the Bostons on Saturday. If tomorrow's game is lost, then Phillippe will again be put on the rubber on Saturday.

♦ ♦ ♦

A "YELLOW STREAK"

When twenty-five-game winner Sam Leever left in pain after the first inning of the second game of the 1903 World Series, the Pirates were effectively down to one reliable pitcher. After Pittsburgh lost game two to Boston, Deacon Phillippe came back after his first game victory to win games three and four and give the Pirates a 3-1 lead. Without any pitching depth, however, Pittsburgh went on to lose the next four games, including two by the overworked Phillippe, and lost the series to Boston 5-3. After the series, baseball writers began to question the story of Leever's sore arm and thought he had "laid down" under pressure. They also questioned the character of Honus Wagner and wondered if he had a bit of a "yellow streak" after having only one hit and making five errors in the last four games and batting only .222 for the series.

Christy Mathewson, the New York Giants' great Hall of Fame pitcher, remembered how Wagner was affected by the claim that he was "yellow" and how he went on to vindicate himself in the 1909 World Series against Ty Cobb and the Detroit Tigers. Mathewson had good reason to respect Wagner, who had a lifetime .324 average against him.

Take Him Out

CHRISTY MATHEWSON

There is another element which enters into all forms of athletics. Tennis players call it nervousness, and ball players, in the frankness of the game, call it a "yellow streak." It is the inability to stand the gaff, the weakening in the pinches. It is something ingrained in a man that can't be cured. It is the desire to quit when the situation is serious. It is different from stage fright, because a man can get over that, but a "yellow streak" is always with him. When a new player breaks into the league, he is put to the most severe test by the other men to see if he is "yellow." If he is found wanting, he is hopeless in the Big League, for the news will spread, and he will receive no quarter. It is the cardinal sin in a ball player.

For some time after "Hans" Wagner's poor showing in the world's series of 1903, when the Pittsburg club was defeated for the World's Championship by the Boston American League club, it was reported that he was "yellow." This grieved the Dutchman deeply, for I don't know a ball player in either league who would assay less quit to the ton than Wagner. He is always there and always fighting. Wagner felt the inference which his team mates drew very keenly. This was the real tragedy in Wagner's career. Notwithstanding his stolid appearance, he is a sensitive player, and this hurt him more than anything else in his life ever has.

When the Pittsburg club played Detroit in 1909 for the championship of the world, many, even of Wagner's admirers, said, "The Dutchman will quit." It was in this series he vindicated himself. His batting scored the majority of the Pittsburg runs, and his fielding was little short of wonderful. He was demonstrating his gameness. Many men would have quit under the reflection. They would have been unable to withstand the criticism, but not Wagner.

From *Pitching in a Pinch or, Baseball from the Inside* by Christy Mathewson with John W. Wheeler (New York and London: G. P. Putnam's Sons, 1912).

◆ ◆ ◆

THAT DAMN *TESSIE* SONG

When Ty Cobb died in 1961, Lawrence Ritter decided that someone needed to act quickly to record the fading voices from baseball's past for future generations of base-ball fans. First published in 1966, Ritter's The Glory of Their Times, *with its won-derful evocation of a nearly lost baseball era, is now regarded as a baseball classic and the standard for the baseball oral history.*

Tommy Leach was one of several former Pirates interviewed by Lawrence Ritter for The Glory of Their Times. *Leach came to Pittsburgh from Louisville in 1900, along with Honus Wagner, Fred Clarke, and several other players, as part of Barney Dreyfuss's eventual takeover of the Pirates. Tommy Leach was only 5 feet 6 inches and never weighed more than 150 pounds, but he led the National League in triples (22) and home runs (6) in 1902, and went on to help the Pirates win four pennants and the 1909 World Series. Here, he talks about how he started in the major leagues and how wild it was in the first World Series against Boston.*

Tommy Leach

LAWRENCE S. RITTER

Listen, when you say the name Wagner to me, you better say *Honus* Wagner. Anybody else, you mention Wagner to them and they know right off who you're talking about. But not me. That very confusion resulted in me almost pulling one of the biggest boners of my whole life.

It happened in 1898. I was a skinny twenty-year-old kid, only 135 pounds, playing third base for the Auburn Club of the New York State League. About a month before the end of the season the owner of the club sent down word that he wanted me to come in and see him. "Uh-oh," I thought, "what the dickens is coming now?"

"I told you I was going to sell you to a Big League club before the sea-son was over," he said, "and I've got a chance to do just that. Two National League clubs want you, and I'm going to let you make the choice. Where would you rather go, Washington or Louisville?"

"Well," I said, "I'd like to talk to the manager first, before I make a de-cision, if you're really going to let me make it. I don't know anything about those clubs, and I'd like to go where I have the best chance."

From *The Glory of Their Times: The Story of the Early Days of Baseball Told by the Men Who Played It* by Lawrence S. Ritter (New York: William Morrow, 1984). Reprinted with permission of Lawrence S. Ritter.

"That's all right," he said. "You won't go until our season is over, anyway. And then you'll report to whichever club you pick."

So I went to the manager. He was a real old-timer. I don't know whatever became of him. He was a drinking man, and they let him go soon after.

I put it to him: "I just want you to tell me where I'll have the opportunity to show what I can do," I said. "I'd like to go where I'll have the best chance to play third base, because I know that's my best position."

"I'll tell you," he said, "knowing what I know, I'd say take Louisville. If you go to Washington, they have a man there who's a darned good third baseman. His name is Wagner."

Well, I didn't know Wagner from beans. So, naturally, I chose Louisville. Our season at Auburn ended a month before the Big League season was over, so in late August of 1898 I reported to the Louisville club.

I hardly had time to get settled before it hit me that this guy the Louisville club had at third base was practically doing the impossible. I'm sitting on the bench the first day I reported, and along about the third inning an opposing batter smacks a line drive down the third-base line that looked like at least a sure double. Well, this big Louisville third baseman jumped over after it like he was on steel springs, slapped it down with his bare hand, scrambled after it at least ten feet, and fired a bullet over to first base. The runner was out by two or three steps.

I'm sitting on the bench and my eyes are popping out. So I poked the guy sitting next to me, and asked him who the devil that big fellow was on third base.

"Why, that's Wagner," he says. "He's the best third baseman in the league."

And when I heard that, did I ever groan. I'm sure it was loud enough to be heard the whole length of the bench. "What chance does a tiny guy like me have here, anyway?" I thought to myself. "Wagner isn't with Washington, he's *here*."

Do you know what happened? There was a Wagner with Washington, all right. But it was *Al* Wagner, Honus' brother. Honus himself was right there in Louisville.

Well, it all turned out for the best, of course, but until it did you can bet I was pretty sore at that Auburn manager for giving me the benefit of his wisdom. It turned out for the best because I wound up in Pittsburgh on one of the greatest teams that ever played. We won the pennant four times in the next ten years or so, and beat Ty Cobb and the Tigers in the World Series the last time.

You see, after the 1899 season the National League cut back from twelve to eight clubs. Louisville was one of the four clubs cut out, but Barney Dreyfuss, who owned the Louisville club, bought the Pittsburgh Pirates and transferred a dozen of us who were with Louisville over to Pittsburgh. So the Pittsburgh club that started the season in 1900 was mostly the same team as the Louisville club that had ended the 1899 season.

And it also turned out that while Honus was the best third baseman in the league, he was also the best first baseman, the best second baseman, the best shortstop, and the best outfielder. That was in fielding. And since he led the league in batting eight times between 1900 and 1911, you know that he was the best hitter, too. As well as the best base runner.

◆

The next year—that would be 1900—we moved from Louisville to Pittsburgh. We had a little trouble getting started that year, and in June we were in last place. Then we started playing the way we should, and we almost won the pennant. Brooklyn beat us out by only a couple of games, even after our bad start.

But we did win it the next three years, in 1901, 1902, and 1903. In 1902 we won the National League pennant by 27½ games over the second-place team. Even in all the years that have passed since then no club in either major league has ever finished that far out in front. That was the year, believe it or not, that I led the league in home runs. I really did. I had six. The next year I did even better: I hit seven. But Jimmy Sheckard beat me out with nine.

Of course, I wasn't a home-run hitter like you see today. The fields were big then, and if you hit a ball between the outfielders and were fast enough, you had a home run. None of those I hit went over the fence.

In 1902, like I said, we won the pennant by 27½ games, and do you know that our starting pitcher pitched the *complete* game in something like 130 out of the 140 games we played that season? Just think of that, and compare it with today. It's hard to believe, isn't it? We had four pitchers, and they just took their regular turn, day after day, and went the distance almost every time: Jack Chesbro, Deacon Phillippe, Sam Leever, and Jesse Tannehill. Four of the best pitchers in baseball!

In 1903 we won the pennant again, the third year in a row, and that was the year we were in the first World Series ever played. The very first there ever was. The American League had started in 1901, but the two leagues couldn't get together to play each other until 1903. I hit four triples in that Series, but it didn't help, because the Boston Red Sox beat us anyway. I think they were called the Boston Pilgrims then, by the way.

That was probably the wildest World Series ever played. Arguing all the time between the teams, between the players and the umpires, and especially between the players and the fans. That's the truth. The fans were *part* of the game in those days. They'd pour right out onto the field and argue with the players and the umpires. Was sort of hard to keep the game going sometimes, to say the least.

I think those Boston fans actually won that Series for the Red Sox. We beat them three out of the first four games, and then they started singing that damn *Tessie* song, the Red Sox fans did. They called themselves the Royal Rooters and their leader was some Boston character named Mike McGreevey. He was known as "Nuf Sed" McGreevey, because any time there was an argument about anything to do with baseball he was the ultimate authority. Once McGreevey gave his opinion that ended the argument: nuf sed!

Anyway, in the fifth game of the Series the Royal Rooters started singing *Tessie* for no particular reason at all, and the Red Sox won. They must have figured it was a good-luck charm, because from then on you could hardly play ball they were singing *Tessie* so damn loud.

Tessie was a real big popular song in those days. You remember it, don't you?

> *Tessie, you make me feel so badly,*
> *Why don't you turn around.*
> *Tessie, you know I love you madly,*
> *Babe, my heart weighs about a pound.*

Yeah, that was a real humdinger in those days. Like *The Music Goes Round and Round* in the 'thirties. Now you surely remember *that* one?

Only instead of singing "Tessie, you know I love you madly," they'd sing special lyrics to each of the Red Sox players: like "Jimmy, you know I love you madly." And for us Pirates they'd change it a little. Like when Honus Wagner came up to bat they'd sing:

> *Honus, why do you hit so badly,*
> *Take a back seat and sit down.*
> *Honus, at bat you look so sadly,*
> *Hey, why don't you get out of town.*

Sort of got on your nerves after a while. And before we knew what happened, we'd lost the World Series.

That year, 1903, was also the year Honus became a full-time shortstop. Up until 1903 he played almost every position on the team, one day at short, the next day in the outfield, the day after at first base. He didn't look like a shortstop, you know. He had those huge shoulders and those bowed legs, and he didn't seem to field balls the way we did. He just ate the ball up with his big hands, like a scoop shovel, and when he threw it to first base you'd see pebbles and dirt and everything else flying over there along with the ball. It was quite a sight! The greatest shortstop ever. The greatest *everything* ever.

We never finished out of the first division the next five years, but we didn't win again until 1909. That year we evened it up with the American League by beating the Tigers in the World Series. They had a good team, too: Ty Cobb, Sam Crawford, Davy Jones, Donie Bush, George Moriarty, and all that bunch.

That was a mighty rough World Series in 1909, you know. Almost as rough as that first one in 1903. There was a lot of bad blood between us and Detroit, especially with that George Moriarty, the Detroit third baseman. He was a tough character.

It so happened that right about that time I started to get bald. Terrible feeling. I was only about thirty years old then. Well, somebody told me that I could stop my hair from falling out if I'd shave it off completely and rub this liniment on my head. I think it was some kind of horse liniment, to tell the truth. So that's exactly what I did, just before the Series started. It was foolishness, but I did it anyway.

Well, in one of the games of the Series—I forgot just which one—I got a single and went to third on a hit by Honus. I'm standing there on third base, not thinking about anything in particular, when this Moriarty suddenly comes over and kicks me in the shin. Just like that.

I looked at him in surprise, and asked him what was the meaning of such a thing. He just walked away, didn't say a word. I had to stay right where I was, of course. I didn't dare get off the base, because if I did they'd tag me out.

A few seconds later I had my back turned and he comes over again, and this time he grabs my cap right off my head. I was embarrassed and I started to laugh.

"Well," I said, "I got it all shaved off the other day." I wanted to explain to him why there was no hair on my head, you know.

But he didn't wait for me to finish. He reached up and slapped me right on top of my bare head. With my own cap, too!

Boy, that was too much. So I turned around and grabbed my cap, and at the same time gave him a good healthy kick in the shins. We were about to really go to it when the game started again, and I think the inning ended on the next pitch, so that was that. Anyway, as you can see, that horse liniment didn't do a heck of a lot of good.

◆

You might think this is all a lot of malarkey, but I really believe baseball was a more exciting game back in those days. It was more rugged, first of all. Take the equipment. We had little gloves that would just fit over your hand. Now they have those big nets, and they catch the ball in the webbing. But we had to catch the ball with our hands.

And the fields. Now the lowest minor leagues have better fields to play on than we had in the major leagues. You never knew how a ball was going to bounce in those days. Lots of times we'd get a rake and go out and rake the ground around our own positions.

The style of play is very different now, too. We used to play a running game, a lot of bunting and base stealing. I stole almost 400 bases in my Big League career, and that wasn't considered much at all. Heck, Fred Clarke stole over 500, and Honus over 700. All of us on one team, mind you. Even the fellows who were considered the power hitters in those days used to run the bases a lot. Like Sam Crawford, the strong boy—he stole about 400 bases, and so did other big guys, like Jake Beckley and Dan Brouthers.

Today they seem to think that the most exciting play in baseball is the home run. But in *my* book the most exciting play in baseball is a three-bagger, or an inside-the-park home run. You used to see a fair number of them in the old days, but now they're the rarest plays in baseball. For sheer excitement, I don't think anything can beat when you see that guy go tearing around the bases and come sliding into third or into the plate, with the ball coming in on a line from the outfield at the same time. Now *that's* something to write home about.

◆　◆　◆

FATHER CHADWICK

Henry Chadwick, who emigrated from England to the United States in 1837 at the age of thirteen, became the foremost pioneer of American baseball. The only journalist elected directly into the Hall of Fame, he has often been called the Father of Baseball. Father Chadwick was a champion of baseball as the national pastime, but his essential contribution to the development of the game was his invention of the box score and numerous statistical categories, including the batting average. Here he argues for a further evolution of the batting average by including "runners forwarded" as the deciding measurement of effective hitting. Using this new category, Chadwick claims that Honus Wagner, who lost the batting title to Cincinnati's Cy Seymour in 1905, was a much more effective hitter. Chadwick's argument was futile, but Wagner, without the assistance of Chadwick, went on to win the batting title for the next four years.

Chadwick's Chat

HENRY CHADWICK

In my correspondence last week I found a letter from the official scorer of a Western college club who, in one of his three questions, asked me this, viz.: "Which batsman would you give the palm to for the best record for really effective batting? To him who excelled in the figures of best percentage of base hits or him who had the best percentage in forwarding runners by his hits?"

The writer stated that in making up his averages for 1905 he had introduced the data of "percent of runners forwarded by base hits," and that in accordance with this latter base of estimate, he found that while batsman No. 1 had had a percentage of base hits of .367 with but .307 from the record of runners forwarded by hits, batsman No. 2, in base hit per cent, had the percentage of .357 in forwarding runners. My reply was that, under the faulty construction of the existing code of playing rules, he had no option but to decide the question in accordance with the only existing rule, viz., that of per cent of base hits, inasmuch as the code did not recognize any other criterion of batting excellence.

National League Batting

In the National statistics of 1905 will be found in the batting averages tables the record awarding the palm of batting superiority for the season to Seymour, of Cincinnati, on the single basis of his figures of .377 in base hit percentage, with Wagner of Pittsburg rated as second on the list, by his per cent of .363. Yet there is no questioning the fact that Wagner led Seymour in the per cent of runners forwarded by hits. But, regarding the real effectiveness of his work for the defense, Wagner was the best batsman of the two. Between Seymour and Chance, of Chicago, too, taking into consideration the defensive work of sacrifice hits and stolen bases, the latter was the most valuable man of the two, inasmuch as Chance had a record of thirty-eight stolen bases to Seymour's twenty-one, and of fifteen sacrifice hits to Seymour's nine, besides which Chance played in fewer games by 115 to Seymour's 149.

From *Sporting Life*, February 3, 1906.

American League Batting

Looking over the American League statistics for 1905, too, I find a similar unjust estimate made. In these latter records, while Lajoie of Cleveland is given the lead as the champion batsman of 1905, by his record of .329 in base hit percentage in sixty-five games, Keeler of New York is placed fifth on the list with .302 in 149 games, with additional defensive record skills of forty-two sacrifice hits to Lajoie's three such hits, besides excelling him in base running.

But as to the really effective batter, Keeler, by his great lead over every other batsman in the country in forwarding runners by hits—the only true criterion of batting excellence—of which the existing code of rules takes no cognizance, is made to rate as fifth on the American records.

Well-Founded Fear

I wonder if the Rules Committee of 1906 is so wedded to the old erroneous basis of estimates to once more refuse to recognize the great need of amendment to the code of data of runners forwarded by base hits. But the committees of the past decade have become so habituated to depending upon the old estimate—"He batted over .300, you know"—that I fear that the long-needed addition has very little chance of adoption.

◆　◆　◆

"THE FINEST FIELD ON EARTH"

Barney Dreyfuss's role in Pittsburgh's baseball history took on an even greater magnitude at the end of the first decade of the twentieth century when he decided to build a new steel and concrete ballpark for the Pirates and their fans. He was determined to get his team out of Exposition Park with its shabby conditions, industrial surroundings, and the constant flooding from the Allegheny River. Dreyfuss wanted a ballpark that would stand as a symbol of civic pride and a modern monument to baseball's self-proclaimed status as the national pastime. Dreyfuss's three-tiered "folly" as it was first dubbed by Dreyfuss's critics, was constructed at the entrance to Schenley Park in Oakland, a rapidly developing cultural area in the city. Six months after construction began, Forbes Field, named after British General John Forbes, opened to great fanfare on June 30, 1909. The Pirates lost their first game at Forbes Field to the defending World Champion Chicago Cubs 3-2, but the ballpark was an overwhelming success and the fans' excitement a harbinger of things to come in the 1909 season.

Pirates Lose First Game on Forbes Field

STAFF REPORTER

GREAT ENTHUSIASM, THOUGH CHICAGO CAPTURES CONTEST

INSPIRING SIGHT FULL OF ACTION

OLD-TIME PLAYERS AND PUBLIC OFFICIALS HELP IN DEDICATION
CEREMONIES

Staid Oakland rang and rang again yesterday afternoon with frenzied cheering from 30,338 throats because of an unparalleled event, the dedication of wonderful Forbes Field, that triumphant exposition of Pittsburgh's sportsmanship.

The enormous throng, a record-breaker in attendance at a baseball game, enthusiasm and other things, intent in paying homage to King Baseball, refused to be subdued, even when Chicago carried off the victory after nine innings of sensational play by a score of 3 to 2.

There may have been other parks opened with ceremonies imposing enough, attended by notables and having the usual "trimmings," but previous events fade into insignificance in comparison with the dedication of grounds the equal of which have never before been seen.

A scene of magnificent inspiration for fan and player alike was presented by the great mass of humanity filling the grandstand tier upon tier, banked in the bleachers and encircling the playing field in solid array. About the four sides of the amphitheater the only break in the shifting mass of color was the strip of concrete wall visible in left field, below the dangling legs of those perched upon it and those wedged tightly below.

Fitting Features of Event

Presence of the most influential figures in the world of balldom and the fact that Chicago, the National League and world's championship team, was opposing the Pittsburgh team, form fitting features of the occasion. Of course, intense interest was taken in each minute of the game, yet the real purpose of enthusiasts was evidently to see that nothing was lacking in proper initiation of the new grounds.

Fans could scarcely help compare surroundings with those of Exposition Park, the field dear to all because of countless memories and associations. Never was a June day fairer. No trace of smoke blurred the sun-bathed lawns, woodlands and drives of Schenley Park spread out on a beautiful panorama of sylvan beauty. To the left were seen the Carnegie Institute and Carnegie Technical schools, while on the horizon glimpses were visible of stately private mansions. It was a scene to make participants forget business cares of a manufacturing city. Birds yet unaccustomed to having their haunts invaded flew across the diamond now and again.

Had the megaphone-armed "fans," men, women and children, proudly enrolled under the title, needed a reminder that it was a gala day, their memory would have been jogged by the brave display of bunting. Flags fluttered and snapped at every gable. Above the topmost boxes white streamers bearing the names of each National League club were alternated with United States ensigns.

The most wonderful spectacle of the day was viewed by those who waited a moment after the last man was out. In an instant outfield and infield were covered by the crowd, converging in orderly lines, as though on parade, on the main entrance gates. Stands and fields were emptied of their thousands in 15 minutes, while, had the crowd been acquainted with the many means of egress, all probably would have been able to leave the grounds in less than 10 minutes.

Society at the Game

Society played a prominent part in the gala event. Handsomely gowned women and daintily garbed girls transformed the occasion into a brilliant affair. Families prominent in the city's professional, religious, educational and industrial life for generations were largely represented. Automobiles lined the curbs of Bouquet Street and the new street opened at the entrance. Women formed no inconsiderable factor in the attendance and were no less enthusiastic than the men.

Spectators began arriving before noon. Before the gates were opened, a mob was clamoring for admission. Every town in Western Pennsylvania was represented in the throngs that, after every seat was occupied, were glad to stand if they could but take part in the celebration. No village was too small to organize a delegation.

It was a half-holiday of necessity in many of the section's greatest establishments. Stores in the Bellefield and Oakland districts closed for the afternoon, and nowhere was there a "boss" so unfeeling as not to accept the venerable "dead grandmother" excuse.

Ready to Handle Throngs

Every detail was found in readiness for their reception when the fans poured into the grounds. Bunting covered unfinished walls, and ferns and palms beautified corners in the spacious corridors. Well-drilled ushers handled the surging crowds quickly and without a cause for complaint. One glance at the glistening turf and smooth base paths assured fast play.

The Pittsburgh Railways Company handled the crowd ably though it was a gigantic task and by Saturday, when the "rough spots" are smooth, there will not be a hitch.

If President Barney Dreyfuss' idea had been to furnish a park so big that Pittsburgh could not fill it, he would have been disappointed. There were no vacant places. Even grandstand aisles were occupied by late-comers.

Considering the attendance, there was little confusion. Placards pointed the way to booths where tickets were purchased for "bleachers," intermediate seats or the grandstand. There were 50 uniformed policemen scattered through the grounds, who added to the dignity of the occasion, but had nothing to do. Boys vending soft drinks were unable to supply the shouted demands of fans whom shouting had made thirsty.

An appreciated feature of "the finest field on earth" was the fact that, owing to their position, the entire grandstand and most of the bleachers were shaded from the afternoon's sun. Seats are of a style and comfort usually found only in theaters.

All Done by Pittsburghers

Planned by Pittsburghers, erected with Pittsburgh money and completed in record time with the city's customary "hustle," it was eminently proper that opening exercises should exceed all expectations. In building a monument epitomizing the stability of modern baseball, Pittsburgh honors herself.

The good nature of spectators afforded an illustration of the manner in which Pittsburghers take their amusements. Jostling and laughingly arguing claims for precedence, the fans flowed into the park and out again. No accidents marred the event.

It was an occasion that drew the most influential men of the baseball world to the city. Among officials present were President H. C. Pulliam and Secretary John A. Heydler of the National League; Secretary John H. Farrell of the National Association of Minor Baseball leagues; Joseph D. O'Brien, president of the American Association; Francis Richter, the owner of "Sporting Life," and President Kilfoyl of the Cleveland American League club.

A. G. Pratt led the cohorts of old-timers, mighty men of the game in their day. Among them were Frank J. Paulson, George B. Logan, Congressman John K. Tener, Dr. M. E. Baldwin, Edward Hanlon, president of the Baltimore baseball club, J. H. Stewart, A. S. Cameron, A. J. Bryan, James W. Gray, Samuel Nicholl, Frank Curry, W. S. Gumbert, Edward Morris, Grant Briggs, John R. Brown, William Clark, Commissioner S. J. Toole, Marr Phillips, P. R. McShannic, Henry Earle, John Menefee, L. N. Moore, Henry Irvin, J. T. Irvin, H. D. Moore, Dr. C. C. Rinehart, Frank Rinehart, Sheriff A. C. Gumbert, and M. A. Kirtchley.

Assisted in Exercises

Officials at the helm of city and county affairs, former players who have attained high places in business life, and men who are actively engaged in guiding the destinies of modern baseball development felt themselves honored by an opportunity to assist in the exercises. Yet it was realized that after all the day and the place were for the common garden variety of "fan."

Ceremonies dignified in their simplicity inaugurated the dedication, if it can be said to have had any beginning, when for two hours previously there had been a bedlam of noise drowning the music of the assembled bands. Officials of the baseball club and old-time ball players followed in the wake of the band in a procession from the home plate to the flagstaff in center field. Behind went Captains Clarke and Chance, leading their players, the white uniformed upholders of Pittsburgh's supremacy each paired with a gray-clad Chicagoan.

Up went the American flag, with above it a banner bearing the magic words, "Forbes Field." All former outbursts of yells and cheerings were as a summer zephyr compared to an equinoctial hurricane in contrast with the thundering roar that burst from the excited thousands waving their hats and handkerchiefs, shrieking and whistling in an apparent frenzy. In every heart was the hope that in the coming months the pennant of the National League and world's championship would be won.

Tribute Paid to Dead

Not even in the elation to the occasion was it forgotten to pay a tribute of respect to the dead. The banners rose above the exalting throngs, but stopped at half-mast, in memory of President L. W. Durham of the Philadelphia National League club, whose funeral takes place today. In consequence, the second clash between Chicago and Pittsburgh will be postponed.

Cornet signals blown by Commodore Charles Zeig, faintly heard amid the uproar, set time for the practice of opposing teams and the beginning of the game. The musician stood in the field and could have been easily heard from every stand if the noise had subsided. The first signal sounded at 2:55 for the Pittsburgh's team batting practice; at 3:15 it announced the visitor's fielding practice; at 3:23 the home team's fielding practice; and at 3:30 the commencement of the game.

After all, "the game's the thing." The eyes of every fan were riveted upon Mayor Magee as he arose in an upper box grasping a new, glistening white ball. Far below, near the home plate, stood Director of Public Safety John Morin. In a flashing curve impelled by the executive arm, the ball dropped to the Pride of Oakland's waiting hands. Perhaps the one-time great ball player is out of practice or more probably he was "over anxious to complete the play," the sporting writer's stock excuse. He muffed!

Borrowing Fred Clarke's cap, Mr. Morin, who used to pitch for the Missoula (Mont.) team, retrieved his error handsomely when he shot the ball across the plate and into Catcher Gibson's glove, Evers, of Chicago, swinging at it ferociously as it passed. Almost five seconds of silence, the first in several hours, accompanied the ceremony, and then, with the game started, the noise began again.

Warm Greeting for Each Pirate

A heart-warming reception greeted each Pittsburgh player. And if the applause for Wagner, Clarke and Leach was a little more thunderous, the team's young blood should remember it is the veterans' due.

As breathless moments succeeded one another—when Chicago forged to the front, and was overtaken and again secured a lead, in the tense instants when a hit or an error meant victory or defeat, or when Miller's smash was thought to have won the game for Pittsburgh, only to have the umpire call it a two-bagger because of the ground rules—the character of Pittsburgh's sportsmanship was tested to the utmost. It emerged stainless, preserving the fans' reputation as good losers. Just one "knocker" in all the mighty horde is said to have been found, but he was forced to subside after a single remark in face of the storm of protest.

◆

Surprise depicted upon faces of the oldest habitues of the games formed one of the most interesting features of the reflex action of attendance figures. Men who have been fans for a score of years stood and gazed dumbfounded about the field surrounded by a dense crowd on every side, each individual yelling an unintelligible nothing.

Interest in the event was confined to no class or creed. Millionaire shouted with mechanic, and office boy with bank president. And high about the roar occasionally shouted the voice of some "sweet young thing."

◆ ◆ ◆

Forbes Field became a palace of delights in 1909 for Pittsburgh baseball fans when the Pirates won their first National pennant since the ill-fated 1903 season. The Pirates finished with a team-high 110 victories and dethroned the powerful Chicago Cubs, winners of the last three National League pennants and two consecutive World Series crowns. After finishing in the first division every year since 1903, including three second-place finishes, Pittsburgh finally had a chance to make up for its disappointing loss in baseball's first World Series. The Pirates, heavy favorites in 1903, were underdogs in 1909 to an experienced and improved Detroit Tigers team that had lost the 1907 and 1908 World Series to Chicago and now seemed ready to claim its first championship. The 1909 World Series turned into a seesaw affair; the Pirates won games one, three, and five and the Tigers won two, four, and six. Barney Dreyfuss then lost a coin toss to decide the site of the seventh and deciding game, which was played in Detroit on October 9, 1909.

Among the many who watched Pittsburgh claim its first World Series championship was Ring Lardner. Before he became a national celebrity and syndicated columnist, Lardner was a sportswriter, mainly for the Chicago Tribune, *where this excerpt from his special report first appeared. Lardner became a legend among sportswriters because he, as Elizabeth Hardwick once wrote, "made literature out of baseball."*

Pirates Outgame Tigers for Title

RING LARDNER

Once more the National League is triumphant. The Pittsburg Pirates today won the championship of the world by beating Detroit in the seventh and deciding game of the series, 8-0.

To Babe Adams must be handed the palm. This young gentleman from Missouri, pitching his first season in the big leagues, was called on by Manager Clarke this afternoon to work for the third time in the series. He had two victories to his credit out of two attempts and was really the only Pirate pitcher who had puzzled Detroit at all. Game to the core, Babe came back and held the Tiger sluggers helpless from start to finish.

It was the only time during the series that Detroit was shut out. The probabilities are the Tigers wouldn't have been blanked if they hadn't been behind almost at the start, but that doesn't make any difference.

From the *Chicago Tribune*, October 10, 1909.

They were beaten and beaten soundly. There were no excuses to offer and not a Detroit player tried to offer any.

The Tigers couldn't win very well without any runs. They had less of a chance after Bill Donovan had handed Pittsburg two tallies in the second inning. It was thought that Donovan had shaken off his title of Wild Bill. But he surely was wild this time. Probably the weather wasn't to his liking. There was something wrong anyhow, and Bill pitched badly enough in the first three rounds to lose any game in the world. He had a lot of luck or the Pittsburgers would have counted many more times than they did.

Mullin Succeeds Donovan

When Bill had proven conclusively to Jennings that he was not the man to go through with it, the boss took him out and substituted George Mullin, the Tiger pitcher who had made the seventh game a necessity. Mullin had done too much. He didn't have any more stuff left with which to fool the Pirates, and he probably knew it when he went in. Pittsburg had the jump and no pitcher in the world could have secured a verdict at this stage. Mullin pitched as hard as he knew how, but the Pirates were full of the pepper that accompanies a nice lead and they were the aggressors from start to finish.

It was not an ideal day for Donovan. Much warmer than Friday and with a sun that came out at intervals and shone brightly, the afternoon was still far from hot, and Bill likes hot weather almost as well as victory. Nevertheless it was policy to pitch him and hold Mullin in reserve. The Tigers had been beaten twice by Adams and they were due to get after him.

Mullin had worked thrice, with two victories and one defeat to his credit, or debit, and the dope was that the pitcher who was not so well known to the hitters would come out ahead. Donovan had beaten Pittsburg in the only game he pitched, so Jennings picked him instead of Mullin because he thought it was time for the Pirates to get wise to the Wabash, Ind., person.

Tigers Play Good Ball

Neither Tiger pitcher could blame his support for the result. Donovan was wholly and solely responsible for the two tallies while he was working and the two Detroit errors were made after the game had been finished to all intents and purposes. The Detroit defense was marvelous. So was that of Pittsburg, although the chances given the Pirate fielders were not as hard as those handed the Tigers. Little Owen Bush played a more than perfect game at shortstop and Wagner's stunts didn't come up to his, even though the big Dutchman performed in a manner nothing short of wonderful. Davey Jones and Sam Crawford were there with some more great outfielding and so was Fred Clarke.

The cripples on both clubs started the game, but before the second inning was over two athletes had to leave the field on account of injuries. Bobby Byrne suffered a sprained ankle and his mates carried him off the field in the middle of the opening round. George Moriarity was hurt in the collision that put Byrne out of it and he lasted only until he had driven to third base the only Tiger who got there.

The two wounds brought Charles O'Leary and Ham Hyatt into the game. Neither of them did anything especially creditable and neither of them was responsible for the ultimate outcome. Even the Detroit bugs hated to see Byrne get his injury in this crucial game, and there were cheers for him by Tiger partisans when he was hurried to the clubhouse. There also were cheers for Moriarity when he limped past the left field stands, unable to do more service for his club.

Injured Back on Battlefield

The injured pair were hurried through their dressing and both returned to the battlefield to watch their brethren wind it up. Byrne forgot his pain in the joy of the hour. Moriarity, however, was a pitiful sight. He had to sit there and watch the downfall of the Tigers without a chance to go out and help them or share in their bereavement.

In the big duel between the stars of the two teams, Wagner and Cobb, the Dutchman was fortunate enough to finish with top honors. He drove all hope from the breasts of Detroit's adherents with his three-base hit in the sixth, and he pulled off things in the field that brought his admirers to their feet in appreciation. Cobb didn't manage to hit a ball on to safe territory, nor did he have any chance to shine in the field.

The work of the Pittsburg defense was perfect. Even Bill Abstein, who had been censured by his team mates and by Pittsburg bugs for his poor work all through the series, butted in with some classy playing and worked around his position like a real first baseman.

There is almost as much noise in Detroit tonight as if the Tigers had won. The Pittsburg partisans evidently came to stay awhile. They were all over the streets in big and loud numbers after the game, and they were certainly celebrating some. They had their own band with them and the band played more noisily than musically. As was perfectly natural there was a general rush for joy water and the natural enthusiasm over the victory was doubled by the almost unlimited flow of White Seal, Ruinart, Bourbon, and Budweiser.

The betting today was 10 to 9 in favor of Detroit and it is needless to say that the supporters of the Pirates made a lot of money at the odds. They are spending it, or most of it, at least. No one was able to buy anything at all this evening unless he is from the city of smoke. One would think this was Pennsylvania instead of Michigan.

The Wolverines are taking the whole thing with becoming cheerfulness, but they can't begin to be as cheerful as those who are celebrating a real victory.

◆ ◆ ◆

THE STARS OF THE SERIES

The dramatic centerpiece for the 1909 World Series was the competition between two of baseball's greatest stars, Honus Wagner and Ty Cobb, both league batting champions in 1909. Wagner clearly outplayed Cobb, outhitting him .333 to .231 and proving his courage in a now legendary confrontation on the base paths. The real story in the series, however, was manager Fred Clarke's decision to start rookie Babe Adams in game one instead of one of his veteran pitchers. Adams went on to win three complete games, including an 8-0 shutout in the seventh and deciding game, and became an instant baseball celebrity. In his long career with Pittsburgh, Babe Adams won 194 games, ranking third behind only Wilbur Cooper and Sam Leever on the all-time Pirate list. A year before the end of his career, he pitched one scoreless inning against the Washington Senators in the 1925 World Series.

John P. Carmichael's My Greatest Day in Baseball, *first published in 1945, is a collection of interviews that originally appeared in the* Chicago Daily News. *Among the forty-seven famous players interviewed were Honus Wagner and Babe Adams, who, not surprisingly, picked the seventh game of the 1909 World Series as their greatest day in baseball.*

Babe Adams

as told to HERBERT F. MCDOUGAL
JOHN P. CARMICHAEL, Editor

About an hour and a half before the first game of the 1909 World Series at Pittsburgh, I was sitting on the bench with the other Pirate youngsters making jokes about how we'd handle the Detroit Tigers if we could get in the series. It was strictly fooling, for we all knew the team was full of stars and we were only kids. I was 21, and never was what you'd call high-strung—just a country boy who had been drawn to the game by all the interest around my home, Mount Moriah, Mo., and the near-by towns of Princeton, and the Shane-Hills from across the line in Kansas. Cy Young and his brother Lon were playing at Spickard. The woods were full of amateurs then.

A Missourian named Ham Hamilton, who was an umpire out on the Pacific Coast, came home the winter of 1904, I think it was, and was hired by the New Missouri Valley League to scout players. He watched me pitch for Mount Moriah and signed me to play with Parsons, Kansas. I did all right that 1905 season and had a trial with the St. Louis Cardinals in 1906 but didn't stick, and signed with Louisville where I lasted a couple of weeks and was shipped to Denver where a Pirate scout signed me in 1907. The Pirates tried me out then and gave me more seasoning at Louisville where I won 22 games in 1908 and was brought back up by the Pirates for the 1909 season.

Fred Clarke, the manager, used me in about 25 games or so, and I won about 12 and lost only three, but that was nothing to the big three on our club: Howard Camnitz, who won 25; Lefty Leifield, who won 19; and Vic Willis, who won 22. And Nick Maddox, with 13 wins, was great in a tight game, and Deacon Philippe, though getting along, was just the man for a World Series game. For relief we had old Sam Leever, as smart as they made them.

It was enough for me that I was on a team with those stars and Hans Wagner and Tommy Leach and George Gibson. Gibson had caught 133 consecutive games for us. I remember when he caught the 111th it broke the world's record.

We had a team that year, and had beaten out the Cubs and Giants by putting on a 16-game winning streak in August to clinch it. What helped us was the way Christy Mathewson beat the Cubs that season. As I remember it he hadn't beaten Mordecai Brown in a pitching duel in four or five years till that season when he turned the tables.

(The record book shows that on June 8, Mathewson beat Brown for the first time since 1903. Editor's note.)

It was Matty's greatest year, as I recall.

(Mathewson won 26 and lost 6 that year for an .806 average, his big league top. He was out several weeks with an injured finger or he might have reached his 1908 tops in games won, 37. Editor's note.)

Nobody ever had a more exciting freshman year I suppose. Playing a double-header against the Giants that summer I played to 35,000 people, which everybody said was the biggest crowd baseball had ever drawn. I remember we won the flag by taking 110 victories, but had to go like mad because the Cubs won 104.

Considering the opposition we had beaten that year we felt we could take the Tigers in the World Series, but the betting was in favor of Hughie Jennings' team. The experts figured that with Ty Cobb and Sam Crawford as the big batting punch, and with such pitchers as Mullin, a 29-game winner; Willett, a 22-game winner; and Summers, a 19-game winner; and Owen Bush, a whirlwind fielder at short, they'd chew us up.

To hear all the talk and read all the papers this Cobb was going to go this time. The Tigers had been licked by the Cubs in the 1907 World Series, four games to one, and again by the same dose in 1908. That meant they had won only two games in the last two World Series and they were raving.

I'd keep hearing how the Cub pitchers had stopped Cobb in the 1907 series, but how he'd broken out and hit them for a .368 average in the 1908 series, and how the Pirate pitchers weren't as good as the Cubs' Brown, Overall, Reulbach, Pfiester, and so on.

But we figured we were the National League champs, who had licked the American League in three of the last four World Series and that not even Cobb could stop us from making it four.

The newspapers had said I was to start the first game because Howard Camnitz was still weak from a throat operation he'd had, but we youngsters all thought that was Fred Clarke just working some pre-game tricks on the Tigers. I was enjoying myself kidding on the bench before the game, free as a bird, when suddenly we looked up and Clarke was standing there and he threw me the ball and said, "You're it."

I caught it and laughed, for he could be pretty funny. But he repeated, "You're it. Come on, kid."

I warmed up. I wasn't a bit excited, though I was sort of anxious about Ty Cobb. We had talked a lot about him, of course. He was in his fifth year with the Tigers and had burned that American League to a crisp. He had had a big year.

(Cobb had hit .377 that season, stolen 76 bases, driven in 115 runs and scored 110 times. He was only 22, although in his fifth season with the Tigers. Editor's note.)

Being too careful, I walked him that first time and Delehanty singled him home, but I got him out the rest of the game—and we won 4 to 1. I gave them 6 hits. The Tigers won the next game and we took the next and it see-sawed, turn about, that way up to the seventh. Clarke pitched me again in the fifth game and I won 8-4. Cobb got a single off me, but no more. They only got six hits, the same as the first game. But Wagner made some errors and Leach bumped into the fence on a long ball from Sam Crawford's bat and Sam got a homer to run the score up to four.

The Tigers won the sixth and we came to the deciding game in Detroit on October 16. I had had two days' rest, but I was young and wanted to pitch it. The weather was cold and raw, and held the crowd down to around 17,000. I remember this because I expected there'd be a sellout for the crucial game. Some friends of mine from northern Missouri had wired me to get them tickets and I didn't think I could, but when I tried I found there was plenty of room.

It wasn't the crowd, or anything much that happened that made this day the biggest I can remember in baseball. It was just that I shut the Tigers out in the big payoff game, and kept their big two, Cobb and Crawford, from getting hits. They were up four times apiece and down four times. I was really never in trouble, for Wild Bill Donovan for the Tigers was wild, walked six men in three innings, and Mullin who came in was about as wild as that and Hans Wagner tore them apart in the sixth inning with a triple that scored two and Fred Clarke stole two bases and we made altogether 11 hits and eight runs, while they were goose-egged and got six hits.

All three of my wins in that series were six-hitters. Eighteen hits, five runs they got in the three games and Cobb only got one hit in 11 times against me.

(Cobb hit only .231 for the series. Editor's note.)

As the last man went out, we raced for hacks that were to take us down to our hotels, where we dressed. The crowd was rushing, too, and here came my friends from Missouri pushing roses at me, and screaming congratulations and saying I was the only man beside Mathewson ever to win three games in a World Series. There was a pin in the handle of the bouquet and it ran into the back of my hand deep. I guess I was thinking about that more than the game as the hack started downtown. I was wondering if it would keep me out of the barnstorming tour we were going to make. It didn't.

My share from the series was $1,745. I read last year that each of the winning Cardinals got around $6,200. That's all right. We lived in a different time, and I enjoyed myself in baseball, pitching, all told, 18 years for the Pirates.

Hans Wagner

as told to CHET SMITH

JOHN P. CARMICHAEL, Editor

When a fellow has played 2,785 games over a span of 21 years it's not the easiest thing in the world to pick out a single contest and say it was his best or that it gave him his biggest thrill. But I was never sharper than in the last game of the World Series our Pirates played with the Detroit Tigers of 1909, and I never walked off any field feeling happier.

It was the afternoon of October 16 and not only a big day for me but for all the sport fans, for on that same afternoon Big Jack Johnson, heavyweight prize-fight champion, knocked out Stanley Ketchel in the 12th round of their battle in San Francisco to retain his crown.

I regard that final game with the Bengals as tops because it meant the end of a grand fight against a bunch of real fighters. I'm still willing to testify that the club of Hughie Jennings and Ty Cobb, of "Wahoo Sam" Crawford and Donie Bush, of Davy Jones and George Moriarity, was a holy terror. And it tickles my vanity to think the Pirates outbattled and defeated them.

Cobb stole two bases in the series, but I was lucky and got six. Cobb made six hits, I made eight.

Ask Ty what happened the day he stood on first and yelled at me, "Hey, Kraut Head, I'm comin' down on the next pitch." I told him to come ahead, and by golly, he did. But George Gibson, our catcher, laid the ball perfect, right in my glove and I stuck it on Ty as he came in. I guess I wasn't too easy about it, 'cause it took three stitches to sew up his lip. That was the kind of a series it was from start to finish. Fred Clarke, our manager, told us we'd better sharpen our spikes since the Tigers would be sure to, and we took him at his word. We were sorta rough, too, I guess.

Cobb surprised the Pirates by playing an unusually clean series, but some of the others weren't so careful.

The trouble started in the first game. Both sides had their jockeys warmed up. The Tigers let us have it and we gave it back to 'em with interest. There was a jawing match on nearly every pitch, and it was a good thing we had two of the greatest umpires who ever worked—Bill Klem and "Silk" O'Loughlin. They were young fellows then, but they knew their business and kept us in line. At least there weren't any riots.

In that first game, Fred Clarke hit a home run off Big George Mullin, who was Detroit's best pitcher that year. I followed Clarke at the plate, and I could see that Mullin was boiling, and anxious to get back at us. I always stood pretty far away from the plate, but this time took every inch I could, figuring Mullin would throw at me. I wasn't wrong. He laid his fast ball right in my ribs. Of course, you can't say a thing like that is deliberate, but our boys reckoned it was, and from that minute the rough-housing was on.

We came into the final game tied up at three apiece. It was played in Detroit, and the night before, the Tiger rooters hired two or three bands to play in front of our hotel and keep us awake, but Clarke fooled 'em by taking us all out to a tavern along the lake shore.

We knew our pitcher was going to be Babe Adams, the kid who had won two of our three victories. Babe was hardly old enough to shave, but Clarke had a hunch on him all along. I'll never forget the look on Adams' face when I told him Clarke wanted him to pitch the opener. He asked me if I wasn't fooling and I told him I wasn't and he hadn't better fool, either, when he got on the mound. What a job he did for us.

I guess I don't have to tell you what the feeling was that last day. "Wild Bill" Donovan, who started for the Tigers, lived up to his name and we got two runs off him in the second. Mullin came in to pitch in the fourth and couldn't find the plate, either. There were two walks and two singles, giving us two more. In the sixth I got my only hit, but it was a three-bagger that drove in Clarke and Tommy Leach, and I kept coming and crossed the plate when Davey Jones made a bad throw from the outfield. We certainly didn't need the run we picked up in the seventh, but it made us eight, and with Adams pitching perfect ball that was the score 8 to 0. But it's far from being the whole story.

On my hit Jones kicked the ball into the overflow crowd, trying to hold it to a double under the ground rules, but O'Loughlin saw him and wouldn't allow it. Another time there was a close play at first and the Tiger runner hit Bill Abstein, our first baseman, in the stomach with his fist. Abstein folded up and Ham Hyatt had to take his place. Another Tiger slid into second and cut Jack Miller on the head and leg. Bobby Byrne, our third baseman, banged into Moriarity so hard that Bobby had to leave the field with a broken ankle, and George, who concealed his injury until the next inning, went to the doctor to have 11 stitches put in his knee. Talk about "bean balls"—they were flying around everybody's head all afternoon.

OLD JUDGE CIGARETTES Goodwin & Co., New York.

Louis Bierbauer, "Godfather" of the Pirates.

(Courtesy of the Pittsburgh Pirates)

The mighty Honus Wagner, believed by many to be the greatest shortstop in baseball history.

(Courtesy of the Pittsburgh Pirates)

(Below) Huntington Avenue Baseball Grounds, Boston, where the Pirates played four games of the first ever World Series.

(Carnegie Library of Pittsburgh)

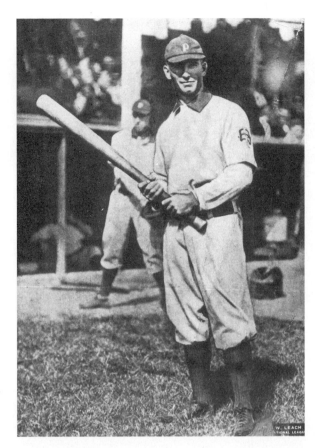

Third baseman Tommy Leach, the first Pirate to lead the National League in home runs with six in 1902.
(Carnegie Library of Pittsburgh)

(Below) Exposition Park, North Side, home to the Pirates through their first three pennant-winning seasons and first World Series.
(Carnegie Library of Pittsburgh)

The heroes of the 1909 World Series: rookie pitcher Babe Adams, player-manager Fred Clarke, catcher George Gibson, and the great Honus Wagner.
(Carnegie Library of Pittsburgh)

(Opposite, top) Pie Traynor, voted by baseball writers in 1969 as the greatest third baseman ever to play the game.
(Courtesy of the Pittsburgh Pirates)

(Opposite, bottom) The Waner brothers look dwarfed standing beside Babe Ruth and Lou Gehrig, but managed to outhit the winning Yankees in the 1927 World Series.
(Courtesy of the Pittsburgh Pirates)

(Opposite, top) Babe Ruth's last hurrah after hitting his final home run at Forbes Field.

(National Baseball Hall of Fame Library, Cooperstown, N.Y.)

(Opposite, bottom) Hank Greenberg's tutelage helped Ralph Kiner become one of the most proficient sluggers in baseball history.

(Courtesy of the Pittsburgh Pirates)

(Right) Joe Garagiola, being treated for a spike wound, kept his sense of humor through the Pirates' dismal 1952 season.

(Copyright, Post-Gazette Archives, *Pittsburgh Post-Gazette*, 2002, all rights reserved; reprinted with permission)

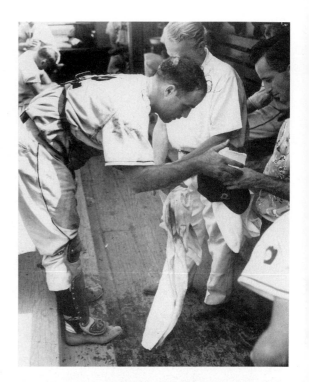

With this swing, Dale Long set a major-league record by hitting a home run in eight consecutive games.

(National Baseball Hall of Fame Library, Cooperstown, N.Y.)

Forbes Field as viewed by the "knothole-gang" fans, who entered through a gate under the right-field stands.

(Courtesy of the Pittsburgh Pirates)

Fans and players mob home plate to celebrate Bob Skinner's dramatic, game-winning home run on Easter Sunday, 1960.

A joyful Bill Mazeroski travels the last few feet to home plate after his dramatic home run of the 1960 World Series.

(Courtesy of the Pittsburgh Pirates)

Steve Blass leaps for joy as Bob Robertson stretches his arms in victory after recording the last out of the 1971 World Series.
(Courtesy of the Pittsburgh Pirates)

(Opposite)

Bill Mazeroski once said that he and Roberto Clemente were teammates "longer than bacon and eggs."
(Courtesy of the Pittsburgh Pirates)

No Pirate ever played with more pride and passion than Roberto Clemente.
(Courtesy of the Pittsburgh Pirates)

The personalities and careers of Steve Blass and Dock Ellis captured the attention of some of the best writers of the 1970s.

(Courtesy of the Pittsburgh Pirates)

Colorful and controversial broadcaster Bob Prince returned to the radio booth just a few weeks before his death in 1985 after being fired ten years earlier.

(Courtesy of the Pittsburgh Pirates)

Danny Murtaugh, the most popular manager in Pirates history.

Danny Murtaugh joins Roberto Clemente and Willie Stargell for an informal moment at the Dapper Dan banquet held in 1972.

(Opposite, top) Willie Stargell, patriarch of the 1979 World Series Champion Pirate "fam-i-lee," hit 475 career home runs, many of them "tape-measure" shots.
(Courtesy of the Pittsburgh Pirates)

(Opposite, bottom) The Pirates celebrate their 1979 World Series comeback, after trailing 3 games to 1 and then defeating Baltimore in the remaining games for the championship.
(Courtesy of the Pittsburgh Pirates)

(Right) Pirate pitcher Jim Gott, second in saves in the 1988 National League season, demonstrates the angry or "crazed" look popularized by baseball's top relievers.

Manager Jim Leyland shares a quiet moment with controversial Barry Bonds, whose career with the Pirates was filled with turbulence, despite two MVP awards.

(Above) The Pirates and Reds line up for the first home game at PNC Park, which, like its true predecessor, Forbes Field, was built strictly for baseball.

(Left) Brian Giles celebrates after his grand slam with two outs in the bottom of the ninth gives the Pirates their most dramatic win of the opening season at PNC Park.

The Greatest World Series Ever and the Damn Yankees

PIE TRAYNOR

The 1909 Pirate championship season marked the end of an era. The Pirates remained respectable for the next decade, but the retirements of Wagner and Clarke, the failure to sign future Hall of Famers George Sisler and Tris Speaker, and a series of disappointing acquisitions prevented Pittsburgh from being a serious contender until the 1920s and the emergence of a new set of Pirate stars. Voted the greatest third baseman of all time by the baseball writers of America, Harold "Pie" Traynor was also one of Pittsburgh's most popular personalities. Elected to the Hall of Fame in 1948, Traynor had a lifetime batting average of .320 in his seventeen-year playing career and was widely admired as one of baseball's greatest defensive players. In the 1920s, Traynor, playing with future Hall of Famers Max Carey, Kiki Cuyler, and the Waner brothers, helped the Pirates to ten straight first-division finishes, including National League pennants in 1925 and 1927, and a World Series victory in 1925. He also managed the Pirates from 1934 to 1939. Traynor was not only remembered as one of baseball's greatest stars, but for his humanity and humor, his trademarks long after his playing career was over.

Hot Corner? Traynor, No Argument

BOB BROEG

Unflinchingly, the greatest of all third basemen, Harold (Pie) Traynor—let followers of Jimmy Collins stand aside—faced and felt the cold steel and hot slides of enemy base-runners. But he shivered with fear one time when he was driving with Charles J. (Chilly) Doyle and the Pittsburgh sports writer told him, "Turn right at the next corner, Pie."

Traynor, who didn't mind getting shaken up out there at the hot corner, was considerably shaken up at Doyle's command for two good reasons: (1) It was absent-minded Chilly who was behind the wheel, and (2) Traynor never drove a car in his life.

When professional baseball turned 100 years, Traynor turned 70, still active enough to be able to don a uniform and conduct summer tryout camps for the Pirates at Forbes Field. One of the reasons he reached three-score-and-ten in such splendid physical condition was his lifelong habit of walking where others would ride.

"I never learned to drive because I was afraid I'd find an excuse not to walk, which I've found so enjoyable, so relaxing and healthful," said the

From *The Sporting News*, August 2, 1969. Reprinted by permission of Bob Broeg.

handsome, silver-haired septuagenarian in cultured tones that are misleading.

Neither by heredity nor environment, instinct nor inclination, is Traynor cultured, but he's gentlemanly and articulate. His precise diction, an altered New England accent, served him well for more than 20 years as a Pittsburgh sportscaster on radio.

From the time he tramped through the snows of suburban Boston as a boy in Framingham and Somerville, through the years when he sat down at the bridge table only when the weather wasn't fit for hunting, Pie has been a physical culture man, as active as the miners and mill hands who were among his warmest admirers in the 14-plus seasons he gave Pittsburgh positively the finest combination third-base glove and bat in baseball history.

Collins Is Pie's No. 1 Rival

Except for the original Collins, a stocky little man who played in the big leagues from 1895 to 1908, there hasn't been another third baseman who has had a call when it came to selecting all-time teams. And Collins didn't have the hitting or fielding figures—or size—to compare with Traynor's.

Traynor was broad-shouldered and rawboned, lithe and supple. He was six feet tall, long-legged and long-armed. He played at 175 pounds and he weighed almost exactly the same at 70 as he did when he took himself off Pittsburgh's playing list, reluctantly, at 37.

Opening day, 1969, living very much in the present, though proudly glorying in the past, Pie stepped out of his apartment in downtown Pittsburgh and surveyed the crowded bus headed for Forbes Field. Mentally, he made note of the bus number and struck out on foot, an uphill three-mile climb to the Schenley district in which Forbes Field is located.

"I didn't push myself," he said, "but I got there before the bus."

As a walking man and part mountain goat, Traynor is incredible. At his playing peak, he confided, he once became lost when hunting in the Wisconsin woods and tramped from 5 in the morning until 9 at night before he found civilization, estimating he'd hoofed about 50 miles.

In his playing years, he'd think nothing of walking from Manhattan's old Alamac Hotel at 71st street to the Polo Grounds at 157th. Once, he and Jewel Ens, a Pirate coach, walked back to the Alamac all the way from Brooklyn's Ebbets Field.

A Brisk Walk—127 Blocks

As recently as the time when both he and this century were in their mid-50s, Pie awakened to find New York bathed in pleasant Indian summer sunshine the early October morning of a Dodger-Yankee World Series. The Pittsburgh broadcaster ate breakfast at his 34th street hotel and began a leisurely walk up Eighth avenue toward Yankee Stadium, located at 161st street.

"En route," he recalled, smiling, "friends in cabs would spot me and stop, but I thanked them. I know the folks in Harlem must have thought I was nuts. The trip took about three and a half hours. Sure, I was tired when I got there, but I was loosened up and relaxed."

The therapy of putting one foot in front of the other—"with motion, there's no emotion," someone once said—was apparent in the longest walk Traynor ever took. Not the longest mileage, but certainly the grimmest and most painful.

In 1938, Pie took a ball club that had only one 15-game winner, relief pitcher Mace Brown, and led the National League so comfortably down the stretch that in September, club officials even ordered a new rooftop press section built for the World Series. Then the Pirates staggered and the Chicago Cubs came on. The seven-game lead dwindled.

At Wrigley Field in late September, ailing-armed Dizzy Dean outfoxed the Pirates with slow stuff, 2-1, cutting Pittsburgh's lead to one-half game. The next day, the Pirates twice blew two-run leads in a game that went into the home tenth tied, 5-5, with darkness casting a gray shadow over the Cubs' park.

By then, Traynor no longer was a player manager, able to inspire his young Buccos with his bat and his glove, but the Cubs' field foreman was their tomato-faced catcher, Gabby Hartnett. It was apparent that the umpires would call the game if relief ace Brown could retire Hartnett.

With two strikes, however, Mace hung a curve and Gabby belted it over the ivy-covered left field fence for a famed homer in the gloaming that put the Cubs into first place to stay.

Traynor walked from Wrigley Field to the Pirates' downtown hotel, accompanied by friend Ens and a young Pittsburgh sports writer, Les Biederman. Not a word was spoken.

"If either of you had said anything, I'd have popped you one," said Traynor, quite understandably out of character.

It was out of character for Pie to be thrown out of a ball game, and there's only one recorded incident of ejection, a bit of unusual news that prompted reporters to question umpire Pete McLaughlin. Why?

"Traynor said, 'I'm sick and tired of such decisions,'" the umpire explained.

Well?

If He's Sick, He's Excused

"Since he wasn't feeling well, I excused him for the day," said McLaughlin, sounding like a junior-grade Bill Klem. "I hated to put him out—such a fine young man, too—but he did throw the ball to the ground, and we're instructed to put out any player who makes a gesture indicating disrespect for any umpire."

Pie is a pleasant, personable man and some thought he was too good-natured or easy-going to be a successful manager, but it's a fact, anyway, that in his five-plus seasons he got the Pirates closer to a pennant in '38—and quite surprisingly—than they were at any time in the long drouth between victory drinks. That is, between 1927, when he was the star third baseman, and 1960, when he was a Pittsburgh-area scout who did a daily stint on radio.

Traynor returned to Pittsburgh in 1944 to go on the air for one year and he stayed for 22, displaying the kind of consistency and durability that had featured his play. Pie's air work was a blessing, financially, because he'd lost in the stock market crash of 1929 and, astonishingly, considering his baseball skill and his double duty as player and manager, the most money he ever made was $14,000 a season.

This, mind you, even though he had a lifetime batting average of .320 after batting over .300 in each of ten seasons. He hit as high as .366 in 1930 and also batted .356, .337 and .342 the three seasons immediately preceding, but he regarded 1923 as his top season.

At 23, the four-season professional hit .338 and collected 208 hits, driving in more than 100 runs for the first of seven times. He had 19 doubles, tied for the league lead with 19 triples and hit 12 home runs. He also scored 108 runs.

"I was the first Pittsburgh player ever to bat .300, score 100 runs, drive in 100 and get 200 hits in the same season," said Traynor, aware that his predecessors included legendary Honus Wagner, the Pirate player with whom he is most closely associated.

Pie has considerable affection for old Honus, who coached for him and with whom he was associated in an ill-fated sporting goods business. But he seemed to reserve his greatest respect for blunt, outspoken Rogers Hornsby.

"Hornsby not only was the greatest righthanded hitter I ever saw," said Traynor, "but he was a good teacher. When I appealed to him for help early in my career, noting that I was hitting long outs with not quite enough power to reach the left field fence often in a big ball park, he recommended a heavier bat. 'You'll go to right field more often,' he said, and he was right.

"I switched to a 42-ounce bat, one of the heaviest in the game, and, as Hornsby predicted, I didn't get around on the ball as quickly. So I began to hit line drives to right field and right-center."

I can recall Pie hitting the ball as tight to the right field line—and as deep—as any righthanded hitter I ever saw.

A Tribute from McGraw

Traynor is understandably a bit sensitive that he doesn't receive more recognition for his hitting, which certainly does speak for itself. But, truthfully, Pie's defensive play was so brilliant that it tended to overshadow his hitting, though the Pittsburgh third baseman's all-round excellence was not lost on John McGraw, the long-time Giants' manager who was Mr. National League for 30 years.

"If," McGraw said in 1929, "I were to pick the greatest team player in baseball today, I would have to pick Pie Traynor."

Sure-handed, quick-fielding and strong-armed, Pie once started four around-the-horn double plays in a game against McGraw's Giants. With Glenn Wright, Pittsburgh's shortstop for five seasons in the mid-'20s, he represented probably the finest left side of an infield ever to choke off opposition hits.

At Pie's peak, there was an old telegraphic play-by-play parody that went like this:

"Smith (or Jones or Hornsby or Hafey) doubled down the left field line, but Traynor threw him out."

Playing virtually even with the bag, Pie could make every play. On balls hit to his left he ranged into the hole, quickly and gracefully. On bunts, he was so alert and adept that batters rarely laid the ball down in his direction.

On pop flies, he ranged from home plate to the field boxes to short left field. And he was positively devastating on the toughest play of them all, the hot backhanded smash over the bag.

"I've seen him make that play barehanded," said Charlie Grimm, a former teammate and opponent who had a ham-sized hand himself. "Pie had the quickest hands, the quickest arm of any third baseman. And from any angle he threw strikes. Playing first base with him was a pleasure—if you didn't stop too long to admire the plays he made."

Hafey Hit Wicked Liners

They even talk about the kind it's hard to believe. That is, Traynor lunging backhanded to his right, gloving a smash and, losing balance, flipping the ball to his bare hand and firing a side-armed strike to first base before taking a header into the dirt.

To the premier third baseman, the hardest-hitting pull-hitter he ever faced was bespectacled Chick Hafey, lean, rawhide slugger of the Cardinals.

"He'd pull the pitch at the last split-second," Pie recalled, "and the ball would be on you in a flash, dipping fiercely or sailing. He was a helluva all-round player who ought to be in the Hall of Fame."

No player of Traynor's generation, or for that matter, no person inside baseball or out could make more valid evaluations than the 70-year-old master of the hot corner. Not necessarily on the basis of native good judgment, but on the basis of experience—and exposure.

Even though in baseball's 100th year and his 50th in the professional phase of the game, he was doing only filmed television commercials and helping run Pirate try-out camps, Traynor was on top of the game he'd first played for coffee and cakes in 1920.

Down at Bradenton, Fla., in spring training, the old guy was out there in uniform, not getting underfoot, but offering encouragement to 5' 4" Freddie Patek, when the little man was thrust into the regular shortstop's job because of Gene Alley's persistent arm trouble. Traynor knows, incidentally, what it means to have a career ended by an arm injury.

Sliding home in 1934, the year he took over as manager of the Pirates in June, Pie tried to elude catcher Jim Wilson of the Phillies. Missing the plate as Wilson missed the tag, he thrust his right arm out to touch the rubber just as the whirling catcher came down on the outstretched arm with both knees.

"I felt something snap and was certain I had a broken arm," Traynor recalled. "I didn't but I couldn't throw well any more."

He played only 59 games in 1935, none in '36 and went to bat just 12 times in 1937.

"With more minor leagues then and more players, you had more seasoned men ready for the majors," he said, "and that's why, with expansion further diluting talent, it's possible now for good players to play longer."

Traynor was explaining, not complaining, because he doesn't permit himself to become marshmallow sticky in sentiment for the "good old days." He's at Forbes Field regularly and he doesn't believe that the game and the guys who play it have gone down the drain.

"The best third baseman I've ever seen is Ken Boyer," said Traynor, mentioning a performer who was voted the National League's Most Valuable Player as recently as 1964. Pie, of course, didn't see Traynor.

"For ten years before Boyer hurt his back, he was out of this world," said the Hall of Fame third baseman enthusiastically. "He made all the plays, hit for power and drove in big runs. Brooks Robinson is another good one. And the most underrated star I've ever seen, white or black, is Henry Aaron."

To Traynor, the best pitcher he ever saw was Washington's Big Train, Walter Johnson, and he's extremely proud of having homered off Johnson his first time up in the 1925 World Series, a conquest that provided the greatest thrill of his career.

◆

Harold Joseph Traynor has had a long love affair with baseball even though when he was six years old and pestering older boys to let him play, they played a dirty trick on the son of an Irish printer in suburban Boston. They put him behind the plate without a mask and the first pitch hit him in the mouth and knocked out two teeth.

There are two versions of how the boy got his nickname. One is that his father hung it on him one day when Harold came home covered with dirt. "You look like pied type," James Traynor supposedly remarked, referring to a jumbled, ink-stained mess.

The other version is that an older boy, a neighborhood idol, began to call him "Pie Face" when the Traynor lad would show up at the grocery store looking for his favorite dish. Traynor long since has outgrown his sweet tooth, but the nickname, hung on him when he was only eight years old, stuck like a hot grounder gloved by the master himself.

As one of eight children, Pie went to work at the age of 12, walking three miles into Boston to serve as a messenger and office boy. By the time World War I broke out, turned down in an effort to enlist, he was put to work checking freight cars with munitions, riding a horse 12 hours a day for six months. Maybe that's why he has preferred to walk, not ride.

Stallings Chased Prospect Away

In 1918, Pie got down off his horse and, at the invitation of a Braves' scout who'd seen him play on the Somerville sandlots, he reported to Braves Field. Someone forgot to tell George Stallings, however, and the Braves' manager angrily chased off one of the finest players the club ever missed.

By 1920, wiser and less timid, though still shy, Pie was scouted by both the Philadelphia Athletics and his favorite team, the Red Sox. The Sox still were his favorites even though they'd traded to Cleveland his personal favorite, Speaker. And that's a clue, in part, as to why Pie thinks Tris was even better than Ty Cobb.

When one Les Bangs, manager of the Portsmouth club of the Virginia League, wired an offer to the tall, young Somerville shortstop, Traynor took the telegram to Ed Barrow, boss of the Bosox for whom he'd worked out. Should he sign?

"Go ahead," Barrow told him. "We've got a working agreement with Portsmouth. If you look good down there, we'll buy you."

The Red Sox tried to buy him, after he'd hit .270 in 104 games, but Pittsburgh wanted him even more. On the strength of a glowing report from scout Tom McNamara, frequently tightfisted Barney Dreyfuss, owner of the Pirates, bought the kid's contract for $10,000, a pretty tidy sum a half-century ago.

Pittsburgh, which had gone through several shortstops since Wagner's retirement three years earlier, gave the 21-year-old Traynor a 17-game look late in the 1920 season. Pie made 12 errors, batted .212, and the Pirates swung an off-season deal by which they obtained baseball's perennial pixy, Rabbit Maranville, Boston's shortstop.

Optioned out to Birmingham, Traynor had a big year, batting .336 and stealing 47 bases. When the Southern Association season ended, the Pirates recalled the infielder as they fought to retain a slender September lead over the Giants. Manager George Gibson played him one game at third base—and it was costly.

Costly not only because young Traynor threw low, allowing Chicago to score the winning run, but, as Max Carey pointed out, even more costly because manager George Gibson hesitated to use the rookie again. He played outfielder Clyde Barnhart at third base.

"Pie could play rings around Barnhart and he didn't get into any of our critical games with the Giants," Carey told writer Lee Greene a few years ago.

Switch from Short to Third

Traynor began the 1922 season at shortstop, with Maranville at second base. But when Bill McKechnie replaced Gibson as manager in midseason, Barnhart returned to the outfield, Maranville moved back to shortstop and Traynor began his long spectacular stand as the cool man at the hot corner.

"The hardest thing in going from shortstop to third base was learning to play that much closer to the hitter," Pie explained. "It was very important to know your hitters and station yourself correctly. A shortstop can always gamble a little because he can see the ball better and gets a better jump.

"Actually, though, I had to learn to play third base twice. When I was young and had good legs, I could play in closer and take more chances. But as I grew older and found my reflexes slowing, I found I was second-guessing myself.

"That's when I started over again, playing back and relying more on my positioning."

It's ironic that Traynor suffered his career-shortening injury as a base-runner. Teammates always thought he'd get it defensively. For all his skill, the clever base-stealing Carey said, Pie never did manage to avoid barreling base-runners, and he was cut now and then.

But he cut into only two pint-sized shares of the World Series, batting a handsome .346 in the seven-game 1925 classic when, down three games to one, the Pirates rallied and finally beat Walter Johnson in the sawdust circus atmosphere of a rainy showdown, 9-7. Pie had two triples and a homer that time, but he had just one double to show for only three hits and batted only .200 when the Yankees routed the Pirates in four straight two years later.

As a handsome bachelor, Traynor was one of the boys with the Pittsburgh cutups of the early '20s, though he couldn't qualify for the famed quartet of Maranville, Grimm, Possum Whitted and Cotton Tierney.

"He wanted in," said Grimm, grinning, "but he couldn't sing."

Winters, he was a lone timber wolf, trekking off to Wisconsin to hunt deer and to fish by cutting a hole through the ice of a Wisconsin lake, dropping a baited line into the water.

"There's nothing like the tug of a big northern pike," Traynor said.

Except maybe romance. In 1931, Pie married Eva Helmer, chief operator of the Havlin, a Cincinnati hotel where the ball club stayed. They had no children.

Traynor lost 20 pounds after the agonizing 1938 season and then lost his job at the end of the next season to Frank Frisch, an old foe for whom he has little regard. Pie moved to Cincinnati, his wife's hometown, but then Pittsburgh radio station KQV called him back to become sports director, and he began the double-duty decades as a sportscaster and Pirate scout.

As the only third baseman elected to baseball's Hall of Fame—Jimmy Collins and Home Run Baker were chosen by the veterans' committee—Pie Traynor was in a class by himself. Take the word of his long-time radio associate, Jack Henry, a reformed Pittsburgh sports writer.

Even in blizzard weather, the walking man of the Golden Triangle never wore a hat. Henry wondered why.

Accused of Stealing Umbrella

"Why, you know, I had my hat stolen at the overcoat exchange," said Traynor. Translated, it meant he'd lost it in a restaurant.

But that had been six years before, hadn't it?

It had, but there'd been another unpleasant experience. Pie, who no longer could look pie in the face, explained with the sad-eyed deadpanned expression that made it difficult to tell when he was telling a tall tale.

"I've never felt the same about a hat since I went to a rack to retrieve one at a restaurant and a gentleman thought I was stealing his umbrella," Traynor told Henry.

But. . . .

"But then the very next day, my wife gave me three umbrellas to take into town for repairs," he said, "and I bumped into the same restaurant patron. He stared at me in disbelief and then muttered, admiringly, 'Man, you sure had a good day today.'"

Indeed. A good day, a good career and a good life, but, say, friend, don't you have the feeling we've been had the way the famous pedestrian was when Chilly Doyle told him to turn right at the next corner?

Big, Little, Young, Old—All Pay Tribute to Pie

ROY MCHUGH

Every few minutes a man in a dark suit would bring a basket of flowers into the room. With one large basket, peppermint carnations and red gladiolas, he paused before two of the mourners and said, "From Lloyd Waner."

Old friends and teammates wherever they were remembered Pie Traynor yesterday. So did people who never knew him at all. Up the wet driveway to the Samson Funeral Home, the cars began coming at noon.

Ken Smith had flown here from the spring training camps in Florida. Well over 60, Ken Smith is the director of the Baseball Hall of Fame at Cooperstown, N.Y. He was in Vero Beach, where the Los Angeles Dodgers train, when he heard that Pie Traynor, the greatest third baseman of all time, was dead.

From the *Pittsburgh Press*, March 19, 1972. Copyright/*Pittsburgh Post-Gazette*, 2002. All rights reserved. Reprinted with permission.

"I'm here for the Hall of Fame, but this is personal, too," said Ken Smith. "This guy, there was nobody like him."

The young and the old, the rich and the poor . . . Pie Traynor appealed to them all. In the first few hours yesterday, a judge and a banker, a police chief and a television executive, a stock broker and an usher at Three Rivers Stadium paid their respects.

A small boy knelt in front of the casket. In the visitors' book after his name, he wrote in parentheses, "fan."

Everyone there had a special recollection of Pie.

A man named George Dyer said, "I used to be a watchman in a building on Liberty Avenue and 30th Street. On his walks, Pie would come out that way, and he always stopped in to see me."

Jimmy Miller, the sports writer, said that when Pie managed the Pirates the two of them sometimes walked from Forbes Field to the Sun-Telegraph Building, downtown, after a game. "Then, especially if the Pirates had lost, Pie would ask if I wanted to walk back," Miller said.

Johnny Boyer, who pioneered the play-by-play broadcasting of Pirate games in the 1930s, told a story about a game at Forbes Field between the broadcasters and the newspapermen in which Pie, long since retired, was to play for the broadcasters. The newspapermen had Steve Swetonic pitching for them and he could still throw a wicked fastball.

"Pie," said Boyer, "I'm scared. I haven't played baseball in years and I just watched Swetonic warm up. He looks tough."

"You're scared?" answered Pie sympathetically. "Well, I'm scared, too. I released that guy when I was manager and he's got better stuff now than he had then."

That was the way Pie talked. Somebody else said, "He'd get people laughing. He elevated the company he was in. He elevated the mood. He never seemed depressed."

And yesterday afternoon the stories about Pie seemed to lift the depression in Samson's Funeral Home.

"Even right now, it's hard to believe he's dead," said Ken Smith.

Eve Traynor, Pie's widow said, "You expect him to wake up and tell a joke. A corny joke. He always complained that I didn't laugh at his jokes. I'd say, 'They're too corny,' and he'd answer, 'You don't understand them.' I'd say, 'I understand them all right, but I heard those stories in grade school.' I never let him get ahead of me."

Dead at 72, Pie Traynor was elevating the mood, the mood of the people who came to mourn him.

"The last time I was here," said Jack Berger, who works for the Pirates in public relations, "I saw Pie. Same room. Pie always liked boxers, and

Cuddy DeMarco had died. Well, Pie started out from downtown to walk here, of course, like he always walked everywhere, but coming out Fifth Avenue a guy driving a bread truck recognized him.

"He gave Pie a lift and he came in here with Pie. He came in here with Pie in his bread truck uniform."

Chances are he was there yesterday, too.

◆　◆　◆

THE 1925 WORLD SERIES

The 1925 World Series between the Pirates and the Washington Senators was one of the most dramatic in baseball history. It had a wonderful cast of characters, including several future members of the Hall of Fame. It also had a great plot line. The Pirates, once they fell behind three games to one, were vilified by the press and public for their lack of skill and courage, even though they had captured the National League pennant from a powerful New York Giants team, winner of four league championships in a row. No team had ever come back from a 3-1 deficit to win a best of seven World Series, but the Pirates rallied to win the next two games against the defending World Champion Senators and set the stage for a seventh and deciding game, played in the fog and rain at Forbes Field. When the Pirates won 9-7 on Kiki Cuyler's dramatic two-out, bases-loaded, two-run double in the bottom of the eighth against the great Walter Johnson, the team was roundly praised for its skill and courage.

World's Title Battle Never Equalled for Thrills, Heroic Action

CHARLES J. DOYLE

BIGBEE'S DOUBLE TO TIE COUNT, CUYLER'S SMASH WITH BASES FULL AND TWO OUT TO GIVE BUCCANEERS TWO-RUN LEAD IN EIGHTH AND SIGHT OF BIG TRAIN JOHNSON VAINLY GIVING HIS ALL ARE AMONG FEATURES

Our wonderful Pirates were crowned champions of the world yesterday, but the real story probably never will be told by human endeavor. In the bright galaxy of writers from near and afar, there was none who could begin to describe the drama which was unfolded in the rain mists of October as the Pittsburgh athletes fought their way to the pinnacle of the

From the *Pittsburgh Gazette-Times*, October 16, 1925. Copyright/*Pittsburgh Post-Gazette*, 2002. All rights reserved. Reprinted with permission.

sport in defeating the Washington team, until last evening, masters of all they surveyed in baseball.

Fifty years of major league play have brought with them flag fights and struggles for the bigger emblems that have hardly been done justice with words, but all of these feature scenes paled into comparative obscurity under the brilliance of the seventh and concluding battle with the Senators—a fight that decided the honor that is the goal of every kid whose fortune it is ever to handle a baseball.

Never in the annals of the sport has there been a contest that had so much drama. The wet stage which autumn provided for the final fight was believed at the start to be a hindrance to fast play, but the quality of the skill displayed by the desperate opponents was not dulled by the rain.

Tide Turns in Eighth

The game ended 9 to 7 in favor of the National League champions, but most of the multitude did not seem to have an exact knowledge of the figures. The fans all knew that the Pirates broke a deadlock in the eighth, and when they were retired, they were leading by two runs, and with only three men to be retired.

What did the Pittsburgh shouters care about the score, so long as they had a two-run margin of victory in the ninth. They had followed the ups and downs of the greatest fight in the history of the game, and when the last of the eighth arrived with the Pirates trailing by a run, the wild-eyed backers of the home boys were not worrying about the score. They wanted one run for a draw, and when little Skeeter Bigbee, cold from the bench, hammered a double against the left-field screen, the men, women and children knew the significance of the tally.

Cuyler Gives Bucs Lead

To attempt to pick the most heroic part in the last grand struggle is much the same as looking for the brightest sunbeam on the dewy grass of a Maytime morning. It was the clean-living, good-natured Hazen Cuyler that unloosed the flood gates of joy with a long hit that produced two tallies that gave us a two-run advantage going into the ninth. This hit will go into history as one of the outstanding markers in the progress of the diamond game—yes, it may be that Cuyler's double with the bases loaded, the score tied, and two out in the eighth, will get the first portal in the Hall of Fame, but, when the boys of the future read about what happened in the past, they will find other high spots that deserve to be ranked with Cuyler's winning hit.

To recount the valid deeds of the Pirates and their worthy foemen—to chronicle their deeds in a meritorious manner, the folds of a big book would not nearly be large enough. If the sport had a Lincoln who could express himself after the fashion of the inspired one when he touched on a more sublime subject at Gettysburg, a better appreciation might be sensed by the reader, but when one reads a two or three-column story on yesterday's spectacle in the Oakland playground, he is apt to feel like those who heard the long speech of the other speaker who that day was on the rostrum with Honest Abe.

Johnson at Last Bows

Through the maze of the mists and rain, a wondrous physical specimen—one of the greatest athletes that ever walked the earth—was expending the last ounce of wondrous energy that had carried him along in 20 years of baseball. If there had been nothing more than the figure of the exhausted Johnson in the drama of the World's Series, fans would have remembered the sad sight until their dying day.

The steady downpour of the last half of the fight gave emphasis to the suffering which the mound star felt as he struggled heroically against the victory-mad kids who had done his bidding in two other games. On several occasions it was apparent that a rescue man might be called upon to relieve the distressed man who has done so much for the sport.

When the base-hit cloud fell upon the soaked patriarch to add to the woes which the skies were dropping upon his tired form, he was indeed sad to behold. Bucky Harris came in to talk with his Grand Old Man. Perhaps Bucky wanted to save Walter further punishment, but there was a marked strain of determination in the tiring veteran.

Carry Sawdust to Mound

On two occasions the soil upon Fogarty Knoll became so treacherous that Johnson had trouble standing solidly while making his pitch. Walter, on those occasions, called for the sawdust. Then he tried to carry on, but there was no allowable move that could be made to thwart the driving Pirates in their wild flight. At times, the battle field was so dark under the persistent drizzle that the journey of the thrown and batted ball was hard to follow by the spectators, and on several occasions, the players, themselves, appeared to be fooled by the course of batted balls. Yet this handicap for the players could not prevent the enactment of a number of plays that would have been cheered to the echo had they been reeled off under the sunshine of a mid-summer day.

Traynor, Cuyler, and Rice were in the front rank in this connection.

Somerville Pie, after unleashing a savage triple into center, which brought us on even terms with the foe when two were out, came through with one of his famous diving assists a moment afterward. Had that run been on the sacks a few seconds later when Roger Peckinpaugh hammered a homer over the left field screen, there is no telling what might have happened at the close.

Players in Desperate Mood

Not since Braddock clashed with the French and Indians back around 1750 has there been such fighting in the relative sectors bordering on the Allegheny and Monongahela rivers. No blood was shed in the most strenuous fight ever staged in baseball, but in the serious business of war the participants seldom move with deeper concentration on the main objective.

The mud-besplattered gladiators of the ball field behaved as though it was a fight to a finish. There was no unsavory or foul tactics on display, but the desperate mood of the contenders was reflected ever in those who are slow to show emotion.

One had only to look at Stuffy McInnis to discern some of the things that were in the minds of the players. Slow to anger, McInnis is known as a modest fellow with quiet aggressiveness: he never quits, but his manner of fighting is not spectacular. Yesterday, McInnis was like a wild Firpo turned loose on the baseball pampas. Hatless part of the time, he pleaded with his mates to overcome the invaders.

Nats Take Early Lead

The hopes of the 40,000 or so who were cheering for Pittsburgh fell heavily in the first inning when old favorites acted in a manner suggestive of a rout at the hands of the invading hosts. Many things of a loose nature happened in the first period before Johnny Morrison was rushed to the relief of the courageous Aldridge, who may have gone to the mound once too often.

The first inning produced four enemy tallies and as Walter Johnson moved toward the mound in his majestic stride, there were many oppressive sighs in the breasts of those who had seen Johnson in action only a week before.

On many occasions, while in their fine batting form, have the Freebooters pounded their way successfully against the handicap of a four-run lead, but in two previous games the athletes were in a pronounced slump against the splendid veteran. But they could not be denied in the all-important fight. Johnson started in a manner that scared all of us who hold Pirate sympathies, but the strain of the strenuous innings soon began to tell on him.

Carey Leads Attack

Much will be written about Cuyler's double with the bases filled (a drive that was scored a home run for four tallies before the umpires decided against the Pirates). Columns will be printed in praise of Pie Traynor, but when the analysis is made, the result will surely show that Capt. Max Carey was the swaying force in bringing Pittsburgh the first world's championship since 1909.

The gallant captain of the Freebooters, game to the core as he refused to consider injuries, set such a dizzy pace against Johnson that the whole Washington club was befuddled. Five times did the brilliant fellow go to the plate, and five times did he get on the throbbing runways. Capping one of the most honorable careers in the game, Carey rose to magnificent heights in the supreme effort of his baseball work. Scoops secured for himself lasting fame through his dazzling exploits of the deciding flight.

Morrison Starts Rally

It was Carey who started the victory march but his mates did not fall into step as soon as he sounded the first notes. We'll pause here to recount that Johnny Morrison—more power to Dewey—started the third inning with a single. Dewey's Texas Leaguer off the servings of the great Walter actually was the beginning of the winning drive, and didn't Morrison race to the plate like a real base runner when Eddie Moore slammed a double to left center!

Carey contributed to the run-making of the third, and he started after Johnson in the fifth with a double, his third hit of the game. In the seventh, Carey came through with another important two-bagger, and in the same inning he scored the tying run amid great excitement when the admirable Traynor socked a triple to center.

Traynor's part is worth special attention in commenting on the causes of victory. Pie was "up there" with Carey on third and two out. Failure to get Scoops in would have been disappointing to Pirate fans, and it might have encouraged the foe to bigger things.

Traynor Near Homer

Pie was grappling carefully and courageously with the eminent pitcher. Johnson served one that was almost ideal for a hard smash and Pie connected for a vicious liner that streaked over second in remarkable velocity. The brilliant Rice, a high class performer in the series, faltered a bit in trying to hold the drive to a single. The ball skipped past Sam, and as it skidded over the grass toward the fence, visions of a homer flashed in many minds. Carey trotted over, and the field was in an uproar as the anxious eyes watched Traynor in his mad scamper around the bases, two being out at the time. Joe Harris ran into the section near the fence, and retrieved the ball. Pie was rounding third as Joe's throw went to his namesake, who was set for a throw to the plate. Bucky sent the ball spinning to Muddy Ruel, and the Somerville greyhound was stopped with what was then the winning tally, but the other run was in and the Pirates were right back in the ball game.

The Pirates went out onto the field, and as Remy Kremer had swung into a beautiful stride on the mound, there was much to encourage the Pittsburgh players and their friends.

Peck Clouts for Circuit

Kremer flashed his diving assist on Ruel, but suddenly a homer fell over the left field screen and the enemy was out in front again and at this late period. Peck, the same efficient player who has faltered so often in the fights for the title, made a big hero of himself with his circuit clout. Kremer retired the side, but the fans knew there was serious business ahead.

Before telling the story of the eighth inning—an inning that will live a delightful memory with Pirate fans—let us pause again to honor a little athlete whose career appears to have been blighted at a time when the boy in question was coming into full possession of his skill.

Skeeter Bigbee is a happy boy tonight. He has had little to cheer him in a baseball way this year, for he has been on the bench throughout most of the summer. In the never-to-be-forgotten eighth, Earl Smith whipped a mighty double to right center after two were out. There was a run we had to have and Ray Kremer was due to bat. Obviously, the Frenchman did not belong at the plate.

Bigbee "Comes Through"

Emil Yde ran out to second to run for Smith, as Bigbee's form came through the rain that made the Pirate dugout difficult of discernment. Little Skeeter faced the task of putting us back where we would have at least an even chance.

Bigbee doesn't look like the mighty Casey at the bat, but the slender sprinter and crack outfielder is a good batsman, regardless of his poor success, a failure that came through sickness.

Well, folks, there was nothing uncertain about the double which Bigbee uncorked against the screen behind Goose Goslin. Skeeter pulled up at second with the winning run. Johnson and Moore had a big duel which Eddie finally won by drawing a fourth ball. Carey came up for his fifth clash with the master of the mound. Three doubles and a single were nicked in his favor 'ere this.

Scoops drove a roller to Peck. The shortstop passed the ball in a hurry to Stanley Harris with the intention of ending the inning by a forceout, but the toss pulled Harris off the bag and the bases were loaded.

In going beyond expectations of his fond friends, Cuyler was heroic to a marked degree. He had to be courageous to match himself with Johnson in the big crisis and when the count came to two strikes and only one ball, his role was a perilous one.

Cuyler fouled off three pitches and then he looked at one that was close to the outside corner. Umpire McCormick gave Cuyler the better of it, to which Johnson offered some objections.

On the succeeding pitch, the excitement rose to a point that was not reached until the game ended. Cuyler drove a wicked liner down the right field line. Bigbee, Moore and Carey tallied in the wild excitement and Cuyler himself went over the plate when the ball became mixed up in the bullpen throng. The Senators protested the homer and won their protest from the umpires. The drive was officially recorded as a two-bagger and Carey and Cuyler were put back on the bases, but the stroke was complete.

Red Oldham and Johnny Gooch went out to worry the foe in the ninth. It wasn't long until the two returned in a blaze of splendor that shone through the dark and misty day. The first man to face Oldham was Sam Rice. Sam looked at a curve ball and was called out. Bucky Harris was a sore leader and he reflected his feelings with a hard smash, but his liner went straight into Eddie Moore's hands. Dangerous Goose Goslin also looked at a curve ball for a third strike. When Umpire McCormick raised his right hand to signify a strike the biggest scene baseball has ever known was staged by the victory-crazed multitude.

Pirates Should Take Rank with the Greatest of Clubs, Runyon Says

DAMON RUNYON

CORSAIRS, WITH SPEED, STRONG DEFENSE, POWERFUL ATTACK AND
MAGNIFICENT COURAGE AND NERVE LIKELY TO ACHIEVE PLACE
WITH GREATEST NINES GAME HAS EVER PRODUCED

In the wildest, and certainly the wettest finish ever seen in a World's Series, the Pittsburgh Pirates struggled through to victory and the baseball championship over the Washington Senators by a score of 9 to 7 yesterday afternoon.

These pallid lines cannot hope to inform the reader of the scene that befell when young Hazen Cuyler, outfielder of the Pirates, came up and slugged one of old Walter Johnson's fast shoots down the first base line, driving home the winning runs.

It was equalled only by a scene produced a moment before when Carson Bigbee, a utility outfielder of the Pirates, batting for Ray Kremer, doubled in the tying run. Both scenes were presented by the 40,000 spectators, most of them exposed to a driving rain.

20,000 Rush on Field

As the game ended, at least 20,000 of these well-soaked spectators poured out into the muddy field, and surrounded the red-coated bandsmen, who shook the water out of their instruments and blared "There'll Be a Hot Time in the Old Town Tonight," which there undoubtedly is. The crowd chased the Pittsburgh Pirates off the field trying to capture some member of the valiant baseball crew that has brought a world's championship to this city. The fans desired to make someone an object of boisterous adulation and they didn't care much who it might be.

They would have preferred Hazen Cuyler, or Carson Bigbee, or "Oil" Smith, the Arkansas man and the talkiest citizen the game of baseball has ever known, whose two-bagger in the eighth after two were out started the Pirates on their way to victory. They would have been satisfied with "Red" Oldham, the left-hander, whose pitching in the final inning held the Senators helpless, or Max Carey, captain of the Pirates, who was a powerful figure in the general assault.

All the Pirates escaped to the club house, however, and the crowd marched behind the band to the Washington bench, and stood with the rain sprinkling their bare heads while the band played "The Star-Spangled Banner." Then they all marched over to the Pittsburgh bench, and the anthem was repeated, with a lady singing in a high soprano.

Cheer, Celebrate for Hour

It was an hour after the game before the crowd finally leaked out of the ball yard, many of them jamming the streets outside the premises for a peek at the triumphant Pirates as they emerged from their club house in street apparel. Tonight the hotels and cafes of the downtown district resound to the joy of Pittsburgh.

It was the seventh and deciding game of the series, with each club having won three games. Before it was over, the spectators could scarcely see the ball through the curtain of misty rain, and the outfielders were mere outlines, vague and shadowy.

Time and again the game was halted while the ball and bats were wiped dry with towels, and twice Walter Johnson asked for a delay that he might get sawdust to scatter around the pitching mound to give his sliding feet a firmer hold. The baselines were channels of mud. The base runners had to keep kicking their cleats free of the wet and clinging earth. Meantime, the spectators were gradually sopping up rain water as they sat on the exposed seats of Forbes Field.

The Washington club got off to a four-run lead in the first inning which seemed to put the Pirates at a hopeless disadvantage, especially against the pitching of the mighty Johnson, who held them as helpless as so many mannequins in two other games.

But it is a fighting crew that Bill McKechnie has assembled here in Pittsburgh, and they kept on fighting until a forlorn hope carried through. Oddly enough, it seemed to me that at no time did the spectators seem to regard the cause as lost. Even when Roger Peckinpaugh broke up a 6 to 6 tie in the first of the eighth inning by knocking a home run over the left field wall, and with but two innings left to the Pirates, the crowd kept bawling encouragement to the home club.

Poor Peckinpaugh's eighth error of the series, which is a new world's record, contributed no little to the last minute shove by the Pirates. His bad toss during the melee of the eighth inning filled the bases. Had the toss been accurate, it would have been the third out of the inning, and would have left the score tied. Let me briefly sum up that Pirates' eighth, leaving out the cheers and the jeers and the nerve-racking tumult from the stands.

With two out, Smith doubled. Emil Yde ran for him. Bigbee, batting for Kremer, doubled to left, scoring Yde with the tying run. Moore walked. Carey hit to Peckinpaugh, whose toss to S. Harris to get Moore at second was high and nobody was put out. Cuyler doubled to right, scoring Bigbee and Moore. Barnhart popped out.

There you have it all in a few words.

Fates Against Peck

Fortune set her face sternly against Roger Peckinpaugh. The baseball writers dripping in the press section were thinking of the drama of the situation when Peckinpaugh broke up the tie in the eighth, because Peckinpaugh had contributed to Washington's distress by muffing an easy fly in the seventh, permitting the Pirates to tie the tally.

His homer glossed over a lot of things for Roger Peckinpaugh in the eighth. It looked as if he was to finally emerge from the series in one of the important roles. The entire Washington bench turned out in the rain to give old Roger a cheer as he trotted in from his trip around the bases after that blow.

But baseball fortune is mighty fickle. A few moments later Roger Peckinpaugh had slipped back into a more dismal pose. It seems strange that one of the greatest infielders that ever lived should wind up with more errors in a series of games than any other player has ever made.

The wet ball seemed to trouble the mighty Johnson more than it did Ray Kremer, Johnny Morrison, or Oldham, but not as much as it troubled Vic Aldridge, the Hoosier state right-hander, who was dismissed from the game in the first inning. Aldridge, like Johnson, had won two games of the series. He could not control the ball, which was not then as wet and slippery as it later became. He gave an illustration of the fickleness of baseball fortune, for Aldridge seemed almost certain to make a good showing on the strength of his past performances.

◆　◆　◆

BIG POISON AND LITTLE POISON

In 1926, with three future Hall of Famers already in their lineup, the Pirates added a fourth when they signed Paul Waner to a major-league contract. After winning the World Series in 1925, the Pirates fell to third place in 1926, but rookie Waner led the team in batting with a .336 average. When the Pirates bounced back to win the pennant in 1927, Waner won the National League's batting title with a .380 average and received the League's Most Valuable Player Award. During his fifteen years in Pittsburgh, Waner won three batting titles and hit over .300 thirteen times. He finished his career with a .333 lifetime average and was elected to the Hall of Fame in 1952.

When Paul Waner signed with the Pirates for the 1926 season, he told them he had a younger brother Lloyd who was quite a ballplayer and recommended that they also sign Lloyd to a contract. In 1927, Lloyd Waner joined his brother Paul in the Pirate outfield and, in his first season, made 223 hits (a rookie record), batted .355, and led the National League in runs scored with 133. In his fourteen years with the Pirates, he batted over .300 ten times, led the league in singles for four consecutive years, and ended his career with a lifetime average of .316. When he was elected to the Hall of Fame in 1967, Lloyd and Paul Waner became the only brothers to be enshrined at Cooperstown.

In this selection from Lawrence Ritter's The Glory of Their Times, *Paul Waner talks about growing up in Harrah, Oklahoma, with his brother Lloyd, their years together with the Pirates, and the 1927 World Series against the Yankees.*

In the piece that follows, from Donald Honig's oral history, The October Heroes, *Lloyd Waner talks about his "broomstick" and "corncobs" childhood and his playing days with Paul, including the "true" story of how they got their "Big Poison" and "Little Poison" nicknames. He also talks about the 1927 World Series and the story, which he refutes, of the Pirates giving up after watching Ruth, Gehrig, and the rest of Murderer's Row in batting practice.*

Paul Waner

LAWRENCE S. RITTER

I come from a little town right outside of Oklahoma City, a town by the name of Harrah. You can spell that backwards or forwards. From there I went to State Teachers' College at Ada. And you can spell that backwards or forwards, too. Which just naturally explains why I've always been a fuddle-dee-dud!

I went to State Teachers' College at Ada for three years, although I didn't really intend to be a teacher. Maybe for a little while, but not forever. What I wanted to be was a lawyer, and I figured sooner or later I'd go to law school. Eventually I was going to go to Harvard Law School, I reckon. That was my ambition, anyway.

But all at once baseball came up, and that changed everything all around. Of course, I was playing ball on amateur and semipro teams all the while I was in high school and college. In those days, you know, every town that had a thousand people in it had a baseball team. That's not

From *The Glory of Their Times: The Story of the Early Days of Baseball Told by the Men Who Played It* by Lawrence S. Ritter (New York: William Morrow, 1984). Reprinted with permission of Lawrence S. Ritter.

true any more. But in those days there were so many teams along there in the Middle States, and so few scouts, that the chances of a good player being "discovered" and getting a chance to go into organized ball were one in a million. Good young players were a dime a dozen all over the country then.

How did they find me? Well, they found me because a scout went on a drunk. Yes, that's right, because a scout went on a bender. He was a scout for the San Francisco Seals of the Pacific Coast League, and he was in Muskogee looking over a player by the name of Flaskamper that Frisco wanted to buy. He looked him over, and sent in a recommendation—that was late in the summer of 1922—and then he went out on a drunk for about ten days. They never heard a thing from him all this while, didn't know anything about him or where the heck he was.

He finally got in shape to go back to the Coast, but on the way back a train conductor by the name of Burns—you know how they used to stop and talk with you and pass the time of day—found out that this fellow was a baseball scout. Well, it so happened that I went with this conductor's daughter—Lady Burns—at school. So naturally—me going with his daughter and all—what the heck—he couldn't wait to tell this scout how great I was. How I could pitch and hit and run and do just about everything. He was such a convincing talker, and this scout needed an excuse so bad for where he'd been those ten days, that the scout—Dick Williams was his name—decided, "Doggone it, I've got something here."

When he got back to San Francisco, of course they wanted to know where the heck he'd been and what had happened. "Well," he said, "I've been looking over a ballplayer at Ada, Oklahoma. His name is Paul Waner and he's only nineteen years old, and I think he's really going to make it big. I've watched him for ten days and I don't see how he can miss."

Then Dick quickly wrote me a letter. He said, "I've just talked to the Frisco ball club about you. I heard about you through this conductor, Burns. I told them that I saw you and all that, and I want you to write me a letter and send it to my home. Don't send it to the ball club, send it to my home. Tell me all about yourself: your height, your weight, whether you're left-handed or right-handed, how fast you can run the hundred, and all that. So I'll know, see, really know."

So I wrote him the letter he wanted, and sent it to his home, not really thinking too much about it at the time. But the next spring, darned if they didn't send me a contract. However, I sent it right back, 'cause my Dad always wanted me to go to school. He didn't want me to quit college. My father was a farmer and he wanted his sons to get a good education.

But they sent the contract right back to me, and even upped the ante some. So I said, "Dad, I'll ask them for $500 a month, and if they give it to me will you let me go?"

He thought about it for awhile, and finally said, "Well, if they'll give you $500 a month starting off, and if you'll promise me that if you don't make good you'll come right back and finish college, then it's OK with me."

"Why surely, I'll do that," I said.

So I told the Frisco club about those conditions. But it didn't make any difference to them. Because they could offer you any salary at all and look you over, and if you weren't really good they could just let you go and they'd only be out expenses. They had nothing to lose.

So out I went to San Francisco for spring training. That was in 1923. I was only nineteen years old, almost twenty, just an ol' country boy. I didn't even know, when I got there, that they had a boat going across to San Francisco. My ticket didn't call for any boat trip. But after the train got into Oakland you got on a ferry and went across San Francisco Bay. Boy, as far as I was concerned that was a huge ocean liner!

◆

I had a good year in the Coast League that first season; hit about .370. Then the next season I did the same thing, got over 200 hits, and batted in about 100 runs. I was figuring by then that maybe I should be moving up to the Big Leagues. Joe Devine, a Pittsburgh scout, was trying to get the Pirates to buy me, but the San Francisco club wanted $100,000 for me, and the Pittsburgh higher-ups thought that that was a little too much for a small fellow like me. I only weighed 135 pounds then. I never weighed over 148 pounds ever, in all the years I played.

So Joe said to me, "Paul, it looks like you'll have to hit .400 to get up to the majors."

"Well, then," I said, "that's just exactly what I'll do."

I was kidding, you know. But darned if I didn't hit .401 in 1925. I got 280 hits that season, and at the end of the year the Pirates paid the $100,000 for me. San Francisco sold William Kamm to the Big Leagues for $100,000 in 1922, and then did the same thing with me three years later.

After I got to Pittsburgh early in 1926, I told Mr. Dreyfuss, the president of the club, that I had a younger brother who was a better ball player than I was. So the Pirates signed Lloyd and sent him to Columbia in the Sally League to see how he'd do. Well, Lloyd hit about .350 and was chosen the league's Most Valuable Player.

The Pirates took Lloyd along to spring training in 1927, mostly just to look at him a little closer. They never thought he could possibly make the team, 'cause Lloyd only weighed about 130 pounds then. He was only twenty years old, and was even smaller than me.

Our outfield that season was supposed to be Kiki Cuyler, Clyde Barnhart, and myself. But Barnhart reported that spring weighing about 260 or 270 pounds. He was just a butterball. They took him and did everything they could think of to get his weight down. They gave him steam baths, and exercised him, and ran him, and ran him, and ran him. Well, they got the weight off, all right, but as a result the poor fellow was so weak he could hardly lift a bat.

So on the trip back to Pittsburgh from spring training, Donie Bush came to me and said, "Paul, I'm putting your little brother out there in left field, and he's going to open the season for us."

"Well, you won't regret it," I said. "Lloyd will do the job in first-rate style."

And he did, too, as you know. We won the pennant that year, with Lloyd hitting .355. I hit .380 myself, and between the two of us we got 460 base hits that season: 223 hits for Lloyd and 237 for me. It's an interesting thing that of those 460 hits only 11 were home runs. They were mostly line drives: singles, doubles, and a lot of triples, because both of us were very fast.

Don't get the idea that we won the pennant for Pittsburgh all by ourselves that year, though, because that sure wasn't so. We had Pie Traynor at third base, you know, and Pie hit about .340 that season. Pie was a great ballplayer, I think the greatest third baseman who ever lived. A terrific hitter and a great fielder. Gosh, how he could dive for those line drives down the third base line and knock the ball down and throw the man out at first! It was remarkable. Those two Boyer brothers who are playing now are both great fielding third basemen, but Pie could do all they can and more. In addition to his hitting and fielding, Pie was a good base runner, too. Most people don't remember that.

◆

I did see Honus Wagner play. I really did. Honus came back as a coach with the Pirates during the 'thirties. He must have been sixty years old easy, but goldarned if that old boy didn't get out there at shortstop every once in a while during fielding practice and play that position. When he did that, a hush would come over the whole ball park, and every player on both teams would just stand there, like a bunch of little kids, and watch every move he made. I'll never forget it.

Honus was a wonderful fellow, so good-natured and friendly to everyone. Gee, we loved that guy. And the fans were crazy about him. Yeah, everybody loved that old Dutchman! If anyone told a good joke or a funny story, Honus would slap his knee and let out a loud roar and say, "What about *that*!"

So whenever I'd see him, the first thing I'd say would be, "What about *that*, Honus," and both of us would laugh. I guess there's no doubt at all that Honus was the most popular player who ever put on a Pittsburgh uniform. Those Pittsburgh fans were always fine fans, did you know that? They sure were. And I presume they still are, for that matter.

I remember soon after I came up, Pie Traynor said to me, "Paul, you're going to be a very popular ballplayer. The people like to pull for a little fellow."

And that's the way it turned out. In all the 15 years I played with Pittsburgh, I was never booed at home. Not even once. The same with Lloyd. No matter how bad we were, no booing. We never knew what it was like to be booed at home. I don't imagine it would help a fellow any.

◆

We won the pennant in 1927, the first year Lloyd and I played together in the Pittsburgh outfield. That was a great thrill for us, naturally. We even brought Mother and Dad and our sister to the World Series. But then the Yankees beat us four straight, so we weren't very happy about Mother and Dad seeing *that*.

The only thing I remember best about that Series is that I didn't seem to actually realize I was really playing in a World Series until it was all over. The first time we came to bat in the first game, Lloyd singled and I doubled, and from then on the two of us just kept on hitting like it was an ordinary series during the regular season. Neither of us was a bit nervous.

Finally, we came into the bottom of the ninth of the fourth game, with the score tied, 3-3. We were playing at Yankee Stadium, and the Yankees had already beaten us three times in a row. Before I knew what had happened, the Yankees had loaded the bases: Babe Ruth was on first base, Mark Koenig on second, and Earle Combs on third. And there were none out. But then Johnny Miljus, who was pitching for us, struck out Lou Gehrig and Bob Meusel, and it looked like we'd get out of it. While he was working on Tony Lazzeri, though, Johnny suddenly let loose a wild pitch that sailed over catcher Johnny Gooch's shoulder, and in came Combs with the run that won the game, and the Series, for the Yankees.

Out in right field, I was stunned. And that instant, as the run that beat us crossed the plate, it suddenly struck me that I'd actually played in a World Series. It's an odd thing, isn't it? I didn't think, "It's all over and we lost."

What I thought was, "Gee, I've just played in a World Series!"

And you know, I think that's the first time I really realized it. It's funny how much your frame of mind has to do with your ability to play ball. I guess I forced myself not to think about playing in a World Series, so I wouldn't get nervous.

◆

After that disastrous World Series, Mom and Dad and Lloyd and I went back to Oklahoma, and darned if they didn't have a parade and all for us in our home town. Everybody was so happy that I was hard put to figure it out. After all, we hadn't won the Series, we'd lost it, and in four straight games to boot.

Well, it turned out there had been a lot of money bet there, but it hadn't been bet on the Pirates against the Yankees. It had been bet on the Waner brothers against Ruth and Gehrig. And our combined batting average for the Series had been .367, against .357 for Ruth and Gehrig. So that's why everybody was so happy.

Well, after that 1927 pennant we never won another one, not one single one, all the years Lloyd and I played in Pittsburgh. Gee, that was tough to take. We ended second about four times, but never could get back on top again. We had good teams, too. You know, Pie, Arky Vaughan, Gus Suhr, Bill Swift, Mace Brown, Ray Kremer, all good boys. But we never quite made it.

It'd just tear you apart. We'd make a good start, but before the season was over they'd always catch up with us. And when you're not in the race any more, it gets to be a long season, really long.

The closest we came was in 1938. God, that was awful! That's the year Gabby Hartnett hit that home run. We thought we had that pennant sewed up. A good lead in the middle of September, it looked like it was ours for sure. Then the Cubs crept up and finally went ahead of us on that home run, and that was it.

It was on September 28, 1938. I remember it like it just happened. We were playing in Chicago, at Wrigley Field, and the score was tied, 5-5, in the bottom of the ninth inning. There were two out, and it was getting dark. If Mace Brown had been able to get Hartnett out, the umpires would have had to call the game on account of darkness, it would have ended in a tie, and we would have kept our one-half-game lead in first place. In fact, Brown had two strikes on Hartnett. All he needed was one more strike.

But he didn't get it. Hartnett swung, and the damn ball landed in the left-field seats. I could hardly believe my eyes. The game was over, and I should have run into the clubhouse. But I didn't. I just stood out there in right field and watched Hartnett circle the bases, and take the lousy pennant with him. I just watched and wondered, sort of objectively, you know, how the devil he could ever get all the way around to touch home plate.

You see, the crowd was in an uproar, absolutely gone wild. They ran onto the field like a bunch of maniacs, and his teammates and the crowd and all were mobbing Hartnett, and piling on top of him, and throwing him up in the air, and everything you could think of. I've never seen anything like it before or since. So I just stood there in the outfield and stared, like I was sort of somebody else, and wondered what the chances were that he could actually make it all the way around the bases.

When I finally did turn and go into the clubhouse, it was just like a funeral. It was terrible. Mace Brown was sitting in front of his locker, crying like a baby. I stayed with him all that night, I was so afraid he was going to commit suicide. I guess technically we still could have won the pennant. There were still a couple of days left to the season. But that home run took all the fight out of us. It broke our hearts.

Well, there's a lot of happiness and a lot of sadness in playing baseball. The last full season that Lloyd and I played together on the Pirates was 1940. That was my fifteenth year with Pittsburgh, and Lloyd's fourteenth. Heck, I was thirty-seven by then, and Lloyd was thirty-four. Of course, we hung on in the Big Leagues with various teams for about five more years, but that was only on account of the war. With the war and all, they couldn't get young players, so I played until I was forty-two, and then my legs just wouldn't carry me any more.

◆

So that's the way it was. Those 24 years that I played baseball—from 1923 to 1946—somehow, it doesn't seem like I played even a month. It went *so fast*. The first four or five years, I felt like I'd been in baseball a long time. Then, suddenly, I'd been in the Big Leagues for ten years. And then, all at once, it was twenty.

You know . . . sitting here like this . . . it's hard to believe it's more than a quarter of a century since Lloyd and I played together. Somehow . . . I don't know . . . it seems like it all happened only yesterday.

Lloyd Waner

DONALD HONIG

Some people find it unusual for two brothers to have gone up to the big leagues and had long careers and in fact ended up in the Hall of Fame together. Well, the way I look at it, Paul and me had an advantage over most kids. There was only two years and eleven months difference in our ages, so we never lacked for somebody to play with. We loved baseball and we played together all the time. Seems we were always swinging something, be it a broomstick or a plain old stick or whatever was handy. Our Dad made sure we had something to swing, and he'd make us a baseball out of old rags and twine.

We were always pitching to each other, be it one of those old rag-and-twine balls, or else corncobs. That's right, corncobs. We would break them in two and then soak them in water so they'd go farther when we hit them. You couldn't help but to develop quick wrists swinging at those things because they broke in every direction. It was almost impossible to throw one straight. Broomsticks and corncobs. That's the beauty of baseball—anybody can play it and it doesn't have to be done too fancy.

◆

Paul went into professional baseball two years before I did. He went out to San Francisco to play in the Pacific Coast League. He told the scout who had signed him about me and the fellow came by a year or so later and signed me to a contract. He said they would give me the same as they gave Paul his first year, which was four hundred dollars a month. I thought I was getting rich—that was big money back then, in 1925.

I was playing for a semipro team in Ada when I signed up. San Francisco promised to pay the team one thousand two hundred and fifty dollars and my Dad the same amount. Dad wanted to use the money to get me through college. I'd promised him I would go to college after the season. Well, San Francisco reneged on the agreement and wouldn't pay the money. Paul talked to Joe Devine who was a scout for Pittsburgh, and Devine said I should get my release and Pittsburgh would sign me. Paul advised me to do it and I did what he said. I got my release and the Pirates signed me. That suited me just fine because Paul was already with the Pirates and naturally I wanted to play with him. I was farmed out to Columbia, South Carolina, in the South Atlantic League, had a big year there and joined Paul in Pittsburgh the next season, 1927.

Reprinted from *TheOctober Heroes: Great World Series Games Remembered by the Men Who Played Them* by Donald Honig by permission of the University of Nebraska Press. © 1979 by Donald Honig.

That was half the fun, I think, playing with old Paul. I sure would have missed him if I had gone with somebody else. He helped me out a whole lot, too. There were some pitchers in the league I was having a little trouble with and he told me what I was doing wrong against them. He got me to open my stance against left-handers so I wouldn't pull away from them. And he would tell me not to pay attention to the pitcher until the ball was delivered so as not to be thrown off by the motion. Paul was always helping me, telling me a lot of little old things that made me a better hitter. The main thing he used to tell me was to hit down at the ball instead of up. He said that would give me a level stroke and I'd hit a lot of line drives. That's the way he did it and he'd hit them through that infield so fast they couldn't see them.

Paul used to lay the bat right on his shoulder and keep it there until the last second, and then with those strong wrists he'd whip it around and make that ball zing. I did it the same way. I never will forget some of the managers around the league saying we couldn't hit the inside pitch because we wouldn't be able to get the bat around on it. But the inside pitch never bothered us; in fact we hit it better. In our first three years together at Pittsburgh, Paul hit .380, .370, .336, and I hit .355, .335, .353, and we averaged better than 220 hits a season apiece. So we were making pretty good contact.

They used to call us "Big Poison" and "Little Poison." A lot of people have thought we had those nicknames because we were "poison" to the opposing pitchers. But that isn't the way it came about. It started in 1927, in New York. We were playing the Giants in the Polo Grounds. There used to be this Italian fellow who always sat in the center-field bleachers. He had a voice on him you could hear all over the ball park. When he hollered out you heard him no matter where you were.

Well, Paul and I were hitting well against the Giants. This one day we came out of the clubhouse between games of a doubleheader and this fellow started hollering at us. What it sounded like was "Big and Little Poison," but what he was really saying was "Big and Little Person." He was a real nice fellow and we would wave at him and he finally became our biggest rooter in the Polo Grounds. We got him an autographed baseball one time. But whenever we came in there he would yell that and the newspapermen finally picked it up, except they thought he was saying "Poison" instead of "Person." It became a newspaper nickname, because no ball players ever called us that. And the name has stuck, right down to this day.

◆

My first year up to the majors was 1927 and darn if we didn't win the pennant. Boy, I thought to myself, this looks like a cinch. But I hung around for eighteen more years and never saw another one.

We played the Yankees in the World Series that year. Of course everybody knows that the 1927 Yankees are supposed to be the greatest team ever put together, what with Babe Ruth, Lou Gehrig, Earle Combs, Bob Meusel, Tony Lazzeri, and the rest of them. The famous story that has come out of the 1927 World Series concerns the first day, when we were supposed to have watched the Yankees taking batting practice. According to the story, which I have read and heard so many times, Paul and me and the rest of us were sitting there watching those big New Yorkers knock ball after ball out of sight and became so discouraged that we just about threw in the sponge right then and there. One story that I've read I don't know how many times has me turning to Paul and in a whispery voice saying, "Gee, they're big, aren't they?"

That was the story. Well, I don't know how that got started. If you want to know the truth, I never even saw the Yankees work out that day. We had our workout first and I dressed and was leaving the ball park just as they were coming out on the field. I don't think Paul stayed out there either. We never spoke of it. I know some of our players stayed, but I never heard anybody talk about what they saw.

I don't know where the story came from. Somebody made it up out of thin air, that's all I can say. Every time I hear that story I tell people it's not so, but it just keeps on going. I don't think Paul ever saw anything on a ball field that could scare him anyway. He was such a great hitter in his own right that he never had to take a back seat to anybody.

This is not to say we weren't impressed by those Yankees during that Series. We sure were. They were just a fine ball club. And Ruth, well, that fellow always impressed you. I can remember when the Yankees let him go and he came over to the National League with Boston. This was in 1935. He was old, he was fat, he couldn't run, and he had lost a lot of his ability up at the plate. But he was still Babe Ruth. He came into Pittsburgh to play and after one of the games, I was leaving the ball park to go home and there's Babe signing autographs, surrounded by this big crowd. I'll swear that half the people who were to the game were waiting for him to sign. I stood there for a while watching and marveling at it. When I went home that crowd was still around him. The next day when I came to the park, somebody told me that Babe finally asked one of the policemen to get him a folding chair and Babe just sat there signing autographs.

"Till how long?" I asked.

"Till nearly ten o'clock at night," the fellow said. "He just sat and sat and sat till he'd made everybody happy."

But that's the way he was. He would never disappoint anybody if he could help it. You don't find them like that very often, I daresay.

It was in Pittsburgh that Babe had his last great day on the field. You could see he was near finished. He still had that beautiful swing, but he just wasn't hitting them anymore. But this one day he upped and amazed everybody. He hit three of them out in one game. The last one was hit farther than any ball I've ever seen. It went over the roof. I was standing in center field watching it go. You would have thought it had a little engine in it. It became a dot against the sky and then disappeared. My, did he hit it. But he could hardly get around the bases. His legs were shot, you see. We hit several balls out to Babe in right field in that game and he could hardly move after them. It was sad watching him out there. Matter of fact, he retired shortly after that game.

But in 1927 Babe was still in top form and he showed very well in that Series. It's true the Yankees beat us four straight, but they didn't run us off the field. There was only one lopsided game, where they beat us 8-1. Otherwise two of those games were settled by one run, and it seems to me that every game was close going into the late innings.

No, I wasn't nervous playing in the World Series. I'll tell you the only time I ever felt that way on a ball field—when I played my first major league game. After that I was never nervous again on a ball field. That's the truth.

I started off the Series in good fashion. First time up, Waite Hoyt hit me with a pitch. Paul doubled me around to third—he had a nice habit of doing that—and I scored on a fly ball. Later on in the game I doubled and came in on a base hit.

Ray Kremer pitched for us and he worked a good game. What beat him was errors. The Yankees got three runs in the third inning and I don't think a one of them was earned. They beat us by a run, 5-4. That was too bad; we should have won it.

In the second game I led off with a triple against George Pipgras. I remember that clearly. George threw me a good fastball and I just laid my bat on it and poked it down the left-field line. Then I scored on a fly ball. That was another close one until the eighth when the Yankees got three runs. I think that score was 6-2.

The third game was the only one where they beat us real bad. It was 8-1. But even so, it was close until the bottom of the seventh when they got six runs. That was one of the things about that Yankee team—they could explode right in your face at any time. Lee Meadows had been going along just beautifully for us for six innings, and then *wham*! Six runs. Babe Ruth hit a home run in that inning with a couple of men on. But do you know, for all their power, they only hit two home runs in the Series—both by Ruth. Do you know who hurt us in that Series? Mark Koenig, the shortstop. He hit .500. We just couldn't keep that fellow off the bases. And he was batting in front of Ruth and Gehrig. That's what did us in more than anything else, that fellow always being on base when those big guys came up. I'll tell you another interesting statistic about that Series somebody recently pointed out to me. In the four games the Yankees struck out twenty-five times to our seven. But all the same, no matter how many things you look at, it's still who scored the most runs, isn't it?

Something people tend to overlook with that Yankee team is their pitching. Everybody talks about Ruth and Gehrig, and well they might, but that was one fine gang of pitchers they had. We saw four of them in the Series—Waite Hoyt, George Pipgras, Herb Pennock, Wilcy Moore. Pennock was rough. In the third game he retired the first twenty-two batters. He had a perfect game going until one out in the eighth. I remember it was Pie Traynor who broke it up. Pennock had fine stuff and A-1 control. Remember, our club had a .305 team batting average that season, but Pennock smoothed us out with very little trouble. He wasn't the type who threw the ball past you—he just made you hit it right at somebody.

The fourth game was a close one all the way and had a very unusual finish. In fact, I wonder if any World Series game ever ended the way this one did. It was played in Yankee Stadium. I led off with an infield hit and came around to score the first run. Later on Ruth hit a home run to put them ahead by two runs, but then we scored two in the top of the seventh to tie it up. It went on into the bottom of the ninth that way, 3-3.

That bottom of the ninth was a real oddball inning. Johnny Miljus was pitching for us. He was a relief pitcher and a real hard thrower. He could burn it in. He started off the inning by walking Earle Combs. Then Koenig beat out a bunt. First and second now, with nobody out. Then Miljus made it even worse by letting go a wild pitch, moving the runners up to second and third, with no outs. And all the Yankees have waiting in line for us are Ruth, Gehrig, Meusel and Lazzeri.

Naturally in a spot like that we put Ruth on. So now it's bases loaded and Gehrig up. But I told you Miljus could really fire the ball, and that's just what he did. He leaned back and let it go. Struck out Gehrig. Then he struck out Bob Meusel. All of a sudden it's two out and the bases are still loaded. Then he got one strike across on Lazzeri. I was standing out in center field and I was beginning to think, "Maybe we'll get out of it yet."

Miljus wound up and he fired the next one, but it went into the dirt and got away from the catcher, Johnny Gooch, and rolled all the way back to the screen. Combs ran home and the game was over. The World Series was over. For a couple of seconds I didn't budge, just stood out there in center field. Couldn't believe it, I guess. It's no way to end a ball game, much less a World Series, on a doggone wild pitch.

That's how they scored it, a wild pitch. But Johnny Gooch said later that he should have caught it. Well, no matter. It was all gone and done with.

We were a little unhappy with the way things had gone. We thought we were going to give a better showing than we did because we were a good hitting team, with Pie Traynor, Glenn Wright, Joe Harris, George Grantham, Clyde Barnhart, Paul and myself. In the Series I hit .400 and Paul .333, which wasn't bad. We outhit Ruth and Gehrig.

Paul and I went into vaudeville that winter. That's right. We were a vaudeville act. We traveled on the Loew's Orpheum circuit. We played ten weeks, going from St. Louis to Baltimore to New York where we played Loew's State for two weeks, then on to Pittsburgh and San Francisco and Los Angeles. Ten weeks altogether. We'd come out on the stage in our uniforms and play catch and tell some jokes about Babe Ruth and the World Series. Paul would go on the stage first and start calling into the wings asking where I was. Finally I'd run out with a ball in my hand and say, "I was running after the ball that Babe Ruth hit." The audience thought that was a good one.

Then we'd play burn-out. That was throwing the ball back and forth at top speed, making it pop in our gloves. Paul would say something like, "Say, you're pretty good." And I would say back to him, "You ought to see my brother." The people got a big kick out of it.

Then we played some music. You see, when we were going to school Paul took some lessons on the saxophone and I tried the violin. I never could get the hang of that thing, but I could carry a tune. So after the jokes and the running around on stage, the orchestra would strike up and we'd get our instruments and play along with them. Once in a while we'd hit the same note as the orchestra, but it didn't make much difference one way or the other because they made sure to play good and loud to cover us.

It was pretty good fun. We got a lot of standing ovations and sometimes had to come out and take a second bow. And we made more money those ten weeks in vaudeville than we did playing baseball for six months.

We did all right. They wanted us to go on for ten more weeks. But that would have thrown us over into spring training and the Pittsburgh ball club wouldn't let us do it. Paul was disappointed; he loved getting out there on the stage. But as far as I was concerned it was just as well. It had been a long season and I figured it was time to get on back home.

◆   ◆   ◆

LARDNER HANDICAPS THE 1927 WORLD SERIES

If Paul and Lloyd Waner really wanted to know who started the story that the Pirates were intimidated by the Yankees before the World Series even began, they should have read Ring Lardner's "Landis Dumps Lardner's Novel 'Serious' Scheme," a syndicated piece that appeared in newspapers around the country, including the October 5, 1927, Pittsburgh Post-Gazette. *Lardner may not have been entirely responsible, but this satirical piece on his scheme to help the "nervous" Pirates by imposing the rules and etiquette of golf and tennis on "the big bruisers from the Bronx" has its fun with the generally held view that the 1927 World Series was an overwhelming mismatch. One of the many ironies of Lardner's essay is that by 1927, Lardner, who established his reputation as a sportswriter during baseball's dead ball era, believed that the live ball and the home run had changed the way baseball was being played, and not for the better.*

Landis Dumps Lardner's Novel "Serious" Scheme

RING LARDNER

RING'S FEELINGS HURT WHEN JUDGE LAUGHS OFF WRITER'S ATTEMPT TO ASSIST DONIE BUSH IN DOWNING YANKS

In a last minute effort to be of assistance to the friend of my youth, Donie Bush, in his ball club's impending brawl with the big bruisers from the Bronx, this handsome writer gained audience last night with Judge Landis and presented a scheme which, if put into effect, may change the entire complexion of the series and probably of all future baseball.

It would be clearly unfair to pit these two teams vs. each other on even terms. The Yankees won the pennant before the season opened and the only thing they have had to worry them since was the remote possibility that one of the other American League teams would trade itself in bulk for

Casey Stengel's Toledo nine and thus introduce the element of competition into what has long been laughingly known as the Ban Johnson circuit. This didn't happen and the Yankees are entering the World Series as carefree as a vegetable dinner. Whereas, on the other hand, the Pirates are nervous. If they ain't nervous, they ain't human. I don't mean to imply that they are scared. If they was the kind of boys that gets terrorized, they would have jumped right out of the league just listening to the Giants talk. But you can't go through with what they have been through and not feel kind of shaky and for that reason I have figured they ought to be given some little handicap to counterbalance the advantage of the Yankees' sang froid.

Lardner's Suggestion

Well, I suggested to the judge that regular baseball rules and customs prevail only when the New York players are doing something, but that when the Pittsburgh athletes are performing either in the field or at bat, the game be played according to the etiquette observed in tennis and golf, the two outdoor sports whose exponents appear to be very sensitive. Judge Landis, who was now dozing off, asked me to jot down a few of the regulations I had in mind so they might be submitted to Messrs. Dreyfuss and Ruppert before game time.

I have kept a copy of same and here they are:

1. The umpire shall request that while a Pittsburgh pitcher is pitching or a Pittsburgh fielder fielding or a Pittsburgh batter batting, the spectators maintain absolute silence.

2. There shall be no booing of a Pittsburgh player at any time.

3. The spectators shall not applaud Pittsburgh errors.

4. When a New York batter hits a ground ball or fly ball to any Pittsburgh infielder or outfielder, there shall be no demonstration of any kind until the play is completed.

True Sportsmanship

5. If a Pittsburgh player is called out when a New York player thinks he is really safe or when a safe hit by a Pittsburgh player is called foul and a New York player thinks it is fair, the New York player shall purposely strike out the next time he comes to bat and then turn to the press stand and smile, as much as to say, "This is true sportsmanship, typical of France."

6. No spectator should be allowed to rise to his feet except between innings.

7. New York players, whether running bases or running after batted balls, shall stop and replace each divot made by their spikes before making another one.

8. In the game called golf it is annoying to most high-class players to have anyone stand close to them or directly behind them while they are making a stroke. Therefore, when Pittsburgh players are about to swing their bats, the New York catcher and the home plate umpire shall betake themselves to one or the other of the two benches and remain there quietly until the Pittsburgh player has swung.

"Well, K. M.," I said to the judge after I had read the above aloud to him, "will you see that these ideas are carried out?"

"Yes," he replied. "Just toss them into the basket there and the maid will tend to them in the morning."

"Is everything Jake with you, judge?" I asked.

"Oh, no," the judge answered. "I like Barney just as well."

"Which reminds me," said I, "That I haven't seen much liquor around here."

"No," agreed the judge. "It looks as if this was to be a Dreyfuss."

Short All Around

Deciding that the high commissioner of baseball was growing a trifle ribald, I ventured downstairs to the crowded Schenley lobby and ran into Jimmy Sheckard, who played left field for Methuselah's club in the days when fly balls had to be caught in the beard.

"What do you think of the series, Sheck?" I shouted in his good ear.

"It ought to be a short series," he said. "Both the managers are short. If you took Bush and Huggins and laid them end to end, the game warden would make you throw them back into the brook."

"I never thought about both of them being so little," I said. "Maybe their success will influence the owners of other major league clubs to hire brief managers."

"Hardly," said Mr. Sheckard, lifting his skirts and beginning an old-fashioned quadrille. "Look at Dave Bancroft and Ray Schalk. They are both midgets, too. But if you took them and laid them end to end, or even side by side, it would be at least a week before you would have to apply for tickets to a world series between the Whitesox and the Braves."

At the end of his dance he asked me who I was picking to pitch today's game.

"Kremer and Hoyt," I replied.

"Just those two?" said Sheck. "I think we Wilcy Moore."

◆ ◆ ◆

The most telltale statistic going into the 1927 World Series may well have been the sea-son total of home runs for the Pirates, who edged out the Cards by 1½ games to win a tight National pennant race, and the Yankees, who ran away with the American League pennant by nineteen games over the Athletics. Led by Paul Waner and Glenn Wright, tied with 9 apiece, the Pirates hit 54 home runs in 1927. The Yankees, led by Babe Ruth's record-breaking 60, hit 158 home runs, including 47 by Lou Gehrig.

After Ruth and Murderer's Row swept the Pirates in four games, Ralph S. Davis, who had covered the 1903 World Series, wrote up the final game of the 1927 World Series in the October 9, 1927, Pittsburgh Press. In "Yanks Win Baseball Champi-onship," Davis, sports editor of the Press, claims that, though the series was disap-pointing, the final game was "one of the most thrilling contests in World Series his-tory." In the same issue of the Press, Babe Ruth, with the help of his ghostwriter Christy Walsh, gives his own assessment of the series in "Bambino Expected Quick End."

Yanks Win Baseball Championship

RALPH S. DAVIS

WILD PITCH ENDS SERIES
BABE RUTH HITS HOMER WITH ONE ON BASE IN FIFTH—TALK OF
CUYLER-CRITZ DEAL RENEWED

It's all over. The world series of 1927 has passed into baseball history and the New York Yankees are the premiers.

They won the honors today in one of the most thrilling contests in all world series history. And yet the finish came in one of the most disap-pointing anti-climaxes the fans have ever seen.

John Miljus was on the mound for the Pirates. He had replaced Carmen Hill earlier in the game. The ninth inning opened with the score tied at three runs each.

Jovo opened the last half of the ninth by passing up Combs, then Mark Koenig dumped the ball towards third and was credited with a hit when Traynor failed to scoop it. Ruth, the busting Babe, was intentionally passed up.

That filled the bases with none out. Pittsburgh hopes were at the zero point. But a mighty cheer went up from the Smoky City contingent in the stands, when Miljus fanned Lou Gehrig, making him swing wildly on the third one. That brought up Bob Meusel, and the hopes revived when he also whiffed.

That made it two out, and the bases still filled. Fans were shouting for Miljus to fan Lazzeri also. After one ball had been called, Miljus let go a wild pitch, which Gooch tried in vain to collar. The ball struck his glove and bounded away over toward the Pirate dugout, while Combs raced home with the run which ended the game and the series.

It was a terrible moment for Pittsburghers, hundreds of whom saw their Buccaneers go down into oblivion as one of the poorest world series teams in the entire history of the classic.

And yet today's game was filled with excitement. It was a battle those who witnessed it will never forget. At the start Carmen Hill and Wilcy Moore were opponents on the slab. Moore went the full route, but Hill was removed for a pinch-hitter and Miljus replaced him.

The Pirates got one run in the first when Lloyd Waner started off with a single to left, advanced to second on Barnhart's out at first and scored on Wright's single.

Tie Score Early

The Yankees lost no time in tying the score, getting one in their half of the opening inning when Combs singled through Grantham, who didn't seem to be able to stoop to make the scoop. Koenig also singled, and Combs stopped at second. He scored when Ruth cracked a single to right.

The Yankees forged to the front in the fifth, and again it was the busting Babe who did the damage. With one out, after Combs had singled, Ruth got one of Hill's low offerings on the nose and clouted it into the right field stands for a home run, scoring Combs ahead of him.

As the game drifted on, it looked as if those two runs would win the game and the series, but the Pirates rallied in the seventh and tied it up. Yankee errors helped them along, Moore failing on Smith's rap. Yde went to first to run for Smith, and Brickell batted for Hill. He hit the ball to Lazzeri, who allowed the ball to slip out of his hand as he attempted to throw it, and all hands were safe. Lloyd Waner sacrificed, and Barnhart's single to center scored Yde. Brickell scored the tying run on Paul Waner's sacrifice fly to Combs.

Zero in Eighth

The eighth was scoreless, and the Pirates died in order in the ninth. Then came that dreadful last half inning, giving the Yankees the title, and sending the Buccaneers home as the first National League world's series team ever to be beaten in straight games.

The Bushmen were off their stride throughout the entire series. But today they appeared more like themselves than in any of the first three games. There was more zip and pep to their work and they hit more nearly normal.

It was a real pity that they had to be nosed out of the game on a wild pitch, and it was doubly pitiful that Miljus had to uncork that wild pitch after the marvelous bit of pitching he had shown but a moment before.

Yanks Too Much

There is no use to try to deprive the Yankees of their laurels. They are a great ball team, and they out played the Pirates in every department throughout the series.

Today's contest was witnessed by a crowd almost, if not quite as large as that of yesterday, despite the fact that throughout the morning rain fell. For a time, it looked like there might be a postponement. The clouds never cleared away, but no rain fell after noon.

The day was dark and dismal, and the sky reflected the feeling of the Pittsburgh team as they wearily wended their way to their dressing room after that terrible pitch.

The Pirates left for home tonight, and by Monday the players will have scattered, some of them never again to be together as teammates. Some changes will be made in the roster before long. Talk of a Cuyler-Critz deal was renewed here, and it would not be surprising if something of the sort were to develop before long.

Bambino Expected Quick End

BABE RUTH

RUTH PREDICTED YANKEES WOULD CAPTURE WORLD TITLE IN FOUR GAMES

Well, it's over and in four straight games, just as I predicted.

But don't let anyone tell you we didn't have to work hard to win. And don't let anyone tell you them babies weren't tough either. When they came back and fought us to a standstill in that last game after losing three in a row, it was proof enough that they're a fighting ball club. Don't make any mistake about that. They'll give anybody a fight anytime they take the field.

And, the man I'm sorriest for in the whole series is John Miljus. There's a pitcher. He has plenty, that fellow, and all the nerve and courage in the world along with it. Losing a ball game and a series on a wild pitch like he did is about the toughest thing that can happen. Particularly after he struck out Gehrig and Meusel with the bases full.

But that's baseball.

It's just one of those breaks that the boys talk about, and we had that one coming to us. The Pirates had theirs earlier when Cy Moore and Tony booted a couple. Otherwise there wouldn't have been any need for that last inning.

Every man on the Yankee team played great ball in the series. Particularly the young fellows. When you start talking about series heroes you've got to give Mark Koenig a vote and Lou Gehrig and Tony Lazzeri along with him. They delivered the goods, and the fact that Lou struck out in that ninth inning doesn't take any of the credit away from him. He played bang up baseball all the way through. A lot of people think the Pirates dogged it.

That's the bunk. They were in there fighting all the time and when the breaks went against them they just gritted their teeth and kept on trying. Fellows like Pie Traynor and Glenn Wright and Joe Harris and the two Waners never will dog it. You can put that down now. They're a game ball club, and a good ball club. The fact that we beat them in four straight games doesn't prove that they're not. We caught them when they were off form and we know it. We're not handing ourselves anything on that score.

There was just one funny incident in that game yesterday. When I came to bat in the fifth Earl Smith said, "What are you thinking of now, Babe?"

"I'm thinking of those bleachers," I said, and right then Carmen Hill put one down through the middle and I socked it for a home run. The next time I came to bat Smitty was on the job.

"Listen, big boy," he said, "think about a pop-up this time, will you?"

There's something about winning in four games that makes me happy and other baseball men too. Maybe now some of the croakers who were howling that the series was fixed to go seven games will stop squawking. That ought to take the wind out of their sails for a while. It always gives me a pain to hear fellows howling about everything being fixed and that's the reason why I'm mighty glad we won the game yesterday.

Again I say it was a great series between two great ball clubs. Miller Huggins deserves a lot of credit for our victory. Huggins never made a mistake during the whole series.

He's a smart guy that chap—and a great manager. But so is Donie Bush. I've heard a lot of folks criticizing Donie since the series opened. They're all wet. It's easy to stand up there in the stands and find fault. But there is not a man in the world who could have done a better job than Donie did. He kept the boys fighting and on their toes, he played the game right all the time, and he never once gave us a break that he could avoid.

You must remember that no manager can go in there and pitch and hit and field 'em. He's a great little guy, Donie Bush, a good manager, and he's got a corking ball team.

We beat them because we had more power and we were lucky enough to get better pitching and better fielding.

Now we're the champions of the world. I believe we deserve to be.

For, and this is no kidding, I believe the Yankees are the best team in baseball today. We've proved it.

◆　◆　◆

RUTH'S LAST HOME RUNS

On Saturday, May 25, 1935, Babe Ruth, now forty years old and days away from his final game as a player, reminded the baseball world of his past greatness with an epic performance at Forbes Field. Released by the Yankees in February, Ruth signed a contract with the Boston Braves as a player and assistant manager because he believed the Braves would eventually appoint him as the team's manager. By the end of May, Ruth was struggling at bat and in the field, the Braves were in last place, and management had reneged on its promise to Ruth. After announcing his retirement, Ruth agreed to play on until the Braves completed their first western trip of the season, which included a swing through Pittsburgh. Ruth, in the third game of the Pirates series, thrilled the 10,000 fans in attendance by hitting three home runs. His third home run was the last of his career and his last hit in the major leagues.

Volney Walsh's dramatic account of the fantastic performance of "the Great Man of Baseball" describes the distance of each home run, from the first, which barely cleared the right-field screen, to the second, which landed in the second deck in right-center field, to Ruth's final home run, a blast that cleared the right-field roof, a feat never accomplished before at Forbes Field.

There's Plenty of Life in the Old Boy Yet;
Drives in Six Boston Runs

VOLNEY WALSH

PARADE OF PITCHERS WITH PEP YOUNG ALSO CRACKING
OUT HOMER WITH TWO ON FEATURES FREE-HITTING CONTEST;
THEVENOW STARS AT BAT

George Herman Ruth—the Great Man of Baseball—lighted the twilight of his career with a fantastic display of home run hitting at Forbes Field yesterday—a gaudy exhibition that was dimmed not one whit because his Boston mates could not prevent the Pirates from winning, 11 to 7.

The Bambino pyramided three home runs, equalling his best previous record set back in the days when he was a young giant and not a man of 40. When he piled on the third and final home run it was the longest drive ever seen in the Oakland flats—a prodigious wallop that carried clear over the right field stands and lit somewhere down in the hollows.

No one before the Great Man ever had been able to hit a ball over that stand since it was erected in 1925. Some of them have done it in practice, but never in a championship game.

The Great Man strode to the plate in the seventh inning to face Guy Bush, off whom he had manufactured his second home run. Bush deliberated with every pitch, threw everything he had on every ball. The Great Man heard three balls called on him and swung at one strike that he missed. Then came a half-speed curve ball. The Great Man unloosened his bat, took a tremendous swing and the ball traveled high and far toward the right field stands. Pirate players stood in their tracks to watch the flight of the ball. It was a home run all the way and when the ball disappeared behind the stands, there was a mighty roar from the crowd of 10,000.

Strength in Old Boy Yet

Ruth trotted around the bases, lifted his cap as he crossed the plate and trotted on through the Pirate dugout to the clubhouse. He had concluded his day's work with one of the great shows for which he is famous and convinced one and all that he is still the mightiest of them all.

His first home run came in the first inning off Red Lucas. That time he whacked a long, towering fly out to right and the ball barely cleared the screen and dropped into the lower deck.

Home Run No. 2 came on the Babe's next appearance at bat in the third inning. By this time, Bush was pitching. That one was a tremendous drive in itself, equalling some of the other record homers Forbes Field has seen. The ball lighted in the second deck of the right field stands out toward center beyond the screen.

Then came the record-breaker, the third and final, but not until the Great Man had sandwiched in a single that drove in a mate.

All in all, Ruth hit three home runs and a single that drove in six of the seven runs the Braves made. Just to show there's life in the old legs yet, he raced from first to third on a single with a great thundering sprint, slid into the bag and was ruled safe.

Braves Have No Pitching

The Braves should have climaxed the Great Man's day by winning the game. But while they had Ruth, they had not pitching and the Pirates piled up doubles and triples with one home run by little Pepper Young to sweep the three-game series.

Not only at bat did the Great Man shine, but he turned in three catches in right field, one of which was a beauty. He picked a line drive off Bush's bat, scampering in toward the infield to pluck the ball out of the air just off his knees.

Ruth caused the Pirates to use three pitchers, for twice when he hit home runs he so upset the Buc chucker that the latter immediately got into another bad hole as though the embarrassment Ruth had caused was not enough.

The Babe's first sock virtually eliminated Lucas from the game. It came after Urbanski had walked and gave the Braves a two-run lead. When Berger and Moore followed with singles, Bush came in and retired the side on a double play.

But Bush was to feel the Ruthian sting later. Up came the Babe again in the third with Mallon on base and his homer that time put the Braves ahead 4 to 0.

Young Drives Home Run

Huck Betts couldn't hold the lead. Thevenow tripled with two on in the fourth and in a moment the Pirates had the score tied 4 and 4. From then on it was a battle between Ruth and the Pirates' slugging. Young's homer, a drive that Wally Berger barely touched in center field in the fifth, accounted for three runs and put the Pirates ahead at 7-5. Bush having pitched out of a bad hole in the fifth when the Great Man punched a single into left to score Mallon and then raced to third on Berger's single.

Ruth's third homer in the seventh, the record-breaker, left the Braves a run in arrears and again Berger and Moore singled, driving Bush to the showers. Waite Hoyt relieved him, allowed Boston to tie the score on Lee's fly to Lloyd Waner, then shut them out the rest of the way.

The Pirates launched what proved the winning rally the same inning. Thevenow doubled with the bases filled scoring all three runners, off Ben Cantwell, who had relieved Betts.

While the Great Man drove in six runs, Thevenow plunked in five for the Pirates with his triple and double.

From Depression
Baseball to Depressing
Baseball

The 1930s, beginning with the death of Barney Dreyfuss in 1932 and closing with the heartbreaking loss to the Cubs in the 1938 pennant race, was a frustrating decade for Pirate fans and a precursor of frustrations to come in the 1940s and 1950s. But no matter how disappointing the baseball season, Pittsburgh had the wonderful voice of broadcaster Rosey Rowswell to entertain its fans. In 1937, sixteen years after Harold Arlen's historic first radio broadcast of a major-league game on KDKA, Rowswell began the first complete season broadcast of Pirate games, including away games that he recreated in the studio from a Western Union tickertape. He continued as the voice of the Pirates until his death in 1955.

On the occasion of Rowswell's death, Harry Keck wrote a moving tribute to Pittsburgh's "Rosey" in remembrance of his great popularity, especially with women fans, and his many colorful expressions, which became commonplace in Pittsburgh households.

Pirates Won't Be the Same without "Most Valuable" Rosey

HARRY KECK

Forbes Field and the Pirate games won't be the same this year now that "Aunt Minnie's" favorite nephew is gone.

Something went out of Pittsburgh with the death yesterday of Albert Kennedy (Rosey) Rowswell, for 20 years broadcaster of the Pirate games.

The first thought that struck me when I heard of the passing of the lovable Rosey was that the Pirates had lost their "most valuable player," the blithe spirit and voice that brought the fans pouring into the park across the years in the face of mediocre performances.

I do not think I am wrong in stating that Rosey's soft persuasive patter over the air waves meant more to the box office than Ralph Kiner's big bat or the individual performance of any player on the field.

No matter how sad the fortunes of his favorite team at the moment, Rosey never gave up until the last man was out—and then only to express confidence that "we'll get them tomorrow."

He never lost his boyish enthusiasm for the game although he spoke in fatherly tones. His Bucs could do no wrong. New arrivals in the city sometimes found fault with the partiality of Rosey's broadcasts, but they never could swerve him from his course, from his homely philosophy that won particularly the hearts of women.

"Sold" Baseball to Women Fans

It was largely due to his bringing the games into the parlor and the kitchen that he created a love for the sport among women and added thousands of new fans who, having suffered "Oh, my aching back" or gloated with Rosey, took to attending ladies' day games and made their menfolks take them on other occasions. Women who before didn't know where second base was located in the diamond learned about the sport and its heroes as they toiled over ironing boards or the kitchen range. They will be among his chief mourners.

Who ever will forget the genuine high glee of this thin but wiry apostle of optimism when a Pirate clouter hit one out of the park or into Greenberg Gardens to the accompaniment of Rosey's little tin whistle and a simulated clattering of broken windows and his chortling:

"Open the window, Aunt Minnie, here she comes! . . . She nev-er made it. Nev-er made it! That's home run No. X for Ralph (or Frankie Thomas or whoever the socker happened to be), right into the old petunia patch!"

Coined Household Expressions

And his "doozie-marooney," his "ol-ld dip-sy doodle" for the third strike against an enemy batter, his "put 'em on and take 'em off" after a Pirate pitcher worked out of a hole with men on bases, and his relieved "just a breeze, just a breeze" when a hostile rally was shut off in the ninth and the Buccos barely won by a whisker. Most of these gems became household expressions.

There were times when it seemed you couldn't walk down a street without hearing every radio blaring Rosey's dulcet tones as he alternately "died" and lived with his Pirates. And, like a Pied Piper, luring the stay-at-homes out to the next game.

He was as good at recreating from telegraphic bulletins in the radio studio where, when things were going against the Pirates, he frequently got up and walked around the chair "for luck." He invoked other superstitions and whammies, too.

I don't remember Rosey (he used to sign his name "Rosey (not a girl) Rowswell") ever having an enemy. That was because he never said an unkind word about a player or an umpire or anybody else. His middle name might just as well have been Charity.

Famed as Speaker and Toastmaster

Rosey was more than a broadcaster. He was famed throughout the land as an after-dinner speaker and toastmaster and traveled far and wide and was in great demand at fancy fees, preaching his sermons of life and reciting poems, many of them his own. It was as a speaker and lecturer and greeting card publisher that he was known before he entered the radio field.

He was always willing and anxious to aid any worthy cause. Year after year he was master of ceremonies at the Sun-Telegraph's Green Pennant games at Forbes Field in the interest of the Western Pennsylvania Safety Council's child traffic safety program.

If anyone had a wider acquaintance in baseball, unless it be Branch Rickey, who has proteges in virtually every league and hamlet in the United States, I do not know who he could have been.

I feel a deep personal loss in the death of Rosey. A "sweeter" guy never lived, one who was always doing nice things and being nice to people. No one will miss him more than the sports writers who were close to him. His passing follows closely on the heels of that of another of the Old Guard in the Forbes Field press box, John L. Hernon, long-time chairman of the local chapter of the Baseball Writers' Association of America, who also will be sadly missed.

How both would have liked to live to see the day when their Pirates would be back on top again!

To paraphrase the words of Rosemary Clooney's popular song, without them this ole house at Forbes Field won't be what it used to be.

May they rest in peace in the Elysian playing fields above.

◆ ◆ ◆

HAVE YOU SENT FOR SERIES TICKETS?

Long before Bob Moose's wild pitch ended Pittsburgh's hopes of returning to the World Series in 1972 and Francisco Cabrera's two-out, two-run single knocked the Pirates out of the 1992 World Series, Gabby Hartnett broke the hearts of Pirate fans with his "homer in the gloaming." The Pirates were so sure they were going to win the pennant in 1938 that management had a World Series press box, dubbed the "crow's nest," added on to the third tier of Forbes Field. Then a hurricane swept along the East Coast, causing four Pirate games in Philadelphia and Boston to be cancelled, and the Pirate pennant drive cooled. Pittsburgh stumbled into Chicago for a three-game series with only a 1½ game lead. On September 28, after losing the first game in the series to Dizzy Dean, the Pirates battled the Cubs to a 5-5 tie into the ninth inning. In the bottom of the ninth, with darkness moving into Wrigley Field and players, umpires, and fans barely able to see the play, Gabby Hartnett hit a two-out, two-strike home run into the left-field stands to put the Cubs into first place, where they would remain for the rest of the season.

This short piece, "World Series Ticket Rush Swamps Pirate Officials," appeared just one week before Hartnett's infamous homer.

World Series Ticket Rush Swamps Pirate Officials

STAFF REPORTER

MAIL ORDERS KEEP OFFICE FORCE BUSY; POSTOFFICE, BANKS HIRE EXTRA HELP TO TAKE CARE OF FANS

Talk about war in Central Europe, an up-and-down stock market and other important world happenings were set aside yesterday locally, as Pittsburgh's pennant-hungry baseball fandom made a mad rush for world series tickets following the Pirate management's announcement that it would accept orders for the big games.

The rush was on. But definitely! Post offices and banks first carried the brunt of the fans' attack to get in line for the baseball classic as they prepared money orders and certified checks for the number of tickets they wanted. Later in the afternoon, ball club officials, headed by Vice President Sam Watters, were staggered by the impact of two large sacks full of mail, carrying the first orders to be dumped on their desks.

Forbes Field offices were closed to all callers and even newspapermen, as Watters and his aide de camps, Bill Gardner, Larry Collier and Wilson Faas, all veterans of former world series games, waded through the first stack of envelopes, and attempted to get them in some semblance of order for later identification and delivery. More men are expected to be added today, when several more thousand orders will be received.

The postoffices and banks were also forced to put on extra help as the fans wasted little time to be first in line to get the reserved and box seats placed on sale. One bank opened a special window to assist the regular department of handling certified checks.

The Pirates' offices in the Flannery Building, under the direction of Jim Long, were also kept busy, with one young fellow doing nothing but answering the telephone to tell the callers that nothing but mail orders, accompanied by certified checks or money orders, covering tickets for three games would be considered. A steady stream of callers, inquiring about this and that, were given attention. None, however, could get through the locked doors of the Forbes Field office.

Everywhere that one went yesterday the question came up: "Have you sent for your series tickets?"

Just how many orders the Pittsburgh club will receive will not be known until the end of the week, but it is safe to hazard a guess that at least 150,000 applications will be made from which about 42,000 or slightly better will be lucky enough to receive tickets.

◆　◆　◆

THE BLOOPER PITCH

Truett "Rip" Sewell pitched for the Pirates from 1938 to 1949. He was Pittsburgh's best pitcher during the 1940s. He tied for the National League lead in 1943 with 21 wins, won 21 games in 1944, helping the Pirates to second place, and finished his Pittsburgh career with 143 victories. But Sewell is best remembered for his blooper, or "eephus," ball. The blooper, delivered with a shot-put motion, floated in an arc that reached twenty-five feet, then suddenly dropped across home plate in the strike zone. It became so popular with the fans that an appearance by Sewell usually meant an attendance increase at the ballpark.

In Donald Honig's Baseball When the Grass Was Real, *an oral history of the game from the 1920s to the 1940s, Rip Sewell tells the story behind the invention of the blooper ball and gives his version of what happened in the 1946 All-Star Game when he threw the pitch to an anxious Ted Williams.*

Rip Sewell

DONALD HONIG

You say you want to know the story of the famous blooper pitch? Well that started with a shot gun blast in the Ocala National Forest on December 7, 1941. So that's a date I'll remember for more than one reason. I was out deer hunting that day. I was walking through the woods when an-

From "Rip Sewell," reprinted from *Baseball When the Grass Was Real: Baseball from the Twenties to the Forties Told by the Men Who Played It* by Donald Honig by permission of the University of Nebraska Press. © 1975 by Donald Honig.

other hunter spotted something moving. What he spotted was me, but he didn't realize that until he had turned suddenly and discharged two loads of buckshot out of a twelve-gauge shotgun at about thirty feet. Caught me in both legs. That shot tore holes in me as big as marbles. One of them smashed up the big toe I pitched off of.

I had to learn to walk all over again, keeping that big toe up when I moved. Naturally my whole pitching motion had to be changed. I had to pitch just like I walked, like I was taking a step forward, all the while keeping that big toe up.

That's how the blooper ball came about, from having to learn to pitch with that motion, like I was walking toward you. I was the only pitcher to pitch off the tip of his toes, and that's the only way you can throw the blooper. It's got to be thrown straight overhand. I was able to get a terrific backspin on the ball by holding onto the seam and flipping it off of three fingers. The backspin held it on its line of flight to the plate. So that ball was going slow but spinning fast. Fun to watch, easy to catch, but tough to hit. It helped me win 21 games in '43 and again in '44.

I was fooling around with Al Lopez in the bullpen one time and started looping the ball and dropping it into his glove. All of a sudden Lopez said, "Why don't you throw that in a game?"

I laughed. "Man, no," I said. "Frisch would get after me, and so would everybody else if I threw it in a game."

Then we were in Muncie, Indiana, playing an exhibition game against the Detroit Tigers. Dick Wakefield was at bat, with two out. Out of a clear blue sky I decided I was going to throw him that blooper ball. So I wound up and let it go. The thing went up in the air, and coming down, it looked like it was going to be a perfect strike. He started to swing, he stopped, he started again, he stopped, and then he swung and missed it by a mile. I thought everybody was going to fall off the bench, they were laughing so hard.

Later I was sitting in the clubhouse, and all the newspaper boys came around to ask me what the hell that was. Maurice Van Robays was sitting next to me. Maurice says, "That's an eephus ball."

Somebody said, "What's an eephus ball?"

Maurice says, "Eephus ain't nothin', and that's what that ball is."

So then they started calling it the eephus pitch. That's the way it got started. I got more funny reactions from that than you can imagine. The fans loved it. And a lot of times some of the players on the opposing team would whistle out to me, when one of their own players was at bat, and make their fingers dive up and down through the air, telling me to throw it. You see, most guys usually swung at it no matter where it was. It was like waving a red flag in front of a bull. Made them mad as hell. It looked like anybody could knock it out, and they always tried.

I had as good control of it as I did of my fastball and curve. I'd spot it around here and there, when they were least expecting it. It reached an arc of about 25 feet.

When I first started throwing that thing I had more trouble from the umpires with it than I did the batters. Some of the umpires said they wouldn't call it a strike, no way. I heard about that and told Frisch. He became concerned because that damn pitch was becoming a drawing card. We had people coming in from West Virginia and Ohio and everywhere else just to see it.

The Pirate management got hold of Bill Klem. He was the supervisor of National League umpires at that time. And of course you know Klem's reputation—the greatest umpire of them all. So he came to Pittsburgh and came into the clubhouse to see me. He told me to get a catcher and a batter and to go out on the mound. We did that, and he got behind the plate to see if it was true the blooper was a strike. I began demonstrating it. He watched me throw it for a while, then he said, "Okay. It's a strike, and I'll see that they call it." From then on they called it.

I guess the most famous blooper pitch was the one I threw to Ted Williams in the '46 All-Star game at Fenway Park. Before the game, Ted said to me, "Hey, Rip, you wouldn't throw that damn crazy pitch in a game like this would you?"

"Sure," I said. "I'm gonna throw it to you."

"Man," he said, "don't throw that ball in a game like this."

"I'm gonna throw it to you, Ted," I said. "So look out."

Well, if you remember that game, they had us beat 8-0 going into the bottom of the eighth. It was a lousy game, and the fans were bored. I was pitching that inning, and Ted came to bat. You know how Ted used to be up there at the plate, all business. I smiled at him. He must've recalled our conversation because he shook his head from side to side in quick little movements, telling me not to throw it. I nodded to him: You're gonna get it buddy. He shook his head again. And I nodded to him again. He was gonna get it. So I wound up like I was going to throw a fastball, and here comes the blooper. He swung from Port Arthur and just fouled it on the tip of his bat.

He stepped back in, staring out at me, and I nodded to him again: You're gonna get another one. I threw him another one, but it was outside and he let it go. Now he was looking for it. Well, I threw him a fastball, and he didn't like that. Surprised him. Now I had him one ball, two strikes. I wound up and threw him another blooper. It was a good one. Dropping right down the chute for a strike. He took a couple of steps up on it—which was the right way to attack that pitch, incidentally—and he hit it right out of there. And I mean he *hit* it.

Well, the fans stood up, and they went crazy. I walked around the base lines with Ted, talking to him. "Yeah," I told him, "the only reason you hit it is because I told you it was coming." He was laughing all the way around. I got a standing ovation when I walked off the mound after that inning. We'd turned a dead turkey of a ball game into a real crowd pleaser.

And he was the only man to hit a home run off the blooper. Ted Williams, in the '46 All-Star game.

◆ ◆ ◆

BASEBALL'S COLOR LINE

Lester Rodney became the sports editor of the Communist Party newspaper, the Daily Worker, *in 1936. When he received his BBWAA card the following year, he became a member of both the Baseball Writers' Association of America and the Communist Party. In 1936, eleven years before Jackie Robinson joined Branch Rickey's Dodgers, Rodney started a vocal campaign to end segregation in major-league baseball. In 1939, as part of this campaign, Rodney sent a questionnaire to all sixteen owners of major-league baseball teams to see if they would give tryouts to Negro League players. The only owner to respond to Rodney's questionnaire was William E. Benswanger of the Pittsburgh Pirates. Rodney's excitement over Benswanger's positive response is expressed in "Pittsburgh Prexy Favors Ending Jim Crow." Benswanger agreed to a tryout for Negro League catcher Roy Campanella, but eventually backed out under pressure from the baseball establishment.*

In 1938, Wendell Smith became sports editor of the Pittsburgh Courier, *one of the most widely circulated African American newspapers in the nation. Smith, like Rodney, worked actively to integrate major-league baseball, and, in a more personal campaign, the Baseball Writers' Association of America. When he argued in 1948 that even Rodney, a self-proclaimed Communist, had a membership card, the BBWAA officially accepted Smith as a member. Twenty-one years after his death, in 1993, Smith became the first African American to enter the writers' wing of the Baseball Hall of Fame when he received the J. G. Taylor Spink Award "for meritorious contributions to baseball writing."*

In 1947, Wendell Smith spent spring training with the Brooklyn Dodgers, at Branch Rickey's expense, as a companion and advisor to Jackie Robinson. When he returned to Pittsburgh, he used his column in the Courier *to support Robinson and raise his voice against racial hatred. Smith's article is an account of Robinson's first*

road trip to Pittsburgh, his encounter with Hank Greenberg, and the beginning of
what Smith hoped would be a new atmosphere of racial tolerance after the early dis-
plays of bigotry by members of the St. Louis Cardinals and the Philadelphia Phillies.

Pittsburgh Prexy Favors Ending Jim Crow

LESTER RODNEY

The first big league magnate has spoken out in favor of admitting Negro baseball players to the game:

The President of the Pittsburgh Pirates of the National League, William E. Benswanger, in response to a query from the *Daily Worker*, says:

"If the question of admitting colored baseball players into organized baseball becomes an issue, I would heartily be in favor of it.

"I think the Negro people should have an opportunity in baseball just as they have an opportunity in music or anything else."

This simple statement by a big league owner, the first of its kind, follows the rapidly mounting flood tide of similar statements by big league managers and players themselves, a tide which threatens to rip away the last flimsy excuse for continuing the shameful discrimination against Negro players in our National Pastime.

Already Managers Bill McKechnie, Leo Durocher, and Doc Protho of the National League have named Negro players with the ability to star in the big leagues and have said bluntly that they would be glad to sign some of them if given permission by the magnates.

In the American League, Managers Haney and Baker have vouched for the fact that there are many Negro stars qualified for big league play and that the situation is entirely up to the owners.

Players too numerous to mention have expressed their admiration for the Negro players. Most of the big leaguers have played with Negro stars in after the season exhibition games and know their caliber.

And now, as the campaign started by the *Daily Worker* sports page three years ago gathers momentum and approaches the final showdown with those Jim Crow magnates who have kept baseball a step behind all other American sports in the fundamental question of sportsmanship, one of the sixteen magnates speaks out for the end of discrimination.

The past three years have seen the fight broaden out, and assume na-

From the *Daily Worker*, August 7, 1939. Reprinted with permission of Lester Rodney.

tional proportions with sports writers, players and fans gradually speaking out as they realize the unfairness of keeping men out of the game because of the color of their skin no matter how fast they could run, how hard they could hit, how far they could throw. It received two of its initial boosts when Joe DiMaggio, the Yankees great star, said that Satchel Paige, Negro League hurler, was the greatest pitcher he had ever faced, and when Ford Frick, president of the National League, told the *Daily Worker* that there was no written ban against the Negro stars and there was an unwritten agreement between the individual club owners.

With the sensational statement by Bill McKechnie that he "knew at least 25 Negro stars good enough" and would "hire some if given permission," the campaign caught fire last month and was followed rapidly by other clean cut statements by managers and players.

Benswanger's statement is another step forward. "If it becomes an issue . . ." says the Pittsburgh owner. It's becoming the liveliest issue in the American sports world today and Benswanger has put himself on the side of the overwhelming majority who want an end to an un-American relic of discrimination in our National Pastime.

The Sports Beat

WENDELL SMITH

Robbie a "Hit" in Pittsburgh

During the three-game series with the Pirates in Pittsburgh the Dodgers found the going rather rough, losing two out of three games to Billy Herman's hustling crew. If the Brooklyn team had anything to be happy about it was the playing of Jackie Robinson who banged out six hits in thirteen trips to the plate. It was the best series Robinson has had and it was obvious to every one who saw him perform that, with some of the early tension gone, he has found himself and from now on is going to be a tough customer for the opposition to deal with.

While such incidents as the St. Louis Cardinal strike threat and the Philadelphia Phillies' name-calling tirade left nasty tastes in the mouths of everyone, the experiences Robinson had with the Pirates prove that all ball players in the majors are not "laying" for him, or "out to get him."

The Pittsburgh club was particularly hospitable and friendly to the

Reprinted by permission of GRM Associates, Inc. From the issue of May 24, 1947, of *The Pittsburgh Courier*. Copyright © 1947 by *The Pittsburgh Courier*; copyright renewed 1975 by *The New Pittsburgh Courier*.

player whom some writers have referred to—without actually checking to find out—as the "loneliest man in baseball." Just why the Pirates treated Robinson more humanly than any other club has thus far is hard to say. It may be that the Pittsburghers are more understanding and reasonable. It may be that they admire him for the way he carries the tremendous load he has on his shoulders, with ease and grace. Or it may be that it is a club made up fundamentally of high-class players who are too big to hit him below the belt because he happens to be of a darker hue.

Whatever the reason, the Brooklyn first sacker left Pittsburgh with a high impression of the Pirates. In fact, he has a great deal of admiration for the team and its famous first baseman, Hank Greenberg.

In the first game of the series, Robinson became involved in a tangle at first base with Greenberg. Jackie laid down a perfect bunt and was setting some kind of a speed record as he zoomed down the line to first base. Pitcher Ed Bahr had to hurry his throw and it pulled Greenberg off the bag. In an attempt to spear the ball, the Pirate first baseman threw out his big arm just as Robinson rounded first and they collided. Jackie lost his balance and took a tumble. He got up, however, and continued on to second base.

That particular play was the type that prejudiced writers and players and big league owners used to say would cause a riot. Those who have fought against the entrance of Negro players into the majors have always contended that the kind of collision that Robinson and Greenberg had would only result in a free-for-all and the "good" name of baseball would be smeared.

That wasn't true, of course, but it was good ammunition to shoot out of a gun of bias. In this particular instance, however, it was just the opposite. Greenberg, as big in his heart as he is physically, later asked Jackie if he had hurt him when they collided.

Conversation Congenial after Collision . . .

"Hope I didn't hurt you, Jackie," the famous home-run hitter said. "I was trying to get that wild throw. When I stretched out to get the ball you crossed the bag at the same time. I tried to keep out of your way but it was impossible."

Robinson, pleased and surprised over Greenberg's explanation, said: "No, Hank, I didn't get hurt. I was just knocked off balance and couldn't stay on my feet."

Assured that he hadn't hurt the personable Negro athlete, Greenberg then asked Jackie how he was getting along.

"How are things going, Jackie?" asked Hank.

"Pretty good," Robinson answered, "but it's plenty rough up here in the big leagues."

Greenberg knew just what Robinson meant. Although they didn't pour it on him as viciously as they have on Robinson, the big first baseman experienced some bigotry and insults when he first came up to the Detroit Tigers from the minors. Many times when he was trying to break in and win a place for himself, Greenberg had to close his ears when they hurled racial epithets at him from the opposing bench. In fact, one time it was so bad that he threatened to clean off the bench of a visiting team with his big bat he swings if they didn't stop putting the racial angle into their bench jockeying.

So Hank has some idea of what Jackie has been going through. He knows how tough it was on him and that it must be ten times tougher on the bronze-faced kid from Pasadena, Calif.

Hank Understands Jackie's Problems . . .

"Listen," Greenberg told Jackie during their conversation, "I know it's plenty tough. You're a good ball player, however, and you'll do all right. Just stay in there and fight back, and always remember to keep your head up."

After offering those words of encouragement, Greenberg went about his business of playing ball and so did Robinson. But Jackie didn't forget what Hank told him. In fact, he was grateful to the Pirate star for showing such an interest in him.

"He sure is a swell guy," Jackie said after the game. "He helped me a lot by saying the things he did. I found out that not all the guys on the other teams are bad heels. I think Greenberg, for instance, is pulling for me to make good."

Teammates' Attitude Improving . . .

Generally, the picture is developing better for Robinson every day. We visited the Dodger dugout and dressing room all three days last week and found the atmosphere much improved over those tense days he experienced when he first joined the club. It appears that the Dodgers are getting used to this "innovation" and that they've come to the realization that "this guy ain't no different than any other guy." There is more warmth towards him these days in both the dugout and the club house. Things are going much smoother and he has actually become a part of the club.

Last Saturday, for instance, Fritz Ostermuller hit him on the arm with a fast ball. The pitch was fast and if he hadn't thrown up his arm, Jackie might have been beaned. At it was, he hit the dirt and for a moment no one in the park knew whether or not he had been injured seriously. When the ball hit him a deathly silence hovered over the entire park. Jackie was on the ground grimacing with pain. Ray Blades, third base coach, ran to his aid and every one of the Dodgers came up off the bench. Robinson finally got up and walked to first base.

It was then that the Dodgers showed they are for their Negro team-mate. It was then that they displayed, probably for the first time, that they regard him as one of them and that they'll go so far as to fight for him. The group of Dodgers standing on the club house steps unloaded their wrath on Ostermuller. They unloosed a volley of threats that must have made his ears turn red, and with Eddie Stankey leading the chorus vowed to "get even."

"Don't forget," they warned, "you guys have to come to bat, too."

"We'll get even with you," growled another Dodger, "and we'll keep you guys in the dirt." They shouted many other things at the Pirate pitcher, the majority of which are unprintable here. But, as profane as they were, the things the Brooks shouted were simply expressions of their regard for Robinson and they sounded good to anyone who once feared that Jackie couldn't win the support of his teammates.

Any idea that Ostermuller had intentionally thrown at him was re-moved soon after by Frankie Gustine, the Pirates' brilliant third baseman. Gustine singled when he came to bat the next inning and while standing on the bag struck up a conversation with Robinson.

"That was a close one, wasn't it, Jackie?" he asked.

"Yeah," Robinson said, "too close for comfort."

"Well, I'll tell you this," Frankie said. "I don't believe he tried to hit you. 'Osty's' fast ball takes off, it jumps in on you and that's what hap-pened in your case. I'm sure he didn't mean it."

Gustine went out of his way to make amends for the Pirate pitcher. In a sense, he was asking Robinson to forgive the pitcher and not to feel that anyone was trying to hurt him. He also threw in a few words of encour-agement, told Robinson he was glad to see him in the majors and then resumed playing.

Jackie Optimistic about Future . . .

So, when Jackie left Pittsburgh Saturday night and headed for Chicago, he had a new perspective and a feeling that things might not be as "rough" in the future as in the past. Although he had no assurance of it he felt that things might be turning in his favor and Branch Rickey's prediction that "these things will work themselves out" was actually coming true.

Even Clyde Sukeforth, the Dodger coach who has been Jackie's staunchest supporter within the Brooklyn organization, sensed the "new atmosphere." We were talking with him in the lobby of the Schenley Hotel, where the Dodgers stay here, Saturday night just before train time, and "Sukey" was particularly pleased with the way things were going, insofar as Jackie's situation is concerned.

"The guys on the team are all for him," said Sukeforth. "You could see that by the way they acted when he got hit." The Dodger coach then smiled and said: "Yes, sir, Mr. Jackie Robinson's going to do all right."

I think he is, too!

◆　◆　◆

THE HIGH HARD ONE

Kirby Higbe had a Hall of Fame career until it was derailed by baseball history and his own personal conduct. When Jackie Robinson crossed baseball's color line in 1947 with the Brooklyn Dodgers, Higbe, who won a team-high seventeen games in 1946, was one of a handful of southerners who told Branch Rickey that they "did not want to play ball with a Negro." A month into the 1947 season, Rickey traded Higbe to the Pittsburgh Pirates.

Higbe's The High Hard One *was written with Martin Quigley, who had collaborated earlier with Joe Garagiola on* Baseball Is a Funny Game. *Published in 1967, three years before Jim Bouton's innovative baseball exposé* Ball Four, The High Hard One *is an uninhibited "tell-all" book about Higbe's life, from his childhood days of throwing "rocks at the colored kids" to the gambling, drinking, and womanizing that ruined his career.*

The Traveling Casino

KIRBY HIGBE

I wouldn't say the other players on the Pittsburgh Pirates led me astray, but I wouldn't call them a steadying influence either. The first year, in 1947, we weren't going any place in the National League race, but we sure had a lot of fun along the way. We loosened up pretty good most every night, and I am sure we did not lose any games that year because we were too tight. We won 154 and lost none in the night league.

From "The Traveling Casino," reprinted from *The High Hard One* by Kirby Higbe with Martin Quigley by permission of the University of Nebraska Press.© 1967 by W. Kirby Higbe and Martin Quigley.

The sports writers called us the "traveling casino" when we were on the road. We usually had a no-limit poker game going, and we played hearts, one of the sharpest card games there is, for a dollar a heart. Some of the players took their girl friends on the road with them.

There were no tears shed when I left Brooklyn. I was told that Mr. Rickey wanted to see me in his office, but he wasn't there to see me. Burt Shotton told me I had been traded to Pittsburgh, and I never did see Mr. Rickey before I left. I was not surprised that he didn't have the heart to tell me himself, because I never thought he had a heart. I guess one of the things that made him great in baseball management was that he regarded players as property, not people. There was no room in any baseball operation he ran for sentiment. That's the way the game is played, on the field and behind the owner's door.

The Brooklyn ballplayers told me I was going to a club with power that would get me plenty of runs—Ralph Kiner, Hank Greenberg, Elbie Fletcher, Jim Russell, and Frankie Gustine. The first five games I started for the Pirates, they got me a grand total of three runs.

When Roger Wolff came to the Pirates from the Indians, he said the only difference between the two leagues was that there was more power in the American League. He started against the Cardinals next day, and they hit five homers off him in three innings. He said, "I must have been hearing about the wrong league. They didn't hit five home runs off me in two months in the American League."

"Don't mind that, Roger," Tiny Bonham told him. "You were just standing too far away from the ball after you threw it."

Speaking of the Cardinals and their hitting in those days, I once threw a change of pace to Stan Musial, who hit the hottest line drive I ever saw right between Hank Greenberg's legs at first. Hank came trotting up and said, "Hig, I should have caught that one." I said, "Hank, if you had caught that one, it would have turned you inside out."

Tiny was our leader in the laugh department. I remember he was always talking about how live the ball was getting. "Hig," he said, "if you hold that ball close to your ear, you can hear that rabbit's heart beating in there." One off-night we were playing an exhibition game in Albany before a huge crowd that overflowed onto the field. One of the Albany players hit one into the crowd. So help me, as the ball went into the crowd, a rabbit ran out. "I told you," Tiny shouted. "That crowd scared that rabbit right out of the ball."

Billy Herman was managing the club. My only criticism of him as a manager is that I think we would have had a better season that year, 1947, if he had played himself at second. He was one of the finest ballplayers I ever saw.

The fans entered into the spirit of things at Pittsburgh. Every time one of our relief pitchers left the bullpen to head for the mound, the fans in the bleachers would offer him a dollar bill and ask him to go to a movie instead.

Often some of our players would continue their loosening-up right up until game time. Once when I started against Ewell "the Whip" Blackwell in Cincinnati, five of our regulars came to the ball park loaded. We went into the fifth inning 0-0. I had two out with the bases loaded on a walk and two errors. The batter hit an easy fly to center. Our fielder made a dash in, the ball dropped behind him, and all four runs scored. I gave the ball to Billy Herman: "Blackwell is hard enough to beat with nine sober ballplayers, but impossible with five drunks." He won that one 12-0.

Before a night game in St. Louis, four or five of us didn't get to the ball park until along about 7 o'clock, when we were supposed to be taking hitting practice. Dixie Howell, my roommate and the only catcher on the club that could handle the knuckleball I had started to throw, still wasn't there. When Billy asked me, I told him I hadn't seen him since noon. We were taking infield practice when Dixie showed up on the field, feeling fine. Preacher Roe was fielding throw-ins for the fungo hitter, and Dixie came charging on the field and threw as good a flying tackle on him as I ever saw in a football game. Just having fun. When the game started, Dixie retired to the back of the dugout and went sound asleep.

We went into the top of the seventh behind 5-4. Billy took our pitcher out for a pinch-hitter and told me to take Dixie to the bullpen and warm up. When he stepped out of the dugout, Dixie said, "Roomie, it is really dark out here." I told him to open his eyes.

In the bullpen I found out the only thing he could catch was a straight ball. We went in to work the bottom of the seventh.

I called to Frankie Gustine, playing third, and told him that if a pop fly went up either he or I, one, would have to catch it, not to count on Dixie.

As long as there was nobody on base, I could throw curves or knucklers until I got two strikes on a batter. Then I would have to come in with a fast ball so Dixie could hold it. Every time I threw a curve or a knuckler, I would see Dixie's fanny charging back to the backstop to retrieve the ball.

I got them out in the bottom of the seventh, and Ralph Kiner hit a home run in our eighth to tie it up. I got them out again in the eighth, and Hank Greenberg hit a home run in the ninth to put us ahead 6-5. The Cardinals had Enos Slaughter, Terry Moore, and Stan Musial coming up in the ninth. We got Slaughter and Moore, and I was two strikes on Stan and had to throw the fast ball. He hit a line shot to left field. Ralph Kiner made one of the greatest catches I ever saw in baseball, to hold the game for us, 6-5.

When I got to the hotel after the game, there was a message in our box for Dixie to see Roy Hamey in his room right away. I went up to Roy's room to see what I could do. Roy said, "Dixie was in bad shape out there tonight, and everybody in the stands knew it."

I said, "We won the game, Roy. Dixie will be all right."

When we got back to Pittsburgh, damn if he didn't go to Roy's office and ask for a raise. Roy told him he was going to send him so far from the big leagues next season that it would take a thirty-five-cent stamp to reach him.

◆

When we went to Chicago some of us would often go to a club called the Chez Paree to see the floor show after the game. One night a few of us went with one of our pitchers who was going with a girl in the chorus line. He said he was going to stick around and wait for her to get off at 4 A.M. When we reminded him he was going to pitch the next day, he said, "Who knows? It might rain tomorrow. If it does, I won't have to pitch. If it don't rain, I might win. So it looks like the percentages are all working for me."

Next morning about eleven o'clock I asked him how he felt. He said, "A little rough. I haven't slept any." He struck out fourteen hitters, drove in two runs, and beat the Cubs 3-0.

I went back with him to the Chez Paree that night. Some gamblers gave him hell for winning. They said, "After we saw you here all night and then go out with that beautiful girl, we didn't think you had a chance to beat the Cubs today."

He said, "Boys, don't ever bet against me when you see me out all night with a beautiful girl. I am just getting loose for the game."

In New York two of our players who were roommates went on a double date with two dolls, night-club dancing and having a few nips. One player liked the other fellow's date better than his, so he danced with her and asked her for a date the next night. She said she was supposed to have a date with his roomie, but she would ditch him. They arranged to meet at the Diamond Horseshoe.

Next day his buddy asked him what he was going to do that night, and he said, "Roomie, I'm going to spend the night with a friend." He went off to meet the gal, who was wearing the same big black hat she was wearing the night before.

The other fellow dropped in at the Diamond Horseshoe about 10 P.M., and the bartender mentioned that his buddy had just left with a beautiful girl with a big black hat.

"He said he was spending the night with a friend," the roomie said, "but he didn't tell me it was a friend of mine.

In 1948 we started right where we left off in 1947. When I walked into the station in Pittsburgh to get on the train for California, three of the boys were sitting at the bar. We got on the train and went right to the club car to begin spring training.

We were staying at the Miramar Hotel in Hollywood in cabanas around the swimming pool. One of our players would come back to his cabana about two every morning and call for the rest of us to join him in a good-night swim. We would hear a big splash, and he would swim around the pool for about five minutes with his clothes on. He must have had some cleaning and pressing bill that spring.

In the morning, getting into the bus to go to the ball park, he would walk right past Billy Meyer, who was our manager that year, and say, "Billy, you've got to have that juice if you want to stay loose." He must have been the most loose ballplayer in the world.

Bing Crosby owned a good part of the Pirates, and he and all of his sons used to work out with us every day. We had many, many movie stars that came to work out with us. Some were pretty good ballplayers, but most of them couldn't hem a hog up in a ditch. They were swell people, and we had a lot of fun.

We went north and played the Giants in Oakland and the San Francisco club in their park. We stayed at the Mark Hopkins and got in shape at the bar at the Top of the Mark. We didn't win too many ball games, but we were batting 1.000 in the night clubs.

When we went back down to Los Angeles for three days, another player and I rented the bridal suite at the Biltmore. Some of those Hollywood parties you hear about looked like Sunday-school picnics compared to the party we had. Just the suite cost $300, not counting what we ordered up, but it was well worth it. We really enjoyed our spring training that year.

We had a pretty good team that year, and I will say that every man on it put out 100 per cent on the field. We were right up in the pennant race all the way until the last three weeks of the season.

I relieved most of that year and set a club record by appearing in 56 games, with an 8-7 record.

Howell had been sent down, but we got another catcher that could handle my knuckle ball. He was another two-fisted double-shot-drinker.

When I went in to relieve, the regular catcher would take off his gear and leave it at the plate for my catcher.

Bill Meyer called on me to start a game against Brooklyn. My catcher said, "Hig, I need a double shot and I'll be okay." So I took him to a bar across the street. His hand was shaking so bad that he couldn't hold the glass. He had to put his mouth down to the glass to drink the first shot. But after the first he got steady enough to raise the glass for the next shot. He got steadier after every double shot. It was quite a game, but he went all the way with me, and we beat them 3-1.

◆

We went back to California for spring training in 1949, this time to San Bernardino, out in the desert a ways from Hollywood. One of the players and I began to go to Hollywood, about sixty miles away, every night after practice. He was one of the roughest, toughest men that ever played in the major leagues. We would get in about 5 A.M. and this fellow would be in my room at 6:30, looking like he had slept twenty hours instead of two, hollering like a bull moose to wake me up. My eyes were so red I think I would have bled to death if I hadn't kept them closed.

One night we stopped at a night club on the way to Hollywood and had a few drinks. Three big guys were picking on a little guy, so my friend said, "Hig, I think I will go straighten those guys out." I told him, "They're pretty big, so I'll go with you." He said, "Sit still. I can handle this."

He went over and said something, and one of them obliged by taking a swing at him. In a minute or two all three of them were on the floor, and he was walking back to our table with the little fellow, saying, "Son, you better stay with me so you won't get hurt." We didn't stay long, because we were asked to leave. If I hadn't been with him, I think he would have cleaned the whole joint out.

After ten nights of that, I couldn't hold out any longer and had to start getting some sleep. He kept on going to Hollywood during all of spring training, but he played every day and did a good job of it.

After working out, some of us would take the hot baths at the Arrow Springs Motel. You would take the elevator straight down to the hot-bath room. One time, while sitting in the hot room, Tiny Bonham was kidding Danny Murtaugh about how ugly he was. Tiny said, "Danny, you sit here long enough and your face will get as soft as putty, then we'll remold it." Danny said, "I'll try it. Anything would be an improvement."

That was the spring I took up handicapping in a serious way. I passed quite a bit of time reading the racing forms and then doing my handicapping. I placed my bets with a nearby bookie. I lost a thousand or more dollars before I bet $100 on a 12 to 1 horse which won. Since I was about even, I decided to quit. When I went to collect, the place was closed, and the people next door told me the law had beat me there and raided the place. I quit handicapping while I was still behind.

Charlie Grimm, managing for the Cubs, did a great relief job that spring. Five players from each of the four major-league clubs training in the Los Angeles area were invited to a big shindig at the Biltmore Hotel. Groucho Marx got each of us players up and gave us a going over with questions about how we met our wives. He was really funny, and it was going his way until he came to old Charlie. They put on the funniest show I ever saw. Charlie stole it from Groucho, and we all felt pretty good that one of our people could stand up against just about the best professional comedian in the business.

We had just got back to open the season in Pittsburgh when I got a phone call at two in the morning from the wife of one of our players. She thought maybe I would know where her husband was. I didn't know, but I told her old Hig would get up and go looking. I knew most of the hang-outs, and I hadn't been to about three of them before I found him sitting at the bar like he owned the world. I said, "Boy, you know what time it is?"

He said, "I am trying to drink enough to get the guts to go home and face my wife."

I said, "Wait until Billy Meyer gets through with you tomorrow."

"All Billy can do is fine me," he said. "I would rather face ten Billy Meyers than one wife. Someday I'll leave this club, but I've got to live with her forever."

◆　◆　◆

GREENBERG GARDENS

Detroit Tiger slugger Hank Greenberg was the first great Jewish-American baseball player in the major leagues. He was at the height of his career in 1941 when he be-came only the second big-league ball player to be drafted into the armed services. He returned from the war in July 1945 and on the last day of the season hit a grand-slam home run to win the pennant for the Tigers. In 1946, at the age of thirty-five, he led the American League in both home runs (44) and runs batted in (127), but in January 1947, because of his age and high salary, he was placed on waivers and claimed by the Pittsburgh Pirates.

In an interview with Lawrence Ritter, Hank Greenberg gives his account of the extraordinary effort made by the new Pirate ownership, headed by John Galbreath, to sign him for the 1947 season, including a willingness to bring in the left-field fence at Forbes Field. Greenberg hit 25 home runs in 1947, but the popular complaint was that everyone was hitting home runs into the Greenberg Gardens except Hank Greenberg.

Hank Greenberg

LAWRENCE S. RITTER

I had a pretty good year the following year, 1946. I hit under .300 for the first time since I'd been with the Tigers, but I still led the league in both home runs and runs batted in.

After the season ended, though, I got one of the biggest shocks of my whole life. In January of 1947, I heard on the radio that I'd been sold to the Pittsburgh Pirates. I wasn't even sold, really. Given away would describe it better. I was waived out of the American League and picked up by Pittsburgh for practically nothing. Evidently nobody else felt they could afford my $75,000 salary.

I couldn't believe it. Detroit was my team. I identified 100 percent with the Tigers. I'd been in the Detroit organization for seventeen years. Only a little over a year ago I'd hit that pennant-winning home run on the last day of the season. And here I was being dumped without even the courtesy of a phone call. I did get a telegram: YOUR CONTRACT HAS BEEN ASSIGNED TO PITTSBURGH IN THE NATIONAL LEAGUE. That's all it said.

I never understood it. Still don't to this day. I've had a sour attitude toward Mr. Briggs ever since. He's the man who must have been responsible. I still remember Mrs. Briggs kissing me good-bye when I went into the army in 1941. But now the war was over. It's an old story: what have you done for me *lately*? In my case it was just lead the league in home runs and runs batted in!

I was so shocked and hurt I quit baseball. Simply quit. I told the press I was retiring and that was that.

John Galbreath, Frank McKinney, and Bing Crosby had just bought the Pittsburgh Pirates. They announced that they had acquired Hank Greenberg—the American League's home-run and runs-batted-in leader —and in a week their advance sale picked up $200,000. So they were very eager for me to play. When I said I was retiring, they were quite unhappy.

From *The Glory of Their Times: The Story of The Early Days of Baseball Told by the Men Who Played It* by Lawrence S. Ritter (New York: William Morrow, 1984). Reprinted with permission of Lawrence S. Ritter.

Mr. Galbreath came to New York and phoned me to have lunch with him. I said, "Mr. Galbreath, I'm not going to play anymore. I've announced my retirement and I mean it."

"I don't want to talk you into playing," he said. "I just want to have lunch with you."

So we had lunch and while we were eating, he said, "Tell me what your objections are to playing in Pittsburgh."

"I don't have my heart in it," I said. "I've played all my career with Detroit and that's home to me. Not to mention things like the fences in your ball park. Pittsburgh has a big ball park. I'm used to a park that's 340 feet down the left-field line. Yours is 380 feet. I don't want to disappoint everybody."

"Don't worry about that," he said. "How far is it in Detroit? 340? Well, we'll make Pittsburgh 340, too. We'll bring the fences in so it'll be 340."

"That's not so important," I said. "There are a lot of things. For instance, I can't ride those trains anymore. The berths are too small. Every time I go in them I get a crick in my back."

"You don't have to go by train," he said. "You can go by plane."

"I can't stand a roommate anymore," I said. "At my age, I don't want to have to deal with roommates."

"Fine," he said. "Don't worry about roommates. We'll give you a suite by yourself on the road."

"Well," I said, "if I ever did play for anybody, they'd have to give me my outright release at the end of the season. I never want to hear on the radio again that I've traded or sold."

"OK," he said, "we'll give you your outright release at the end of the season."

Everything I mentioned, he said, "Don't worry, we'll take care of it. We'll work it out"

So finally I said, "Well, you wouldn't pay me enough, anyhow."

"We'll pay you whatever you want. What did you get last year?"

"$75,000."

"What do you want for this year?"

"I'd say $100,000."

"Fine," he said, "you got it."

When he got through offering me all this, what could I do? He talked me into playing, so I went and played one more year.

I doubt if I really earned my salary on the field that year, even though I hit 25 home runs and drove in about 75 runs. I brought in a lot of money at the gate, however, and I think I earned my pay by training my own successor, so to speak. I worked a lot with Ralph Kiner, who was still a baby then, and helped him become the great home-run hitter he eventually became. I still feel as close to Ralph as if he were my own son.

Ralph had a natural home-run swing. All he needed was somebody to teach him the value of hard work and self-discipline. Early in the morning, on off-days, every chance we got, we worked on hitting.

"Let me ask you something," I said to him. "In a 150-game season, let's say you go to bat four times a game. That's 600 times at bat. Let's say you get two decent swings each time at bat. That's 1,200 swings. If you stand here at home plate and you make the pitcher throw strikes, don't you think that with 1,200 swings you'll hit 35 balls out of the park?"

"Sure," he said.

"Well," I said, "that's all there is to it. You know you're going to get 1,200 swings. Now the secret is to make the pitcher throw strikes. If you learn the strike zone, you're automatically going to have 35 home runs a season. It's as simple as that."

He learned the strike zone and instead of hitting 35 home runs, he hit over 50 twice and led the league seven straight years. Except for Babe Ruth, no one has ever hit as many home runs per time at bat as Ralph Kiner.

At the end of the '47 season, the Pirates kept their word and gave me my release, and then I really did quit playing. The passage of time and changes in the game have pushed me way down in terms of number of home runs hit, but when I retired in 1947, my 331 lifetime home runs were *fifth* on the all-time list; the only ones who had hit more home runs than me were Babe Ruth, Jimmie Foxx, Mel Ott, and Lou Gehrig, in that order.

◆

As a player, I often had fans and opposing players taunting me, calling me names. For at least ten years I hardly played in a ball park where there wasn't some loud-mouthed fan popping off with anti-Jewish remarks. In the minors—the Piedmont League, the Texas League—and for many years in the majors, too, my religion was seen as an appropriate topic for ridicule.

However, I think that *helped* me more than it hurt. I was a very sensitive, fired-up ballplayer, and when they got on me that way, it brought out the best in me. I played all the harder.

In my mind, by the way, players belong in a different category than fans. It was considered fair game to try to probe for a guy's weak spot so you could catch his attention and destroy his concentration. Joe McCarthy used to have two third-stringers on the Yankee bench—we called them bench jockeys—whose main job was to ride the opposition and try to get their goat.

When opposing bench jockeys taunted me, was it really anti-Semitism or just a psychological ploy to distract me? Probably some of both, but in my opinion it was mostly a psychological ploy. After all, Al Simmons heard similar insults about his Polish ancestry and Joe DiMaggio about his Italian heritage. Babe Ruth was called a "big baboon," and much worse, and Zeke Bonura "banana nose." In all honesty, I couldn't then and I can't now single out the insults aimed at me as any different from all the others. I think they were all the same kind of thing.

You want to talk about real bigotry, that was what Jackie Robinson had to contend with in 1947. Teammates asking to be traded rather than play with him, opponents threatening to strike rather than play against him; in many places he couldn't eat or sleep with the rest of the team. I never encountered anything like that.

I was with Pittsburgh in the National League that year, so I saw it close up. Brooklyn was leading the league and we were in last place, they were beating our brains out, and here's some of our guys having a good time yelling insults at Jackie! I had to put up with little more than a mild hazing compared with what he went through.

◆　◆　◆

RALPH KINER

From his rookie season in 1946, when he first led the National League in home runs, until he was traded to the Chicago Cubs in June 1953 by Branch Rickey, Ralph Kiner was a larger-than-life-figure on some of the worst teams in Pirate history. During those dark years, the only thing that kept fans at Forbes Field in the late innings of yet another Pirate loss was the chance to see Kiner bat one more time. His Hall of Fame numbers include winning or sharing the National League home-run title in each of his seven full seasons with the Pirates. In 1949, he hit 54 home runs, only two short of Hack Wilson's National League record (since shattered by Mark McGwire, Barry Bonds, and others). He was so proficient at hitting home runs that his ratio of 7.1 at bats is second only to Babe Ruth among players in the Hall of Fame.

In the May 1950 issue of Sport *magazine, Ralph Kiner, in an "as told to" article with Al Stump, the Ty Cobb biographer, responds to those asking if he will break Babe Ruth's home-run record. At the time of the article Kiner had hit 168 home runs in his first four big-league seasons, something no one had done before in baseball history. His response is hardly surprising, but his thoughts on what will likely hap-*

pen to the first player to hit 61 home runs are remarkable, considering Roger Maris's fate in 1961.

The Home Run I'd Hate to Hit

RALPH KINER

Will I break the Babe Ruth home-run record? That's the question I get from all sides these days, sometimes a dozen times a day, from everybody from the kids in ragged pants who hang around the clubhouse to white-haired old ladies of 80. All I can tell them is what I believe: "I might—with luck."

You can't escape the fact that no ballplayer can get close to or match the Babe's 60 homers in one season without everything going in his favor. Jimmy Foxx, among many others, can vouch for that. Foxx was on his way to surpassing the Babe in 1932, but sprained his wrist in August. He got only three homers that month. At that, he finished with 58 for the season, as close as anybody has come to the record. I haven't discussed it with him, but Foxx may agree with my theory that the Babe's record just might not be beaten for many more years. Not unless everything goes 100 percent right or thereabouts through 154 games for some extra-lucky guy. Because the Babe, of course, was one-in-a-lifetime hitter. And his mold is broken.

Babe's big 60 has stood up since 1927 against the best whacks of Hornsby, Simmons, Ott, Wilson, Foxx, Gehrig, Greenberg, Mize, DiMaggio, and Williams, just to skim the top sluggers. The combined major-league seasons of these 10 total more than 140, or enough to sink hundreds of records. But it hasn't been enough to beat the Babe's.

The record was set in a day-ball era. The night-owl life we lead today not only favors the pitcher but also crowds games so close together that you don't step up to the plate as bright-eyed and ready as you should be.

It was set by a man who got plenty of chances to hit because he played on one of the highest-scoring teams in history and had terrific wallopers batting fore and aft of him.

Your favorite hitter and mine was a left-hander, who had an undeniable advantage over a right-hander because of the peculiar construction of major-league parks.

And Babe Ruth was that rarest of all guys with a bat—one who re-

From "The Home Run I'd Hate to Hit," by Ralph Kiner, as told to Al Stump, in *Sport*, May 1950. Reprinted by permission of Ralph Kiner.

mained just as strong and dangerous in September as he was in May. We mere mortals who have followed him have a habit of slacking off in power in the midsummer months, when the temperature is 90° and the bat feels like a lead pipe on your shoulder. The most amazing part of the Ruth record is that he was still KO'ing the ball every other day right through the final stretch.

There's one other hazard that you don't hear much about. I know it's there because I face it every day. It isn't Rex Barney's smokeball or Ken Heintzelman's sneaky change-of-pace screwball. Or even Johnny Sain's five (count 'em) varieties of curves. The best way I can describe this hazard is to say that it's written on the faces and in the letters of thousands of fans who ask the inevitable question: "Will you beat the Babe's record . . . etc."

Most of them, you see, are hoping and perhaps praying that you don't wreck baseball's greatest legend. In their hearts, they are pulling against you. When I reach 50 homers, as I did in 1947 and again last year, and start getting nervously close, most of my mail is on just one subject. Out of 200 or 300 letters a week, more than half are of what you might call the discouraging type. Some fans get bitter about it.

"I hope you never make it," one of them sizzled at me. "You're not worthy to replace Ruth!"

Others let me know that if I ever do make the mistake of hitting 60, I'll never be popular again. These are mostly the older fans who best remember and love Babe Ruth. And what a tribute they pay him. Outside of a very few Presidents and maybe Will Rogers, no American who has passed on has such a faithful following.

After you soak up repeated doses of this sentiment, you begin to feel the psychological effect. Maybe, *if* a man reached No. 59 in the homer derby, he'd be smart to stop there. Or else!

On the other hand, the younger generation is inclined to pull for a new mark. One lad wrote me a 26-page typewritten letter of instructions on how to reach it. "All you have to do," he explained, "is hit more home runs over the right-center fence. It's no further than left-center, and you hit them there all the time."

It probably wouldn't satisfy this fan to explain that I've hit only four or five major-league homers in my life to right field, including none at all at Forbes Field, because all my power is naturally to left. But, in view of other comments, I appreciated his interest just the same.

The Editors of *Sport* have asked me to speak frankly on the subject of my baseball future. This is as frank as I can make it. If it should fall to my

lot to do as well as the Babe, which is a much longer shot than my boost-
ers seem to believe, it would be a supreme thrill. Nothing I can think of
would match it, except perhaps playing in a World Series. But home run
No. 61—that's different. Any ballplayer who puts No. 61 out of the park
would have to be more sad than glad. I think a lot of people in the stands
that day, as well as the man who did the deed, would suddenly feel a lot
older. Although that one blow would be worth more money than anything a player could accomplish, it's the homer anybody would hate to hit.

When I was skipping meals and homework to play ball around the
sandlots in Alhambra and nearby Pasadena, California, the Babe was the
hero of all the kids. All of us saw some Ruth in ourselves. I don't remember keeping track of my singles or doubles, but there was a wall in our
basement that had a mark for each round-tripper I got in schoolboy
games.

Later, Babe Herman took me into Los Angeles to meet the Babe at
Wrigley Field, where he was making some movie scenes. It was the only
time I met him. He didn't say much except to grunt "hello" and wish me
luck.

But that was enough, brother!

I've got a further feeling that, if and when his record is topped, it won't
change the feeling of the public a bit. After the first shock wears off,
people will still remember him long after they've forgotten his successor.
It's like the invention of the airplane. Probably you don't remember who
improved on the first model, but you can't forget the Wright Brothers. The
same way, Babe Ruth has a perpetual patent on the home run, and the
best the rest of us can do is infringe on it a little.

Furthermore, I don't think anybody will approach his lifetime record
of 714 homers—730 if you count the 15 he hit in various World Series,
plus one in the 1933 All-Star game.

◆　◆　◆

BRANCH RICKEY DAYS

*When Branch Rickey was forced out of the Dodger organization at the end of the
1950 season, he was hired by John Galbreath to take over the operation of the Pittsburgh Pirates. As he arrived in Pittsburgh, he loudly proclaimed, "We're pointing
toward 1955. That's when the bells will start ringing as the red wagon comes down
the street." But Rickey's teams never caught fire and, during his five-year plan, the
team finished next to the last in 1951 and dead last for the next four years. Rickey's*

1952 team, losers of 112 games, was so bad that manager Bill Meyer told his players "You clowns can go on What's My Line *in full uniform and stump the panel."*

Al Abrams, a Pittsburgh native who worked for the Pittsburgh Post-Gazette *for over fifty years and had seen the best and the worst of Pirate baseball, drew upon his considerable experience as a sportswriter to point out that the recent run of bad baseball in Pittsburgh had not begun with Rickey. But even Abrams had no idea of how bad things would get in 1952.*

Sidelights on Sports

AL ABRAMS

Old First Division Days

It was the once proud boast of the late Barney Dreyfuss, "Pittsburgh is a first division town; I'm a first division man and I want my clubs to finish in the first division."

The little man who built baseball in Pittsburgh backed up his boast by finishing in the first division in 26 of his 31 years. Six of his clubs won pennants and six finished second.

After his death in 1932, Bill Benswanger, Dreyfuss' son-in-law, carried on the first division tradition. The Pirates won no additional pennants but Bill's clubs finished among the upper four in 11 of 15 seasons.

Four Pirate teams since 1932 finished second and the 1938 club, under Pie Traynor, lost the flag after the club had built a world series press stand. (Remember?)

The Dreyfuss dynasty, spanning 47 seasons from 1900 to 1946 inclusive, thus offered 37 first division finishes in 47 years.

Contrast this now with the dolorous gait of Pittsburgh clubs since the new management took over in 1947. Only one fourth place finish in five years with the sixth offering little hope of betterment.

One can't blame the oldtime Pirate fan for beefing. He became accustomed to first division baseball under the Dreyfuss regime and hasn't had much of it since.

Let's Look at the Record

To make the records official we went to the books to verify the big league baseball given the town by Dreyfuss and his successor as compared with the type we have had to suffer with of late.

From the *Pittsburgh Post-Gazette*, April 29, 1952. Copyright/*Pittsburgh Post-Gazette*, 2002. All rights reserved. Reprinted with permission.

The following table shows how the Pittsburgh club finished under each regime.

	1	2	3	4	5	6	7	8
Dreyfuss (1900–31)	6	7	7	6	3	1	1	1
Benswanger (1932–46)	0	4	1	6	2	1	1	0
New Deal (1947–51)	0	0	0	1	0	1	2	1

Again the words of the astute Dreyfuss come back to us:

"I don't always win the pennant but I usually can make it close for the team that does. Why shouldn't a club finish in the first division? It's a disgrace to finish in the second division!"

Barney Had His Critics, Too

No baseball owner ever lived who didn't have his critics. Despite the fine class of first division ball he dished out annually, Dreyfuss was not without his blasters.

And, what do you think the beef was? First division ball wasn't good enough for the majority of fans. They wanted a pennant winner.

If I heard it once I heard it said a thousand times back in the old days that Dreyfuss wasn't interested in winning pennants.

"He's a shrewd businessman," the critics would snort. "He'd rather finish second, third or fourth and not have to pay his players too much money."

There's no pleasing some baseball fans, win, lose, or finish last.

A Cutting Retort

The Pirates of today have been taking plenty of razzing from both the fans and the writers but the unkindest cut of all came from the typewriter of Warren Brown, Chicago scribe.

Brown had plenty of chances to observe the Bucco fledglings in spring training and in the games played with the Cubs so far. That he doesn't think much of the team is evident by his early estimation of the club that it is one of the worst he has ever observed.

Warren relates the story about two fans passing by the press box on their way out of a ball park. One of them observed that a Pirate rookie looked "pretty good" but should be sent to a minor league team for more seasoning.

His companion came back with the following.

"Where can you find a more minor league team than the one he's with right now?"

◆ ◆ ◆

BASEBALL IS A FUNNY GAME

In 1952, Joe Garagiola reached the depths of his professional baseball career when, after being traded to the Pirates during the previous season, he played on arguably the worst Pirate team in its modern history. The following year, Garagiola was one of the players sent by Branch Rickey to the Chicago Cubs with Ralph Kiner in one of the most shocking trades in Pirate history.

During his career, Garagiola kept notes on the funny things that happened to him as a ballplayer. In 1960, with the help of St. Louis writer Martin Quigley, he published his anecdotes in Baseball Is a Funny Game. *The book includes the story of the way Garagiola found out that he was part of the Kiner trade. In 1977 Garagiola wrote "Were the Pirates the Worst Ever? Maybe So" to commemorate the twenty-fifth anniversary of his 1952 Pirates.*

Inside the Clubhouse

JOE GARAGIOLA

The keeper of the clubhouse is each player. He spends more time here than in his own home during baseball season. It's where twenty-five guys battle every day but have to live like one. It's a continually changing scene, the clubhouse, because trades are such an important part of base-ball. It is in the clubhouse that trade announcements are usually made.

The big Ralph Kiner trade between the Pirates and the Cubs was finally announced in the clubhouse. I was with the Pirates and had reported for the day's game as usual (and in 1953 that took courage) but had a feeling that something unusual was going to happen. We had been hearing ru-mors, but what really made us feel something was going to happen was the presence of newspapermen in the press box. It was only 11:30 and they were in the press box already. On a normal day most of the writers wouldn't get there until the sixth inning because nothing was going to happen before then anyhow. The Pirates took batting practice at the usual time, and the Cubs would start their practice at 12:30. At 12:20 both man-agers called their teams off the field. I remember the time so well because I remember turning to George Metkovich and saying, "George, remember the time and date, 12:20 on June 14, 1953 . . . this is history. We will see

From "Inside the Clubhouse," in *Baseball Is a Funny Game* by Joe Garagiola with Martin Quigley (Philadelphia: J. B. Lippincott Company, 1960). Reprinted with permission of Joe Garagiola.

the biggest deal in baseball, with both teams going off the field it must be twenty-five Cubs for twenty-four Pirates and cash."

Fred Haney was the Pirates manager then, and when the whole team was seated in the clubhouse, he said, "We have just made a trade." (This was the biggest understatement since Stan Musial said he thought he could hit.) Sitting on a trunk, I never dreamed I was in on it. I thought I was set for a couple reasons. I had a good year in 1952, hitting .272, twenty-two points higher than I had ever hit, I had played in 112 games and had showed up for 154 (and when you lose 112 like we did showing up was worth something); I had made a lot of luncheons, and I had done the extra things like catching batting practice.

The first player Haney told was Ralph Kiner. "I hate to see you go, but you are the man they wanted. I think it will be better for all concerned. Thanks for everything." Kiner admitted that the deal didn't surprise him too much. The next player was Howard Pollet. Howard knew about it because he was to have pitched the night before but was bypassed because of the pending deal. George Metkovich, an outfielder, was next. The Catfish knew it because Haney had mentioned the possibility of the deal to him.

I'm sitting back wondering how many are involved. Is it really a twenty-five for twenty-four deal? What are we getting? After all, I knew I had that good year in 1952, and a couple days before I had a meeting with Mr. Rickey to back up my confidence. Mr. Rickey, a very dramatic speaker, had grabbed those bushy eyebrows, looked up to the sky, and said, "By Judas Priest, Joe, we're turning the corner. We're coming out of the wilderness, and you, my boy, figure in my plans."

I could see Haney deliberate and think hard what he was going to say next. A lump almost came to his throat as he spoke softly the next three words, "*Where's the Dago?*" (They hardly ever use your name in the clubhouse.)

I thought he meant Pete Castiglione, the infielder, so I hollered, "Which one, me or Castiglione?" (thinking I knew all the time).

Haney said, "You! You're the one."

"Me, you must be kidding! I figure in the Pirate plans and, besides, my wife did the home stand shopping yesterday."

"No, it's you Dago. I couldn't tell you anything because I didn't know until this morning. Got anything you want to say?"

"Yeah, if anybody wants to get off this club, rent my apartment. Bill Howerton and Bill McDonald had it before me." (Gene Hermanski, a Cub who was in the deal, took it and lasted about two years.) With that we loaded our stuff, walked through one door and through another, and we were Chicago Cubs. That's a typical day—a Pirate in the morning, a Cub in the afternoon. Confusing? Well, follow it through. Here I was with the Chicago Cubs in Pittsburgh leaving for New York that night and my family was in Pittsburgh heading back for home in St. Louis until I find a house for them in Chicago. You never know what's going to happen behind those clubhouse doors.

Behind those doors the moods can go from New Year's Eve to a Dead on Arrival morgue scene in a matter of minutes.

Were the 1952 Pirates the Worst Ever? Maybe So

JOE GARAGIOLA

One of my favorite events on baseball schedules is Old-Timers' Day. Many clubs hold theirs in connection with an event, like the 20th anniversary of winning a pennant.

With that in mind, I don't see how the Pittsburgh Pirates can pass up the chance to mark the 25th anniversary of the 1952 Pirates. As a member of that team, I feel we made genuine contributions to baseball, not only in Pittsburgh, but elsewhere.

Let's take the matter of batting helmets. We were the first big league team to wear them. The theory was that when pitchers threw at batters, the batters' heads would be protected. But with hitters like we had, pitchers never felt the need to throw at us.

The first test didn't involve a pitcher and a batter. One of our baserunners was the front part of a double play and didn't duck when the shortstop threw to first. To us, the play was typical. But the runner wasn't hurt, which did a lot for the helmet business.

Almost Out of the League

Since the 1952 Pirates are now a quarter-century old, maybe I should present our credentials. It's not fair to compare us to expansion clubs. They are bad because they're new. Pittsburgh had been in the National League 65 years when we came along.

We did not win the pennant that year. We finished 22½ games behind Boston, and Boston finished next to last.

Last-place clubs sometimes have one area where they do better than other clubs. Not us. No matter what the category, we had an iron grip on

From the *New York Times*, February 20, 1977. Reprinted with permission of Joe Garagiola.

last place. As Branch Rickey, our General Manager said, "This team finished last on merit."

We had the worst record in the National League, and the worst home record on the road. We were last in batting. Our hitters struck out more than those on any other team. We had the lowest fielding average, a statistic that some people think doesn't prove anything. In our case, it did. We also led the league in errors. You knew we would miss the ball; the suspense and excitement came because you didn't know how.

Several years ago, a big-league pitching coach said to me, "You laugh about that bad ball club in Pittsburgh, but what about those poor guys who had to do the pitching for you?"

Poor guys? Don't you believe it. As the catcher, I was the safest guy on the field. The batters made sure the ball stopped about 4 feet from me.

Our pitchers carried their part of the load. We had the worst team earned-run average in the league, gave up the most bases on balls and struck out the fewest opponents. We did have one 14-game winner, Murry Dickson. He was our ace, and he lost 21. No member of our staff won more than he lost.

Strikeout Artist Strikes Out

In May 1952, Ron Necciai struck out all 27 batters in a nine-inning game for our minor league farm. In his next game, he struck out five in one inning (his team, like ours, had trouble fielding). He was 20 years old, 6 feet 5 inches and fast. And wild. We called him up, and he walked more than he struck out.

It's a standard gag on bad ball clubs that while some ball clubs might look good on the field, "ours looks good in the hotel lobby." With us, not even that was true. John Berardino looked more like an actor, which he is now on daytime television. Dick Hall was 6 feet 6 inches, but weighed only 180 pounds. Hall was one of baseball's finest relief pitchers for many years, but we used him at third base. Does that tell you something?

Certain things we did well. On special-events days around the league, we were usually the attraction. As a result, we got good in things like wheelbarrow racing, and relay throwing from the outfield to the plate.

But even then, we ran into embarrassments. One day there was a throwing contest for catchers, testing the arms for accuracy by throwing from home plate into a barrel at second base. Clyde McCullough, Ed Fitzgerald and I were the catchers on our team. We were all entered. The winner was Sam Narron, one of our coaches, who had retired as a player five years before.

I would like to see the 1952 Pirates go back, if for nothing else, to test the fans. They could give us our old uniforms, our same numbers, let us walk around the field and see if the fans recognize us. Oh, to see a shoe-string catch of a bat on a bunt play; to see a pop fly drop and hear the reason was that it hit an air pocket—The good old days.

I understand if the Pirate management doesn't bring back the 1952 club on its silver anniversary. It will probably decide to celebrate the 50th anniversary of the 1927 club, which won the National League pennant.

But I'd like to remind management that the 1927 Pirates lost to the Yankees in four straight. We saved the city of Pittsburgh from that kind of embarrassment. We clinched last place on opening day . . . during the singing of the national anthem.

◆ ◆ ◆

LONG STREAK

After spending nearly a decade in the minor leagues, Dale Long finally played his first full season in the big leagues in 1955 at the age of twenty-nine. Going into the 1956 season, his only notoriety came from Branch Rickey's failed experiment in 1951 to convert Long into a left-handed catcher. But from May 19 to May 28, 1956, Long accomplished something that had never been done before in baseball history when he homered in eight consecutive games. Long's heroics so captured the imagination of America that he was invited to appear on the Ed Sullivan Show. *Nagged by injuries after his amazing feat, he struggled the rest of the year and was traded by the Pirates to the Cubs during the 1957 season. Long appeared in the 1960 World Series, but as a pinch-hitter for the Yankees against the Pirates.*

32,221 See Long Set HR Mark

AL ABRAMS

BOB FRIEND STOPS BUMS ON 2-HITTER TO WIN 8TH, 3-2

Dale Long rewrote his amazing home run record and Bob Friend twirled a two-hitter last night at Forbes Field as the equally amazing Pirates bumped off the Brooklyn Dodgers, 3-2, before a delirious throng of 32,221.

The largest night game turnout since July 21, 1950, saw Long ram out his eighth home run in as many consecutive contests to crack his own mark of seven which he set only last Saturday in Philadelphia.

He Homers in Fourth

The big first sacker's blow came in the fourth inning with none on base, but it tied the score at 2-all. It barely cleared the barrier in right center at a point approximately 380 feet from the plate.

No sooner had Long's bat connected with the ball than a roar came from the monster throng. The customers cheered the historic clout all the while Dale circled the bases and then did something never seen in the history of Forbes Field.

To a man, woman and child, the 32,221 fans gave Long a standing ovation that lasted for several minutes, meanwhile holding up the game.

The modest Dale, all but mobbed by his teammates, acknowledged the greetings by going to the top step of the Pirate dugout and doffing his cap several times while the mob roared.

Oh, Well, He Fanned Twice

This was Long's only hit of the game but it was enough to become historic. On three other trips to the plate, he struck out twice and bounced out to Peewee Reese who was playing second base in the exaggerated shift the Dodgers used every time Dale came to the plate.

Sharing equal billing with Long in the winning heroics was Friend who recorded his eighth triumph of the season against two defeats. It was Bob's sixth straight win at Forbes Field. He didn't allow a hit after the third inning when Gilliam singled to right.

Outside of an unusual streak of wildness, Friend mastered the hard-hitting Dodger lineup like he owned them. He walked six men, five of them coming as the first batters in an inning but outside of the first none of these proved harmful.

Snider Hits Homer

Jim Gilliam was the recipient of Friend's first gift and he romped home in front of Duke Snider when the latter blasted a ball over the right center field fence at a point between the Dreyfuss monument and the iron gate. This was even longer than Long's terrific wallop last week.

The homer gave the Brooks a 2-0 lead behind the talented Carl Erskine but the Bucs chipped away to one run in the second. Long's homer to tie in the fourth and the game winning tally in the fifth on Hank Foiles' triple and Bob Skinner's pinch single.

Overlooked in the general excitement was Dick Groat's sensational fielding at short and two remarkable one-handed catches by Duke Snider in center field.

The victory was the Pirates' fourth in a row, seventh in the last eight, and 11th in the last fourteen to further cement their hold on third place in the standings.

◆   ◆   ◆

TWELVE PERFECT INNINGS

On May 26, 1959, at Milwaukee County Stadium, Harvey Haddix pitched what has been described as "the greatest game in baseball history." Facing the Milwaukee Braves, with future Hall of Famers Eddie Mathews and Hank Aaron in the lineup, Haddix pitched twelve perfect innings, retiring thirty-six batters in a row before losing 1-0 in the bottom of the thirteenth. When told by a reporter that his pitching performance was historic, Haddix replied, "All I know is that we lost the game. What's so historic about that?" A year later Haddix would become the winning Pirate pitcher in the seventh and deciding game of the 1960 World Series.

As Lester J. Biederman, long-time sportswriter for the Pittsburgh Press *and special correspondent for* The Sporting News *explains below, the game ended in some confusion. Even the final score was a matter of contention, and was not officially determined until the following day.*

Haddix Loses "Greatest Game"

LESTER J. BIEDERMAN

PIRATE LEFTY HURLS 12 PERFECT INNINGS BEFORE BOWING, 2-0

Harvey Haddix, a slightly built 33-year-old Pirate left-hander, lost the greatest game ever pitched in the long history of baseball here last night but he took the defeat like the man he is.

Haddix regretted the loss of the one-hit game more than he appreciated the glory of pitching 12 perfect innings before the Braves won the bitterly contested battle in the 13th inning on an error, an intentional walk and a "double."

"I knew I had a no-hitter because the scoreboard was in plain view but

I wasn't so certain about it being a perfect game." Haddix calmly related the details of baseball's finest pitching spectacle.

"I thought perhaps I might have walked somebody in the early innings but going down the stretch, my main idea was to win. We needed this one badly to keep going."

The Braves went up and down in one-two-three order for the first twelve innings as the 19,194 fans realized they were witnessing one of the epics of baseball. Many of the fans cheered each Brave putout but when the Milwaukeeans finally broke through in the 13th inning, the local fans began yelling for the victory.

Error Gives Braves Breakthrough

Felix Mantilla hit an ordinary grounder to Don Hoak in the Braves' 13th inning and in Hoak's haste to keep Haddix's streak going, he threw low into the dirt and the ball skipped off Rocky Nelson's left foot for an error.

Ed Mathews sacrificed Mantilla to second and Haddix gave up his only walk of the night, an intentional pass to the major leagues' leading batter, dangerous Hank Aaron.

Joe Adcock, who had fanned twice and grounded out the other two times, picked on Haddix's second pitch—a high slider—and sent it into right center.

Bill Virdon and Joe Christopher raced to the spot and Virdon made a frantic leap but the ball barely cleared the fence about 375 feet away. The fans roared as Haddix and his Pirate teammates walked off the field heart-broken at the sudden turn of events.

But the excitement still wasn't ended. Mantilla, who was on second, scored easily but Aaron rounded second base then cut across the pitcher's mound for the Braves' dugout.

Adcock, seeing the umpire's signal for a home run, simply kept on running and passed Aaron between second and third base. The umpires stood on the field as Fred Haney and their coaches tried to regroup their runners.

Finally, Aaron and Adcock began retracing their steps from third to second but actually Adcock was out when he passed Aaron. Adcock thus received credit for a double and a run batted in.

Bucs' 12 Hits to No Avail

The run was unearned. Thus Haddix lost, 1-0, on one hit, although his teammates nicked Lew Burdette for 12 safeties but just couldn't score.

(The score last night was announced as 2-0, but Warren Giles, president of the National League, today ruled that the official score was 1-0. Giles ruled that Joe Adcock, who hit a three-run "homer," would be credited with a two-base hit because he didn't touch all the bases and the Braves given one run since that was all they needed to win.)

The Pirates could have won the game in the third inning when they bunched three singles. But Roman Mejias tried to go from first to third on Haddix's sharp rap off Burdette's leg.

The ball rolled a few feet toward second base, but Johnny Logan grabbed it and made a fine throw to third to nail Mejias. Dick Schofield, who singled three times off Burdette, came through with a single but Virdon flied out.

Nelson had singled in the second inning and was rubbed out on Bob Skinner's double-play ball. Mejias singled in the fifth and this time Haddix rolled into a double play.

Burdette peeled off the next ten batters before the Pirates made a bold bid for victory in the ninth inning. Virdon singled to center with one out, held first as Smoky Burgess flied out but rolled to third on Nelson's single to right. But Skinner grounded out to Adcock.

Haddix took the mound to meet the test of nine perfect innings as he faced the Braves in their half and he did. It was very easy as he fanned two of the three batters.

Hoak singled with one out in the 10th but didn't move. Schofield scratched a single off Burdette's bare hand to open the 11th but Virdon, after trying to bunt, forced him. Then Burgess hit into a double play.

Bill Mazeroski singled with two gone in the 12th but Hoak forced him, and Schofield turned up with his third hit after two were out in the 13th. But Virdon grounded out.

Haddix struck out eight, all in the first nine innings and the only walk issued by either pitcher in the 13 innings was the intentional pass Haddix yielded to Aaron in the final frame.

If both teams can come down to earth tonight, Warren Spahn will pitch against Vern Law.

A Miracle Season
and the End of an Era

EASTER MIRACLE

After the heartbreaking trades, losses, and general misery of the 1950s, Pirates fans had trouble imagining a brighter future for the team. But disappointment and failure are no match for miracles—and a miracle is exactly what Pittsburghers got in 1960. The incredible events began, appropriately enough, on Easter Sunday. The Bucs were playing a doubleheader against the Cincinnati Reds, and a crowd of 16,196 fans cheered Bob Friend's first-game shutout as the Pirates won, 5-0. In the second game, though, things turned around, and the Pirates were losing by that same 5-0 score. Most of the fans had already left the ballpark by the time the Pirates came to bat in the bottom of the ninth. There were no "Beat 'em Bucs" banners waving on April 17, 1960, no Benny Benack band, and no choruses, led by Bob Prince, of "The Bucs Are Going All the Way," but the Pirates rallied to win the game in a dramatic fashion that would be their trademark for the rest of the season—carrying the miracle right into the 1960 World Series.

Bucs Bump Reds Twice, 5-0, 6-5

JACK HERNON

BOB'S HOMER WINS IN 6-RUN NINTH; FRIEND'S 4-HITTER TAKES OPENER

Bob Friend pitched a four-hit shutout for a 5-0 victory in the first game but it was just an Easter Sunday sidelight at Forbes Field yesterday.

What happened while Friend was cooling out from his first victory was—well, just about unbelievable. Especially the scene at home plate where Skinner was welcomed after his ninth inning home run ended a six-run inning and brought a 6-5 victory over Cincinnati.

There must have been a thousand kids and grownups there trying to pat Skinner on the back at the same time.

Rousing finishes have come to be expected at Forbes Field but not anything like this one.

Newcombe Injured

The Pirates had been shut out for eight innings on five hits by Don Newcombe and Raul Sanchez. Big Newk had to leave the game in the fifth inning after one of Bill Virdon's three hits slammed into his right wrist. Sanchez took over and pitched until the ninth inning.

Then Bill Henry came on to throw for the Reds.

He got one batter out before Smoky Burgess singled to center. Hurrying Joe Christopher ran for him.

Virdon singled to center putting Joe on third and he hurried home when Bill Mazeroski singled to left. Virdon hustled into third on the play.

Hal Smith, who caught Friend in the first game, went up to hit for Joe Gibbon, the fifth of Danny Murtaugh's staff on duty. Whoom! And the Bucs were behind only 5-4. Smitty jumped on a high pitch and slammed it out of the joint in deep left center field for three runs.

Ted Wieand replaced Henry and he retired Don Hoak. But Dick Groat, who was in the first game up to his neck, brought breath to the Buc rooters with a bouncing single to center.

Hit, Skip, and Victory

It was his first hit in the nightcap and brought up Long Bob. Skinner had a two-strike, one-ball count when he sent a long belt to right field. It hit the base of the pipe on the right-field screen and skipped happily into the hands of fans in the seats out that way.

It brought Gibbon his first triumph and the Pirates their third in the four-game set with Cincy.

Before the fireworks, the Reds picked on Ben Daniels for three runs, nudged out a pair against Fred Green and Don Gross and were blanked by George Witt and Gibbon, who was making his major league debut.

The Reds counted in the first inning when Vada Pinson singled on the infield and went to third on another single by Gus Bell. The fleet outfielder scored after Bob Clemente, who rapped a two-run homer off Joe Nuxhall to give Friend a two-run edge in the first game, grabbed Frank Robinson's fly.

Daniels Leaves

In the third, Daniels departed. He walked Pinson and Bell looped a single to left. Then Robinson cracked one to left scoring Pinson and Lee Walls singled to send Bell home. Green replaced Bennie.

The last pair of Cincy tallies ran over in the fifth. After two out, Walls walked. Gross took over on the mound after Green appeared to have a kink in his arm. Ed Bailey greeted the new pitcher with a run-scoring double. Billy Martin singled for the second score.

But then the Pirates had the last go at it and came up with six.

In the first inning of the opener Groat singled against Nuxhall and got a free ride on Clemente's line-drive homer over the wall in left-center field.

To make it easier for Friend, Skinner doubled to right in the third inning. Groat rode him home and took second on a throw to the plate. An infield out put the "Cap" at third and he counted after Dick Stuart flied to Bell.

The last marker was posted against Claude Osteen in the eighth inning on a pair of booming triples off the wall in left-center by Clemente and Stuart.

◆ ◆ ◆

"THE BUCS ARE GOING ALL THE WAY"

Long before his "terrible towel" fame as the voice of the Pittsburgh Steelers, Myron Cope made his living as a sportswriter with the Pittsburgh Post-Gazette *and as a freelance writer in national magazines.*

Written with Cope's usual flair, this feature article on the phenomenal 1960 baseball season in Pittsburgh gives readers the inside story of the pennant-hungry Pirates and their miracle season. It also serves up a detailed account of the historical circumstances, from the dark days of Branch Rickey to the controversial trades and acquisitions of his successor, Joe L. Brown, that shaped the league-leading Pirate ball club into a perfect fit for spacious Forbes Field and its devoted mill-town fans.

What's Got into the Pirates?

MYRON COPE

In March 1947, seven months after a syndicate headed by portly Indianapolis banker Frank E. McKinney had bought control of the Pittsburgh Pirates, McKinney speculated that it might take five years to build the Pirates into a pennant contender, although he was hopeful that the job could be done in three.

In 1952, when McKinney had long since staggered from the Pirate scene, his successor as president, John W. Galbreath, said, "I can see the future forming for us now. Another rough year is coming up, but by 1953 we should start moving in the right direction."

The year 1953—and 1954 and 1955—saw the Pirates standing stock-still in last place. Branch Rickey, Galbreath's general manager, had charted

From the *Saturday Evening Post,* September 17, 1960. Reprinted with permission of Myron Cope.

a five-year plan of development to get the Pirates into contention by 1956. A question was put to him, "If by 1956 the Pirates still are in seventh or eighth, what then?"

Rickey's answer was, "I'd be a sick man, baseballically and physically." A year prior to 1956 he withdrew from active management of the club, thereby preserving his "baseballic" and physical health.

In 1957 Ford Frick, the commissioner of baseball, singled out Pittsburgh as a harrowing example in telling a Congressional committee about the financial risks that club owners run. He said that the Pirates, who had been spending lavishly for players, had lost $1,537,303 in five years. He might have added that they still had nothing to show for it. From 1950 through 1957 Pittsburgh finished last five times, tied for last once and placed seventh twice.

Now all this has changed. Front runners in the National League for most of the season, the Pirates have become the team to beat. Although not endowed with exceptional speed, they run bases with a boldness that rattles their enemies. Lacking power, they swat ground balls that hop crazily over the heads of waiting infielders. They may literally rap more hits to the opposite field—that is, right-handed hitters to right field and left-handed hitters to left field—than they do to their natural fields.

On defense they execute such stunts as this rare infield maneuver with runners on first and second in a bunt situation: Third baseman Don Hoak charges the bunt and whirls and fires the ball to shortstop Dick Groat covering third, who fires to second baseman Bill Mazeroski covering first.

Pirate outfielders have been seen to scale the ivy-covered Forbes Field wall, thrust a hand wrist-deep into the vines and come down holding the baseball aloft victoriously.

From their dugout the eager Pirates fill the air with a cacophony of yapping that does not cease until the last man is out. The ardent home crowds, which held up commendably even during the losing years, have multiplied in size and zeal. Parents bringing small children to Forbes Field have become so entranced by the action that the public-address announcer has spent almost as much time describing lost youngsters as announcing relief pitchers.

For all their excitement, the fans recognized the possibility of a late-season collapse. However, they were confident that Pittsburgh, a city that has not had a pennant winner in thirty-two years, was solidly back in the picture for some years to come.

For one thing, a hard core of players whom the Pirates first began collecting and rearing twelve years ago has matured. Says Bill Turner of the

Pirate farm staff, "It's as simple as planting a garden. One day the flowers are going to pop."

Actually the flowers began popping two years ago, when the Pirates shot up from the cellar to second place. In 1959, when the club tailed off to fourth place, it seemed that the upsurge had been comparable to the brief twelve-hour blooming of the cactus. This season, however, fortified by trades, the Pirates burgeoned for fair.

Today's team is the handiwork of three general managers—Roy Hamey, Branch Rickey and Joe Brown—who, one after the other, were hired by the club's wealthy absentee owners and told to see what the devil could be done to improve the situation. In earlier times the situation had been mostly good. From 1900 until his death in 1932, hustling, German-born Barney Dreyfuss operated the Pirates successfully, winning half a dozen National League championships and finishing out of the first division only six times.

The Pirates were Dreyfuss's livelihood. He ran the club on its own capital and would have sold it had he been able to make a big enough profit.

Dreyfuss willed the Pirates to his widow, Florence, and for the next fourteen years the club was run by his son-in-law, Bill Benswanger, a mild, bespectacled musicologist who knew his baseball as well as his Bach.

One summer day in 1946 Frank McKinney—who later became chairman of the Democratic National Committee—walked into Benswanger's office without an appointment and said, "Are you willing to sell the Pirates?" McKinney and his three partners—Ohio realtor John Galbreath, entertainer Bing Crosby and Pittsburgh attorney Thomas P. Johnson—were prepared to pay roughly $2,000,000 for 70 per cent of the Pirate stock. The widow Dreyfuss had wanted to sell, and promptly did.

On August eighth, the day McKinney's combine took over, the Pirates lay in last place, twenty-two and a half games behind the first-place Brooklyn Dodgers. Bill Benswanger says the chief trouble was that the players had been wrangling among themselves. Boston lawyer Robert Murphy had chosen Pittsburgh as the city in which to drive an opening wedge in his abortive attempt to organize a ballplayers' trade union and had split the Pirates into two political camps.

Anyway, Frank McKinney and his new general manager, hefty Roy Hamey, sought to lift the Pirates by purchasing fading celebrities—such as Hank Greenberg, Dixie Walker and Hugh Casey—at outrageous prices. They kept on buying players with the desperation of a gambler who doubles his bets to recoup his losses. By July 19, 1950—the date on which McKinney sold his Pirate stock to partners John Galbreath and Tom

Johnson—his regime had put $850,000 into bonuses to youngsters and invested roughly $1,000,000 in player purchases. Despite all this, the Pirates climbed no higher under McKinney than fourth place—in 1948— and were down in the cellar when he pulled out.

Four months later Roy Hamey also left. He had made two contributions to Pittsburgh's pennant contenders of the distant future. His scouts had signed Vernon Law and Bob Friend, the aces of today's pitching staff. Ironically, in view of all the Pirates' heavy spending on boys who never amounted to anything, Law had been paid a bonus of only $2000. Friend got $15,000.

Branch Rickey, the celebrated builder of baseball dynasties at St. Louis and Brooklyn, was lured to Pittsburgh by Galbreath with a $100,000 salary even before Hamey had time to write his resignation. Rickey at once began stocking Pirate farms as though he were casting a battle scene for Cecil B. DeMille. In his first year Rickey signed approximately 300 prospects, shelling out almost $400,000 in bonuses. Although the number of signings declined considerably thereafter, the Pirates continued to lose money and ball games, remaining firmly anchored in last place.

Yet Rickey sowed a few promising seeds. Under his management Pirate scouts tracked down first baseman Dick Stuart, second baseman Bill Mazeroski, left fielder Bob Skinner and shortstop Dick Groat. Further, Rickey also poached legally—and effectively—on Brooklyn Dodger farms, drafting right fielder Roberto Clemente and relief pitcher Elroy Face from minor-league clubs where the Dodgers had been seasoning them. The Pirates of 1960 were taking shape.

When Rickey retired after the 1955 season to an advisory role, with the largely honorary title of chairman of the board, a brisk young protégé of his took over. This was Joe L. Brown, who immediately courted unpopularity with the Pittsburgh baseball public by declaring, "I am a Rickey man!"

Joe Brown, the son of comedian Joe E. Brown, is a tall, tanned, erect man who favors close-cropped haircuts, gaucho shirts and sport jackets. At forty-two he still often is mistaken for a ballplayer by the urchins lurking for autographs outside Forbes Field. In his five years at Pittsburgh he has made two dozen player deals, of which the great majority drew critical disapproval or yawns of indifference. As matters turned out, however, only one was an outright flop. In 1957 Brown traded pitcher Bob Purkey to Cincinnati for pitcher Don Gross. Gross subsequently developed shoulder trouble and has been farmed out, while Purkey remains a starter for the Reds.

A few days after Brown took charge of the Pirate front office, an underling, older than he, spoke to him frowning. "Joe, we're way behind in our work here," the man said.

Brown smiled brightly at him, "Well, catch up!" he said and walked off.

Brown himself has energetically sought to catch up with the rest of the National League. Speaking and moving with a crisp, staccato manner, he is a self-admitted busybody who one minute may be directing the groundskeeper to mop up a couple of puddles he has detected under the third-base grandstand, the next minute sitting in the dugout spewing tobacco juice on the steps while gossiping with players.

He is not inhibited by the unwritten rule that general managers must not fraternize with the help. "If I don't go down to the dugout," he says, "how the devil am I supposed to know what's going on? Besides, this is how I learn how you make the double play, how you hold the ball. I like to nose around."

On a July night in 1958 Brown was nosing around the Los Angeles Coliseum before a game between the Pirates and Dodgers. He parked himself *kerplunk* in the Pirate bull pen. There he watched, fascinated, while pitching coach Bill Burwell, a red-faced, bespectacled old-timer, patiently taught Vern Law a new fast-ball delivery and a deceptive body rhythm.

"Law had lost his fast ball a few years before because of a sore arm," Brown recalls. "He'd become a breaking-ball pitcher. In the meantime his arm had recovered, but he'd forgotten how to throw his fast ball. He was coming down as he would with his curve—with his arm tight to his body, his elbow in."

At season's end a front-office executive, dissatisfied with Law's fourteen-twelve record, said, "Let's trade him. He'll never be much better than a .500 pitcher." Brown responded by showing how Law's record had improved since Bill Burwell began to revise his form. Law had cut his earned-run average from 5.02 to 3.97 and had won five of his last six starts. So Brown kept him. The next season Law won eighteen games and lost only nine. This year he had eighteen victories by August eighteenth.

As a trader, Brown at first confined himself to relatively insignificant deals, but early in 1959 he sat down with Cincinnati general manager Gabe Paul in a New York hotel room and hammered out a seven-player exchange. Brown swapped slugger Frank Thomas—a home-grown Pittsburgh favorite—utility infielder Jim Pendleton, pinch hitter Johnny Powers and a one-eyed pitcher named Whammy Douglas for third baseman Don Hoak, catcher Smoky Burgess and pitcher Harvey Haddix.

News of the trade flashed over radio and television at midnight. At Brown's home in Pittsburgh the telephone began ringing and did not stop until three A.M. "Has your husband gone crazy?" Pirate fans kept demanding of Joe's wife, Din.

Upon his return, his wife told him, "Next time you swing a big deal, Trader Brown, kindly be at home to answer the telephone."

Nobody heckles Brown about that deal any more. Thomas hit a sickly .225 for the Reds in 1959 and was traded to the Chicago Cubs at season's end. Pendleton, Powers and Douglas disappeared into the minors. Meanwhile Hoak and Burgess have firmly established themselves in the Pittsburgh line-up, while Haddix has contributed some well-pitched games.

A month prior to the Cincinnati trade, Brown stood up at the winter draft meeting, sucked in his breath and called out "Rocky Nelson!" A titter ran through the room. Nelson, a bald, craggy-faced, garrulous veteran, had been in professional baseball since 1942 and had had nine major-league trials. He played first base competently and in the minors he hit with ease, averaging as high as .418. In the big leagues, though, he had mostly ridden benches—and then trains carrying him back to the bushes.

Joe Brown had put in a long apprenticeship in the bushes too. At the age of twenty, when he was an end on the U.C.L.A. football team, he had quit college to become assistant business manager of a Class D baseball club in Lubbock, Texas. During his seventeen-year climb to his present job, he had dragged infields, taken tickets, driven team buses. He had also learned something about evaluating players, as the case of Rocky Nelson was to prove. Platooning at first base with Dick Stuart, Nelson has become a definite asset to the Pirates, averaging around .300 as a hitter.

"Nothing at Pittsburgh has given me as much personal satisfaction as drafting Rocky Nelson," says Joe Brown today. "I was the only man in our organization who thought of him. Our scouts spent better than a month going over reports on possible draftees, but Rocky's name was not on their list. I simply could not believe that a guy would have his minor-league record and not have ability."

Brown gives much of the credit for the blooming of players at Pittsburgh to manager Danny Murtaugh. Says Brown, "Danny has the patience to go along with a player not until he fails, but until he succeeds."

Brown's luck has held up on the deals he made for the current season. During the interleague trading period last winter he gave the Athletics catcher Hank Foiles and two farm hands—shortshop Ken Hamlin and pitcher Dick Hall—in exchange for cash and Hal Smith. Smith was a catcher the A's had been trying to convert into a third baseman. With the Pirates he has proved to be a capable receiver, platooning with Smoky Burgess, and he has hit close to .300 for most of the season.

Twelve days after Brown acquired Hal Smith, he struck a bargain with

St. Louis general manager Bing Devine that befuddled sports writers and baseball men. On paper, at least, the Pirates desperately required additional pitching and long-ball hitting. So what did Brown do? He airily traded a starting pitcher, Ron Kline, for a minor-league pitcher, Tom Cheney, and a center fielder—Gino Cimoli—who had averaged less than seven home runs per season in four years of major-league ball.

Well, in St. Louis Kline's curve ball began hanging high, and in midseason manager Sol Hemus relegated him to the bull pen. In the meantime, Murtaugh, the Pirate manager, had alternated the right-handed Cimoli in center field with left-handed Bill Virdon, another bargain Brown finagled from the Cardinals four years earlier. Both men cover Forbes Field's vast outfield with darting speed and hit satisfactorily, if not with power.

"Power does not win pennants," declares Joe Brown as he surveys his deals that have enabled Murtaugh—his manager since August 1957—to platoon center fielders, first basemen and catchers. "Balance does."

On May twenty-seventh he relieved the Cardinals of Wilmer (Vinegar Bend) Mizell, a southpaw who, according to gossip among players, had gone as sour as his nickname. Vinegar Bend promptly won eight games and lost only two in a little more than ten weeks as a Pirate. While he was doing so, a footnote to Brown's Kline-Cimoli coup developed. Tom Cheney, the "throw-in" on the deal, became a major-league pitcher after ten weeks of seasoning on Pittsburgh's Columbus farm.

Brown has sought to fit the Pirate personnel to sprawling Forbes Field, the toughest park in the majors for right-handed sluggers. The left-field wall starts at 365 feet, with a twenty-five-and-one-half-foot scoreboard to clear, and falls away to 457 feet in center field. Brown, recognizing the futility of gunning for the wall, has assembled a team of lightweight line-drive hitters. The Pirates have been well down the National League list in home runs this year, but have been leading the circuit in base hits.

Many of the hits, especially at home, have come on ground balls that skitter through the infield. The Pittsburgh ground crew, obviously by no mere whim, sees to it that the infield grass grows no higher than one inch. The infield clay is treated with only the barest trace of sand and thus remains firmly packed. Periodically the infield is rolled with a one-ton roller.

Last season, Ted Kluszewski, then with the Pirates, said to groundskeeper Eddie Dunn, "Say, Eddie, I have a friend who would like to borrow your infield formula. He's building highways over in Ohio."

Pittsburgh's deft infielders, playing seven times as many games at Forbes Field as their opponents, have an obvious edge in coping with the hard surface. Joe Brown is all innocence when asked if he planned things that way. He concedes that the ground may be a trifle hard—there is no rule specifying infield composition—but vaguely explains that this is because a canvas cover must be kept on the field to hedge against the threat of rain. He talks as though Pittsburgh summers—the city had only 3.8 inches of rain in June and 2.9 in July—are comparable to the rainy season in Pago Pago.

Whatever the case, the infield fits in perfectly with the gadfly tactics the Pirates employ in wearing down their opponents. Dizzy Dean has likened this team for sheer spirit to the St. Louis Gashouse Gang of 1934. "Them Pirates are hungry," says Diz. "They travel in packs, like wolves."

Wolves? Actually the Pirates address one another by such nicknames as Tiger, Crane, Duck, Hawk, Doggie, Quail, Kitten, Bug and Chicken. They are the only team in the league so schoolboyish as to have a captain. Dick Groat, who holds that rank, came to the Pirates in 1952 from Duke University, where he had been All-American basketball player. He addressed everyone, even cub sportswriters, as sir, covered little ground at shortstop and hit rather mildly. Within five years he lost his hair, stopped saying sir, became a shortstop of remarkable instincts and hit .315.

Groat captains such unusual athletes as Vernon Law, a Mormon elder who does not drink even tea or coffee because he regards them as harmful stimulants, and teetotaling Smoky Burgess, who looks less like an athlete than like a traveling man for a farm-implement company. Burgess, a rotund little North Carolinian with a slick of sparse black hair and small, pudgy hands, sits by the hour in hotel lobbies chatting companionably with old ladies. At bat he reaches over his head or down to his shins for pitches and clouts them into the right-field seats.

Similarly, Roberto Clemente, the Pirates' Puerto Rican right fielder, profanes the rules of form unconscionably. A born showman who fairly quivers with excitement when Pirate fans affectionately shout, "*Arriba! Arriba!*" he stands off to the side of line drives and spears them with a whirling, one-handed motion more commonly seen in *jai alai frontóns*. When he runs the bases, his arms and legs flailing in every direction, he pays no more attention to Frank Oceak, Pittsburgh's third-base coach, than he would to a cigar-store Indian.

Occasionally Oceak has taken Clemente to task for ignoring his stop signs. "I sorry, Fronk," says Clemente in wide-eyed apology. "Next time I look." Next time he does not look, but somehow scores.

Captain Groat's forces range from Don (The Tiger) Hoak, a former middle-weight boxer who stalks in livid rage to the mound and censures his own pitchers in language that would raise the hair on a seal, to left fielder Bob Skinner, a gangling, easygoing philosopher who is unruffled by the vocal *aficionados* who inhabit Forbes Field's one-dollar left-field bleachers. A pendulum-smooth batter but a slightly awkward fielder, Skinner was booed ferociously by the bleacherites one night for a bumbling performance. "Shucks," he said later, "if I had to sit up there and watch me, I'd boo me too."

With fitting incongruity, a third-string rookie catcher, Bob Oldis, has become one of the Pirates most in demand for radio and television interviews. "We don't expect no Cubs to knock off no Milwaukee or no L.A. for us," he piped recently in a scratchy voice. "We gotta knock off them Milwaukees and L.A.'s by ourselfs. We gotta shake some kinda' bush and get some kinda' hits—and, by golly, one o' these days we're gonna be some kinda' happy with 'at World Series money."

Compensating for their lack of power with savvy, the Pirates are always dangerous. Twenty-two of their first sixty victories this season were achieved by rallies that took place in the seventh inning or later. "We adjust to the opposition's pitcher," explains Don Hoak. "We study him, we pin down what he's throwing and by the seventh inning, we know him."

Frankie Gustine, a former Pirate infielder who owns a popular tavern a block from Forbes Field, complains, "The fans used to start coming into my place in the eighth inning. Now they wait till the last man is out."

From a broader standpoint, the patience of Pirate fans has been monumental. Pittsburgh has been waiting since 1927—longer than any other major-league city—for a pennant. The Pirates seemed to have it made in 1938, when they held a five-game lead on September eighth. Bill Benswanger, then the club's president, had workmen erect a $35,000 press box to accommodate newspaper reporters for the World Series. Series-ticket orders were accepted. But the Pirates' margin dwindled to a half game. On the afternoon of September twenty-ninth at Wrigley Field in Chicago, Gabby Hartnett drove a home run into the dusk to drop them irrevocably into second place.

Pittsburgh fans went on waiting. In recent years they had to endure tortures to which few baseball cities have been put. In 1951, for example, they winced at the Pirates' Singer Midget infield, a combination averaging just over five and a half feet in height, and in 1952 they writhed at the carryings-on of Branch Rickey's youth movement, the Rickeydinks.

In 1953 the Rickeydinks' catcher, Vic Janowicz, a former All-American halfback at Ohio State, missed three foul balls in one game. When he began circling under a fourth—which he eventually grabbed—a leather-lunged fan behind home plate cried, "Signal for a fair catch, you bum!"

In July 1955, Fred Haney, then the Pirates' manager, wrote in *The Saturday Evening Post* [July 30, 1955] that "the Pirates haven't driven me nutty—yet!" He concluded, "I can detect progress . . . The seven other teams are growing older. The Pirates are just growing up."

While they grew, Pittsburghers continued to support them with the racking devotion that junkies have for dope. In fact, since the day in 1946 when the Dreyfuss family sold the club into absentee ownership, Pirate attendance has surpassed the million mark seven times. Only twice—in 1954 and 1955—did the turnstile count, like the team itself, trail the league. In the latter year, it fell to 469,397, but the next season, when the Pirates escaped from eighth place to seventh, attendance soared to 949,878.

Now that the Pirates have matured, Forbes Field's one-season attendance record of 1,517,021, set in 1948, appears certain to be far outdistanced this season. Neither serious unemployment among Pittsburgh's steelworkers nor abominable parking facilities at the ball park have deterred the fans.

Forbes Field, a fifty-one-year-old double-decked structure, stands hemmed in between the University of Pittsburgh campus and a fraying residential district. Householders in the web of narrow streets behind the ball park rent parking space in their back yards and front lawns—and in some cases have torn out front porches to accommodate more cars. Parking rates sometimes go as high as five dollars per car. One operator places folding chairs along the curb of the street, preventing motorists from parking and thereby forcing them into his lot. Nevertheless, on come the crowds.

The upward curve of Pirate fortunes this season was matched by a similarly sharp increase in beer-guzzling in the stands. Pennsylvania law forbids the sale of beer in ball parks, but spectators have been free to bring their own, and Pirate fans came fortified as never before. In teams of two, three and four, they carried immense coolers, wash tubs and garbage cans stocked with beer. Rowdyism occurred nightly, almost inning by inning.

Finally, on the night of August ninth, prohibition came to Forbes Field. Waves of police were flung into every entrance to challenge fans down to their last six-packs. Louis Rosenberg, Pittsburgh's director of public safety, had hurled a Volstead curve "in the knowledge," as he put it, "that excitement will run high and restraint may be lacking" down the home stretch of the pennant race. With mercy toward none, Rosenberg even forbade sports writers to drink beer in the press box.

Beer aside, Forbes Field has been a contentious place this year. By the end of June more Pirates had been thrown out of games by umpires than were ejected all last season. Up in the stands Pirate broadcaster Bob Prince has had his own private war. Prince may on occasion be seen leaning out of his radio booth, which hangs from the second tier, and jawing cantankerously with a fan who, equipped with a transistor radio, sits above him and raucously second-guesses his broadcasts.

But much of the commotion at Forbes Field has, of course, been sheer exuberance, as exemplified by the man with a flowing beard who sometimes honks the Pirates to victory with a duck call. For a stretch of seven games, a six-piece band sponsored by a brewery blew up a happy storm behind home plate, its members decked out in white dinner jackets, scarlet trousers and straw skimmers with green bands. The Pirates lost five of the seven games, however, and players decided that the brewery combo was a jinx. At the team's request the music-making was discontinued.

Through the roaring madness that blankets Forbes Field there has run a theme of steady, methodical baseball. The 1960 Pirates have been men of purpose. On the night of July first, for instance, they were locked in a 3-3 tie with the Dodgers in the tenth inning. Roberto Clemente was on first base with two out. Dick Stuart, the batter, blooped a soft single to short right field.

Clemente set sail as though Stuart had driven the ball deep into the right-center pocket. Frank Howard, the Dodgers' clumsy right fielder, was so astonished to see Clemente digging for home that he threw wildly, and Roberto scored the winning run standing up.

In the clubhouse later, Clemente explained himself. "I have sore foot," he said. "I no want no play any more tonight, so I try to end game."

◆　◆　◆

THE 1960 WORLD SERIES

It was a World Series to make Yankee fans despair and Pirate fans dance in the streets of downtown Pittsburgh in a Mardi Gras frenzy. The miracle that had begun on Easter Sunday continued throughout the season with dramatic come-from-behind victories. It culminated when the Pirates clinched their first National pennant since 1927 and once again faced a powerful Yankee team in the World Series, led this time by Mickey Mantle, Roger Maris, Whitey Ford, and Yogi Berra. In an exciting, improbable sequence of lopsided Yankee wins and closely fought Pirate victories, baseball's world championship was finally decided in a riotous seventh game that ended with the most dramatic home run in World Series history. As the following three articles—all from the same issue of the Pittsburgh Press—*illustrate, Pittsburgh could not get enough of its new champions.*

Pirate Champs "Team of Destiny"

LESTER J. BIEDERMAN

MAZ, SMITH HOMERS KILL YANKEE HOPES
NELSON ALSO BOMBS AS HADDIX GAINS WIN IN 10-9 FINALE

Team of Destiny? Well, can you think of a better word to describe the brand new World Champion Pirates?

This surely was a team of destiny with tremendous spirit and un-matched desire. They bolted through the National League like true champions, then carried the power-packed Yankees to seven games before beating them yesterday at Forbes Field, 10-9, with their very own weapon, the home run.

And with it, they won the greatest prize baseball has to offer—the world championship in their first opportunity since 1927 when the same Yankee organization humiliated them in four straight games.

Mark it: Debt repaid in full.

Until yesterday, the Pirates had hit only one home run (Bill Mazeroski in the opener) to eight for the Yankees in their first six games. Then after the American Leaguers blasted a pair in this vital seventh game, the Pirates saved their best two shots until they needed 'em.

Hal Smith came through with a dramatic three-run blast over the left-field wall with two outs and the Pirates trailing 6-7 in the eighth inning that rocked old Forbes Field and brought the 36,683 fans up screaming.

The Yankees tied it in the top of the ninth but this was only temporary.

Then when Bill Mazeroski drilled Ralph Terry's second pitch over the left-field wall leading off the ninth inning to crack the 9-9 tie and bring Pittsburgh its first world championship since 1925 with a 10-9 victory, there was a thunderous ovation awaiting Maz and his teammates when he finally touched home plate.

There have been similar scenes at Forbes Field all season long but none that meant as much as this one.

The whirlwind finish was as dramatic as any World Series game in many years. Yet it seemed the Mazeroski game-winning homer was a little anti-climatic after Smith's two-out, three-run homer that came with such swiftness it almost numbed the fans before they really cut loose.

The Pirates and their fans figured the game was over then and there but the Yankees tied it in the ninth only to allow Maz to become the hero with his home run that sailed majestically over the left-field wall and sent the crowd into a frenzy never matched in this city.

This blow touched off a celebration in Pittsburgh that lasted far into the night and was heard round the world.

The Pirates simply had one more last-inning rally left in their systems and they gave the Yankees a dose of it. They won 23 games during the year in their final turn at bat and this time they proved that lightning can and does strike more than once.

By the time Maz circled the bases and was escorted to the dugout, the fans had started swarming on the field, making it difficult for the Yankees to drudge silently and solemnly to their clubhouse.

The game started out as a duel between Vern Law, trying for his third victory despite a lame right ankle, and Bob Turley, who won the second game here.

Rocky Nelson gave Law a fast 2-0 lead when he homered in the first inning after Bob Skinner walked and in the second inning, the Pirates chased Turley when Smoky Burgess led off with a single.

They filled the bases on Bill Stafford with a walk and Maz's safe bunt, but when Stafford took Law's bouncer and started a double play, it appeared he was home safe. However, Bill Virdon cracked a two-run single and now Law enjoyed a 4-0 lead.

Bill Skowron spoiled the shutout with a right-field homer in the fifth but when Bobby Richardson singled and Tony Kubek walked to open the sixth, Danny Murtaugh felt Law's ankle was acting up and he called in Roy Face.

Face retired Roger Maris but Mickey Mantle singled for one run and Yogi Berra drilled a three-run homer into right field and the Yankees had a 5-4 lead.

Bobby Shantz protected this margin expertly and then Face yielded two more runs in the eighth on a walk, Skowron's scratch single, John Blanchard's looping single to center and Cletis Boyer's double to left.

But in their half of the eighth, the Pirates got a break, a big break. Gino Cimoli dropped a pinch-single into right and Kubek waited for Virdon's grounder, but it took a bad hop and hit him in the throat.

Instead of one on or a double play, the Pirates now had runners on first and second and the fans were screaming. Dick Groat singled for a run and Jim Coates relieved Shantz. Skinner sacrificed but Nelson flied out and fans moaned.

Then came another real break. Roberto Clemente grounded to Skowron but Coates didn't cover first base and Clemente beat it for a hit, Virdon scoring.

This seemed to breathe new life into the Pirates and they took advantage of it as they've done so often during the season.

Coates had two strikes on Smith and even had him swing and miss strike two but the husky catcher took dead aim on a 2-2 low fast ball and the moment he connected everybody knew the destination—Schenley Park.

When Smith touched home plate with the run that gave the Pirates a 9-7 edge, the customers were limp from excitement.

But the Yankees still had some fight left. Bob Friend came in to pitch the ninth and Richardson singled and so did pinch-hitter Dale Long. Exit Friend, enter Haddix. Maris fouled out but Mantle singled for a run.

Berra hit a sharp grounder down the first base line but Nelson grabbed it, stepped on first and tried to tag Mantle but Mickey slid back safely as the tying run crossed the plate.

Maz didn't keep the fans waiting long in the Pirate ninth. He took the first pitch for a ball, them met a high fast ball and sent it sailing over the left-field wall and the Pirates became the champions of baseball.

No game today!

City Bats Cleanup in Series

JACK MCNAMARA

If Pittsburgh has some kind of a hangover today, why shouldn't it?

The celebration started at 3:36 P.M. yesterday with the crack of Mazeroski's bat and police were still trying to get the celebrants to go home to bed at 4 A.M. today.

A few people did sleep last night in the world's happiest city, but not since Colonel Bouquet saved Fort Pitt has there been such joy unconfined in the Triangle.

V-J Day Scene Downtown

People who had seen samples of such happy madness before compared it to V-J Day, New York Times Square on New Year's Eve and New Orleans in the Mardi Gras.

It seemed that Pittsburgh police and firemen under safety director Louis Rosenberg were the only ones at work, and for the most part they

From the *Pittsburgh Press*, October 14, 1960. Copyright/*Pittsburgh Post-Gazette*, 2002. All rights reserved. Reprinted with permission.

were able to stand by quietly with big smiles on their faces and watch the crowd whooping it up.

Nobody will ever know for certain, but Mr. Rosenberg estimated the crowd in the Golden Triangle at 300,000.

There would have been more if he hadn't shut off inbound traffic from both the Liberty and Fort Pitt tunnels at 9 P.M. when he decided the "saturation point was reached."

At the beginning officials feared a complete breakdown of law and order and Mr. Rosenberg, in an unprecedented move, appealed by radio and television for suburban residents to stay out of the City and for the Downtown crowds to disperse.

But despite the revelry only 28 celebrants were arrested, 20 of them for too much imbibing and eight on disorderly conduct charges.

There was some minor vandalism and a few injuries, but for the most part, the crowd was just out to celebrate the winning of the world's baseball championship.

Grandma Has Her Fling

Young folks predominated but there were Pirate fans of all ages—from babes in arms to the little gray-haired grandmother who walked the length of Fifth Avenue spinning a noisemaker.

At 9 o'clock, hours after the Pirates' 10-9 victory, the City seethed from end to end, traffic ceased even to creep and a police lieutenant radioed to headquarters:

"This is preposterous!"

It was a night of contrasts . . . while the fans let down their hair, five people quietly sat before a television set in the lobby of the Pittsburgher Hotel watching Senator Kennedy and Vice President Nixon debate events of less world shaking import than "WHO WON THE WORLD SERIES?"

There was the cocktail set sipping Old Fashioneds on the sidelines and watching the throng set a new world's record for spilling beer in the streets.

And typist Connie Grebeck was "so excited" she abandoned her desk in the Grant Building, dashed into the street and dumped an armload of scrap paper in the lap of a passing motorist.

White collar workers leaned far out of office building windows while showering a continuous cloudburst of IBM cards on the revelers below.

An occasional telephone book thumped into that sea of head and shoulders. A three-piece combo—bugle, paint bucket, and soup spoon—played "There's No Tomorrow" while two North Side brothers, Archie and

Louie Lidey, drove along Smithfield Street bashing in the roof of their car with sledge hammers.

"We sold this heap for $25," shouted Louie. "We got to deliver it in the morning . . . and I don't know what the owner's going to say when he sees it, either."

At the onset of the celebration, Smoky Burgess quietly left Forbes Field and made his way through the melee to a Forbes Field parking lot.

He reached the car without a single person recognizing him.

Shortly after Mazeroski swung from the garters to end "Yankee aggression" for 1960, autos-turned-floats were clogging Pittsburgh streets.

Traffic coughed and wheezed homeward. But many of the drivers were only going home to pick up their families and head back into the city.

The din of blaring auto horns reached its crescendo at 6:30, but Ruth Elizior was waiting for the latecomers.

A private secretary with Blue Cross, Ruth was one of thousands who stayed after work to "let off steam."

"I called up girl friends and told them I had my car downtown. I said, 'Let's celebrate.'"

She had one complaint—"not enough noisemakers around."

Downtown variety stores broke out their Halloween stock of rattles and horns and did a land office business.

"They're buying anything that goes boom, toot, or wheeee!" said sales girl Pat Crook.

When the stores closed, do-it-yourself parades and pep rallies were breaking out all over the City. "Musicians" sported such instruments as hall trees (with hats still on them), road signs, and the Lidey brothers' loud but very flat car roof.

Business college student Mary Gallagher groaned at it all. "I don't think I'll ever get out of this town alive," she said.

Understandably, Pharmacist Geri Kelly at a drug store in Gateway Center reported a run on aspirin.

"They're buying the large size bottles," she said, taking two for herself.

Manager Dave Lipman joined her, declaring, "This is like Broadway and 42nd . . . only ten times worse."

On every street and square pandemonium reigned.

Youngsters, businessmen, men in working clothes and ladies in fine furs threw their heads back and marched and marched and marched.

And the confetti piled up.

It packed like soft snow under trolley wheels. Those cars that did roll set fire to paper streamers draped over their cables.

Such was the tumult and shouting that a woman resident of the 8400 block of Frankstown Avenue phoned Desk Sgt. Charles Ryan and remanded:

"Do something about all that noise. I can't stand it."

Another woman phoned the police to report her husband "missing."

"He went to the tavern to watch the last two innings on TV," she explained. "That was the last time I saw or heard from him four hours ago."

Chances are he was snake-dancing in Grant Street or stomping through the Hilton "Lookin' for Yankees."

Both Democratic and Republican campaign headquarters were buttoned up for the night. But the fans of Mazeroski took up the election year slack by booming Billy for president.

Eight emergency fire fighting units were posted in potential "hot spots" around the City.

Sam Gross, of Economy, came to town dressed in a barrel with these words painted across the front:

"I bet on the Yankees."

But the bravest man in town was Lee Bracey, a Yankee fan from Wood Ridge, N.J. He stationed himself on a Penn Avenue corner with a sign announcing, "They were lucky."

Series Greatest—Even Beats 1925 Win over Johnson

CHESTER L. SMITH

OUR CHAMPS ARE MOST BENEVOLENT—GAVE NY RECORDS—
KEPT CHAMPIONSHIP

While the Community was rapidly coming apart at the seams last night, the atmosphere in Jerry's Joint for Juices and Jerks was one of commendable calm.

Jerry himself absent-mindedly spooned a martini in a small glass as he spoke.

"These have been days to tear men's hearts out by the roots," he said, half to himself and half to those of his clients who were listening. "And they haven't been so easy on the women, either. A fellow just didn't know whether to organize another parade or promote a panic."

From "The Village Smithy," in the *Pittsburgh Press*, October 14, 1960. Copyright/*Pittsburgh Post-Gazette*, 2002. All rights reserved. Reprinted with permission.

Several heads nodded and one voice interrupted to say, "Yes, and when Mazeroski hit that home run it did more than win a World Series. It got my missus back to the kitchen. We have had a sinkful of dirty dishes for a week and after Wednesday's game she was so spent she guessed we would open a few cans tonight and that would be all, and it was. Now I guess we'll get back to eating regular rations."

Over in the far corner, the boys were listening to a world traveler, baseball-wise, who had the floor.

"I date back to the 1920's," he was saying. "I remember the Series in '25, in the rain, when the Pirates put the hammer on Walter Johnson in the eighth inning, just as they did on those Yankee pitchers today. Up to now I've always said that was the most exciting Series game I ever watched. But that time the Senators didn't come back and tie the score like the Yankees did, and it wasn't necessary for anybody to hit one out of the park. Washington went down one-two-three and that was it.

"So this game tops that one and becomes the greatest of all the Series games.

"Then there was that playoff between the Giants and the Dodgers when Bobby Thomson hit his home run in the ninth. That topped all baseball I had ever seen for excitement in the stands and tension out on the field. I recall that while Thomson was running around the bases someone in a Giants' suit ran out to the third base coaches' box where Leo Durocher was jumping up and down and hugged him and kissed him.

"I tried to see what was happening out there and in the Pirate dugout while Maz was going around the bases, but lordy, you couldn't find Maz or Frank Oceak or Mickey Vernon, the coaches. Even the Pirates' bench disappeared when that mob broke loose from the stands. You'd a-thought they were giving away something for free."

"They were—the Pirates, I mean," observed Jerry, who is a wit if there ever was one. "They were giving those Yanks all those World Series records they set—in return for the winner's share of the loot."

Murtaugh Unshaken by Yanks' Boast

One of Jerry's patrons had had the good fortune to be on the Pirate bench before the game, he reported. A reporter friend had taken him over to meet Danny Murtaugh, and while he was talking to the manager, another reporter came by and said to Danny, "I understand that Yogi Berra and some of the Yanks said they had the better team no matter who wins the Series. Any comment?"

It seems that Danny answered, "No comment—except I'll be satisfied with the winner and let them argue over the rest," and went right on with a discussion he was holding regarding the merits of the professional brand of basketball as compared to the college variety.

(Editor's note: this Murtaugh is a versatile sort; he has some tips on bowling in case you're interested.)

As the evening wore on at Jerry's the guests got to comparing notes as to just where they happened to be when the now historic homer was stroked. A few had been in Forbes Field. Others were caught in their offices or places at work. Several had been at home.

"The funniest thing happened," said one. "My wife gave a scream, marched out of the house and across the lawn and kissed Mr. Fawcett, our neighbor. She hadn't even spoke to Mr. Fawcett since a year ago last May when he accidentally ran over her lilies of the valley with his power mower."

"Our auditor threw the report on the day's receipts out with the stuff from the wastebaskets we dumped out the window," a gentleman up front disclosed. "We all went home happy, but we're going to be 'til noon tomorrow catching up."

A Tree Grows in Pittsburgh

A customer heard of what he thought was a nice gesture. After the game an elderly man in his block had picked up his grandson and the two of them visited a nearby nursery and bought a tree. Together they brought it home and planted it.

"The old man told me that back in 1925, when the Pirates won their last one, his grandpop and he had also planted a tree to commemorate the great event. He had never forgotten the incident and made up his mind to duplicate the gesture if and when the occasion arose."

"That was real thoughtful," Jerry cut in to say, "but I'm glad everybody didn't wait for our boys to win to plant a tree. We'd be living in a desert."

So the night came and went in Jerry's in a most circumspect manner.

Jerry broke it up and officially ended the baseball season when he passed out the morning line on the morrow's football games. It was then very late.

◆ ◆ ◆

DAMN PIRATES

*The immediate reaction of the Yankees to their loss in the 1960 World Series was to
fire Casey Stengel, who couldn't double-talk his way out of losing his job. Years later,
Pittsburgh's dramatic victory still lingers uncomfortably in the minds of Yankee players and fans. Billy Crystal has never forgiven the Pirates for making his beloved Mick
cry, and the late Stephen J. Gould once said that his friends knew they should never
bring up the 1960 World Series if they wanted to remain his friends. Yogi Berra, on
the occasion of the Yankees' disappointing loss in the 2001 World Series, comforted
Yankee fans by reminding them, in a* New York Times *article, of the Yankees heartbreaking loss in 1960: "Nobody took it harder than Mickey Mantle—it was the only
time I'd ever seen him cry."*

*Pulitzer Prize-winning columnist Dave Barry grew up near New York City, but
he rooted for the Pirates in the 1960 World Series. In his essay, "Our National Pastime," Barry offers an explanation for his allegiance that Pirate fans everywhere
would find perfectly understandable: The Yankees are evil, and God wanted
Mazeroski to hit his home run.*

Our National Pastime

DAVE BARRY

As I ponder the start of yet another baseball season, what is left of my
mind drifts back to the fall of 1960, when I was a student at Harold C.
Crittenden Junior High ("Where the Leaders of Tomorrow Are Developing the Acne of Today").

The big baseball story that year was the World Series between the New
York Yankees and the Pittsburgh Pirates. Today, for sound TV viewership
reasons, all World Series games are played after most people, including
many of the players, have gone to bed. But in 1960 the games had to be
played in the daytime, because the electric light had not been invented
yet. Also, back then the players and owners had not yet discovered the
marketing benefits of sporadically canceling entire seasons.

The result was that in those days young people were actually interested in baseball, unlike today's young people, who are much more interested in basketball, football, soccer and downloading dirty pictures from

the Internet. But in my youth, baseball ruled. Almost all of us boys played in Little League, a character building experience that helped me develop a personal relationship with God.

"God," I would say, when I was standing in deep right field—the coach put me in right field only because it was against the rules to put me in Sweden, where I would have done less damage to the team—"please please PLEASE don't let the ball come to me."

But of course God enjoys a good prank as much as the next infallible deity, which is why, when He heard me pleading with Him, He always took time out from His busy schedule to make sure the next batter hit a towering blast that would, upon re-entering the Earth's atmosphere, come down directly where I would have been standing, if I had stood still, which I never did. I lunged around cluelessly in frantic, random circles, so that the ball always landed a minimum of 40 feet from where I wound up standing, desperately thrusting out my glove, which was a Herb Score model that, on my coach's recommendation, I had treated with neat's-foot oil so it would be supple. Looking back, I feel bad that innocent neats had to sacrifice their feet for the sake of my glove. I would have been just as effective, as a fielder, if I'd been wearing a bowling shoe on my hand, or a small aquarium.

But even though I stunk at it, I was into baseball. My friends and I collected baseball cards, the kind that came in a little pack with a dusty, pale-pink rectangle of linoleum-textured World War II surplus bubble gum that was far less edible than the cards themselves. Like every other male my age who collected baseball cards as a boy, I now firmly believe that at one time I had the original rookie cards of Mickey Mantle, Jackie Robinson, Ty Cobb, Babe Ruth, Jim Thorpe, Daniel Boone, Goliath, etc., and that I'd be able to sell my collection for $163 million today except my mom threw it out.

My point is that we cared deeply about baseball back then, which meant that we were passionate about the 1960 Pirates-Yankees World Series matchup. My class was evenly divided between those who were Pirates fans and those who were complete morons. (I never have cared for the Yankees, and for a very sound reason: The Yankees are evil.)

We followed every pitch of every game. It wasn't easy, because the weekday games started when we were still in school, which for some idiot reason was not called off for the World Series. This meant that certain students—I am not naming names, because even now, it could go on our Permanent Records—had to carry concealed transistor radios to class. A major reason why the Russians got so far ahead of us, academically, during the Cold War is that while Russian students were listening to their teachers explain the cosine, we were listening, via concealed earphones, to announcers explain how a bad hop nailed Tony Kubek in the throat.

That Series went seven games, and I vividly remember how it ended. School was out for the day, and I was heading home, pushing my bike up a steep hill, listening to my cheapo little radio, my eyes staring vacantly ahead, my mind locked on the game. A delivery truck came by, and the driver stopped and asked if he could listen. Actually, he more or less told me he was going to listen; I said OK.

The truck driver turned out to be a rabid Yankee fan. The game was very close, and we stood on opposite sides of my bike for the final two innings, rooting for opposite teams, him chain-smoking Lucky Strike cigarettes, both of us hanging on every word coming out of my tinny little speaker.

And of course if you were around back then and did not live in Russia, you know what happened: God, in a sincere effort to make up for all those fly balls he directed toward me in Little League, had Bill Mazeroski—Bill Mazeroski!—hit a home run to win it for the Pirates.

I was insane with joy. The truck driver was devastated. But I will never forget what he said to me. He looked me square in the eye, one baseball fan to another, after a tough but fair fight—and he said a seriously bad word. Several, in fact. Then he got in his truck and drove away.

That was the best game I ever saw.

◆　◆　◆

DR. STRANGEGLOVE

Slugger Dick Stuart played in Pittsburgh from 1958 to 1962, and, in his short stay with the Pirates, achieved a notoriety beyond his limited accomplishments. After hitting sixty-six home runs in one of his minor-league seasons, he did lead the Pirates in home runs for three consecutive years, but he also led them in strikeouts for four years in a row, including a league-high 121 in 1961. But his real claim to notoriety was his disdain for fielding. "Dr. Strangeglove" routinely led the league's first basemen in errors and, if positioned in the outfield, had an unfortunate knack of catching fly balls on the bounce.

For Danny Peary's Cult Baseball Players, *John Sayles, who directed* Eight Men Out *and played Ring Lardner in the film, wrote about his childhood decision, out of all sense and reason, to make Dick Stuart his baseball idol.*

Dick Stuart

JOHN SAYLES

I once did an experiment in Biology in which we imprinted baby chicks just out of the shell on something other than their mothers. The first thing they saw moving and making noise became their mother figures and role models. It could have been a lab assistant or windup toy or a vacuum cleaner (though the latter tends to be dangerous when chicks are very little). There is a similar sensitive period in the life of a baseball fan, usually coming between the ages of five and ten, when he imprints on a certain team and certain player. I was vaguely entering the age of reason when I became aware that you were supposed to have a "favorite team." There was much playground discussion around these decisions, and a certain amount of violence. A kid in my first grade hit another in the face with a gooey stick (a branch with sap still running out of it—a favored weapon in class wars) because the other kid wouldn't agree that the Cubs were going to win the World Serious. That the Cubs weren't going to *play* in the World Serious didn't seem to matter.

At this point, I'd never really sat down and watched a whole professional ball game on TV, but there was a big hayfield across the street where, every day the weather permitted, you played baseball. If you were a boy kid, that's what you *did*, like cows gave milk and Davy Crockett shot at bad guys. I was tall for my age and wouldn't go away, so I got to play with kids two, three, sometimes four years older, quantum leaps for a first-grader. This caused even more pressure to have opinions on teams and players. My brother liked the Yankees, so that was out, the Dodgers and Giants had already split for California, and the Mets hadn't made the scene yet. I chose the Pirates, I think because I liked their uniforms in the baseball-card pictures. Being a Pirates fan in upper New York State in the fifties wasn't as sociopathic as being a Cubs fan there (or being a Cubs fan anywhere), but it was unusual.

So one day I turned on the TV and there was my favorite team, the Pittsburgh Pirates, in the uniforms I thought were so neat. I don't know whom they were playing or where, but it was late in the game when this big guy gets up and WHAM(!) wins it with a shot over the center-field wall. *Way* over. There was no instant replay in those days, but I feel like I

"John Sayles on Dick Stuart," from *Cult Baseball Players: The Greats, the Flakes, the Weird, and the Wonderful*, edited by Danny Peary (New York: Simon and Schuster, 1990). Reprinted with permission of John Sayles and Danny Peary.

saw it over and over again. And that was it—I was imprinted on Dick Stuart.

Stuart was one of a crop of big bangers that operated in the late fifties and early sixties. Big guys (Stuart was 6' 4") can't field much maybe, can't run much, strike out a lot, but when they got hold of one—forget it. Downtown. Frank Howard was in business then, and Ted Kluszewski, Joe Adcock, and Walt Dropo still, and Cash, Long, Colavito, Killebrew, Gentile, Gordy Coleman—mostly white guys with muscles who they'd stick at first base or bury in the corners of the outfield. When they came up with men on, it was always exciting.

Stuart had the misfortune of playing the meat of his career in spacious Forbes Field, where the fences were high and far, far away. He hit a lot of doubles and long outs while he was there from 1958 through 1962. How he would have hit playing half his games in a smaller park is one of the eternal what-ifs of baseball. Ask Ralph Kiner, who was before my time but must have been some piece of work to have put as many out of Forbes as he did. But one of Dick Stuart's charms was that he was not with the program. A power hitter with a slash-and-run team in a slash-and-run ballpark, a guy who had one of his worst years in 1960 when the Pirates won the pennant and just three singles and no RBIs when they beat the Yankees in the Series, an intensely bad fielder on a club with gloves like Groat, Mazeroski, Virdon, and Clemente.

What he did have was muscle and an implacable ability to do one thing well and nothing else. He could hit. Boys are obsessed with muscles, with who can "take" whom, who can throw the hardest and hit the farthest. The subtleties of baseball come later. Though watching Roberto Clemente was always thrilling, trying to play like him never worked out—all I could manage was the swinging at bad pitches. And though I could hit line drives steadily, my feet at that age were obscenely big and hard to move—I knew Roberto had never been thrown out at first on a clean single to right.

What big leaguer was that slow?

Dick Stuart, who stole only two bases in ten years of major league ball (and with those the element of surprise must have helped).

For some reason the first glove I owned weighed more than my head and had fingers as thick as my wrist. I couldn't hold the thing up, much less field grounders with it.

What big leaguer could mangle an easy roller like me?

Dr. Strangeglove, the man who once got an ovation in Fenway for successfully picking up a hot dog wrapper that had blown onto the field. The awfulness of Stuart's fielding has not been exaggerated. In his first seven seasons he led his league's first basemen in errors five times outright and was coleader the other two years despite playing just 64 and 101 games in the field. His 29 errors in 1963 almost tripled that of his nearest competitor.

Who just didn't have it some days, who never quite became the next Kiner, much less the next Ruth? Me and Dick Stuart.

The lure of Dick Stuart was the lure of potential, the lure of all longball hitters. Couple men on base and just one swing—just one fat pitch—just one good year in a ballpark with friendly fences and you're in the history books. When you're seven years old, everything is potential, and I wasn't the only one who thought he'd explode one of those years.

Stuart got a trade made in heaven in '63, going to the Red Sox of Fenway Park, where punch hitters like Felix Mantilla would end up before retirement and poke twenty or more balls over the left-field wall. The Green Monster beckoned and Stuart answered with 42 homers (and a league-leading 118 RBIs) and 33 homers (and 114 RBIs) in two seasons. Boston was a pretty sad team then, usually so far out of the race that Stuart's fielding was more entertaining than frustrating, and he was popular there. If he was a disappointment to the fans, he wasn't the *special* disappointment he'd been to Pirate fans, who'd been fed on the rumor that he'd hit 66 homers one season in the minors. Red Sox fans *breathe* disappointment, so Stuart was nothing new.

He was human, so clearly human in a game that works hard to create heroes, and I think that's why the early imprinting with me survived the trades. As life got more complicated, as baseball rules and teams began to change, it was comforting to know that someone out there was still going for the fence every time up, trying to win it all with one good shot. He hit 228 homers for the Pirates, Red Sox, Phillies (in 1965 for his final full season), Mets, Dodgers, and Angels (with whom he attempted a comeback in 1969) while averaging over 100 strikeouts for every full season. He couldn't field. He couldn't run. But every couple days, boy, runners on base and Dick Stuart at bat, and WHAM!

For*get* it.

Downtown.

• • •

For Roberto Clemente, the 1960 season was the turning point of his career. Bitter at being snubbed in the voting for the National League's Most Valuable Player Award, won by teammate Dick Groat, Clemente went on to have a Hall of Fame decade. As a team, the Pirates were out of miracles, and failed to win another championship in the 1960s after their year of destiny. But over the next ten years, Clemente, soared to four batting titles, nine Gold Glove awards, and finally, in 1966, was named the National League's Most Valuable Player.

When nineteen-year-old rookie Bill Mazeroski joined the Pirates in 1956, Clemente was twenty-one and in his second year with the team. The two future Hall of Famers would play together until 1972; Mazeroski retired at the end of the season and Clemente's tragic death occurred just a few months later. In "My 16 Years with Roberto Clemente," published just thirteen months before that unforgettable plane crash, Mazeroski gives his account of Clemente's career and personality, including Clemente's struggle to overcome the attempts of the press to portray him as a hot dog on the field and a malcontent in the clubhouse.

My 16 Years with Roberto Clemente

BILL MAZEROSKI

Sometimes it seems as if Roberto Clemente and I have been teammates longer than bacon and eggs. He came up to the Pirates in 1955 and I followed a year and a half later, so we've been sharing the same clubhouse for 16 years, probably longer than any two players still active. You get to know a person in 16 years—his strengths and weaknesses, how he plays the game and how he feels about it, when he hit the high spots and when he was low.

In 16 years you also become a good judge of his talents, the ways he can win for a club. And there are very few players who can win a baseball game in as many different ways as Roberto Clemente.

He's the total ballplayer. A lot of players are tagged superstars when they are really just super-hitters. Take Willie McCovey. A super-hitter, but he can't run and field exceptionally well. He's adequate in those areas and he hits 40 or so home runs and drives in over a hundred most years, but I

From "My 16 Years with Roberto Clemente," by Bill Mazeroski as told to Phil Musick, from *Sport*, November 1971. Reprinted with permission from Bill Mazeroski.

wouldn't call him a superstar. No, when you're discussing superstars, you're talking Willie Mays, Henry Aaron and Clemente.

There are no flaws in Clemente's game. He hits the ball more viciously to the opposite field than anyone I've ever seen. He throws the ball accurately over 400 feet and he has few peers as a baserunner. And he is as fine a rightfielder as Willie Mays is a centerfielder, to me the supreme compliment.

In my mind, Mays is the greatest player of the last 25 years and I rank Clemente behind him, right behind him. Roberto hasn't hit as many home runs as Mays or Aaron, but they have played in hitters' parks, while he spent 14 seasons looking into the biggest centerfield expanse in the major leagues at Forbes Field. He realized Forbes Field was built for line-drive hitters and he tailored his batting style to it from the beginning. Mays steals more bases than Roberto but outside of that and the long ball there is very little from which to choose between them.

When I first saw Clemente play in 1956 he hadn't matured physically, wasn't the hitter he would later become, but anyone who saw him throw knew he was something special.

During those first few years he was always happy, full of vinegar, a guy who trailed laughter wherever he went. He was one of the first really fine players to come from Puerto Rico and he struggled hard with his English. There were a lot of players on the club then who had never known anyone who spoke a foreign language and we used to laugh at his broken English and he laughed with us. We also laughed at some of his ways.

It didn't take long to discover that he was sort of superstitious, which he is to this day. One game in my rookie year he doubled his first three times at bat but the fourth time, with two out and a man on second and us a run behind, he bunted. After the game, the manager, Bobby Bragan, asked him: "How come you bunted?" In that fractured English, Roberto said, "Well, the law of averages was against me to hit another double."

In 1960, he thought a band was jinxing us. At most of the home games a dixieland combo used to play a song called "Beat 'em, Bucs" and before long the whole town was singing it. When we went to Chicago for the last two games of the season, the band went with us. The Cubs were in last place, but they beat us twice and when we got back home Roberto said, "Keep that band out of here. Every time they play we get beat." He just knew if the band played, we'd lose.

He doesn't tell everyone about his superstitions now because we needle him quite a bit. He'll wear a certain shirt and if we win that day, he won't change it until we lose. He had a hell of a time this year when we won 11 straight games.

Roberto's carefree outlook on life began to change when the press started to misunderstand him when he talked about his injuries. When he was hurt he had trouble explaining himself because of the language problem and everyone thought he was jakin'.

I don't think he's ever jaked. He just could do things when he was hurt as well as the rest of us could when we were healthy, and people would see this and decide he was dogging it. They thought he used the basket catch because Mays did and everything he did in the outfield was exciting, so right away to some writers he was a hot dog who jaked.

Stories were written to that effect and he went through some years when he didn't trust writers, and I don't blame him. Some of them put words in your mouth and that's what they did to him when he was younger. They tried to make him look like an ass by getting him to say controversial things and then they wrote how the Puerto Rican hot dog was popping off again. He was just learning to handle the language and he couldn't express what he felt or thought and it frustrated him. Writers who couldn't speak three words of Spanish tried to make him look silly, but he's an intelligent man who knows people and knows the game.

I watched him grow up and mature in those years. When things went wrong he used to give into his anger, bang bats around, kick his helmet, break things. But time mellowed him some and he throws himself into controversies less quickly, is more controlled now.

We've always been friendly—in 16 years we've never spoken a cross word—but as we got older, we got closer. It's just been the last four or five years that we've really been close friends, close enough to agitate each other. He likes to talk about some of the long balls he's hit and he's always telling the kids: "Ask Maz, he was there." They'll ask me and I'll tell them: "Nah, he didn't hit that one very good" and he'll go grumping around about that "dumb Polack doesn't know what he's talking about."

One thing about him hasn't changed over the years. He's the same person to the clubhouse boys that he is to the league president. He doesn't hang around with the big shots, the superstars. He's remained pretty much himself and nothing's gone to his head, ever.

That's why he's gotten involved in some controversies. He was always outspoken and he hasn't changed. You never have to guess where you stand with Clemente. He's very expressive and he lets everyone know exactly how he feels. The older players used to resent it when he talked about being hurt until they realized he was an extrovert, that it was his natural way. If he's hurt, he says so and then goes out and does what he gets paid to do.

He didn't think he got enough credit when we won the pennant and the World Series in 1960—and he didn't—and he said so. When he thought some writers were unfair to him, he said so. He thought he was underrated (for years both he and Aaron were vastly underrated) and after awhile, he let the world know it. That's his way. Some people call it honesty.

He worked as hard as anyone on the club in 1960, but he finished eighth in the voting for the Most Valuable Player award. It was probably the biggest disappointment of his career, and he had a right to be disappointed. He hit .314 and he played in all but eight games. He was just starting to come into his own then and he couldn't understand getting so little consideration for the MVP award. It affected him as a person, made him bitter. I think it was three or four years before he got over it. We had Dick Groat and Don Hoak run 1-2 in the balloting, but Roberto was as valuable to us as either of them. Groat missed a month with a broken wrist and Dick Schofield hit about .360 filling in for him. That year we had a different kind of a club than we did this year. Somebody different picked us up every day, there weren't any stars.

Don't get me wrong, Clemente doesn't need defending by anybody, his record speaks for itself: An All Star 12 times, a Gold Glove winner nine times, the league's leading hitter four times. Still, he gets bum-rapped.

In recent years Roberto hasn't always played in the second games of doubleheaders and in day games following night games, and there's been some grumbling from the press and the public. But when you're older you just don't bounce back as quick as you once did. If my bat was slow and I needed a rest, I still stayed in the lineup because I figured I produced primarily with my glove. But Clemente, even when he's run down, is still supposed to do it all. I was glad to see him rest because when he sat out a game, it meant three or four when he would be at his best. And he's always had trouble sleeping, so much so that one time he said: "When I wake up in the mornings, I pray I am still asleep."

In 16 years you see a lot of players play this game and I don't get real excited every time some young phenom comes along and captures the public's imagination, but in my time no one has played baseball with more skill, enthusiasm and grace than Clemente. Even now, at his age, he never shies away from danger, never gives anything but 100 percent. This year in Houston he saved a one-run game for Steve Blass by running full blast into the wall to pull down a ball that would have gone above the white line for a game-winning home run.

◆

He's kind of sentimental about the Pittsburgh people and when they booed him some last year and earlier this season, he told me it hurt him to think they'd do it after all this time. He didn't like it and neither did I. He hears the boos. A lot of players like to say they don't, but there's no way you can close your ears to it. Nobody can.

Chances are good that he'll be hearing the fans one way or the other, though, for a few more years. He hasn't slowed down very much at 36 and he's got one of those slim builds like Stan Musial had that allows a guy to play longer.

Roberto managed in Puerto Rico last winter, but I don't think he'll manage when he finally retires. He probably would have the type of trouble Ted Williams had in Washington, wanting the players to do things as well as he could. But there just aren't many Ted Williamses or Roberto Clementes. On the other hand, Roberto knows the game well and the players know he's a hell of a person.

In 16 years you build a lot of memories and some of the ones I'll hang onto the longest will include Roberto Clemente.

◆　◆　◆

THE END OF AN ERA

At the end of the 1960s, construction began on Three Rivers Stadium, and with its completion on July 16, 1970, Forbes Field, one of the greatest landmarks in baseball history, was scheduled for the wrecking ball. The Pirates played their last games at the decaying ballpark on June 28, 1970, in a doubleheader with the Chicago Cubs— the same team that played Pittsburgh when "Dreyfuss's Folly" opened in 1909. After Bill Mazeroski fielded the last out of the last game, Forbes Field began to fade into history and legend. It was demolished in 1972.

The selections from Daniel L. Bonk's "Ballpark Figures: The Story of Forbes Field," tell the story of the historical circumstances leading to the demise of the aging ballpark and the nostalgia that has lingered ever since its demise. The segment that follows is drawn from a 1995 interview with Art McKennan, who had been the public address announcer at Forbes Field since 1948. Here, he also talks about his memories of two of the ballpark's fading legends.

Ballpark Figures: The Story of Forbes Field

DANIEL L. BONK

Twilight Years (1945–1970)

The era of new ownership in Pittsburgh coincided with the end of World War II, the start of Pittsburgh's urban renewal called the "Renaissance," the western expansion of baseball, and new developments in Oakland. Each played a role in the demise of Forbes Field.

In 1945, Pittsburgh Mayor David L. Lawrence joined with Pittsburgh's wealthiest and most Republican native, Richard K. Mellon, in a major effort to revitalize the region. Their efforts resulted in the redevelopment of the Golden Triangle, the lower Hill District, and the near North Side. The latter included construction of Three Rivers Stadium, an idea first proposed by the Allegheny Conference for Community Development in 1955.

Baseball franchises were the envy of growing western cities in the 1950s. Beginning in 1953 with the Boston Braves' move to Milwaukee, baseball entered an era when cities openly wooed franchises by offering special incentives including municipally financed stadiums. Before the decade was out, the St. Louis Browns, Philadelphia Athletics, Brooklyn Dodgers and New York Giants would follow the lure of public assistance, perks, and financing to Baltimore, Kansas City, Los Angeles, and San Francisco. The franchises that stayed put, like the Pirates, found themselves increasingly viewed by the community as a public institution rather than a private enterprise.

The Pirates, in contrast to franchises like cross-state rivals, the Philadelphia Phillies, never publicly solicited for a new stadium. Instead, the combined needs of Pittsburgh's urban renewal and the ever-increasing appetite of the University of Pittsburgh for Oakland real estate made it easy for the Pirates to rid themselves of a costly maintenance liability. A vocal proponent of a new stadium was ex-Pirates' President Bill Benswanger, who argued the futility of maintaining the old ballpark: "It's an exposed building and winter and weather take their toil." In 1958, Pitt's chancellor proposed the purchase of Forbes Field for $3 million with an agreement to lease it back to the Pirates for 10 months to four years. Pitt ultimately bought the field and leased it to the Pirates for 12 years.

On June 28, 1970, the Pirates played the last game at Forbes Field

From "Ballpark Figures: The Story of Forbes Field," *Pittsburgh History* 1993.

against the same team they faced in the first game, the Chicago Cubs. The second largest crowd (40,918) in Forbes Field history attended. They watched Bill Mazeroski record the last out by fielding a ground ball from Don Kessinger and stepping on second base to force out Willie Smith.

Epilogue

Forbes Field survives today in bits and pieces. A section of the ivy-covered wall stands besides Pitt's Katz Business School. The 457-foot mark remains a memorial to Dreyfuss's conviction that his ballpark not be known as a place where a man could hit a cheap home run. Across the street from that section of wall is Pitt's Forbes Quadrangle building. Inside the main lobby, the home plate from Forbes Field is encased in Plexiglass and set in the floor.

◆

Most Pittsburgh fans didn't fully realize what was being lost, caught up as they were in another pennant race and the media-whipped euphoria that accompanied the opening of Three Rivers. As the years passed, its inadequacies, coupled with the almost idolic reverence baseball fans have for the surviving classic ballparks, have combined to magnify the loss. What's more, Three Rivers was hailed for its versatility, but Forbes Field must certainly be considered to have been its equal. Besides hosting professional baseball, Pitt, Carnegie Tech, Duquesne University, and the Steelers played football at Forbes Field. It was the place where one went to watch a wrestling show or a boxing match. The Pittsburgh Symphony, Civic Light Opera, and various popular entertainment acts played there. The park saw numerous political rallies, religious congregations, prayer services for departing GIs, and even the circus which used to play at Exposition Park. The broad scope of events meant that just about every Pittsburgher experienced its special feel.

Yet its reputation survives primarily for one sport. In 1969, Benswanger lamented that Forbes Field "was a little bit different from any other ballpark. The fan sits back and looks out on a green terrain that doesn't include factories. There are thousands of people who will regret its passing; that's human nature. I don't know of a better playing field. But it can't last forever."

Bill James, a noted baseball historian, summed up precisely what no longer exists: "Forbes was regarded for many years somewhat the way Dodger Stadium is regarded today, as the crown jewel in the diamond tiara. It was never the biggest, but it seemed, somehow, the best—the sight lines were the best, it contained and expressed the enthusiasm of the crowd the best; it was just the best place to watch a baseball game."

An Interview with Art McKennan

JIM HALLER and ED LUTERAN

ED & JIM: The destruction of Forbes Field must have been a serious loss to you personally.

ART: Right before the last doubleheader played at Forbes between the Bucs and the Cubs, I told everybody that I was going to stay in the park all night, just like sitting up with a dying friend. I just wanted to look over the place for the last time. I really didn't want to leave. I wanted to hold the hand of my dying friend. That is how I felt.

I grew up at Forbes Field. I had been going there for more than 50 years, and it meant a great deal to me. However, the city needed an all-purpose stadium to house the Steelers in order to keep them here. The Steelers had never had their own field to play on. Seemingly, they were always "borrowing" Forbes Field or Pitt Stadium. I think that is why Three Rivers Stadium is better for viewing football than baseball. But it is plastic to me.

However, when we moved into the place in 1970, it was a joy because the working facilities were far superior to Forbes Field. Restaurants and toilet facilities were far better in the new park. The University [of Pittsburgh] had purchased Forbes Field and just let it run down. Why would they put any money into it? It was scheduled for demolition, plain and simply. By 1970, it was totally tired and rundown.

The major regret I have with Three Rivers Stadium is that center field is not open for viewing the city the way the original plans called for. It would have cost a lot more money to open the stadium in center field than to close it the way they did. That seems strange to me.

E&J: Would real grass make you feel better about the stadium?

ART: No. The Steelers ruined the grounds at Forbes Field every year. They had to re-sod the field every spring. The place always looked like a patch quilt. The Steelers would do the same thing in Three Rivers Stadium. Putting in new sod every year is horribly expensive. Mayor Sophie Masloff had a great idea a few years ago when she suggested a separate baseball park for the Pirates. It was just ill-timed. However, they have it in Kansas City and other places.

◆

E&J: If there is anyone who should know this, it is you, Art. Why did the Pirates retire Billy Meyer's number "1"?

From *Baseball in Pittsburgh* (SABR, 1995). Reprinted with permission of Jim Haller and Ed Luteran.

ART: Because the Pirate organization truly loved the man. I have asked a number of people who should know, and they all said the organization was fond of him and always has been. They wanted to do him a special favor. He had one great season as a Buc manager in 1948. The team was in contention for the pennant up to the final couple weeks. It lost to the Boston Braves with ex-Buc Bob Elliott leading the way. Meyer had Danny Murtaugh playing second and Stan Rojek playing short. Kiner was in left with Wally Westlake in center. Frankie Gustine played third. It was a very good team.

E&J: How well do you remember Dino Restelli?

ART: The greatest flash in the pan ever: 12 homers in 1949. It seemed like he hit them all in his first two or three weeks here. Chilly Doyle of the Pittsburgh *Sun-Telegraph* wrote a story about Restelli later that said that he was not as good as his father's spaghetti. His dad owned a restaurant on the West Coast. Restelli was a lot like Johnny Rizzo, only Rizzo lasted longer. Vince DiMaggio was similar to both. Vince struck out with more style and poetry than any other right-handed batter I ever saw. He was beautiful.

Winning It All— and Losing Much More

The 1971 World Series will always be remembered as Roberto Clemente's showcase. For the record, he fielded perfectly, batted .414, homered in the seventh and deciding game (won by the Pirates 2-1), and was the overwhelming choice for the Most Valuable Player award. At the age of thirty-seven, "the Great One" had finally found his vindication. But the World Series may not have gone to Pittsburgh without the brilliant pitching of Steve Blass and a clutch performance by twenty-one-year-old rookie pitcher Bruce Kison. After the Pirates were down 2-0 in the series, Blass pitched a complete game 5-1 victory, then repeated his feat in the seventh game. Kison (who, after game seven, was rushed back to Pittsburgh by private jet for his wedding) intimidated the Orioles in game four and became the winning pitcher in the first night game ever played in the World Series. The Pirates' come-from-behind victory in the 1971 World Series and the contributions of Clemente, Blass, and Kison were celebrated in the Pittsburgh newspapers.

Clemente Drives Pirates to Title

BILL CHRISTINE

Roberto Clemente needs another automobile like he needs a stronger throwing arm. Cadillacs and foreign sports cars are accumulating at his Puerto Rican home faster than flies swarming to a dropped ice-cream cone, and later this week the Pirates' superb right fielder will be handed the keys to a Dodge Charger.

"Roberto, if you don't get that car, I'll buy you one myself," Willie Stargell was saying yesterday in Baltimore. Stargell's cash reserve is safe. *Sport* magazine, the donor, couldn't have possibly honored anyone else after Clemente's 12th World Series hit, a fourth-inning home run, had fired the Pirates to their 2-1 victory over the pseudo-invincible Orioles in the championship seventh game.

Oh, Steve Blass might have been a contender for the wheels, because he pitched two Series games which had the Orioles talking to themselves, but it was Clemente who inspired the Pirates from start to finish. Every game the Bucs won—three in Pittsburgh and finally, breaking the home-field rut which had prevailed throughout the first six, the finale in Baltimore—Clemente was a pivotal performer.

"I'll bet you Harry Dalton (the Baltimore general manager) would trade half his ball club for Clemente," Don Leppert, the Pirates' first-base coach, said. "He'd probably split his club house down the middle, and give us a choice of either side, to get that guy into an Oriole uniform."

Leppert's only regret is that Clemente didn't have the chance to truly excel in the field. Other than his eye-popping throw to the plate in the sixth game, Clemente was required to field no more than ordinary chances.

"Brooks Robinson had that great Series with the glove in 1970," Leppert said, "but you've got to be lucky to field like he did. By that, I mean you've got to get the tough chances, and if Roberto had some in this Series, he really would have shown them something."

The populace of Baltimore must feel that Clemente showed them enough. The 37-year-old veteran gave the Pirates a 1-0 lead off Mike Cuellar yesterday by bashing a 390-foot homer over the fence in left-center in the fourth inning. Clemente's homer came after the Baltimore left-hander had retired the first eleven men to face him. Clemente also homered in Saturday's 3-2 loss to the Orioles and yesterday's blast marked the first time this year he had homered on successive days.

Clemente admitted afterward that he was especially gung-ho for this Series. After the pennant playoff with the Giants, in which Stargell had gone 0-for-14, Clemente said to his wife Vera on the eve of the Series, "Willie's not hitting. I'm going to have to play real good against Baltimore just in case."

Stargell, who batted only .208 in the Series, picked an opportune time to get his fifth and final hit. After leading off the eighth with a single on a grounder that stayed down and skipped to the left of Mark Belanger, Stargell churned home on Jose Pagan's double to left center, a shot which hit the fence at about the same spot where Clemente's homer traveled.

"I musta looked like a runaway beer truck going around the bases," Stargell said. "It was a hit-and-run, and I had to stop at second to make sure the center fielder wasn't going to catch the ball. Once I got going again, though, I said to myself, 'There's nothing that's gonna stop me from making home plate.'

"I don't know yet whether (Frank) Oceak (the Pirates' third-base coach) was holding me or sending me. I had my head down as I was going to third."

Then Stargell smiled. "Course," he said, "a guy with my wheels can afford to take chances. I stole 40 bases this year."

Stargell slid home, but the play wasn't close and Boog Powell cut off the relay throw from Mark Belanger. Merv Rettenmund, the center fielder, juggled the ball on his original throwing motion, and by the time he recocked, the Orioles had lost their chance of flagging the runner.

Blass, who threw a four-hitter to go with his three-hitter in the third game against Baltimore, got into only two real jams. In the second, a walk and an error by Bob Robertson on a grounder put runners at first and second with one out. Blass escaped when Belanger hit sharply to Dave Cash, who turned it into a double play.

The other spot was the eighth, when Baltimore snapped the shutout and put the tying run on second with only one out.

Elrod Henricks and Belanger singled and Tom Shopay, a pinch-hitter, bunted them into scoring position as Blass, with a force-out play at third, threw to first instead. One run scored on Don Buford's grounder to Robertson, but Blass ended the threat by retiring Dave Johnson on a grounder to Jackie Hernandez, playing in the hole, exactly where the ball was hit.

"When I was in the American League," Hernandez said, "I used to play Johnson the other way, more as an up-the-middle hitter. But our scouting reports on the Orioles indicated that Johnson, especially with less than two strikes, likes to pull the ball."

The Pirate sleuths—Howie Haak, George Detore, and Harding Peterson—were rewarded for their work. "There's only one American League shortstop, Gene Michael of the Yankees, who plays Johnson in the hole," Haak said. "But after watching the Orioles, we decided that this was the right place to have the shortstop."

The Pirate clubhouse was relatively devoid of the usual Series-clinching shenanigans, although four cases of champagne and 15 cases of beer were on ice. A few players were tossed into the showers, but the squirting of the bubbly was kept at a minimum.

Someone offered Clemente, a light drinker, a soft drink, but the Pirate star was splurging. He already had a bottle of beer in his hand.

"This championship means more to me than the one we won in 1960," Clemente said. "My father is 91 and my mother is 87, and this victory was meant for them. When they get to be that age, you are not sure how much longer they can go on, so I am glad we got this one now."

During an earlier conversation with Wes Parker of the Dodgers, Clemente had mentioned his parents. Yesterday morning at Memorial Stadium, there was a telegram from Parker waiting for Clemente. It read: "Win it for your parents."

Despite the hitting of Clemente, Manny Sanguillen (who had 11 hits, second only to Clemente on both teams) and Robertson, it was the pitching that won the Series for the Pirates. There was strong mound work—twice by Blass, once each from Bruce Kison and Nellie Briles—in each game the Pirates won.

In the windup, Blass was given more trouble from Earl Weaver, the canny Oriole manager, than he was from any of the Oriole bats. In the first inning, Weaver complained to plate umpire Nestor Chylak, claiming that Blass wasn't placing his foot on or next to the pitching rubber. Again, at the end of the fifth inning, Weaver reiterated his protest to Chylak.

"He was trying to bother the pitcher, but there is nothing wrong with doing that," Clemente said.

Why would Weaver do a thing like that?

"He was trying to win," said the man who now has a car for every day of the week and two for Sunday.

Pitching Did It

ROY MCHUGH

Steve Blass was telling them how he threw mostly sliders after getting his rhythm in the first inning, et cetera, giving them all those technical details that baseball writers like to carry off and present to their readers as jewels, when suddenly in the middle of a sentence he stopped, mouth agape.

"It's all over . . ." he said.

"We won the World Series . . ." he said.

"I'm very happy to be a part of the Pittsburgh Pirates' no-name pitching staff," he said.

By holding the Baltimore Orioles to one run and three hits in the third game and to one run on four hits in the seventh game of the World Series, Blass is a threat to turn the no-name pitching staff into a one-name pitching staff.

He did not receive a call from President Nixon yesterday, but Officer Kirchner of the Connecticut State Police was on the clubhouse phone with the information that Governor Thomas Meskill had been trying to get in touch with him and Miles Blodgett sent a telegram.

In case you hadn't heard, Miles Blodgett is the first selectman of Falls Village, Conn., where Blass votes.

And, though Clemente will get the sports car awarded to the most valuable player in the Series, there are those who believe that Blass, at the very least, rates a motorbike.

Billy the Kid

"Clemente was great," said Baltimore Manager Earl Weaver, "but all I know is that without Blass we might be popping corks."

Later on, Weaver thought of something else he knew—that Bruce Kison's relief pitching on the night the Pirates evened the Series at two games apiece had not done the Orioles any good.

"The biggest thing actually," Weaver said, "was this kid Kison walking out of the bullpen after we get three runs in the first inning and shutting us out for six. He kept us from blowing the game open."

Bruce Kison is 21 and when the Orioles aren't calling him "this Kison" they are calling him "that kid." He is certainly no respecter of persons. From the Pirate bullpen, Dave Giusti watched him "knocking guys down or hitting them and not being scared to go back inside with a little better stuff." Earl Weaver said, "I'd hate to pick him as the Series hero, but that's it."

Danny Murtaugh said, "If there had to be a turning point, it was the six innings Kison pitched. He gave us a chance to go ahead in that game. I imagine if I was a sports writer I'd say that Kison's pitching was the turning point, but the most pressure-packed game was the third game. Steve Blass won the third game, and if we'd lost, after losing the first two, it would have been the crusher."

Manny Believed

What everyone agreed on was that the no-name pitching staff saved the Pirates' necks. The hot bats of Clemente and Manny Sanguillen notwithstanding, the Pirates went through the Series without ever scoring more than five runs in any one game.

The no-name pitching staff, more anonymous than ever after Murtaugh subtracted a sore-armed Dock Ellis from the rotation, was not supposed to win with that kind of hitting. Hindsight now enables Sanguillen to laugh at such an idea.

To the Pirate catcher, "no-name," in fact, seems a misnomer. Without even pausing to think, he rattled off the names of Blass, Kison, Giusti, Bob Moose, Nelson Briles, Luke Walker, and Bob Johnson. "When Kison won a game, everybody surprised," he said. "Everybody surprised because Nelson Briles pitch a good game. Well, I don't surprised, 'cause I believe in my pitchers."

Blass, by the way, was still waiting for the Governor to call as dusk settled over Memorial Stadium in Baltimore. Somebody else called, but it wasn't the Governor. The call wasn't even for Blass, who happened to be standing on Danny Murtaugh's desk when the phone rang.

On the chance that it might be the Governor, he picked up the receiver and said, "Wally's Delicatessen." Blass always answers the phone that way after winning the seventh game of the World Series.

◆ ◆ ◆

"ALL OUR HEARTS ARE SADDENED"

For the Pirates, the 1972 season, with the exception of Roberto Clemente's three thousandth major-league hit, was bitterly disappointing. After repeating as Eastern Division champions, they lost a heartbreaking fifth and deciding playoff game to the Reds on a wild pitch in the bottom of the ninth. Of course, the worst was yet to come for Pirate fans and the baseball world. Less than three months later, at 9:22 P.M. on December 31, a DC-7 cargo plane filled with supplies for the victims of a devastating earthquake in Managua crashed into the Atlantic minutes after takeoff, killing everyone on board, including Roberto Clemente.

This selection from "Adios Amigo Roberto," in Samuel O. Regalado's Viva Baseball!, *draws attention to Clemente's place in baseball's fabled history as the perfect athlete cut down by death at the height of his glory as well as to Clemente's stature in Puerto Rico as a national hero and his outspoken legacy for Latin American ballplayers.*

Adios Amigo Roberto

SAMUEL O. REGALADO

> *Only one thing could ever really stop Roberto Clemente, and it did.*
> —*Milton Richman,* Springfield (Massachusetts) Daily News

> *Greater love hath no man than this, that a man lay down his life for his friends.*
> —*John 15:13*

Vera Clemente sat quietly at home as hope faded away. Manny Sanguillen was inconsolable and assisted in a desperate search for his friend. Indeed, Puerto Rico's first day of 1973 was an anxious one as crowds gathered on the beaches of San Juan offering prayers that Roberto Clemente might still be alive. Only twenty-four hours earlier, the great outfielder had been gathering food and supplies to be flown to Nicaragua where a devastating earthquake had killed thousands of citizens and rendered many others homeless. Clemente, who headed a relief program, had worked tirelessly to aid his fellow Latins. His interest in Nicaragua stemmed from a visit in November when he took a Puerto Rican amateur team there for a tournament. Warmly greeted, he befriended a young boy who had lost his legs in an accident. Through Clemente's efforts, funds were raised to supply his newfound friend with artificial limbs. His long-time comrades were not surprised by Clemente's sensitivity in these matters. Because of his efforts, he was dismayed to learn after the Nicaraguan earthquake that National Guardsmen had stolen many of the supplies intended for the afflicted. Clemente thus decided to accompany the December 31 relief flight to assure that all goods reached their intended destinations. With only a skeleton crew, the Pittsburgh outfielder boarded the weathered DC-7 on New Year's Eve bound for Managua.

Within minutes of taking off the plane crashed into the sea, taking Clemente and four others with it. "It's not possible," repeated a shocked Vera Clemente after learning of the accident shortly past midnight. As Coast Guard crews panned the rough waters off San Juan for survivors, islanders prayed that their hero and his colleagues were safe. In Pittsburgh, many of Clemente's teammates were informed of the accident as New Year's Eve parties wound down. Steve Blass and Dave Giusti "kept pacing in and out of our rooms, past each other." In another part of Pittsburgh, Al Oliver sat, trembling in his recliner as he listened to the news on the radio. By midmorning the world realized that Clemente was gone.

Puerto Ricans were devastated. Inaugural day ceremonies for incoming governor Rafael Hernández Colón were canceled. In his first speech, the governor-elect lamented, "Our people have lost one of their glories. All our hearts are saddened." By the second day of the new year eulogies poured in. "I don't think we as teammates knew him as well as we could have," said pitcher Steve Blass. "He was so much more than a great baseball player." Commissioner Bowie Kuhn saw in Clemente "the touch of royalty."

Pittsburgh's citizens also mourned their fallen hero. News of Clemente's death brought disbelief. "All of a sudden the New Year seems kind of hollow," announced Allegheny County Commissioner Leonard Staisey. "Greetings just don't ring quite right." Another grieving baseball fan claimed that "nobody will ever replace that guy. When I first heard about it I was in a daze. It brought a tear to my eye." The Puerto Rican community in New York City was equally stunned. "Roberto was proud to be a

Puerto Rican," said one resident. "He never forgot his people." Another claimed, "We have lost a man who was a glory to Puerto Rico." Among the finest eulogies came from a child who viewed Clemente as a personification of all Latins. In honor of the Puerto Rican, the five-year-old wrote that he named his dog "'Puerto Rico' because nice people live there. . . . Clemente lived there." The *Washington Post* added its condolences by suggesting that the scoreboard at Three Rivers Stadium change its message from "Roberto Clemente, 1934–1972" to "a man of honor played baseball here." Looming high above Pittsburgh, a neon sign that usually advertised a local beer product simply read "Adios Amigo Roberto."

Roberto Clemente's relief aid program for the people of Managua continued as a memorial fund in his honor. President Richard Nixon was among the contributors. Indeed, in addition to writing a personal check of $1,000, the president met with some Pirates officials and players to help organize the campaign. Donations continued in the ensuing weeks accompanied by letters eulogizing the Pirate star. "I only wish this check could reflect the many thrilling moments Roberto has given me," wrote one Pittsburgh fan. An eighteen-year-old Pennsylvanian penned, "He'll never lift his cap or even smile. Oh, we'll miss him for a long, long while."

Only fifteen months earlier, Roberto Clemente's career was at its peak. A self-proclaimed "old man" at thirty-seven, he led the 1971 Pittsburgh Pirates to a division title and then past San Francisco in the National League championship series. Their World Series opponents, the Baltimore Orioles, however, were a powerfully balanced club led by sluggers Frank Robinson and Boog Powell. The Orioles pitching staff was an even more impressive lot. The starting rotation of Jim Palmer, Miguel "Mike" Cuéllar, Dave McNally, and Pat Dobson had won twenty games each that year. Furthermore, the Orioles compiled 101 wins and were making their third successive trip to the series. Understandably, they were favored to take the fall classic, but few observers recognized the depth of the Pittsburgh right fielder's passion to win.

By then Clemente carried outstanding credentials. The winner of four batting crowns and the 1966 Most Valuable Player Award, he was well on his way toward collecting his 3,000th hit (which turned out to be the final hit of his career the following year). In addition, he owned a bevy of Gold Glove awards and had been named to the National League All-Star squad eleven times. In his only World Series appearance, eleven years earlier, he batted .310. Yet, Clemente remained frustrated because the limelight still eluded him. The 1971 World Series changed that.

Always fiery, he used the fall classic as a public forum. "Nobody in this game does anything better than me," he proclaimed—and he set out to prove it. The entire series was one of shifting momentum. Pittsburgh, after dropping the first two games, rebounded to take the next three. Baltimore evened the series in game six to force a climactic finale. Roberto Clemente was already the big story. Playing like a man possessed, he carried a .440 average that included a home run, a triple, and two doubles. In addition, his defense sparkled and he used every opportunity to exhibit his fielding prowess. At one point, when there appeared to be no Baltimore scoring threat, he launched a powerful throw from the right-field corner to home plate. Players from the Baltimore dugout gasped. "It's got to be the greatest throw I ever saw," remembered second baseman Davey Johnson. "One second he's got his back to the field at the 390 mark, the next instant here comes the throw, on the chalk line." Clemente's actions also inspired his teammates. "You watch Roberto and you can't help getting all psyched," claimed outfielder Gene Clines. "There's the old man out there busting his ass off on every play and every game. Look, I'm twenty-five. If he can play like that, shouldn't I?"

By game seven, all eyes were on Clemente. Indeed, for the Pittsburgh star, the contest was truly symbolic. For years he had fought against stereotypes that cast him and other Latins as absurd, hypochondriacal, and unintelligent. Similarly, he battled social habits and restrictions that he believed belittled not just Puerto Ricans but all people of color. Finally, he sought to win what he felt he earned but had been denied—recognition. Clemente did not fail his supporters. In the fourth inning he broke the scoreless duel by pummeling a home run. Behind Steve Blass's four-hitter, the Pirates won the deciding contest and Clemente ended a remarkable series performance with a .414 batting average. His selection as the World Series Most Valuable Player was obvious.

However, Clemente's greatest satisfaction appeared to come in the locker room as the Pirates celebrated. "I want everyone in the world to know that this is the way I play all the time," shouted Clemente. He then shared his reflections on the past. "All season, every season, I gave everything I had to this game. The press call me a crybaby, a hypochondriac . . . they say I'm not a team player. Now everyone knows the way Roberto Clemente plays." As he paused for questions, one journalist queried if the series victory was his greatest moment. "The greatest moment in my career is now, this precise instant, when I'm going to answer your question." he responded. "This is the first time I've ever been able to have all of you together in one room, and I want to tell all of you that you're a bunch of good-for-nothing bums! Now that I've got that off my chest, you'll see a different Roberto Clemente. I won't complain about anything anymore."

Clemente's satisfaction was complete. Earlier on national television he addressed his parents in Spanish: "On this the proudest day of my life I ask your blessing." Clemente's postgame interviews characterized his career. He was both proud and humble, angry and happy, unreasonable and understanding. Most of all, he demonstrated his contribution as a pioneer in the emergence of Latin players, seeking equality and recognition for them when it was not popular to do so. Moreover, his dreams did not end there.

For years Roberto Clemente had sought to create a sports complex to serve as a training ground for young Puerto Rican athletes whose dreams included participation in Pan-American games, the Olympics, and, of course, professional baseball. "He never forgot where he came from," Vera Clemente claimed. "Roberto used to see that when he was little, that kids like him had nothing." Not until the 1980s did Clemente's Ciudad Deportiva (Sports City) develop as a functional operation, but many young Puerto Ricans, such as Rubén Sierra, whose stardom lay in the future, expanded their skills at a complex that also encouraged family cohesiveness. By then, many of Clemente's contemporaries, such as Orlando Cepeda, Vic Power, and Félix Millán, had contributed their time in reverence of his legacy.

The passing of Clemente marked a transitional period for Latins as the first generation of post-integration players gave way to a younger group. Felipe Alou retired in 1974, Luis Aparicio in 1973, Orlando Cepeda in 1974, and Juan Marichal in 1975. Like Clemente, these Latin players helped cushion the trauma of acculturation and built a foundation for Latin hopefuls of the future. Furthermore, Clemente's outspoken opinions and leadership brought greater notoriety to the Latin plight in North America. The Puerto Rican's recognition reached a crescendo when, shortly after his death, the Baseball Writers Association of America elected him to the Hall of Fame—the first Latin to be inducted. In 1974 Clemente also won election in the Negro Baseball Hall of Fame.

Clemente's induction into the Hall of Fame in Cooperstown, however, did not come without controversy. At the center of the arguments was the process of his election. Two days following his death, the Hall of Fame Board of Directors amended their five-year eligibility rule to allow early induction for the late Pittsburgh outfielder. Criticizing the format as "steamroller" methodology, writer Dick Young chose to abstain in the voting process. Bill Broeg voted against Clemente's induction on the pretense that Clemente "didn't need the special privilege of an extra election to bypass the Hall of Fame's five-year wait for selection." Others, however, reacted sharply to the criticism. In his column for *Newsday*, Ed Comerford chided his colleagues; any dissenter should be "flogged, broken on the rack, and then condemned to cover croquet tournaments the rest of his unnatural life." He then pointed out that "justice demands" Clemente's enshrinement. Arthur Daley of the *New York Times* agreed that "any baseball writer who fails to mark his ballot affirmatively should have his buttons snipped off while being drummed out of the regiment." Larry Claflin of the *Boston Herald* was more direct. "Roberto Clemente belongs in the Baseball Hall of Fame. He belongs there now, not five years from now," he maintained. "No Latin American ball player has ever been enshrined in Cooperstown. There could be no better candidate to be the pioneer than Clemente." On March 31, 1973, Roberto Clemente captured the necessary votes. Later, the commissioner's office instituted an annual trophy given to the major league player who was both an outstanding athlete and an exemplary citizen in honor of Clemente.

◆ ◆ ◆

STEVE BLASS

Roger Angell, the senior fiction editor for the New Yorker, *began writing baseball essays for the magazine in the early 1960s. His essays, also collected in several volumes, now span five decades of baseball history. Though he likes to think of his baseball writings as fan essays, he is widely regarded as the game's most eloquent and thoughtful commentator. His essays range from an appreciation of the beauty and timeliness of the game itself to an understanding of the stupidity and greed that threaten to ruin the game for its fans.*

In April 1975, Roger Angell visited Steve Blass, one of the heroes of the 1971 World Series. Blass was now out of baseball because, after the 1972 season, he suddenly and inexplicably lost the ability to throw strikes, and retired two years later. The resulting essay is one of Angell's finest in its detailed and sympathetic portrait of Blass's baseball tragedy and its effect on his personal life. The title of the essay, "Gone for Good," is indicative of Blass's pitching career, but it doesn't tell the rest of the Blass story—his re-emergence in 1984, with Bob Prince, as a commentator for Pirate games, and his subsequent role, since 1986, as color analyst for Pirate broadcasts.

Gone for Good

ROGER ANGELL

The photograph shows a perfectly arrested moment of joy. On one side—
the left, as you look at the picture—the catcher is running toward the
camera at full speed, with his upraised arms spread wide. His body is tilting toward the center of the picture, his mask is held in his right hand, his
big glove is still on his left hand, and his mouth is open in a gigantic shout
of pleasure. Over on the right, another player, the pitcher, is just past the
apex of an astonishing leap that has brought his knees up to his chest and
his feet well up off the ground. Both of *his* arms are flung wide, and he,
too, is shouting. His hunched, airborne posture makes him look like a man
who just made a running jump over a sizable object—a kitchen table, say.
By luck, two of the outreaching hands have overlapped exactly in the
middle of the photograph, so that the pitcher's bare right palm and fingers
are silhouetted against the catcher's glove, and as a result the two men are
linked and seem to be executing a figure in a manic and difficult dance.
There is a further marvel—a touch of pure fortune—in the background,
where a spectator in dark glasses, wearing a dark suit, has risen from his
seat in the grandstand and is lifting his arms in triumph. This, the third
and central Y in the picture, is immobile. It is directly behind the overlap-
ping hand and glove of the dancers, and it binds and recapitulates the lines
of force and the movements and the theme of the work, creating a composition as serene and well ordered as a Giotto. The subject of the picture,
of course, is classical—the celebration of the last out of the seventh game
of the World Series.

This famous photograph (by Rusty Kennedy, of the Associated Press)
does not require captioning for most baseball fans or for almost anyone
within the Greater Pittsburgh area, where it is still prominently featured
in the art collections of several hundred taverns. It may also be seen, in a
much enlarged version, on one wall of the office of Joe L. Brown, the general manager of the Pittsburgh Pirates, in Three Rivers Stadium. The date
of the photograph is October 17, 1971; the place is Memorial Stadium, in
Baltimore. The catcher is Manny Sanguillen, of the Pirates, and his leap-
ing teammate is pitcher Steve Blass, who has just defeated the defending
(and suddenly former) World Champion Baltimore Orioles by a score of 2-
1, giving up four hits.

I am not a Pittsburgher, but looking at this photograph never fails to

From *Once More Around the Park: A Baseball Reader* by Roger Angell (Chicago: Ivan R. Dee,
2001). Reprinted by permission of Roger Angell.

give me pleasure, not just because of its aesthetic qualities but because its high-bounding happiness so perfectly brings back that eventful World Series and that particular gray autumn afternoon in Baltimore and the wonderful and inexpugnable expression of joy that remained on Steve Blass's face after the game ended. His was, to be sure, a famous victory—a close and bitterly fought pitchers' battle against the Orioles' Mike Cuellar, in which the only score for seven innings had been a solo home run by the celebrated Pirate outfielder Roberto Clemente. The Pirates had scored again in the eighth, but the Orioles had responded with a run of their own and had brought the tying run around to third base before Blass shut them off once and for all. The win was the culmination of a stirring uphill fight by the Pirates, who had fallen into difficulties by losing the first two games to the Orioles; Steve Blass had begun their comeback with a wonderfully pitched three-hit, 5-1 victory in the third game. It was an outstanding Series, made memorable above all by the play of Roberto Clemente, who batted .414 over the seven games and fielded his position with extraordinary zeal. He was awarded the sports car as the most valuable player of the Series, but Steve Blass was not far out of the running for the prize. After that last game, Baltimore manager Earl Weaver said, "Clemente was great, all right, but if it hadn't been for Mr. Blass *we* might be popping the corks right now."

I remember the vivid contrast in styles between the two stars in the noisy, floodlit, champagne-drenched Pirate clubhouse that afternoon. Clemente, at last the recipient of the kind of national attention he had always deserved but had rarely been given for his years of brilliant play, remained erect and removed, regarding the swarming photographers with a haughty, incandescent pride. Blass was a less obvious hero—a competent but far from overpowering right-hander who had won fifteen games for the Pirates that year, with a most respectable 2.85 earned-run average, but who had absorbed a terrible pounding by the San Francisco Giants in the two games he pitched in the National League playoffs, just before the Series. His two Series victories, by contrast, were momentous by any standard—and, indeed, were among the very best pitching performances of his entire seven years in the majors. Blass, in any case, celebrated the Pirates' championship more exuberantly than Clemente, exchanging hugs and shouts with his teammates, alternately smoking a cigar and swigging from a champagne bottle. Later I saw him in front of his locker with his arm around his father, Bob Blass, a plumber from Falls Village, Connecticut, who had once been a semipro pitcher; the two Blasses, I saw, were wearing identical delighted, nonstop smiles.

Near the end of an article I wrote about that 1971 World Series, I mentioned watching Steve Blass in batting practice just before the all-important seventh game and suddenly noticing that, in spite of his impending responsibilities, he was amusing himself with a comical parody of Clemente at the plate: "Blass . . . then arched his back, cricked his neck oddly, rolled his head a few times, took up a stance in the back corner of the batter's box, with his bat held high, and glared out at the pitcher imperiously—Clemente, to the life." I had never seen such a spirited gesture in a serious baseball setting, and since then I have come to realize that Steve Blass's informality and boyish play constituted an essential private style, as original and as significant as Clemente's eaglelike pride, and that each of them was merely responding in his own way to the challenges of an extremely difficult public profession. Which of the two, I keep wondering, was happier that afternoon about the Pirates' championship and his part in it? Roberto Clemente of course, is dead; he was killed on December 31, 1972, in Puerto Rico, in the crash of a plane he had chartered to carry emergency relief supplies to the victims of an earthquake in Nicaragua. Steve Blass, who is now thirty-three, is out of baseball, having been recently driven into retirement by two years of pitching wildness—a sudden, near-total inability to throw strikes. No one, including Blass himself, can cure or explain it.

The summer of 1972, the year after his splendid World Series, was in most respects the best season that Steve Blass ever had. He won nineteen games for the Pirates and lost only eight, posting an earned-run average of 2.48— sixth-best in the National League—and being selected for the NL All-Star team. What pleased him most that year was his consistency. He went the full distance in eleven of the thirty-two games he started, and averaged better than seven and a half innings per start—not dazzling figures (Steve Carlton, of the Phillies, had thirty complete games that year, and Bob Gibson, of the Cards, had twenty-three) but satisfying ones for a man who had once had inordinate difficulty in finishing games. Blass, it should be understood, was not the same kind of pitcher as a Carlton or a Gibson. He was never a blazer. When standing on the mound, he somehow looked more like a journeyman pitcher left over from the nineteen thirties or forties than like one of the hulking, hairy young flingers of today. (He is six feet tall, and weighs about one hundred and eighty pounds.) Watching him work, you sometimes wondered how he was getting all those batters out. The word on him among the other clubs in his league was something like: Good but not overpowering stuff, excellent slider, good curve, good change-up curve. A pattern pitcher, whose slider works because of its location. No control problems. Intelligent, knows how to win.

I'm not certain that I saw Blass work in the regular season of 1972, but I did see him pitch the opening game of the National League playoffs that fall against the Cincinnati Reds, in Pittsburgh. After giving up a home run to the Reds' second batter of the day, Joe Morgan, which was hit off a first-pitch fastball, Blass readjusted his plans and went mostly to a big, slow curve, causing the Reds to hit innumerable rainmaking outfield flies, and won by 5-1. I can still recall how Blass looked that afternoon—his characteristic feet-together stance at the outermost, first-base edge of the pitching rubber, and then the pitch, delivered with a swastikalike scattering of arms and legs and a final lurch to the left—and I also remember how I kept thinking that at any moment the sluggers of the Big Red Machine would stop overstriding and overswinging against such unintimidating deliveries and drive Blass to cover. But it never happened—Blass saw to it that it didn't. Then, in the fifth and deciding game, he returned and threw seven and one-third more innings of thoughtful and precise patterns, allowing only four hits, and departed with his team ahead by 3-2—a pennant-winning outing, except for the fact that the Pirate bullpen gave up the ghost in the bottom of the ninth, when a homer, two singles, and a wild pitch entitled the Reds to meet the Oakland A's in the 1972 World Series. It was a horrendous disappointment for the Pittsburgh Pirates and their fans, for which no blame at all could be attached to Blass.

My next view of Steve Blass on a baseball diamond came on a cool afternoon at the end of April this year. The game—the White Sox vs. the Orioles—was a close, 3-1 affair, in which the winning White Sox pitcher, John McKenzie, struck out seventeen batters in six innings. A lot of the Sox struck out, too, and a lot of players on both teams walked—more than I could count, in fact. The big hit of the game was a triple to left center by the White Sox catcher, David Blass, who is ten years old. His eight-year-old brother, Chris, played second, and their father, Steve Blass, in old green slacks and a green T-shirt, coached at third. This was a late-afternoon date in the Upper St. Clair (Pennsylvania) Recreation League schedule, played between the White Sox and the Orioles on a field behind the Dwight D. Eisenhower Elementary School—Little League baseball, but at a junior and highly informal level. The low, *low* minors. Most of the action, or inaction, took place around home plate, since there was not much bat-on-ball contact but there was a shrill nonstop piping of encouragement from the fielders, and disappointed batters were complimented on their overswings by a small, chilly assemblage of mothers, coaches, and dads. When Chris Blass went down swinging in the fourth, his father came over and said, "The sinker down and away is *tough*." Steve Blass has a longish, lightly freckled face, a tilted nose, and an alert and engaging expression. At this ball game, he looked like any young suburban father who had caught an early train home from the office in order to see his kids in action. He looked much more like a commuter than like a professional athlete.

Blass coached quietly, moving the fielders in or over a few steps, asking the shortstop if he knew how many outs there were, reminding someone to take his hands out of his pockets. "Learning the names of all the kids is the hard part," he said to me. It was his second game of the spring as a White Sox coach, and between innings one of the young outfielders said to him, "Hey, Mr. Blass, how come you're not playing with the Pirates at Three Rivers today?"

"Well," Blass said equably, "I'm not *in* baseball anymore."

"Oh," said the boy.

Twilight and the end of the game approached at about the same speed, and I kept losing track of the count on the batters. Steve Blass, noticing my confusion, explained that, in order to avert a parade of walked batters in these games, any strike thrown by a pitcher was considered to have wiped out the balls he had already delivered to the same batter; a strike on the 3-0 count reconverted things to 0-1. He suddenly laughed. "Why didn't they have that rule in the NL?" he said, "I'd have lasted until I was fifty."

Then it was over. The winning (and undefeated) White Sox and the Orioles exchanged cheers, and Karen Blass, a winning and clearly undefeated mother, came over and introduced me to the winning catcher and the winning second baseman. The Blasses and I walked slowly along together over the thick new grass, toting gloves and helmets and Karen's fold-up lawn chair, and at the parking lot the party divided into two cars—Karen and the boys homeward bound, and Steve Blass and I off to a nearby shopping center to order one large cheese-and-peppers-and-sausage victory pizza, to go.

Blass and I sat in his car at the pizza place, drinking beer and waiting for our order, and he talked about his baseball beginnings. I said I had admired the relaxed, low-key tenor of the game we had just seen, and he told me that his own Little League coach, back in Connecticut—a man named Jerry Fallon—had always seen to it that playing baseball on his club was a pleasure. "On any level, baseball is a tough game if it isn't really fun," Blass said. "I think most progress in baseball comes from enjoying it and then wanting to extend yourself a little, wanting it to become more. There should be a feeling of 'Let's go! Let's keep on with this!'"

He kept on with it, in all seasons and circumstances. The Blasses' place in Falls Village included an old barn with an interestingly angled roof, against which young Steve Blass played hundreds of one-man games (his four brothers and sisters were considerably younger) with a tennis ball. "I had all kinds of games, with different, very complicated ground rules," he said. "I'd throw the ball up, and then I'd be diving into the weeds for pop-ups or running back and calling for the long fly balls and all. I'd always play a full game—a made-up game, with two big-league teams—and I'd write down the line score as I went along, and keep the results. One of the teams always had to be the Indians. I was a *total* Indians fan, completely buggy. In the summer of '54, when they won that record one hundred and eleven games, I managed to find every single Indians box score in the newspapers and clip it, which took some doing up where we lived. I guess Herb Score was my real hero—I actually pitched against him once in Indianapolis, in '63, when he was trying to make a comeback—but I knew the whole team by heart. Not just the stars but all the guys on the bench, like George Strickland and Wally Westlake and Hank Majeski and the backup third baseman, Rudy Regalado. My first big-league autograph was Hank Majeski."

Blass grew up into an athlete—a good sandlot football player, a second-team All-State Class B basketball star, but most of all a pitcher, like his father. ("He was wilder than hell," Blass said. "Once, in a Canaan game, he actually threw a pitch over the backstop.") Steve Blass pitched two no-hitters in his junior year at Housatonic Regional High School, and three more as a senior, but there were so many fine pitchers on the team that he did not get to be a starter until his final year. (One of the stars just behind him was John Lamb, who later pitched for the Pirates; Lamb's older sister, Karen, was a classmate of Steve's, and in time she found herself doubly affiliated with the Pirate mound staff.)

The Pittsburgh organization signed Steve Blass right out of Housatonic High in 1960, and he began moving up through the minors. He and Karen Lamb were married in the fall of 1963, and they went to the Dominican Republic that winter, where Steve played for the Cibaeñas Eagles and began working on a slider. He didn't quite make the big club when training ended in the spring, and was sent down to the Pirates' Triple A club in Columbus, but the call came three weeks later. Blass said, "We got in the car, and I floored it all the way across Ohio. I remember it was raining as we came out of the tunnel in Pittsburgh, and I drove straight to Forbes Field and went in and found the attendant and put my uniform on, at two in the afternoon. There was no *game* there, or anything—I just had to see how it looked."

We had moved along by now to the Blasses' house, a medium-sized brick structure on a hillside in Upper St. Clair, which is a suburb about twelve miles southeast of Pittsburgh. The pizza disappeared rapidly, and then David and Chris went off upstairs to do their homework or watch TV. The Blass family room was trophied and comfortable. On a wall opposite a long sofa there was, among other things, a plaque representing the J. Roy Stockton Award for Outstanding Baseball Achievement, a Dapper Dan Award for meritorious service to Pittsburgh, a shiny metal bat with the engraved signatures of the National League All-Stars of 1972, a 1971 Pittsburgh Pirates World Champions bat, a signed photograph of President Nixon, and a framed, decorated proclamation announcing Steve Blass Day in Falls Village, Connecticut: "Be it known that this twenty-second day of October in the year of our Lord 1971, the citizens of Falls Village do set aside and do honor with pride Steve Blass, the tall skinny kid from Falls Village, who is now the hero of baseball and will be our hero always." It was signed by the town's three selectmen. The biggest picture in the room hung over the sofa—an enlarged color photograph of the Blass family at the Father-and-Sons Day at Three Rivers Stadium in 1971. In the photo, Karen Blass looks extremely pretty in a large straw hat, and all three male Blasses are wearing Pirate uniforms; the boys' uniforms look a little funny, because in their excitement each boy had put on the other's pants. Great picture.

Karen and Steve pointed this out to me, and then they went back to their arrival in the big time on that rainy long-ago first day in Pittsburgh and Steve's insisting on trying on his Pirate uniform, and they leaned back in their chairs and laughed about it again.

"With Steve, everything is right out in the open," Karen said. "Every accomplishment, every stage of the game—you have no idea how much he loved it, how he enjoyed the game."

That year, in his first outing, Blass pitched five scoreless innings in relief against the Braves, facing, among others, Hank Aaron. In his first start, against the Dodgers in Los Angeles, he pitched against Don Drysdale and won, 4-2. "I thought I'd died and gone to Heaven," Blass said to me.

He lit a cigar and blew out a little smoke. "You know, this thing that's happened has been painted so bad, so tragic," he said. "Well, I don't go along with that. I know what I've done in baseball, and I give myself all the credit in the world for it. I'm not bitter about this. I've had the greatest moments a person could ever want. When I was a boy, I used to make up those fictitious games where I was always pitching in the bottom of the ninth in the World Series. Well, I really *did* it. It went on and happened to me. Nobody's ever enjoyed winning a big-league game more than I have. All I've ever wanted to do since I was six years old was to keep on playing baseball. It didn't even have to be major-league ball. I've never been a goal-planner—I've never said I'm going to do this or that. With me, every-thing was just a continuation of what had come before. I think that's why I enjoyed it all so much when it did come along, when the good things did happen."

All this was said with an air of summing up, of finality, but at other times that evening I noticed that it seemed difficult for Blass to talk about his baseball career as a thing of the past; now and then he slipped into the present tense—as if it were still going on. This was understandable, for he was in limbo. The Pirates had finally released him late in March ("outrighted" him, in baseball parlance), near the end of the spring-train-ing season, and he had subsequently decided not to continue his attempts to salvage his pitching form in the minor leagues. Earlier in the week of my visit, he had accepted a promising job with Josten's, Inc., a large jew-elry concern that makes, among other things, World Series rings and high-school graduation rings, and he would go to work for them shortly as a traveling representative in the Pittsburgh area. He was out of baseball for good.

Pitching consistency is probably the ingredient that separates major-league baseball from the lesser levels of the game. A big-league fastball comes in on the batter at about eighty-five or ninety miles an hour, com-pleting its prescribed journey of sixty feet six inches in less than half a sec-ond, and, if it is a strike, generally intersects no more than an inch or two of the seventeen-inch-wide plate, usually near the upper or lower limits of the strike zone; curves and sliders arrive a bit later but with intense ro-tation, and must likewise slice off only a thin piece of the black if they are to be effective. Sustaining this kind of control over a stretch of, say, one hundred and thirty pitches in a seven- or eight-inning appearance places such excruciating demands on a hurler's body and psyche that even the most successful pitchers regularly have games when they simply can't get the job done. Their fastball comes in high, their curves hang, the rest of their prime weapons desert them. The pitcher is knocked about, often by an inferior rival team, and leaves within a few innings; asked about it later, he shrugs and says, "I didn't have it today." He seems unsurprised. Pitching, it sometimes appears, is too hard for *anyone*. Occasionally, the poor performance is repeated, then extended. The pitcher goes into a slump. He sulks or rages, according to his nature; he asks for help; he works long hours on his motion. Still he cannot win. He worries about his arm, which almost always hurts to some degree. Has it gone dead? He worries about his stuff. Has he lost his velocity? He wonders whether he will ever win again or whether he will now join the long, long list—the list that awaits him, almost surely in the end—of suddenly slow, suddenly sore-armed pitchers who have abruptly vanished from the big time, down the drain to oblivion. Then, unexpectedly, the slump ends—most of the time, that is—and he is back where he was: a winning pitcher. There is rarely an explanation for this, whether the slump has lasted for two games or a dozen, and managers and coaches, when pressed for one, will usually mutter that "pitching is a delicate thing," or—as if it explained anything—"he got back in the groove."

In spite of such hovering and inexplicable hazards, every big-league pitcher knows exactly what is expected of him. As with the other aspects of the game, statistics define his work and—day by day, inning by inning—whether he is getting it done. Thus, it may be posited as a rule that a major-league hurler who gives up an average of just over three and a half runs per game is about at the middle of his profession—an average pitcher. (Last year, the National League and the American League both wound up with a per-game earned-run average of 3.62.) At contract-renewal time, earned-run averages below 3.30 are invariably mentioned by pitchers; an ERA close to or above the 4.00 level will always be brought up by management. The select levels of pitching proficiency (and salary) begin below the 3.00 line; in fact, an ERA of less than 3.00 certifies true quality in almost exactly the same fashion as an over-.300 batting average for hitters. Last year, both leagues had ten pitchers who finished below 3.00, led by Buzz Capra's NL mark of 2.28 and Catfish Hunter's 2.49 in the AL. The best season-long earned-run average of the modern baseball era was Bob Gibson's 1.12 mark, set in 1968.

Strikeouts are of no particular use in defining pitching effectiveness, since there are other, less vivid ways of retiring batters, but bases on balls matter. To put it in simple terms, a good, middling pitcher should not surrender more than three or four walks per game—unless he is also striking out batters in considerable clusters. Last year, Ferguson Jenkins, of the Texas Rangers, gave up only 45 walks in 328 innings pitched, or an average of 1.19 per game. Nolan Ryan, of the Angels, walked 202 men in 333 innings, or 5.4 per game; however, he helped himself considerably by fanning 367, or just under ten men per game. The fastball is a great healer.

At the beginning of the 1973 season, Steve Blass had a lifetime earned-run average of 3.25 and was averaging 1.9 walks per game. He was, in short, an extremely successful and useful big-league pitcher, and was understandably enjoying his work. Early that season, however, baseball suddenly stopped being fun for him. He pitched well in spring training in Bradenton, which was unusual, for he has always been a very slow starter.

He pitched on opening day, against the Cards, but threw poorly and was relieved, although the Pirates eventually won the game. For a time, his performance was borderline, but his few wins were in sloppy, high-scoring contests, and his bad outings were marked by streaks of uncharacteristic wildness and ineffectuality. On April 22, against the Cubs, he gave up a walk, two singles, a homer, and a double in the first inning, sailed through the second inning, and then walked a man and hit two batsmen in the third. He won a complete game against the Padres, but in his next two appearances, against the Dodgers and the Expos, he survived for barely half the distance; in the Expos game, he threw three scoreless innings, and then suddenly gave up two singles, a double, and two walks. By early June, his record was three wins and three losses, but his earned-run average suggested that his difficulties were serious. Bill Virdon, the Pirate manager, was patient and told Blass to take all the time he needed to find himself; he reminded Blass that once—in 1970—he had had an early record of two and eight but had then come back to finish the season with a mark of ten and twelve.

What was mystifying about the whole thing was that Blass still had his stuff, especially when he warmed up or threw on the sidelines. He was in great physical shape, as usual, and his arm felt fine; in his entire pitching career, Blass never experienced a sore arm. Virdon remained calm, although he was clearly puzzled. Some pitching mechanics were discussed and worked on: Blass was sometimes dropping his elbow as he threw; often he seemed to be hurrying his motion, so that his arm was not in synchronization with his body; perhaps he had exaggerated his peculiar swoop toward first base and thus was losing his power. These are routine pitching mistakes, which almost all pitchers are guilty of from time to time, and Blass worked on them assiduously. He started again against the Braves on June 11, in Atlanta; after three and one-third innings he was gone, having given up seven singles, a home run, two walks, and a total of five runs. Virdon and Blass agreed that a spell in the bullpen seemed called for; at least he could work on his problems there every day.

Two days later, the roof fell in. The team was still in Atlanta, and Virdon called Blass into the game in the fifth inning, with the Pirates trailing by 8-3. Blass walked the first two men he faced, and gave up a stolen base and a wild pitch and a run-scoring single before retiring the side. In the sixth, Blass walked Darrell Evans. He walked Mike Lum, throwing one pitch behind him in the process, which allowed Evans to move down to second. Dusty Baker singled, driving in a run. Ralph Garr grounded out. Davey Johnson singled, scoring another run. Marty Perez walked. Pitcher

Ron Reed singled, driving in two more runs, and was wild-pitched to second. Johnny Oates walked. Frank Tepedino singled, driving in two runs, and Steve Blass was finally relieved. His totals for the one and one-third innings were seven runs, five hits, six bases on balls, and three wild pitches.

"It was the worst experience of my baseball life." Blass told me. "I don't think I'll ever forget it. I was embarrassed and disgusted. I was totally unnerved. You can't imagine the feeling that you suddenly have no *idea* what you're doing out there, performing that way as a major-league pitcher. It was kind of scary."

None of Blass's appearances during the rest of the '73 season were as dreadful as the Atlanta game, but none of them were truly successful. On August 1, he started against the Mets and Tom Seaver at Shea Stadium and gave up three runs and five walks in one and two-thirds innings. A little later, Virdon gave him a start in the Hall of Fame game at Cooperstown; this is a meaningless annual exhibition, played that year between the Pirates and the Texas Rangers, but Blass was as wild as ever and had to be relieved after two and one-third innings. After that, Bill Virdon announced that Blass would probably not start another game; the Pirates were in a pennant race, and the time for patience had run out.

Blass retired to the bullpen and worked on fundamentals. He threw a lot, once pitching a phantom nine-inning game while his catcher, Dave Ricketts, called the balls and strikes. At another point, he decided to throw every single day in the bullpen, to see if he could recapture his groove. "All it did was to get me very, very tired," Blass told me. He knew that Virdon was not going to use him, but whenever the Pirates fell behind in a game, he felt jumpy about the possibility of being called upon. "I knew I wasn't capable of going in there," he said. "I was afraid of embarrassing myself again, and letting down the club."

On September 6, the Pirate front office announced that Danny Murtaugh, who had served two previous terms as the Pirates' manager, was replacing Bill Virdon at the helm; the Pirates were caught up in a close, four-team division race, and it was felt that Murtaugh's experience might bring them home. One of Murtaugh's first acts was to announce that Steve Blass would be given a start. The game he picked was against the Cubs, in Chicago, on September 11. Blass, who had not pitched in six weeks, was extremely anxious about this test; he walked the streets of Chicago on the night before the game, and could not get to sleep until after five in the morning. The game went well for him. The Cubs won, 2-0, but Steve gave up only two hits and one earned run in the five innings he worked. He pitched with extreme care, throwing mostly sliders. He had another pretty good outing against the Cardinals, for no decision, and then started against the Mets, in New York, on September 21, but got only two men out, giving up four instant runs on a walk and four hits. The Mets won, 10-2, dropping the Pirates out of first place, but Blass, although unhappy about his showing, found some hope in the fact that he had at least been able to get the ball over the plate. "At that point," he said, "I was looking for even a little bit of success—one good inning, a few real fastballs, anything to hold on to that might halt my negative momentum. I wanted to feel I had at last got things turned around and facing in the right direction."

The Mets game was his last of the year. His statistics for the 1973 season were three wins and nine defeats, and an earned-run average of 9.81. That figure and his record of eighty-four walks in eighty-nine innings pitched were the worst in the National League.

I went to another ball game with Steve Blass on the night after the Little League affair—this time at Three Rivers Stadium, where the Pirates were meeting the Cardinals. We sat behind home plate, down near the screen, and during the first few innings a lot of young fans came clustering down the aisle to get Steve's autograph. People in the sections near us kept calling and waving to him. "Everybody has been great to me, all through this thing," Blass said. "I don't think there are too many here who are thinking, 'Look, there's the wild man.' I've had hundreds and hundreds of letters—I don't know how many—and not one of them was down on me."

In the game, Bob Gibson pitched against the Pirates' Jerry Reuss. When Ted Simmons stood in for the visitors, Blass said, "He's always hit me pretty good. He's really developed as a hitter." Then there was an error by Richie Hebner, at third, on a grounder hit by Kent Reitz, and Blass said, "Did you notice the batter take that big swing and then hit it off his hands? It was the swing that put Richie back on his heels like that." Later on, Richie Zisk hit a homer off Gibson, on a three-and-two count, and Blass murmured, "The high slider is one of *the* hittable pitches when it isn't just right. I should know."

The game rushed along, as games always do when Gibson is pitching. "You know," Blass said, "before we faced him we'd always have a team meeting and we'd say, 'Stay out of the batter's box, clean your spikes—anything to make him slow up.' But it never lasted more than an inning or two. He makes you play his game."

A little later, however, Willie Stargell hit a homer, and then Manny

Sanguillen drove in another run with a double off the left-field wall ("Get out of here!" Steve said while the ball was in flight), and it was clear that this was not to be a Gibson night. Blass was enjoying himself, and it seemed to me that the familiarities and surprises of the game had restored something in him. At one point, he leaned forward a little and peered into the Pirates dugout and murmured, "Is Dock Ellis over in his regular corner there?'" but for the most part he kept his eyes on the field. I tried to imagine what it felt like for him not to be down in the dugout.

I had talked that day to a number of Blass's old teammates, and all of them had mentioned his cheerfulness and his jokes, and what they had meant to the team over the years. "Steve's humor in the clubhouse was unmatched," relief pitcher Dave Giusti said. "He was a terrific mimic. Perfect. He could do Robert Kennedy. He could do Manny Sanguillen. He could do Roberto Clemente—not just the way he moved but the way he talked. Clemente loved it. He could do rat sounds—the noise a rat makes running. Lots of other stuff. It all made for looseness and togetherness. Because of Steve, the clubhouse was never completely silent, even after a loss." Another Pirate said, "Steve was about ninety percent of the good feeling on this club. He was always up, always agitating. If a player made a mistake, Steve knew how to say something about it that would let the guy know it was OK. Especially the young guys—he really understood them, and they put their confidence in him because of that. He picked us all up. Of course, there was a hell of a lot less of that from him in the last couple of years. We sure missed it."

For the final three innings of the game, Blass and I moved upstairs to general manager Joe Brown's box. Steve was startled by the unfamiliar view. "Hey, you can really see how it works from here, can't you?" he said. "Down there, you've got to look at it all in pieces. No wonder it's so hard to play this game right."

In the Pirates' seventh, Bill Robinson pinch-hit for Ed Kirkpatrick, and Blass said, "Well, *that* still makes me wince a little." It was a moment or two before I realized that Robinson was wearing Blass's old uniform number. Robinson fanned, and Blass said, "Same old twenty-eight."

The Pirates won easily, 5-0, with Jerry Reuss going all the way for the shutout, and just before the end Steve said, "I always had trouble sleeping after pitching a real good game. And if we were home, I'd get up about seven in the morning, before anybody else was up, and go downstairs and make myself a cup of coffee, and then I'd get the newspaper and open it to the sports section and just—just soak it all in."

We thanked Joe Brown and said good night, and as we went down in the elevator I asked Steve Blass if he wanted to stop off in the clubhouse for a minute and see his old friends. "Oh, no," he said. "No, I couldn't do that."

After the end of the 1973 season, Blass joined the Pirates' team in the Florida Instructional League (an autumn institution that exists mostly to permit the clubs to look over their prime minor-league prospects), where he worked intensively with a longtime pitching coach, Don Osborn, and appeared in three games. He came home feeling a little hopeful (he was almost living on such minimal nourishments), but when he forced himself to think about it he had to admit that he had been too tense to throw the fastball much, even against rookies. Then, in late February, 1974, Blass reported to Bradenton with the other Pirate pitchers and catchers. "We have a custom in the early spring that calls for all the pitchers to throw five minutes of batting practice every day," he told me. "This is before the rest of the squad arrives, you understand, so you're just pitching to the other pitchers. Well, the day before that first workout I woke up at four-thirty in the morning. I was so worried that I couldn't get back to sleep— and all this was just over going out and throwing to *pitchers*. I don't re-member what happened that first day, but I went out there very tense and anxious every time. As you can imagine, there's very little good work or improvement you can do under those circumstances."

The training period made it clear that nothing had altered with him (he walked twenty-five men in fourteen innings in exhibition play), and when the club went north he was left in Bradenton for further work. He joined the team in Chicago on April 16, and entered a game against the Cubs the next afternoon, taking over in the fourth inning, with the Pirates down by 10-4. He pitched five innings, and gave up eight runs (three of them unearned), five hits and seven bases on balls. The Cubs batted around against him in the first inning he pitched, and in the sixth he gave up back-to-back home runs. His statistics for the game, including an ERA of 9.00, were also his major league figures for the year, because in late April the Pirates sent him down to the Charleston (West Virginia) Charlies, their farm team in the Class AAA International League. Blass did not ar-gue about the decision; in fact, as a veteran of more than eight years' ser-vice in the majors, he had to agree to the demotion before the parent club could send him down. He felt that the Pirates and Joe Brown had been extraordinarily patient and sympathetic in dealing with a baffling and ap-parently irremediable problem. They had also been generous, refusing to cut his salary by the full twenty percent permissible in extending a major-league contract. (His pay, which had been ninety thousand dollars in 1973, was cut to seventy-five thousand for the next season, and then to sixty-three thousand this spring.) In any case, Blass wanted to go. He needed continuous game experience if he was ever to break out of it, and he knew he no longer belonged with a big-league club.

The distance between the minors and the majors, always measurable in light-years, is probably greater today than ever before, and for a man making the leap in the wrong direction the feeling must be sickening. Blass tries to pass off the experience lightly (he is apparently incapable of self-pity), but one can guess what must have been required of him to summon up even a scrap of the kind of hope and aggressive self-confidence that are prerequisites, at every level, of a successful athletic performance. He and Karen rented an apartment in Charleston, and the whole family moved down when the school year ended; David and Chris enjoyed the informal atmosphere around the ball park, where they were permitted to shag flies in batting practice. "It wasn't so bad," Blass told me.

But it was. The manager of the Charlies, Steve Demeter, put Blass in the regular starting rotation, but he fared no better against minor-leaguers than he had in the big time. In a very brief time, his earned-run average and his bases-on-balls record were the worst in the league. Blass got along well with his teammates, but there were other problems. The mystery of Steve Blass's decline was old stuff by now in most big-league-city newspapers, but as soon as he was sent down, there was a fresh wave of attention from the national press and the networks; and sportswriters for newspapers in Memphis and Rochester and Richmond and the other International cities looked on his arrival in town as a God-given feature story. Invariably, they asked him how much money he was earning as a player; then they asked if he thought he was worth it.

The Charlies did a lot of traveling by bus. One day, the team made an eight-hour trip from Charleston to Toledo, where they played a night game. At eleven that same night, they reboarded the bus and drove to Pawtucket, Rhode Island, for their next date, arriving at about nine in the morning. Blass had started the game in Toledo, and he was so disgusted with his performance that he got back on the bus without having showered or taken off his uniform. "We'd stop at an all-night restaurant every now and then, and I'd walk in with a two-day beard and my old Charleston Charlies uniform on, looking like go-to-hell," Blass said. "It was pretty funny to see people looking at me. I had some books along, and we had plenty of wine and beer on the bus, so the time went by somehow." He paused and then shook his head. "*God*, that was an awful trip," he said.

By early August, Blass's record with Charleston was two and nine, and 9.74. He had had enough. With Joe Brown's permission, he left the Charlies and flew West to consult Dr. Bill Harrison, of Davis, California. Dr.

Harrison is an optometrist who has helped develop a system of "optome-therapy," designed to encourage athletes to concentrate on the immediate physical task at hand—hitting a ball, throwing a strike—by visualizing the act in advance; his firm was once retained by the Kansas City Royals base-ball team, and his patients have included a number of professional golfers and football players. Blass spent four days with him, and then rejoined the Pirates, this time as a batting-practice pitcher. He says now that he was very interested in Dr. Harrison's theories but that they just didn't seem to help him much.

In truth, nothing helped. Blass knew that his case was desperate. He was almost alone now with his problem—a baseball castaway—and he had reached the point where he was willing to try practically anything. Under the guidance of pitching coach Don Osborn, he attempted some unusual experiments. He tried pitching from the outfield, with the sweep-ing motion of a fielder making a long peg. He tried pitching while kneel-ing on the mound. He tried pitching with his left foot tucked up behind his right knee until the last possible second of his delivery. Slow-motion films of his delivery were studied and compared with films taken during some of his best games of the past; much of his motion, it was noticed, seemed extraneous, but he had thrown exactly the same way at his peak. Blass went back and corrected minute details, to no avail.

The frustrating, bewildering part of it all was that while working alone with a catcher Blass continued to throw as well as he ever had; his fastball was alive, and his slider and curve shaved the corners of the plate. But the moment a batter stood in against him he became a different pitcher, espe-cially when throwing a fastball—a pitcher apparently afraid of seriously injuring somebody. As a result, he was of very little use to the Pirates even in batting practice.

Don Osborn, a gentle man in his mid-sixties, says, "Steve's problem was mental. He had mechanical difficulties, with some underlying mental cause. I don't think anybody will ever understand his decline. We tried everything—I didn't know anything else to do. I feel real bad about it. Steve had a lot of guts to stay out there as long as he did. You know, old men don't dream much, but just the other night I had this dream that Steve Blass was all over his troubles and could pitch again. I said, 'He's ready, we can use him!' Funny . . ."

It was probably at this time that Blass consulted a psychiatrist. He does not talk about it—in part out of a natural reticence but also because the Pirate front office, in an effort to protect his privacy, turned away inquir-ies into this area by Pittsburgh writers and persistently refused to com-ment on whether any such therapy was undertaken. It is clear, however, that Blass does not believe he gained any profound insights into possible unconscious causes of his difficulties. Earlier in the same summer, he also experimented briefly with transcendental meditation. He entered the program at the suggestion of Joe Brown, who also enrolled Dave Giusti, Willie Stargell, pitcher Bruce Kison, and himself in the group. Blass repeated mantras and meditated twice a day for about two months; he found that it relaxed him, but it did not seem to have much application to his pitching. Innumerable other remedies were proposed by friends and strangers. Like anyone in hard straits, he was deluged with unsolicited therapies, overnight cures, naturopathies, exorcisms, theologies, and amulets, many of which arrived by mail. Blass refuses to make jokes about these nostrums. "Anyone who takes the trouble to write a man who is suffering deserves to be thanked," he told me.

Most painful of all, perhaps, was the fact that the men who most sympathized with his incurable professional difficulties were least able to help. The Pirates were again engaged in a close and exhausting pennant race fought out over the last six weeks of the season; they moved into first place for good only two days before the end, won their half-pennant, and then were eliminated by the Dodgers in a four-game championship play-off. Steve Blass was with the team through this stretch, but he took no part in the campaign, and by now he was almost silent in the clubhouse. He had become an extra wheel. "It must have been hell for him," Dave Giusti says. "I mean *real* hell. I never could have stood it."

When Blass is asked about this last summer of his baseball career, he will only say that it was "kind of a difficult time" or "not the most fun I've had." In extended conversations about himself, he often gives an impression of an armored blandness that suggests a failure of emotion; this apparent insensitivity about himself contrasts almost shockingly with his subtle concern for the feelings of his teammates and his friends and his family, and even of strangers. "My overriding philosophy is to have a regard for others," he once told me. "I don't want to put myself over other people." He takes pride in the fact that his outward, day-to-day demeanor altered very little through his long ordeal. "A person lives on," he said more than once, smiling. "The sun will come up tomorrow." Most of all, perhaps, he sustained his self-regard by not taking out his terrible frustrations on Karen and the boys. "A ballplayer learns very early that he can't bring the game home with him every night," he said once. "Especially when there are young people growing up there. I'm real proud of the fact that this thing hasn't bothered us at home. David and Chris have come through it all in fine shape. I think Karen and I are closer than ever because of this."

Karen once said to me, "Day to day, he hasn't changed. Just the other morning, he was out working on the lawn, and a couple of the neighbors' children came over to see him. Young kids—maybe three or four years old. Then I looked out a few minutes later, and there was whole bunch of them yelling and rolling around on the grass with him, like puppies. He's always been that way. Steve has worked at being a man and being a father and a husband. It's something he has always felt very strongly about, and I have to give him all the credit in the world. Sometimes I think I got to hate the frustration and pain of this more than he did. He always found something to hold on to—a couple of good pitches that day, some little thing he had noticed. But I couldn't always share that, and I didn't have his ability to keep things under control."

I asked if maintaining this superhuman calm might not have damaged Steve in some way, or even added to his problems.

"I don't know," she said. "Sometimes in the evening—once in a great while—we'd be sitting together, and we'd have a couple of drinks and he would relax enough to start to talk. He would tell me about it, and get angry and hurt. Then he'd let it come out, and yell and scream and pound on things. And I felt that even this might not be enough for him. He would never do such a thing outside. Never." She paused, and then she said, "I think he directed his anger toward making the situation livable here at home. I've had my own ideas about Steve's pitching, about the mystery, but they haven't made much difference. You can't force your ideas on somebody, especially when he is doing what he thinks he has to do. Steve's a very private person."

Steve Blass stayed home last winter. He tried not to think much about baseball, and he didn't work on his pitching. He and Karen had agreed that the family would go back to Bradenton for spring training, and that he would give it one more try. One day in January, he went over to the field house at the University of Pittsburgh and joined some other Pirates there for a workout. He threw well. Tony Bartirome, the Pirate trainer, who is a close friend of Steve's thought he was pitching as well as he ever had. He told Joe Brown that Steve's problems might be over. When spring training came, however, nothing had altered. Blass threw adequately in brief streaks, but very badly against most batters. He hit Willie Stargell and Manny Sanguillen in batting practice; both players told him to forget it. They urged him to cut loose with the fastball.

Joe Brown had told Blass that the end of the line might be approaching. Blass agreed. The Pirate organization had been extraordinarily patient, but it was, after all, in the business of baseball.

On March 24, Steve Blass started the second game of a doubleheader against the White Sox at Bradenton. For three innings, he escaped serious difficulty. He gave up two runs in the second, but he seemed to throw without much tension, and he even struck out Bill Melton, the Chicago third baseman, with a fastball. Like the other Pirates, Dave Giusti was watching with apprehensive interest. "I really thought he was on his way," he told me. "I was encouraged. Then, in the fourth, there were a couple of bases on balls and maybe a bad call by the ump on a close pitch, and suddenly there was a complete reversal. He was a different man out there."

Blass walked eight men in the fourth inning and gave up eight runs. He threw fifty-one pitches, but only seventeen of them were strikes. Some of his pitches were close to the strike zone, but most were not. He worked the count to 3-2 on Carlos May, and then threw the next pitch behind him. The booing from the fans, at first scattered and uncomfortable, grew louder. Danny Murtaugh waited, but Blass could not get the third out. Finally, Murtaugh came out very slowly to the mound and told Blass that he was taking him out of the game; Dave Giusti came in to relieve his old roommate. Murtaugh, a peaceable man, then charged the home-plate umpire and cursed him for the bad call, and was thrown out of the game. Play resumed. Blass put on his warm-up jacket and trotted to the outfield to run his wind sprints. Roland Hemond, the general manager of the White Sox, was at Bradenton that day, and he said, "It was the most heartbreaking thing I have ever seen in baseball."

Three days later, the Pirates held a press conference to announce that they had requested waivers from the other National League clubs, with the purpose of giving Blass his unconditional release. Blass flew out to California to see Dr. Bill Harrison once more, and also to visit a hypnotist, Arthur Ellen, who has worked with several major-league players, and has apparently helped some of them, including Dodger pitcher Don Sutton, remarkably. Blass made the trip mostly because he had promised Maury Wills, who is now a base-running consultant to several teams, that he would not quit the game until he had seen Mr. Ellen.

Blass then returned to Bradenton and worked for several days with the Pirates' minor-league pitching coach, Larry Sherry, on some pitching mechanics. He made brief appearances in two games against Pirate farmhands, and threw well. He struck out some players with his fastball. After the second game, he showered and got into his Volkswagen and started north to join his family, who had returned to Pittsburgh. It was a good trip, because it gave him time to sort things out, and somewhere along the way he decided to give it up. The six-day waiver period had expired, and none of the other clubs had claimed him. He was encouraged about his pitching, but he had been encouraged before. This time, the fastball had been much better, and at least he could hold on to that; maybe the problem had been mechanical all along. If he came back now, however, it would have to be at the minor-league level, and even if he made it back to the majors, he could expect only three or four more years before his effectiveness would decline because of age and he would have to start thinking about retirement. At least *that* problem could be solved now. He didn't want to subject Karen to more of the struggle. It was time to get out.

Of all the mysteries that surround the Steve Blass story, perhaps the most mysterious is the fact that his collapse is unique. There is no other player in recent baseball history—at least none with Blass's record and credentials—who has lost his form in such a sudden and devastating fashion and been totally unable to recover. The players and coaches and fans I talked to about Steve Blass brought up a few other names, but then they quickly realized that the cases were not really the same. Some of them mentioned Rex Barney, a Dodger fastball pitcher of the nineteen-forties, who quit baseball while still a young man because of his uncontrollable wildness; Barney, however, had only one good year, and it is fair to say he never did have his great stuff under control. Dick Radatz, a very tall relief pitcher with the Red Sox a decade ago, had four good years, and then grew increasingly wild and ineffective. (He is said to have once thrown twenty-seven consecutive balls in a spring-training game.) His decline, however, was partially attributable to his failure to stay in shape. Von McDaniel, a younger brother of Lindy McDaniel, arrived suddenly as a pitcher with the Cardinals, and disappeared just as quickly, but two years' pitching hardly qualifies as a record. There have been hundreds of shiningly promising rookie pitchers and sluggers who, for one reason or another, could not do their thing once they got up to the big time. Blass's story is different. It should also be understood that this was not at all the somewhat commonplace experience of an established and well-paid major-league star who suffers through one or two mediocre seasons. Tom Seaver went through such a slump last summer. But Seaver's problems were only relatively serious (his record for 1974 was 11-11), and were at least partly explicable (he had a sore hip), and he has now returned to form. Blass, once his difficulties commenced, was helpless. Finally, of course, one must accept the possibility that a great many players may have suffered exactly the same sort of falling off as Blass for exactly the same reasons (whatever they may be) but were able to solve the problem and continue their athletic careers. Sudden and terrible batting and pitching slumps are mysterious while they last; the moment they end, they tend to be forgotten.

What happened to Steve Blass? Nobody knows, but some speculation is permissible—indeed, is perhaps demanded of anyone who is even faintly aware of the qualities of the man and the depths of his suffering. Professional sports have a powerful hold on us because they display and glorify remarkable physical capacities, and because the artificial demands of games played for very high rewards produce vivid responses. But sometimes, of course, what is happening on the field seems to speak to something deeper within us; we stop cheering and look on in uneasy silence, for the man out there is no longer just another great athlete, an idealized hero, but only a man—only ourself. We are no longer at a game. The enormous alterations of professional sport in the past three decades, especially the prodigious inflation of franchises and salaries, have made it evident even to the most thoughtless fan that the play he has come to see is serious indeed, and that the heart of the game is not physical but financial. Sport is no longer a release from the harsh everyday American business world but its continuation and apotheosis. Those of us (fans and players alike) who return to the ball park in the belief that the game and the rules are unchanged—merely a continuation of what we have known and loved in the past—are deluding ourselves, perhaps foolishly, perhaps tragically.

Blass once told me that there were "at least seventeen" theories about the reason for his failure. A few of them are bromides: He was too nice a guy. He became smug and was no longer hungry. He lost the will to win. His pitching motion, so jittery and unclassical, at last let him down for good. His eyesight went bad. (Blass is myopic, and wears glasses while watching television and driving. He has never worn glasses when pitching, which meant that Pirate catchers had to flash him signals with hand gestures rather than with finger waggles; however, he saw well enough to win when he was winning, and his vision has not altered in recent years.) The other, more serious theories are sometimes presented alone, sometimes in conjunction with others. Answers here come more gingerly.

He was afraid of injury—afraid of being struck by a line drive.

Blass was injured three times while on the mound. He cracked a thumb while fielding a grounder in 1966. He was struck on the right forearm by a ball hit by Joe Torre in 1970, and spent a month on the disabled list. While trying for his twentieth victory in his last start in 1972, he was hit on the point of the elbow of his pitching arm by a line drive struck by the Mets' John Milner; he had to leave the game, but a few days later he pitched that first playoff game for the Pirates and won it handily. (Blass's brother-in-law, John Lamb, suffered a fractured skull when hit by a line drive in spring training in 1971, and it was more than a year before he recovered, but Blass's real pitching triumphs all came after that.)

He was afraid of injuring someone—hitting a batter with a fastball.

Blass did hit a number of players in his career, of course, but he never caused anyone to go on the disabled list or, for that matter, to miss even one day's work. He told me he did not enjoy brushing back hitters but had done so when it was obviously called for. The only real criticism of Blass I ever heard from his teammates was that he would not always "protect" them by retaliating against enemy hitters after somebody had been knocked down. During his decline, he was plainly unable to throw the fastball effectively to batters—especially to Pirate batters in practice. He says he hated the idea of hitting and possibly sidelining one of his teammates, but he is convinced that this anxiety was the result of his control problems rather than the cause.

He was seriously affected by the death of Roberto Clemente.

There is no doubt but that the sudden taking away of their most famous and vivid star affected all the Pirates, including Steve Blass. He and Clemente had not been particularly close, but Blass was among the members of the team who flew at once to Puerto Rico for the funeral services, where Blass delivered a eulogy in behalf of the club. The departure of a superstar leaves an almost visible empty place on a successful team, and the leaders next in line—who in this case would certainly include Steve Blass—feel the inescapable burden of trying to fill the gap. A Clemente, however, can never be replaced. Blass never pitched well in the majors after Clemente's death. This argument is a difficult one, and is probably impossible to resolve. There are Oedipal elements here, of course, that are attractive to those who incline in such a direction.

He fell into a slump, which led to an irreparable loss of confidence.

This is circular, and perhaps more a description of symptoms than of the disability itself. However, it is a fact that a professional athlete—and most especially a baseball player—faces a much more difficult task in attempting to regain lost form than an ailing businessman, say, or even a troubled artist; no matter how painful his case has been, the good will of his associates or the vagaries of critical judgment matter not at all when he tries to return. All that matters is his performance, which will be measured, with utter coldness, by the stats. This is one reason that athletes are paid so well, and one reason that fear of failure—the unspeakable "choking"—is their deepest and most private anxiety. Steve Blass passed over my questions about whether he had ever felt this kind of fear when on the mound. "I don't think pitchers, by their nature, allow themselves to think that way," he said. "To be successful, you turn that kind of thought away." On the other hand, he often said that two or three successive well-pitched games probably would have been all he needed to dissipate the severe tension that affected his performances once things began to go badly for him. They never came.

The remaining pieces of evidence (if, indeed, they have any part in the mystery) have been recounted here. Blass is a modest man, both in temperament and in background, and his success and fame were quite sudden and, to some degree, unexpected. His salary at the beginning of 1971—the year of his two great Series wins—was forty thousand dollars; two years later it was ninety thousand, and there were World Series and playoff checks on top of that. Blass was never thought of as one of the great pitchers of his time, but in the late sixties and early seventies he was probably the most consistent starter on the Pirate staff; it was, in fact, a staff without stars. On many other teams, he would have been no more than the second- or third-best starter, and his responsibilities, real and imagined, would have been less acute.

I took some of these hard questions to Blass's colleagues. Danny Murtaugh and Bill Virdon (who is now the Yankees' pilot) both expressed their admiration for Blass but said they had no idea what had happened to him. They seemed a bit brusque about it, but then I realized, of course, that ballplayers are forever disappearing from big-league dugouts; the manager's concern is with those who remain—with today's lineup. "I don't know the answer," Bill Virdon told me in the Yankee clubhouse. "If I did, I'd go get Steve to pitch for me. He sure won a lot of big games for us on the Pirates."

Joe Brown said, "I've tried to keep my distance and not to guess too much about what happened. I'm not a student of pitching and I'm not a psychologist. You can tell a man what to do, but you can't *make* him do it. Steve is an outstanding man, and you hate to quit on him. In this business, you bet on character. Big-league baseball isn't easy, yet you can stand it when things are going your way. But Steve Blass never had a good day in baseball after this thing hit him."

Blass's best friends in baseball are Tony Bartirome, Dave Giusti, and Nelson King (who, along with Bob Prince, was part of the highly regarded radio-and-television team that covered the Pirate games).

Tony Bartirome (*He is forty-three years old, dark-haired, extremely neat in appearance. He was an infielder before he became a trainer, and played one season in the majors—with the Pirates, in 1952*): "Steve is unique physically. He has the arm of a twenty-year-old. Not only did he never have a sore arm but he never had any of the stiffness and pain that most pitchers feel on the day after a game. He was always the same, day after day. You know, it's very important for a trainer to know the state of mind and the feelings of his players. What a player is thinking is about eighty percent of it. The really strange thing is that after this trouble started, Steve never showed any feelings about his pitching. In the old days, he used to get mad at himself after a bad showing, and sometimes he threw things around in the clubhouse. But after this began, when he was taken out of a game he only gave the impression that he was happy to be out of there—relieved that he no longer had to face it that day. Somehow, he didn't show any emotion at *all*. Maybe it was like his never having a sore arm. He never talked in any detail about his different treatments—the psychiatry and all. I think he felt he didn't need any of that—that at any moment he'd be back where he was, the Blass of old, and that it all was up to him to make that happen."

Dave Giusti (*He is one of the great relief pitchers in baseball. He earned a BA and an MA in physical education at Syracuse. He is thirty-five—dark hair, piercing brown eyes, and a quiet manner*): "Steve has the perfect build for a pitcher—lean and strong. He is remarkably open to all kinds of people, but I think he has closed his mind to his inner self. There are central areas you can't infringe on with him. There is no doubt that during the past two years he didn't react to a bad performance the way he used to, and you have to wonder why he couldn't apply his competitiveness to his problem. Karen used to bawl out me and Tony for not being tougher on him, for not doing more. Maybe I should have come right out and said he seemed to have lost his will to fight, but it's hard to shock somebody, to keep bearing in on him. You're afraid to lose a friend, and you want to go easy on him because he is your friend.

"Last year, I went through something like Steve's crisis. The first half of the season, I was atrocious, and I lost all my confidence, especially in my fastball. The fastball is my best pitch, but I'd get right to the top of my delivery and then something would take over, and I'd know even before I released the ball that it wasn't going to be in the strike zone. I began worrying about making big money and not performing. I worried about not contributing to the team. I worried about being traded. I thought it might be the end for me. I didn't know how to solve my problem, but I knew I *had* to solve it. In the end, it was talking to people that did it. I talked to everybody, but mostly to Joe Brown and Danny and my wife. Then, at some point, I turned the corner. But it was talking that did it, and my point is that Steve can't talk to people that way. Or won't.

"Listen, it's tough out there. It's hard. Once you start maintaining a plateau, you've got to be absolutely sure what your goals are."

Nellie King (*A former pitcher with the Pirates. He is friendly and informal, with an attractive smile. He is very tall—six-six. Forty-seven years old*): "Right after that terrible game in Atlanta, Steve told me that it had felt as if the whole world was pressing down on him while he was out there. But then he suddenly shut up about it, and he never talked that way again. He covered it all up. I think there *are* things weighing on him, and I think he may be so angry inside that he's afraid to throw the ball. He's afraid he might kill somebody. It's only nickel psychology, but I think there's a lost kid in Steve. I remembered that after the '71 Series he said, 'I didn't think I was as good as this.' He seemed truly surprised at what he'd done. The child in him is a great thing—we've all loved it—and maybe he was suddenly afraid he was losing it. It was being forced out of him.

"Being good up here is *so* tough—people have no idea. It gets much worse when you have to repeat it: 'We know you're great. Now go and do that again for me.' So much money and so many people depend on you. Pretty soon you're trying so hard that you can't function."

I ventured to repeat Nellie King's guesses about the mystery to Steve Blass and asked him what he thought.

"That's pretty heavy," he said after a moment. "I guess I don't have a tendency to go into things in much depth. I'm a surface reactor. I tend to take things not too seriously. I really think that's one of the things that *helped* me in baseball."

A smile suddenly burst from him.

"There's one possibility nobody has brought up," he said. "I don't think anybody's ever said that maybe I just lost my control. Maybe your control is something that can just go. It's no big thing, but suddenly it's gone." He paused, and then he laughed in a self-deprecating way. "Maybe that's what I'd like to believe," he said.

On my last morning with Steve Blass, we sat in his family room and played an imaginary ball game together—half an inning of baseball. It had occurred to me that in spite of his enforced and now permanent exile from the game, he still possessed a rare body of precise and hard-won pitching information. He still knew most of the hitters in his league, and probably as well as any other pitcher around, he knew what to pitch to them in a given situation. I had always wanted to hear a pitcher say exactly what he would throw next and why, and now I invited Blass to throw against the Cincinnati Reds, the toughest lineup of hitters anywhere. I would call the balls and strikes and hits. I promised he would have no control problems.

He agreed at once. He poured himself another cup of coffee and lit up a Garcia y Vega. He was wearing slacks and a T-shirt and an old sweater (he had a golfing date later that day), and he looked very young.

"OK," he said. "Pete Rose is leading off—right? First of all, I'm going to try to keep him off base if I can, because they have so many tough hitters coming up. They can bury you before you even get started. I'm going to try to throw strikes and not get too fine. I'll start him off with a slider away. He has a tendency to go up the middle and I'll try to keep it a bit away."

Rose, I decided didn't offer. It was ball one.

"Now I'll throw him a sinking fastball, and still try to work him out that way. The sinking fastball tends to tail off just a little."

Rose fouled it into the dirt.

"Well, now we come back with another slider, and I'll try to throw it inside. That's just to set up another slider *outside*."

Rose fouled that one as well.

"We're ahead one and two now—right?" Blass said, "Well, this early in the game I wouldn't try to throw him that slow curve—that big slop off-speed pitch. I'd like to work on that a couple of times first, because it's early and he swings so well. So as long as I'm ahead of him, I'll keep on throwing him sliders—keep going that way."

Rose took another ball, and then grounded out on a medium-speed curveball.

Joe Morgan stood in, and Blass puffed on his cigar and looked at the ceiling.

"Joe Morgan is strictly a fastball hitter, so I want to throw him a *bad* fastball to start him off," he said. "I'll throw it in the dirt to show it to him—get him geared to that kind of speed. Now, after ball one, I'll give him a medium-to-slow curveball and try to get it over the plate—just throw it for a strike."

Morgan took: one and one.

"Now I throw him a *real* slow curveball—a regular rainbow. I've had good luck against him with that sort of stuff."

And so it went. Morgan, I decided, eventually singled to right on a curve in on the handle—a lucky hit—but then Blass retired his next Cincinnati hitter, Dan Driessen, who popped out on a slider. Blass laid off slow pitches here, so Sanguillen would have a chance to throw out Morgan if he was stealing.

Johnny Bench stood in, with two out.

"Morgan won't be stealing, probably," Blass said. "He won't want to take the bat out of Bench's hands." He released another cloud of cigar smoke, thinking hard. "Well, I'll start him out with a good, tough fastball outside. I've got to work very carefully to him, because when he's hot he's capable of hitting it out anytime."

Ball one.

"Well, the slider's only been fair today . . . . I'll give him a slider, but away—off the outside."

Swinging strike. Blass threw another slider, and Bench hit a line single to left, moving Morgan to second. Tony Perez was the next batter.

"Perez is not a good high, hard fastball hitter," Blass said. "I'll begin him with that pitch, because I don't want to get into any more trouble with the slider and have him dunk one in. A letter-high fastball, with good mustard on it."

Perez took a strike.

"Now I'll do it again, until I miss—bust him up and in. He has a tendency to go after that kind of pitch. He's an exceptional offspeed hitter, and will give himself up with men on base—give up a little power to get that run in."

Perez took, for a ball, and then Blass threw him an intentional ball—a very bad slider inside. Perez had shortened up on the bat a little, but he took the pitch. He then fouled off a fastball, and Blass threw him another good fastball, high and inside, and Perez struck out, swinging, to end the inning.

"Pretty good inning," I said, "Way to go." We both laughed.

"Yes, you know that *exact* sequence has happened to Perez many times," Blass said. "He shortens up and then chases the pitch up here."

He was animated. "You know, I can almost *see* that fastball to Perez, and I can see his bat going through it, swinging through the pitch and missing," he said. "That's a good feeling. That's one of the concepts of Dr. Harrison's program, you know—visualization. When I was pitching well, I was doing that very thing. You get so locked in, you see yourself doing things before they happen. That's what people mean when they say you're in the groove. That's what happened in that World Series game, when I kept throwing that big slop curveball to Boog Powell, and it really ruined him. I must have thrown it three out of four pitches to him, and I just *knew* it was going to be there. There's no doubt about it—no information needed. The crowd is there, this is the World Series, and all of a sudden you're locked into something. It's like being plugged into a computer.

It's 'Gimme the ball, *boom*! Click, click, click . . . *shoom*!' It's that good feeling. You're just flowing easy."

◆　◆　◆

BOB PRINCE: HOW SWEET IT WAS

Bob Prince joined Rosey Rowswell in the Pirate radio booth in 1948. After Rowswell's death in 1955, Prince took over the role of lead announcer and stayed in that position until, to the dismay of many fans, he was fired after the 1975 season. In his many years as the voice of the Pirates, he became as colorful as the beloved Rowswell and far more opinionated and controversial.

Bob Smizik's aptly titled "The Prince of Pittsburgh" focuses on the Prince legend and his bittersweet return to the Pirate radio booth just before his death in 1985. A year later, Prince received, posthumously, the Ford C. Frick Award and joined Mel Allen, Red Barber, and other broadcasting greats in the Hall of Fame. Had Prince been at the induction ceremony in Cooperstown, he, no doubt, would have exclaimed, "How sweet it is!"

The Prince of Pittsburgh

BOB SMIZIK

20 YEARS AGO, PIRATES AND KDKA FIRED A LEGEND

It has been 10 years since Bob Prince's death and 20 years since he was unceremoniously—and incredibly—ejected from the Pirates' broadcasting booth. Baseball died a little bit in Pittsburgh on that day. So did Bob Prince.

A generation has grown up since Prince was fired by KDKA and the Pirates after the 1975 season, which means there are thousands, maybe tens of thousands, who know little of this unforgettable man. It's time to take a look back at a true Pittsburgh legend.

The only part of Bob Prince's body bigger than his mouth was his heart. He was a flamboyant, hard-living, mammoth-hearted loudmouth, who loved to have fun and loved to do good. He wore the flashiest, loudest clothes he could find and his taste in cars was about the same.

He was famous for his spending habits. He never met a check he didn't want to pick up. It was not uncommon for him to walk by a table where some friends or acquaintances were having a few drinks, throw down some money and say, "Drink on that for a while."

He was adored by waiters, bartenders, doormen, parking lot attendants and cabbies because there might never have been a bigger tipper. Generally speaking, he didn't believe in carrying $1 bills.

Pirates announcer Steve Blass said, "I just ran into a guy the other day who used to park cars at St. Clair Country Club. He said, 'When everyone else was giving me $2, Prince was giving me $10.'"

Lanny Frattare and Milo Hamilton were brought in to replace Prince and Nellie King after the 1975 season. It would be understating the case to say their job was difficult. But even in ways they might never have expected, replacing Prince was next to impossible.

Frattare said, "My first few years in the National League, it wasn't as though the people in other ballparks and press rooms were rude to me, but there wasn't the same warmth to me that there was for Bob. Then I finally realized that Bob was famous for tipping big bucks. He had an impact that way. He wasn't trying to be financially flamboyant but to make sure that the people who were working around him and not as well paid were taken care of."

Prince enjoyed a good deed as much as a good joke. He drained every drop of life out of his 68 years. He made friends everywhere he went— from the powers of corporate Pittsburgh, to the religious leaders of the area, to the common man in the street. He was a bigger celebrity than most of the baseball players he reported on.

There was no middle ground on Prince the announcer. You either loved his homey style or hated it. No one knew that better than Prince.

Once he exited a dinner table to get ready for a broadcast by saying, "You'll have to excuse me. There are a million people waiting to turn me off."

But Prince the man was hard to dislike. His mission in life often seemed to make friends.

The quintessential Prince story tells a lot about the man.

It was 1965, and Prince already was famous for his willingness to do anything. He had been a swimmer in college and fancied himself quite a man in the water. Someone bet him he couldn't jump from his third-floor window in the Chase Hotel in St. Louis to the pool below. Over the years the story has come to be a jump from his third-floor balcony. But it was no balcony from where he started his famous leap. It was a window sill.

"He had to clear about 12 feet of pavement," Pirates trainer Danny Whelan was quoted as saying in Myron Cope's book, *Broken Cigars*.

"It was strictly a blotter job, believe me."

It wasn't. "I cleared by about four feet," Prince would fondly recall of what was his most famous stunt.

There was more to Prince than the man who was on stage all the time. He was a tireless worker for charities, a strong supporter of the underprivileged. He raised thousands of dollars for the Allegheny Valley School.

He also took under his wing Radio Rich, the orphaned, poorly educated, good-hearted young man who hung around his broadcasting booth. When it became clear to Prince that Rich was a good person who would have trouble supporting himself in life, he became Rich's support. He saw to it Rich could run a tab in certain Downtown restaurants, a tab that Prince picked up. He took care of his medical expenses and paid him a salary to be his statistician. Rich became so central to Prince that he, too, became a bit of a Pittsburgh legend.

Sally O'Leary, the Pirates assistant director of public relations, knew Prince almost as well as anyone. They met more than 30 years ago when O'Leary worked for an advertising agency Downtown and Prince was doing commercials.

"He'd call me if there were problems and we got to know each other," O'Leary recalled. "He got to know about my interest in baseball and he knew that I dearly would love to have the job I have now. He knew I had applied with the Pirates. One day he told me there was an opening and he said, 'I'll see you get the job.' He set up the interview and I got the job."

Doesn't sound like much, just one friend helping another. But there was more.

"He knew I'd have to take a big pay cut to go from the ad agency to the Pirates," O'Leary said. "He said not to worry about it. He made me his baseball secretary and supplemented my income year-round."

If you knew Prince, you knew there was more.

"He sent me on a vacation every year," O'Leary said. "First-class air fare and hotel."

Prince began announcing Pirates games in 1948 as the No. 2 man to Rosey Rowswell. When Rowswell died in 1954, Prince became the No. 1 broadcaster. He had a series of partners, with Jim Woods and Nellie King being with him the longest.

Prince was in his prime in 1964 when Blass joined the Pirates.

"When I came up one of the first persons I related to and felt a need to relate to was Bob Prince. As much as perhaps players, coaches and manager. He was that big of a persona for the Pittsburgh Pirates. It was a compliment for him to ask you for an interview or to have time for you. I see players now when a broadcaster asks for time, it's somewhat of a bother."

If Prince knew that was his place, he didn't often let on it was. He could be humble, particularly around the players and particularly when he was doing his job.

"He always got along with the players very well," Blass said. "He made a point to. He wasn't just going through the motions and being condescending. He had the background and the posture and the stance to say whatever he wanted. If he felt someone was dogging it, he'd say, 'Come on, donkey, when are you going to start playing?'

"That was very unusual for an announcer. You had to have some time in and some stature and credibility before you started doing that."

There has never been another person in public life in Pittsburgh like Prince.

"He was his own man," said Blass, who later worked in a broadcast booth with Prince. "He was full-throttle all the time. He had his own set of standards and practices and he believed in himself. Whatever he wanted to do, he did. He'd walk into a fire hall in Munhall or a board room at U. S. Steel and be equally effective and welcome."

Prince was almost 30 years on the job when the 1975 season ended. He was a Pittsburgh institution. Looking back, it hardly seems possible he was fired, along with King. It hardly seems possible anyone would dare make such a move. But fire him is what KDKA did—with approval from the Pirates.

"It kind of killed him," King said. "He came into people's back porches and kitchens every night of the summer for all those years. There was such a bond with the people. To cut it off like that and not to let him say it had been a great run was just too bad.

"Myron Cope just retired. They let him say goodbye. They did it right. They never gave Bob that chance."

"It devastated him," O'Leary said. "There was no warning. No one expected it. I know he was thrilled by the response of the fans."

There was an outrage in the town that was hard to believe. KDKA and the Pirates were inundated with complaints. The fans organized a parade of support for Prince and King. Thousands came to watch it.

Prince was hired by ABC to be part of their Monday night broadcasts the next season. It didn't work out. He was hired the following year by the Houston Astros. It didn't work out. He wasn't the same out of Pittsburgh.

He was brought back in 1984 to be part of a cable broadcasting team. Blass was his partner. Prince hadn't changed.

"We were playing in the Andy Russell Golf Tournament at Laurel Valley in Latrobe on a game day," Blass said. "Bob had a helicopter land on the 18th fairway after our round. We landed at the parking lot at Three Rivers Stadium at 7:28 [seven minutes before game time]. He walked into the booth and began announcing at 7:35 like he had been at the stadium all afternoon."

In 1985, Prince was brought back to the radio booth. He was a dying man, although it wasn't publicly known, when he called his first game. But the magic was still there.

"It was almost painful to hear him speak," said King. "His voice was slurred and he couldn't follow the action. But even so, there was something in that voice that made you want to listen. He was truly unique."

Prince was introduced to the crowd his first night back and there was a thundering ovation. What transpired next was incredible.

In the first inning—Prince's first inning back in the radio booth—the Pirates scored nine runs.

He was dead a few weeks later. But the legend lives on.

"He was a broadcaster who transcended the role of broadcaster," Blass said.

"He was one of a kind," O'Leary said. "There'll never be another Bob Prince."

◆　◆　◆

DANNY MURTAUGH

Danny Murtaugh had a decent career as a major-league ballplayer, including a four-year stint with the Pittsburgh Pirates from 1948 through 1951. His baseball fame, however, began in 1957 when he replaced the volatile Bobby Bragan as Pirate manager. Possessed of an uncommon modesty and an Irish wit, Murtaugh was as famous for his hangdog looks and his ability to spray tobacco juice on an unsuspecting reporter's shoes as he was for his handling of the pitching staff. After meeting baby-faced rookie Bruce Kison for the first time, Murtaugh told reporters "I was born looking older than he does." In his fifteen seasons at the helm, he became the first Pirate manager to win two World Series, in 1960 and 1971. His career win total of 1,115 ranks second to Fred Clarke on the all-time Pirates list. Nationally syndicated sports columnist Thomas Boswell wrote "Murtaugh: Manager and Man" only a year before Murtaugh's death at the age of fifty-nine.

Murtaugh: Manager and Man

THOMAS BOSWELL

Danny Murtaugh may be the least impressive looking person in baseball. His whole body seems rumpled and older than its 58 years. His craggy, hawk-nosed face looks like something slept on it and forgot to straighten the covers.

In Pittsburgh's dugout manager Murtaugh seldom moves and often appears asleep. His coaches go to the mound to make pitching changes. Even chewing out an umpire seems like too much effort. After a game he sits in a rocking-chair and sips milk.

Murtaugh is a teetotaler, a grandfather, with a heart condition, an Irishman so outwardly mild that his players seem to do as they please.

When the Pirates clinched their fifth East Division title in six years and their fourth straight in complete seasons under Murtaugh ('70, '71, '74, '75) this week, it was easy for Murtaugh to be overlooked as he usually is. He didn't mind. "We're kind of quiet around here," he said yesterday.

The Baltimore Orioles needed only two words to sum up Murtaugh's tactical style in their "book" on Pittsburgh before the 1971 World Series. "No surprises," it said.

Few of baseball's famous managers can match Murtaugh's record. Even fewer have left an example for living as he has.

For the record, Murtaugh is 16th among managers in career winning percentage and 26th in career victories. In eleven full seasons, not counting three partial years, he has finished first five times and won two world titles, Pittsburgh's only ones in 50 years.

More distinguished than what he has done is the way he has done it. "He is one of the most loved men in baseball," said Bob Brown, Baltimore's public relations chief.

While such firebrand managers as Billy Martin and Leo Durocher win some games, make more enemies, raise a fuss and move on, Murtaugh has his job "for as long as he wants it," says Pirate general manager Joe Brown.

Where others leave a won-lost record behind, Murtaugh has exemplified a whole set of principles on how to behave properly. "Two angry men don't get anywhere" is his axiom.

"Patience seems to become me," he said yesterday. "I used to be fiery.

From the *Washington Post*, September 28, 1975. © 1975, *Washington Post*. Reprinted with permission.

The Irish blood. But I learned to control my emotions long ago." Somewhere in two arduous decades of playing and managing in the minors, Murtaugh learned the wisdom that "he who would be calm must take on the appearance of calm."

Murtaugh was not always the patron saint of those with acid indigestion. In 1947, at 29, he was still an inveterate minor leaguer, fond of all-night poker, horse racing and a bit of night life. After one all-nighter he learned several lessons from his Boston Brave manager Billy Southworth, a model for a mild-mannered, just man.

One spring training eve Murtaugh and roommate Ernie White spent an entire night finding ways to distribute $700 that Murtaugh had won at the track. They reported unshaven to the ballpark the next day, without intersecting with their roadside motel room.

"Have a good night's sleep, fellows?" asked Southworth.

"Sure, skip," fibbed Murtaugh. "Like babies."

"That's good," said Southworth. "I was afraid you might have been disturbed by the tractor-trailer that crashed through your room in the middle of the night."

The experience sobered Murtaugh. "Ernie and I wouldn't have made it if we'd been in that room," he recalls. He went on the next season to have his best year, a .290 average and 52 votes for Most Valuable Player, with Pittsburgh. He also learned the soft-spoken approach.

He needed it. Murtaugh's career reached bottom in 1955 when he was fired as Charleston manager. He caught on as a Pirate coach in 1956 but only after one Tom Tatum turned up his nose at the job. Murtaugh was named Pittsburgh manager for the final two months of 1957 but only after Clyde Sukeforth turned it down.

The job was a sure dead end. The Pirates wanted eight weeks of silence, managing by benign neglect, so fans and players could forget the tirades of brash Bobby Bragan who presaged his dismissal by serving orange drinks to the umpires.

Murtaugh quickly established his style—conservative on the field, understanding off it, the opposite of Bragan. In three years the Pirates were world champs, just one of three times Murtaugh (who has retired three times for his health) has taken the reins and turned the Bucs from patsies to champs.

During a game Murtaugh has almost always been invisible. He has few, if any, tactical theories of his own. He knows the standard baseball percentages inside out and plays by them most of the time.

"Murtaugh plays middle-of-the-road baseball," said Baltimore super scout Jim Russo. "He doesn't use his team's speed . . . plays for the big inning . . . seldom bunts before the middle innings and doesn't hit-and-run much. He lets his hitters hit."

Murtaugh's strengths, analyzed Russo, are his touch with pitching staffs, especially pulling pitchers at the right time, and his infinite patience with slumping players. "And," Russo adds, in what is almost an involuntary response from baseball men, "He's one of my favorite people."

"If a player thinks a bad game or two will pull him out of the lineup, he can't function," said Murtaugh. "This year we stuck with Richie Zisk (the crowd howled) and now he's red hot." In fact the Pirate team is red hot, having won 24 of 37 since a 2-12 August road trip.

Pitchers, baseball's temperamental children, respond particularly well to Murtaugh's fatherly confidence building. The Bucs' pitching is second in the NL in ERA, yet Russo insists, "They're not that good. It's Danny's touch. They don't even have a 20-game winner."

"Danny's a keen observer of people and appraiser of talent," said Syd Thrift, Oakland's minor league director. "And people say he has an iron hand inside that velvet glove.

"We've ridden many a mile together through the minors looking for free agents," said Thrift. "I see him clear. He can manage other men because he knows how to manage himself. Isn't that the toughest job in life?"

◆ ◆ ◆

"WE ARE FAM-I-LEE"

In 1979, the Pirates closed out the decade by winning their second World Series championship of the 1970s. The victory was a throwback to the 1925 World Series, because for the second time in club history, Pittsburgh rallied from a 3 games to 1 deficit to win the championship. There was also a striking similarity to the 1971 World Series. The opponent, once again, was a heavily favored Oriole team, managed by Earl Weaver, the seventh and deciding game was played at Baltimore's Memorial Stadium, and the deciding blow was struck by another future Hall of Fame Pirate who turned the playoffs and the World Series into his personal showcase. It was the year of "Pops" Stargell and the Pirate "fam-i-lee."

The selections that follow begin with two sections on the 1979 playoffs and World Series from Roger Angell's "Wilver's Way." Pittsburgh's own Dan Donovan and Pat Livingston make their contributions, and the concluding piece, "Where I Come From, Where I Am Going," is based on an interview of Stargell conducted by Eliot Asinof, author of the celebrated Eight Men Out.

Wilver's Way

ROGER ANGELL

The Cincinnati Reds showed grit in the first two games of their playoffs against the Pirates, forcing each of them into extra innings before succumbing by 5-2 in eleven and 3-2 in ten. (The Reds, by the way, won their division this year with a new manager, John McNamara, and a new third baseman, Ray Knight; their immediate predecessors were Sparky Anderson and Pete Rose. Unawed by his burdens, Knight batted .318. The club also got some useful work from Tom Seaver, who won eleven straight games in midsummer.) The opener was an austere, tautly played game, with thoughtful, excellent pitching by Seaver and John Candelaria, and two behemoth home runs, by George Foster and Willie Stargell; the latter's, a three-run shot against Tom Hume, won the game. Game Two was much less rewarding, thanks to some ghastly base-running on both sides. I was watching these encounters on television, and neither game aroused me as much as it should have, given the close scores. Perhaps the trouble had to do with the prim, doubt-stricken Cincinnati fans, who maintained a disapproving silence whenever their team fell behind. At one moment, while the NBC cameras panned across the silent, staring thousands, Joe Garagiola murmured, "This is not a painting."

The third game, an afternoon affair at Pittsburgh, which I attended, was delayed by a heavy rainstorm (a gruesome meteorological omen, had I only known it) but then began in lively fashion, when the Pirates got a run in the first inning on pure zeal. The lead-off man, Omar Moreno, walked, and stole second on the very next delivery by the Cincinnati pitcher, Mike LaCoss. Tim Foli then hit a high bounder to Dave Concepcion, on which Moreno unexpectedly proceeded to third, slithering under the startled shortstop's peg. Then he scored on a fly. In the third, Phil Garner, the dandy Pittsburgh second baseman, saved a run by diving on his belly to knock down Concepcion's single behind the bag, and in the bottom of that inning Stargell and Bill Madlock each hit home runs. The Reds, by contrast, looked corpselike at the end, as Bert Blyleven went the distance for the Pirates, who won by 7-1, to take the pennant. All year at Three Rivers Stadium, the field loudspeakers blasted out the Pirates' theme song during the seventh-inning stretch—a thumping, catchy disco-rock number, "We Are Family," by the Sister Sledge group. This time, with

From *Once More Around the Park: A Baseball Reader* by Roger Angell (Chicago: Ivan R. Dee, 2001). Reprinted by permission of Roger Angell.

the late-summer shadows deepening and the championship at last in hand, the wives of the Pirate players suddenly moved forward from their seats, just behind the screen, and clambered up onto a low, curving shelf that rims the field behind home plate. At first, there were only a few of them, but more and more of the young women ran down the aisles and were pulled up onto the sudden stage, and then they were all dancing together there arm in arm, jiving and boogieing and high-kicking in rhythm, in their slacks and black-and-gold scarves and long, ballplayer-wife's fur coats, all waving and laughing and hugging and shaking their banners in time to the loud music. It was terrific. Since then, I have heard cynical comments about this party, and wry suggestions from writers and fans that the much repeated and much reported Pittsburgh theme song and the players' evident closeness and joy in one another were nothing more than a publicity device, and reminders that *all* winning teams are families, for as long as they win. I don't agree. It is true that the smallest flutter of a spontaneous incident—in sports, or anywhere else in public life in this country—is now seized upon and transformed at once into a mass-produced imitation or a slogan or an advertising gimmick. Bill Hagy was appearing on a television commercial in Baltimore during the playoffs and showed up repeatedly on local TV interviews and game shows. I have no doubt that by next summer two or three major-league teams will come up with organized fans' cheering sections and letter-cheers, in imitation of the Orioles, or even a wives' cheering-and-dancing group in imitation of the Pirates. It is dispiriting, but we can't let ourselves miss the moment of humor and exultation when it does come along, or deny its pleasure. I thought about the Pirates' family when I visited the Cincinnati clubhouse after the last playoff game and saw the Reds preparing to depart for the winter. Joe Morgan was taking off his Reds uniform for the last time. He will venture into the free-agent market this year, but he is thirty-six now, and he had had a disappointing season, batting .250 and looking much slower afield; he had gone hitless in the playoffs. Just three years ago, Morgan and his teammates destroyed the Yankees in the World Series for their second World Championship in a row, and Joe Morgan was named the Most Valuable Player in the National League for the second straight year. That team was a family, too—the Big Red Machine—and now there was almost nothing left of it. But surely nobody understands all this better than the ballplayers themselves—the players and their wives—for that is the nature of their business. Injured, traded, slumping, benched, or simply playing for the wrong team, they are forever, or nearly forever, falling short of their best expectations, while their youth and their skills inexorably fade. Most big-league players never get to play in a World Series at all. When it does happen, then—the unexpected great year, when a whole team comes together, against all the odds, and wins—it should be celebrated, for the good times almost surely will not last. Why not dance?

◆

The Pirates won the last two games by scores of 4-0 and 4-1, and their sustained aplomb and courage in winning the championship against such unlikely odds made the World Series the most satisfying event of this eventful baseball year, which is as it should be. At the same time, it must be said that the sixth and seventh games, like the fifth, were unsatisfying entertainments. In all these games, the Orioles gave up the eventual winning run in the sixth or seventh inning, and the Pirates then went on and increased their lead in the late going. It should take nothing away from the Pirates' triumphant, unrelenting style of play to recall that the Orioles died at the plate in these three games, scoring two runs in the twenty-seven innings and never really mounting anything that could be called a threat along the way. Their cleanup hitter, Eddie Murray, went hitless in his last twenty-one times at bat. Baltimore was no better afield, making five errors in the three games and, more significantly, repeatedly failing to come up with the big play. True baseball fans are insatiably, and properly, critical in their demands, and most of them, I think (I exempt the Pittsburgh fans, of course), will look back on this Series with a sense of disappointment because of these unexpected Orioles failures. This was a flat spell but certainly not a collapse. The Orioles are a young and wonderfully talented team—Eddie Murray is twenty-three years old and has already hit seventy-nine major-league home runs—and I think we will be watching them again in October in the years just ahead.

What we remember about baseball after the game or the season is over is its marvelous moments—the sudden situation that offers a flashing succession of difficulties and chances and possibilities, all in the space of a second or two, and is then abruptly and sometimes shockingly resolved. That and the players' own moments—the images of the best of them that we carry with us into the coming winter. All of us, of course, will keep hold of our picture of Willie Stargell's home run against Scott McGregor, which won the last game. The Orioles were leading, 1-0, in the sixth, and McGregor had been pitching so well, spotting the ball and throwing a lot of sinkers, that a lot of the now terribly doubtful Baltimore fans must have begun to allow themselves to think that the one run just might be enough. (Tekulve, still waiting in the bullpen and all the more formidable, somehow, because of his brief recent loss of form, meant that there probably wouldn't be more than one run.) Bill Robinson's sixth-inning single was only the fourth Pirate hit of the evening. He led off first base as McGregor delivered the next pitch to Stargell—a low curve (a little *too* low, McGregor said later, for Stargell is a murderous low-ball hitter)—and Wilver hit it to deep right field, a high-sailing fly ball that descended just beyond the fence and just above Ken Singleton's leap and stretch and momentarily arrested empty reach. I have seen Willie Stargell hit so many home runs over the years (so many of them this fall, in fact) that I can run off the reel of this one again and again in my head, like a home movie: the preparatory forward double whirl of the bat, with his shoulders tilting and leaning forward, and with the weight of his body low and evenly placed on his feet but still somehow leaning, too—everything leaning—and then all of it abruptly rotating back in the opposite direction like an immense wheel, as weight and shoulders and arms and bat unwind together on the swing, and the circling, upswooping bat almost negligently intercepts the ball and disposes of it, and the body, finishing up, opens and rises, with the arms flying apart and the broad chest turning and facing out toward the field (as if it were watching the ball, too, along with the rest of us) while the bat, held only in the right hand now, softly finishes the circle and comes to a stop in the air behind the batter.

Willie won it all—the game and the Series, and the Most Valuable Player award for the Series, and a fistful of Series slugging records, and, best of all, something like a permanent place in our national sporting regard—and there is a special pleasure in all that, a thump of the heart, because of his way of doing things, because of the kind of man he is. Stargell's triumphs this fall were a perfect recompense for 1971, when the Pirates also beat the Orioles in a seven-game Series but one in which he played a very small part. Although he had led his league that year in home runs and had batted in one hundred and twenty-five runs, he went hitless in the playoffs and then batted only .208 in the Series, driving in one run. His sufferings at the plate were almost too painful to watch, but, as I wrote later, he endured this stretch of pop-ups and strikeouts and weakly topped grounders with unruffled calm—no bat-tossing, no puzzled head-shaking, not a word of explanation or complaint to the press. Near the end of that Series, I approached him in the clubhouse and asked how an intense, proud competitor like him could endure these disappointments and humiliations with such composure. Stargell's son, Wilver, Jr., who was then about four years old, was playing at his father's feet in the dressing cubicle, and Willie nodded toward the boy and said, "There's a time in life when a man has to decide if he's going to *be* a man."

Whew, It's Over! Bucs Are Champs

DAN DONOVAN

If the Pirates' 4-1 win over the Baltimore Orioles in the seventh game of the World Series was dramatic, well, that's the only way it could be.

"When we fell behind three games to one," said right-fielder Dave Parker, "I could feel something dramatic building. And it couldn't be more dramatic than this."

The Pirates battled the Orioles tooth and nail last night, starter Jim Bibby throwing strike after strike until Rich Dauer hit one of them over the left-field wall for a 1-0 lead in the third.

And things were tense still when Bill Robinson singled with one out in the sixth, bringing Stargell, who already had two hits on the night, up to bat with a man on.

"Jim Rooker and I were talking about Willie hitting a home run out in the bullpen," said catcher Ed Ott. "Then he hit it. It was high. It hung up there so long. Rooker and I were pulling it, pulling it."

The home run fell in the bullpen, right next to the two Pirates.

"I don't know how many people realize how close (Oriole right-fielder Ken) Singleton came to catching it," Rooker said. "He reached over the wall and almost got it."

"He (Baltimore pitcher Scott McGregor) threw me a breaking ball," Stargell said. "I didn't want to commit myself on the pitch too soon. I was out in front of it, but I got the bat speed that I wanted. At first, I didn't think it would travel that far. When it did, I was just thrilled. I can't think of any series that's been as exciting as this one."

Besides excited, Manager Chuck Tanner was confident.

"When Willie hit that home run, I thought we had it, because I thought we had enough pitching to hold them," he said.

Tanner was right, even though the Orioles seriously threatened in the eighth after reliever Grant Jackson walked two consecutive batters with one out.

Tanner brought in Kent Tekulve, who first faced Terry Crowley, the left-hander who burned him in the Pirates' 9-6 loss to the Orioles last Saturday.

"I didn't think about how this was the seventh game of the World Series, and how every move was in the limelight," Tekulve said. "I just thought about what I had to do."

From the *Pittsburgh Press*, October 18, 1979. Copyright/*Pittsburgh Post-Gazette*, 2002. All rights reserved. Reprinted with permission.

First baseman Stargell came over, Tekulve said, "to tell me to relax and be myself."

"I said, 'Teke, show the people why you're the best in the National League,'" Stargell said. "'And if you don't think you can do that, then you play first and I'll pitch.'"

But Tekulve did the pitching, getting Crowley to bounce out to second base for the second straight game.

He intentionally walked Singleton to load the bases, then pitched to Eddie Murray who was riding an 0-20 streak.

Murray hit a line drive to right field, the kind that Parker normally catches easily.

"But I slipped—three times," Parker said. "The turf kept giving way."

"I thought, 'I hope his legs don't fail him now,'" Tekulve said. "But he's made those plays all year and somehow I knew he'd get it."

Once he did get it, the last Oriole threat was over.

Tekulve struck out two of the three right-handed hitters, giving him 10 strikeouts in his nine World Series innings.

And he had the benefit of two extra runs scored in the top of the ninth. Phil Garner, who hit .500 for the World Series, doubled to lead off the inning.

He stayed there when Tekulve's bunt didn't work, and the Orioles brought in Mike Flanagan to pitch to Omar Moreno.

Moreno, who finished the Series hitting .333, was 0-8 against Flanagan, with four strikeouts, but this time he singled up the middle to score Garner. The final run came in when Robinson was hit on the finger by Dennis Martinez with the bases loaded.

The game ended with a fly ball to Moreno that Tekulve never saw.

"I threw the ball and did not see the catch," Tekulve said. "I was so wrapped up in the game that it didn't hit me until the ball was in the air and Omar caught it. I then thought, 'World Championship; it's ours and nobody can take it away.'"

Finally, the drama was over.

Stand-Up Pirates Set Down Birds

PAT LIVINGSTON

For four games of the 76th World Series, the Pirates bungled their way against the Baltimore Orioles. A fan might have been justified in wondering if they were impostors.

He might have asked, even, if the real Pirates would please stand up.

They did stand up, first in Game 5 at Three Rivers Stadium, their backs to the wall, in a sudden-death situation, and they didn't sit down until they had won the World Series.

And last night, before an incredulous, disbelieving crowd at Municipal Stadium, the Pirates, for the second time, beat the Orioles in a World Series, repeating their victory of 1971, this time with a stirring three straight victories which revealed to the world how good Manager Chuck Tanner's Pirates can be.

You will read more about the Pirate victory elsewhere on these pages, but it should be noted here that long before the Pirates came to Baltimore, long before the Bucs were into the heart of the season, Tanner had been proclaiming them as the best 25-man squad he had ever been associated with in baseball.

And last night the Pirates proved Tanner to be some kind of prophet.

Tanner didn't need the Pirates to confirm his own biased evaluations, but a doubting world had to be shown, and Tanner's charges showed it, leaving no question about their status among the contenders.

The Pirates won because they had the superior pitchers, the superior hitters and, certainly superior fielding, once the weather had eased up enough to thaw the ice out of their frozen fingers.

From the start, it had been the type of series most fans, and both managers, had predicted it would be—suspenseful, thrilled-packed moments and garlands of air-tight pitching.

The only flaws in the jewels that made up the 1979 World Series were the erratic, inconsistent play of both teams in Game 1, which might justifiably be attributed to the inclement weather, and the appearance of Kent Tekulve in Game 4, when the Pirate reliever pitched in a manner that was totally out of character with his season-long performance.

But there is always the chance of less than perfection, even when two fine teams get together, and Baltimore had its moments, too, that would better be forgotten.

From the *Pittsburgh Press*, October 18, 1979. Copyright/*Pittsburgh Post-Gazette*, 2002. All rights reserved. Reprinted with permission.

The fielding of Doug DeCinces, which gave the Pirates a couple of opportunities to save face, was one of those. The decline of the hitting of Eddie Murray, the Orioles' clean-up batter, after Game 2 was another.

The fact that the Pirates' makeshift pitching rotation had thoroughly handcuffed the Orioles, believed by many to be the best team in baseball, was sure to leave bitter memories among the noisy, imploring bleacherites, who had become symbolic of the baseball fever that had gripped the city on the Chesapeake.

The Pirates' pitching was magnificent. Save for the four innings when the Orioles were able to put more than two runs on the scoreboard, Tanner's pitchers, lightly regarded everywhere but in Pittsburgh, dominated the action.

As a matter of fact, in 53 of the Series' 63 innings, the under-rated Bucs' pitchers sent the frustrated, muttering Orioles back to the dugout without as much as a single run to show for their futile, plate-side efforts.

That was the kind of pitching that the country expected of Jim Palmer, Mike Flanagan, Scott McGregor and Dennis Martinez, the highly touted Baltimore pitchers.

Instead, the Pirates got theirs from Bert Blyleven, Jim Bibby, John Candelaria, Kent Tekulve, Jim Rooker, Grant Jackson, and Don Robinson, the ailing right-hander who had one unfortunate, depressing inning in three outings.

There were over-reactions by the press, as usual, in any World Series.

A Baltimore sports editor, John Steadman, deplored the Pirates' exploitation of something as sacred as "the family" in an athletic connotation. "A cheap grandstand play, a sickening put-on, a bad pun," he called it in his News-American column. "The Orioles haven't been gagging themselves to keep from ridiculing 'The Family' reference, but it must be amusing."

And, after the Orioles had taken a 3-1 lead at Three Rivers Stadium, the collective press was ready to bestow the label of genius, of all things, on Earl Weaver, the colorful Baltimore manager. For four games, every move that Weaver made worked as if he had orchestrated it in some mythical Vahalla.

Changing his lineup, perhaps out of sheer desperation, he got a four-for-four game out of his replacement shortstop, Kiko Garcia, and a two-for-two game, including a home run, out of Benny Ayala, his substitute left fielder.

Every time the dandy little genius sent a pinch-hitter up to the plate, he got a man on base, either through a walk, a hit or an error. But, as later events in the series were to prove, it was not genius, or careful planning, or even coincidence. It was sheer luck, and luck, as any discerning gambler can tell you, is an ungrateful and fickle companion.

And the national press had ridiculed Omar Moreno, who, in his first 12 at bats, had collected only a single hit. "Omar the Outmaker" they had branded him, but after last night—after Moreno had capped his first World Series with 10 hits in his last 21 at bats—nobody was laughing at the bashful Panamanian outfielder.

Still, it was a memorable series, one that will live long in the memories of the fans of Pittsburgh and Baltimore whose hearts went out, not only to the Pirates who finally won it, but to Tanner, the tragedy-stricken figure who had borne up so well during the loss of his mother. It would have been a great script, and a great World Series, no matter which team had won it.

"Where I Come From, Where I Am Going"

ELIOT ASINOF

Wilver Dornell Stargell, at the age of 38, won most every prize usually reserved for far-younger athletes. He was co-winner (with Keith Hernandez) of the 1979 National League Most Valuable Player Award. He won *Sport* magazine's World Series MVP Award. He was acclaimed by *The Sporting News* as The Man of the Year.

More to the point, however, "Pops" Stargell is probably the first MVP to be recognized for his leadership in the lockerroom. The statistics will show that Willie's bat won a multitude of games for the Pittsburgh Pirates, including the seventh game of the 1979 World Series. But almost everyone on the Pirates will say that the Pops paternalism—his awarding of stars to be stuck on Pirate caps, his selection of "We Are Family" as the team's theme song—won more games for the Pirates than did his windmilling, black bat.

Three months after the World Series, Willie was still basking in its glow. I met him in his $200-a-day suite at New York's Hotel Pierre on Fifth Avenue. He was surrounded by his agent, Dan Shedrick; his lawyer, David Litman; and a dozen photographers and newsmen, their microphones thrust at him as though he were an astronaut, who had, moments before, stepped off a rocketship from Mars. The Sister Sledge group was there to celebrate their "We Are Family" album, and so was Willie's grandmother, a stately Seminole. The phone never stopped ringing. I felt like I'd just

From *Sport*, April 1980. Reprinted with permission of Eliot Asinof.

entered the Marx Brothers' chaotic stateroom in the movie, *A Night at the Opera*.

"Relax . . . have a beer," Willie greeted me, apologizing for all the confusion. He seemed not at all unnerved as people babbled around him. He was polite and deferential to everyone, towering over us all like a jolly, black giant.

"It's been this way all week," said Dan Shedrick, "but he glides through all the hullabaloo with the patience of a saint."

Just like in the lockerroom, I thought. Minutes later, seated at a table amid the room's confusion, we began our conversation.

SPORT: I see you in the middle of all this hoopla and I think of what life was like for you 20 years ago, a teenage black kid just beginning to play pro ball in the rural Southwest.

STARGELL: Oh, it was pretty rough, all right. There were times when I felt my life was on the line. But I can't think about that now. I don't want to let that beat me in any way.

SPORT: The way I read it, your problems down there were not only emotional, but physical as well. You couldn't even eat properly, could you?

STARGELL: Yeah. Blacks weren't allowed in the restaurants with the white ballplayers. The others brought us cheeseburgers to eat in the bus after they ate steaks and green vegetables. Man, I cried every night.

SPORT: That first year [Roswell, N.M.], you came home 35 pounds underweight.

STARGELL: What hit me then was my surprise at the prejudice. I'd never been exposed to it. I grew up in Alameda, California, outside of San Francisco. I went to school with whites.

SPORT: It can make a man bitter.

STARGELL: You have to come to a decision as to who you are and what you intend to do with your life. It was my crossroad. I mean, I was real mixed up about it for a while. I would call home almost every night. My stepfather, he would say it was all right if I decided to come home. And my mom, she was very supportive. I knew I had to make the big decision—either play ball or go back home. But I wanted to play ball so badly, I said to myself I wasn't going to let nothing interfere. Nobody had the right to stop me from trying, anyway. Especially if I was qualified. I mean, I wasn't expecting to become president of General Motors. I didn't ever feel qualified to achieve that. I just wanted to play ball.

SPORT: Did you think you could make it?

STARGELL: I didn't think I *couldn't*. What it got down to was for me to take that big chance in life. I mean, I'd been working at the Chevrolet plant in California, making $250 a week. Everyone asked if it was feasible for me to leave that job, a thousand dollars a month, and risk it all for another job that made only $175 a month. But I wanted to do something with my life and money couldn't buy those feelings. There are too many people who never take the chance. They play it safe. There are others who try, but they break if things get too tough. You have to learn to bend but not break. You have to seize the opportunity when it comes along, even if it's going to be tough. And that means not letting yourself dwell on the negative aspects—which is always too easy to do.

SPORT: If your experience is really tough, how do you avoid not dwelling on the negative?

STARGELL: Well, it's hard not to be angry, but it's just as important for a person to do what he has to do in order to achieve. Rather than take such a negative stand, I've got to feel sorry for those people, and anyone like them today. You take someone who goes around hating, that person has to work at it, and from a negative standpoint, it's going to tax his entire nervous system, excite his blood pressure, maybe. What a waste that is.

SPORT: Being the club leader also means you must take a player to the woodshed when someone is malingering or creating problems. How do you do this without creating ill feeling?

STARGELL: There is no such thing as anybody taking anyone to the woodshed. You are talking about grownup men.

SPORT: Are you saying that the Pirates never have any lapses?

STARGELL: Well, I've never seen a case where a guy goes out and plays less than what he is capable of doing. Now there are certain days when one isn't at 100 percent, and there are days when a guy is only working on 50 percent, but we expect him to come out and give 100 percent of 50 percent.

SPORT: So you have never disciplined a teammate?

STARGELL: Well, you can see certain things at times. But you ask and give the guy the opportunity to say what he feels is wrong. There are times when there are problems at home and it can affect a guy. Somebody in the clubhouse will listen to what the guy has to say.

SPORT: Would it be wrong to imply that you are the one man that other Pirates come to in need?

STARGELL: The emphasis that is put on me as the leader of the Pirates is exaggerated. There are so many other guys to go to. What happens when I need someone to talk to? I don't lock myself in a closet and talk to myself. There are guys I can go to with a problem and I do.

SPORT: What guys are you close to?

STARGELL: Everybody.

SPORT: How good a ballplayer were you as a kid?

STARGELL: Oh, I had a lot of learning to do, but I sure had a lot of desire. I learned to take advice. Sometimes I did things the way I thought it best for me, but I always listened.

SPORT: Where were you weak?

STARGELL: Al Kutcher, my manager at Roswell, saw I had trouble catching pop flies at first base. He worked with me till I licked it. The next year, at Grand Forks, N.D., I was shifted to the outfield and I had trouble throwing. Outfielders throw differently than first basemen—an overhand throw so the ball doesn't tail off at the end. I really learned how to throw there as an outfielder.

SPORT: I noticed you have a unique grip, that you hold the bat with your little finger loose at the end. Why?

STARGELL: That started my first year with Pittsburgh in spring training in 1962. I was hitting the regular way with my fingers tight on the bat, inside the nub, and I built up a tremendous callus on the outside of the little finger. It hurt so much that in order to keep playing, I just let the finger lift off the end. It took the pressure off the callus.

SPORT: But when it healed, didn't you go back to the regular grip?

STARGELL: No. I got to like it this way and decided to keep on hitting with the finger loose. If I changed, it would mess me up psychologically. I could feel full freedom to drive my hands through the way I liked. It keeps my swing fluid.

SPORT: Do you know any other hitters who do that?

STARGELL: Well, Johnny Bench does. I think there are more.

SPORT: Did you always wind up when you swung? That big intimidating windmill move, is that yours and yours alone? Why do you do it?

STARGELL: I don't know when that started. It was after I turned pro. It relaxed my wrists and elbows, it loosened my shoulders.

SPORT: Would you say that it also causes you to strike out a lot?

STARGELL: I strike out because I commit myself early. Big swingers have that tendency. I don't sit back and wait on a pitch. I see it leave the pitcher's hand and I commit before I can be sure of what the pitch is. It's an aggressive action. The power comes out of the commitment.

SPORT: The question comes up about your being 38.

STARGELL: I'm *39* in March.

SPORT: About how long can you keep playing? I know Lou Brock retired at 40.

STARGELL: When *is* the point where you're supposed to stop? Why do people say at some certain year you're supposed to retire? I mean, who's to say that? Some say to me, "you're old, you're going to be 39," all that nonsense. I'm thinking maybe they give up on themselves at 38. This guy or that guy comes up and tells me how old I am. I know how old I am. But I also know what I can do. *He* doesn't. If I stood around listening to what other people tell me, I'd have been out of baseball three years ago.

SPORT: I remember how sad it was when Maury Wills retired at 40. I suppose the Dodgers thought Bill Russell was better at 23 than Wills was at 40. So they put Maury out to pasture.

STARGELL: It has a lot to do with what's in a ballplayer's mind. What he thinks of himself. And *how* he thinks of himself. In my case, I feel so good about what I'm doing. I enjoy it so much. I don't think about how old I am.

SPORT: Okay, Willie, here you are, about to be 39 and doing very well as a ballplayer. Better, in fact, as the years go by, understanding more about yourself, enjoying the fun of it all. How do you see yourself in the future? In 1982, say?

STARGELL: Why should I think of 1982 when I haven't even begun 1980 yet?

SPORT: I know, you live from year to year.

STARGELL: No, not year to year, but right *now*. Day to day.

SPORT: Just to speculate, though: do you see yourself still playing in 1982? Or, maybe, as a manager?

STARGELL: I'm too realistic for that.

SPORT: After all these years, has your concentration on the field flagged at all?

STARGELL: I know there's a tendency to relax, but I still love the game so much, it's like I was still a kid out there. To me, playing ball is like being a farmer. He's got to respect the earth, the land he works. That's the only way a farmer can be rewarded—for the crops to grow. With me and baseball, I know I cannot take the game for granted. I've got to keep concentrating out there, to keep working, day in and day out. It doesn't matter if I'm hurting or what, the thing is not to let up. I know there will be times when it all seems to fall apart. Things go wrong for you. Like when we were playing the Cubs at the tail end of the season, and I threw a ball over Bill Madlock's head and a man scored from first with the winning run. And then I got up in the bottom of the ninth with a chance to save the game, and I struck out. I felt like I could jump right out of a window, you know?

SPORT: As a former minor league player myself, I don't see how you can avoid the horror of suffering over a lousy day.

STARGELL: Well, you shake it off and go back out there clean the next day. I came into the game without ulcers and I'm going to leave the game without ulcers. People say I keep a lot of stuff inside me, but don't you believe it. I just won't let a lot of that bad stuff *get* inside me. But what is there gets out.

SPORT: Mostly the joy?

STARGELL: Absolutely. And what could possibly be more fun? I mean, the whole sports scene is such a joy. You can see it all in Pittsburgh, of course. The Pirates and now the Steelers. The way they bring people together from all walks of life.

SPORT: Do you know, Willie, in two more years you'll have played 20 years for the Pirates.

STARGELL: My home is in Pittsburgh. I'm there with my wife and kids, friends, neighbors. I'm part of the city. Sure, the team, too. How can I leave that?

SPORT: Some do—like Pete Rose—for the money.

STARGELL: Well, you know, we *are* a family. I don't remember how long we had that going on the club. I can't see living through the long season in any other way. Can you imagine what it must be like coming into a lockerroom with everyone pushing only for himself? We used to play that Sister Sledge record in there. Then one rainy day with the people in the stands, waiting, they put the words to the song on the scoreboard, and everyone sang along. It was really terrific. The fans adopted the song. The whole thing was very spontaneous. You couldn't dream it up as a PR thing and make it work. It had to be this way, the way it was with us in Pittsburgh all last season.

Trouble, Transition, and a New Beginning

The Pirate promotion for 1980 was an optimistic "Two in a Row and Two Million Fans," but the ball club fell short on both counts. By mid-decade, with the team playing poorly and management facing a financial crisis, the Galbreath family finally decided to put the Pirates up for sale. There was also serious talk about moving the franchise to another city.

David Nightingale's "The Pirate Problem" appeared in the September 9, 1985, issue of The Sporting News, *just as the Pirates were about to finish in last place in the Eastern Division for the second straight year. They would end the season with a dismal 773,500 attendance figure. Nightingale, a senior correspondent for* TSN, *details the many circumstances leading up to the crisis, ranging from the problems with Three Rivers Stadium and "rust belt" depression to poor personnel decisions, the city's negative racial attitudes, and fan perceptions—induced by drug allegations and millionaire salaries—that players were spoiled rotten. The front-page photograph in* The Sporting News *of empty seats at Three Rivers Stadium and the banner declaring "Empty Seats, Empty Hopes" were clear indicators that the Pittsburgh Pirates of the 1980s had become the poster child for a baseball franchise in trouble after its remarkable record in the 1970s.*

The Pirate Problem

DAVID NIGHTINGALE

Next year is supposed to be the 100th season in which Pittsburgh has been a member of the National League.

What if they gave a centennial party and nobody came?

Don't laugh.

Recently, the Pittsburgh Pirates decided to offer their partisans a fantasy camp, a week in the sun that would enable fans to pay for the pleasure of matching muscles with past Pirates heroes.

Only seven people signed up.

Why? It could be lack of interest, lack of money or lack of heroes, perhaps all of the aforementioned.

At any rate, the fantasy fiasco was a microcosm of the troubles that have befallen this once-proud franchise.

You remember the Pirates of the 1970s—the Lumber Company? The Bucs had a .569 victory percentage for the decade—an average of 92 wins

From *The Sporting News*, September 9, 1985. Reprinted with permission of *The Sporting News*.

a season, six division crowns, two National League pennants and two world titles.

Let's hear that 1979 theme song one more time: "We Are Fam-Mi-Lee!"

Now, however, six years later, it's a different tune: a dirge.

If you believe Rand McNally, Pittsburgh is the best place to live in the United States.

But as far as baseball is concerned, Three Rivers Stadium has become a funeral parlor.

You can see it in the mournful performances of the last-place ball club and in the mournful faces of the few who choose to attend what has turned into a season-long wake.

The team drew 773,500 customers in 1984, the second-lowest total in the major leagues. The team lost $6 million.

This year, the team needed to sell 1.3 million tickets to break even. It currently is on an attendance pace of 800,000. The 500,000-fan deficit will send the 1985 red ink into eight figures.

The team is for sale.

But nobody in Pittsburgh wants to buy it—not for anything more than fire-sale prices.

And if nobody buys the Pirates and keeps them here, then, says Rand McNally, this city will drop to "the second-best place to live" in the United States.

Pittsburgh Chamber of Commerce, take note.

"We really had the city turned on after our World Series victory in '79," said Dan Galbreath, the team president. "So in 1980, we were riding with the promotion: 'Two in a Row and Two Million Fans.'

"If ever there was a chance to get on a roll, that was it. But we didn't."

Oh, but they did.

Starting in 1980, the Pirates got on a roll called Murphy's Law: Anything that can go wrong will go wrong

Even Murphy himself must be chuckling over the revelation that former Pirates employee Kevin Koch apparently was a lot more than just Paul Parrot, the team mascot. Minus his feathers, Koch allegedly served as courier between the friendly neighborhood drug suppliers and the Three Rivers' locker rooms.

"Clearly, the lack of fan support is the problem," said Galbreath, who succeeded his father, John, as team president in 1970, nearly 25 years after the family purchased the club.

"I've tried mightily to analyze the causes. I've spent a lot of sleepless nights considering what we could have done differently. And I've reviewed the list of excuses why fans won't support us."

The list includes:

- Three Rivers Stadium itself, which has access problems and a high amusement tax.
- The ailing economy of the Pittsburgh area.
- A series of bad player deals.
- Too many black players on the team.
- The recent spate of drug allegations.
- The Pirates' players' attitude.
- The theory that Pittsburgh was, is and always will be a "football town."
- A series of smaller, miscellaneous reasons, like alleged penny-pinching, the firing of late radio announcer Bob Prince, absentee ownership and the inevitable comparisons of the Galbreaths to Steelers owner Art Rooney.

"Many of our troubles have been present for a long time, but they all have grown, and now they've all come together," said Joe Brown, who recently was rehired as general manager.

Some say his job is more that of undertaker than caretaker.

"All of them combined have created a problem that we can no longer solve," said Galbreath. "I would accept the responsibility (for failure) if I thought we weren't trying to do our job. But aside from some bad player deals, I don't have answers as to what we could have done differently.

"Maybe what it will take to make things happen here is for the Galbreaths to step aside. But so far, we can't even do that. It's been frustrating and depressing that no one else in Pittsburgh has been willing to come forward, take over and go on.

"Perhaps all concerned will grant some relief to (eventual) new ownership. The new owners will need it. But the irony is not lost on me that if certain relief had been granted to us, the 'Pirate problem' might not exist in the first place."

Galbreath conceded some early warning signs were visible as long as 13 years ago:

- In 1972, when the Pirates drew 75,000 fewer customers than in 1971—a world championship season. (A rule of thumb in the majors is that attendance should always increase the year after you field a winner.)

- In 1974, when the team won a division title, its fourth in five years, it played before only 1.1 million fans.
- In 1978, when the paid customer count was only 946,000, despite an unparalleled five-year record of consistency (the team's East Division finishes from 1974-78 were 1-1-2-2-2).

"The average major league team today needs almost two million attendance to meet its nut," said Pirates Manager Chuck Tanner. "I'm not sure a team in Pittsburgh will ever be able to draw that many. But we should do 1.5 million or 1.6 million if we're competitive. And I think we could be competitive, just like the Minnesota Twins, but without a lot of million-dollar salaries."

Right now, however, the Pirates are a long way from being competitive—and light years from drawing 1.5 million. And the disenchantment of the would-be customers has turned from silent finger-tapping into a deafening drumbeat.

Why don't the fans attend games here? Let us count the excuses.

Take Me Out of the Ball Park

Nearly two decades ago, when Pittsburgh decided it had to have a new facility for its professional sports teams, one of the plans was to build Three Rivers Stadium in the middle of the water—where the Allegheny and the Monongahela rivers meet with the Ohio—on a man-made island serviced by a variety of bridges.

"The U. S. Defense Department rejected that plan," Brown said. "They said if somebody blew up the stadium, it would shut down traffic on all three of the rivers."

So the stadium was built on a mainland corner, on land west of the Allegheny and north of the Ohio.

Still, there are a lot of people in these environs who wish somebody would blow it up.

"The ingress and egress is terrible at Three Rivers," said the Houston Astros' Phil Garner, a former Pirate. "If 25,000 people go there for a game, most of them will still be there two hours after the game."

"Getting to Three Rivers is a problem because of road construction bottlenecks, poor exits and lack of decent public transportation," said Bruce Keidan, sports editor of the *Pittsburgh Post-Gazette*. "Oh, sure, there's a new subway system to the north side. It goes right past the stadium. But there's no subway station at the stadium."

"Three Rivers Stadium is a litany of broken promises," said Dan Galbreath.

Original city plans called for dressing up the area around the ball park with a hotel, a marina, a theme park, restaurants, a shopping mall, a $29 million science exposition center and a people mover.

None of the aforementioned has been built, although the stadium has been in use since 1970.

"Also, when the stadium opened, the pipes froze for lack of insulation," Galbreath said. "Concession booths couldn't operate because they lacked water lines, and joints weren't caulked, permitting leakage between different levels."

By the time the first fans arrived, they felt short-changed and ripped off.

"Why?"

"Because, despite the unsolved problems, the stadium still came in over cost," said Galbreath. "So that developed a local mind-set that this was a 'rich man's plaything.'

"It doesn't matter that even in the Pirates' bad years the stadium still generates a minimum of $750,000 a year in tax revenues—plus 1,000 jobs and $35 million a year worth of business for the city. It doesn't seem to matter that the stadium doesn't cost the taxpayers a cent because, among Pittsburgh residents, the mind-set remains that they are subsidizing us."

Further, money that the Pirates might have spent to improve the team had to be spent to improve the stadium. "And, finally, we couldn't afford it any more," said Galbreath.

"Outsiders asked us why we didn't make some money on the side, why we didn't book events like rock concerts and motorcycle races to help pay our bills," he added. "The reason was simple: The city imposed a 10 percent amusement tax (which still exists). And the rock groups took one look at that tax and bypassed us; they got themselves booked into Cleveland or Cincinnati instead.

"So a few years ago we had to sue the city to force it to take over the stadium operation. The lawsuit was the worst possible public relations move for us, but we had to do it or go broke."

"The stadium became a political football," Brown said. "In Chicago or New York, you don't need political support to operate a team. But in the third- or fourth-smallest city in baseball, you need it to survive. Because if the politicians aren't with you, they're against you, and they change public perspective of you."

Land of Thin Wallets

The 1985 Pittsburgh Pirates sold 6,000 full and partial season tickets—down 400 from the previous year. Compare that with the totals of three division rivals—Phillies (17,500 full), Cubs (7,500 full, 17,500 partial) and Cardinals (9,600 full).

One reason for Pittsburgh's troubles is lack of corporate ticket support.

"Local businesses were very generous in one respect: They bought $15 million worth of ball-park advertising over a 10-year span," said Galbreath. "But the corporations don't buy many tickets to our games. I don't know why."

Galbreath, however, knows why many individuals don't buy tickets—lack of money.

"It isn't that we don't have a ton of loyal followers," said Tanner, who lives in nearby New Castle, Pa. "Our radio surveys indicate that people listen to Pirate games for an average of 5½ innings, compared to 2½ innings for the average listener to Dodger radio broadcasts.

"The problem is that many of our fans can't afford to come to the games. Remember that this area was hit hard by the recession. At a time when the national unemployment average was 12 percent, it was close to 25 percent here."

"Officially, the recession—here it was a depression—may be over," said Brown. "But the area still hasn't recovered. The population in Pittsburgh proper is down 10 percent. And while many have returned to their jobs, their buying power is less than it used to be."

"Maybe a guy has gone back to work and has managed to save a hundred bucks," said Tanner. "But instead of spending it on some ball games, maybe he thinks he'd better hold on to it in case hard times come back again."

"Baseball has the lowest cost, on a per-game basis," said Brown. "But, let's face it: For $200, a fan can buy a complete Steeler football season—10 games at the stadium and 10 games on free home television. It would cost him nearly twice that much to buy a baseball season ticket."

Downward Dealing

To employ an ancient cliche, blaming all of the Pirates' current problems on Harding (Pete) Peterson, the former general manager, is like saying the Johnstown flood was caused by a leaky toilet in Altoona.

But somebody out there had to pull a few wrong chains. All of that talent from the Pirates' farm system didn't exactly flush itself out of town.

Former Pirate John Candelaria used to refer to Peterson as a "bozo" and an "idiot," but you have to take Candelaria with a grain of salt because the pitcher was using his mouth, instead of his left arm, as a device to get traded, which he finally accomplished last month when he was dealt to California.

Still, during Peterson's reign, the following did—and didn't—happen:

- The Pirates refused to swap Al Oliver to Montreal for Gary Carter in 1977.

- Slugger Tony Armas and pitchers Rick Langford and Doug Bair were among those sent to Oakland in 1977 for infielders Phil Garner and Tommy Helms. Peterson should get the benefit of the doubt on that one. The A's may have received more talent, but the acquisition of Garner was cement for the Pirates' 1979 world champions.

- Pitchers Bert Blyleven, Rick Honeycutt, Dave Dravecky and John Stuper were shipped out of town for a song. The Pirates' current roster doesn't include a single player acquired from any of those deals.

- Outfielder Mike Easler was traded to Boston for pitcher John Tudor in 1983. "We already had the best pitching staff in the division before 'Bozo' made that deal," said Candelaria. "What we needed at the time was hitting." Easler batted .313 for the Red Sox in 1984.

- Tudor then was dispatched to St. Louis after the 1984 season for outfielder George Hendrick. Tudor is a probable 20-game winner for the Cards this year. Henrick was virtually given to California last month by Brown.

- Free agents Gene Tenace and Amos Otis were signed when they were over the hill.

- The front office publicly questioned the ability of Dave Parker in 1983, thus considerably reducing his trade value. Parker fled town, via free agency, after that campaign and has been a mainstay in Cincinnati for the past two years.

But the last straw, in the eyes of Pirates fans, came when Peterson sent Dale Berra and rookie prospect Jay Buhner to the Yankees last winter for outfielder Steve Kemp and infielder Tim Foli. On paper, that looked like a pretty good deal—until Kemp showed up for spring training with a scar on his shoulder and Peterson admitted he was unaware that Kemp had undergone surgery during the off-season.

Wrong Ethnic Mix

There's a plaque in the Pirates' locker room at Three Rivers Stadium dedicated to the late Bob Moose, a former Bucs pitcher. It reads: "A great competitor who had desire, confidence, class and style, but above all, the ability to be color-blind when it came to people from origins other than his own."

In this less-than-perfect corner of the world, Moose was different. The Pittsburgh area (populated primarily by first-, second- and third-generation European immigrants) does not have a national reputation for color blindness.

Also, the word around baseball is that the Pirates have had too many black players for their own good for a long time.

"When I played my first game for Pittsburgh, after coming over from Oakland, the plate umpire asked me how it felt to break the color barrier," said Garner.

Ever-candid Bill Madlock, who is black, jumped quickly to Haak's defense. "Howie told the truth," said Madlock, the Pirates' third baseman until just a few days ago. "If the population in our area were reversed—if there were more blacks than whites here, the blacks wouldn't come out to see an all-white team."

"Pittsburgh is a difficult town for blacks," said Brown. "The scene changed dramatically here with the passage of the Fair Employment Practices Act. All of a sudden, you saw black faces in unions. And the ethnics in the Pittsburgh area felt threatened, economically, by the emergence of the black worker. So it was hard for many of them to accept a black idol on the baseball field despite the fact Roberto Clemente, Willie Stargell and Parker were our most popular players at their respective times.

"There's a huge irony to this, of course. In our heyday, during the '70s, we had six black or Latin starters—exactly the same number as the Cincinnati Reds.

"But nobody ever screamed about the Reds being too black for the simple reason that they had two white superstars, Pete Rose and Johnny Bench. Our top white players then were Richie Zisk and Richie Hebner, both talented, but not superstars."

"I think the Pirates have problems because the team has failed to develop a product that the fans can identify with," said Garner. "Pittsburgh is blue-collar, Middle America, and the current baseball product just doesn't fit that market. Bill Mazeroski fit the mold, but he was the last. The Steelers can get away with playing a lot of blacks because football is a team game. But in baseball, the fans want to be able to identify with the individuals. And the product the Pirates are selling now . . . Well, it's like trying to sell swimsuits in Alaska."

Turned Off by Cocaine

There's a statue of shortstop Honus Wagner, the Pirates' legendary "Flying Dutchman," gracing the concourse outside Three Rivers Stadium.

According to legend, Wagner didn't smoke, didn't chew and didn't go with girls who did.

That's ironic, because when a local supplier of illegal chemicals refers to a "Dutch treat," he means: "Meet me at Honus Wagner's statue after the game, and I'll deliver your cocaine."

It may or may not be a bad rap, but Three Rivers Stadium still is known around baseball as the "National League Drugstore."

"We have been assured by baseball officials and by law enforcement agencies that the drug trafficking here is no worse than anywhere else in the majors," Brown said.

"Maybe so, but I'll be damned if I'm gonna support any player's drug habit," said local resident Joe Stachowski, who said the only time he comes close to Three Rivers Stadium during the baseball season is to let passengers out of his taxi.

The names of former Pirates Parker and Berra surfaced during the recent conviction of cocaine dealer Dale Shiffman. So did the name of Koch, the former team mascot.

Former Pittsburgh players Lee Lacy and Al Holland have given grand jury testimony about the local drug scene, as have current players Lee Mazzilli and Rod Scurry. And Scurry twice has undergone treatment for drug abuse.

Beyond that, another time bomb is ticking. The trial of alleged drug dealer Curtis Strong, the former caterer at Philadelphia's Veterans Stadium, is coming up soon. Strong's attorney, Adam Renfroe Jr., has promised to parade "a whole mess of ball players" to the witness stand.

"If the problem is everywhere, as we're told, then I don't know why the FBI had to target this city," Brown said with a sigh. "From a public relations standpoint, we got the dirty end of the stick."

Disenchanted Players

There are no highs in the Pittsburgh locker room these days. In fact, many of the Pirates feel lower than a worm's tummy.

"I know I'm a professional and I'm expected to blot out all the crap and just do my job on the field," Madlock said during his last days as a Pirate. "Well, that's easier said than done.

"We don't know who is going to own us or where we'll play next year. There's no excitement on the field because there's nobody in the stands. Guys are walking around here like they're stepping on eggshells because of the (drug) situation.

"What leaves your head spinning, though, is that all of this stuff has come down in just the last two years. How could it happen so fast?"

When Brown returned as general manager this summer, he sought out the opinion of catcher Tony Pena.

"Joe, our team has the worst attitude in baseball," Pena told him.

"The Pittsburgh players are either confused or depressed," said pitcher Kent Tekulve, a Pirates bullpen fixture for years who is now with the Phillies. "No one on that team feels comfortable. The 'family' feeling is gone. There's a larger gap now between the front office and the players than there ever was."

Tekulve escaped the Pirates, of course, via a midseason trade. Madlock found the same escape route.

"You know, Madlock has been mouthing off a lot lately," Galbreath said not long before the Pirates traded the four-time N.L. batting champion to the Dodgers. "Now maybe you can get away with that if you're doing a job. But Madlock wasn't hitting, and he was sloppy fat. Then Joe Brown hauled him on the carpet a couple of weeks ago and told him: 'Look, you aren't worth a cent on the trade market these days. So if you're hoping we'll send you away, you'd better lose that gut and bust your butt and start hitting.' I don't know if Joe's words had any effect. But, right after that chat, Madlock was named National League Player of the Week."

Disenchanted by Players

The man on the street in Pittsburgh really doesn't seem to care for the Pirates—because of the players' high salaries, because of their losing record, their attitude and because, of all things, the Pittsburgh Steelers.

"Maybe I'm unreasonable," said Stachowski, the taxi driver who avoids Three Rivers Stadium during baseball season. "But I figure if a baseball player makes 500 grand, he'd damned well better get a hit every time up and catch everything hit at him."

"I believe the public perception is that the Pirates are a bunch of highly overpaid ingrates," said local attorney Carl Barger.

That perception was enhanced this season by the performance of outfielder "Joggin'" George Hendrick, whose attempts to beat out infield grounders often were terminated after only 45 feet.

"I'll be accused of making this deal to save money," Brown said after trading Hendrick, Candelaria and Holland to the Angels. "But money was not as much of a factor as getting rid of two players whose less-than-perfect attitudes had a negative effect on both our team and our fans."

Keidan, the *Post-Gazette* sports editor, agreed. "The people in this city can't abide players who don't bust their tail when they're making that much money," he said.

On the other hand, the National Football League's Steelers are deemed by local fans to be working hard. And no one seems to dwell on the Steelers' salaries.

Said Barger, the Pittsburgh attorney: "To the average fan, the Pirates come off as an enemy of the city while the Steelers come off almost as a friend."

"That's the paradox, isn't it? Galbreath said with a wry smile. "We are having our problems, and the Steelers are having increased success. The thing to do in Pittsburgh these days is to not be a Pirate fan. But it's considered macho to be a Steeler fan."

"The Steelers are representative of the character of the local populace," Brown said. "The charm of baseball is the individual. The physical nature of football appeals more to those who do physical work—as in this area. But I still don't know why this should translate to what I perceive as a tremendous negative attitude toward the Pirates."

Final Nitpicks

- The Galbreaths are penny-pinchers who are failing to provide the town with a big baseball hero.

"We gave them three exciting superheroes in three different eras—Clemente, Stargell and Parker," said Dan Galbreath. "What more do they want? We gave them Parker, and they booed him out of town.

"As for spending, our team payroll was second or third in the majors in the early 1980s. And we paid big money to (Jason) Thompson and Kemp and Hendrick, too. All right, so the deals for Kemp and Hendrick were bad ones. But at least they were indicative of our willingness to spend."

- The Pirates never should have fired the late Bob Prince, the team's radio announcer.

"The firing (a joint decision by the team and radio station KDKA) did hurt some because Bob was extremely popular, and in a small town you need a cheerleader behind the microphone," Brown said. "We wouldn't be out of the woods (in regard to sagging attendance) if we had kept Prince—but we probably would have been better off."

"I was sorry we had to let Prince go," said Galbreath. "But, frankly, Bob just wasn't the same announcer as a decade earlier. The broadcasts had become the 'Bob Prince Show,' not Pittsburgh Pirates baseball."

• The Galbreaths are absentee owners (they live in Columbus, O.) and don't care about the club.

"Considering the time, effort and money we've put into the team in the last 40 years, I get a little tired of that one," Dan Galbreath said. "I think the situation is more of a comparison of my father with Art Rooney, who seems to be the patron saint of the whole city. I have great respect and admiration for Mr. Rooney, but I don't think that my father—an eminently successful businessman in his own right—should have to suffer by being compared.

"Hey, the Steelers went nearly 40 years (from 1933 through 1971) without winning a damned thing. But did Art Rooney catch hell here? Of course not.

"Why? Because he's Irish, and he's Catholic and he's lovable. In this city, he can do no wrong."

◆　◆　◆

JIM GOTT IN RELIEF

Pittsburgh's baseball franchise was rescued from becoming the New Orleans Pirates when the Galbreath family sold the ball club in late 1985 to Pittsburgh Associates, a group made up of corporate and private investors. The Pirates, thanks to the efforts of Mayor Richard S. Caliguiri, also received concessions and loans from the city of Pittsburgh. By the late 1980s, they started to become an interesting team again, thanks to new manager Jim Leyland and an influx of talent that included Barry Bonds, Bobby Bonilla, and Andy Van Slyke.

After a second-place finish in 1988, the Pirates even caught the eye of Pulitzer Prize-winner and avid baseball fan George F. Will, who saw his first major-league game at Forbes Field in 1950. In his national bestseller Men at Work: The Craft of Baseball, *Will highlighted Pirate Jim Gott in a chapter called "The Pitcher." The following excerpt portrays Gott, who finished the 1988 season with a National League second-best thirty-four saves, as an example of the manic personality that often seems to be part of the make-up of the modern-day relief pitcher.*

The Pitcher

GEORGE F. WILL

Jim Leyland was Gott's manager. The pipe-smoking Leyland is a lean, fine-featured man with salt-and-pepper hair and mustache. When strong sunlight causes him to squint, the crow's-feet at the corners of his eyes crinkle like those of a captain who has just stepped onto the conning tower of a submarine. The Pirates are on the low side in terms of complete games because, Leyland says, "We've got two real horses down there." By "down there" he means the bull pen. The horses snorting and pawing the dirt were then Jeff Robinson and Jim Gott. "Sometimes—and I don't mean this negatively—your real good short relievers, after they've established themselves, they save games on their reputations alone." That is just one of the hard-to-quantify benefits. "There's not enough said about the impact a short reliever has on the entire ball club. If you've got a guy down there who's a stopper, it's a big mental edge. When you bring him in your whole team picks up because they know the game is pretty much over. It makes them more on their toes defensively. They make plays they normally might not make because they know he's going to be around the plate and save the game. There are so many edges when you've got that guy down there." One of them is that a strong reliever also produces a ripple effect through a pitching staff, making the rest of the staff, and the rest of the team, better. The starters need not husband their energies quite as much as they might otherwise do. The batters feel less pressure to pile up big innings early.

One of the men whose task it was to control Gott was catcher Mike LaValliere, known as Spanky. LaValliere is built to be a catcher. The Pirates' 1989 media guide says he stands 5 feet 10 inches. The media guide is fibbing. He is about 5 feet 7 and weighs 200 pounds. This human fire hydrant won a Gold Glove in 1987 when he had a .992 fielding percentage with just two passed balls in 867.1 innings and led the league in throwing out base runners (49 of 115 for a .426 percentage). In 1988 he was named to the *Sporting News* postseason all-star team. He has one of baseball's drier wits. When asked if he tells Leyland when he thinks the starting pitcher is running out of gas, he responds, "More often than not the opposing hitters let us know. If we see the names on the backs of our outfielders too much, that's a pretty good indication." LaValliere adds, "With Jeff (Robinson) and Jim in the bull pen, I get more aggressive with

From *Men at Work: The Craft of Baseball* (New York: Macmillan, 1990). Reprinted with the permission of George F. Will.

the starting pitchers. I don't go into a game thinking that I've got to throw some off-speed stuff so they'll still have a little bit of a fastball in the eighth and ninth innings. With us, it's basically to get 'em to the sixth."

"My time," says Gott, "is the eighth and ninth." It sure is. In his first two full seasons as a closer (1987–88) he never pitched a three-inning stint. Short stints are not for artistry. The canvas is too small. Pitching at its most elegant is (in words Roger Angell used to salute Catfish Hunter) "a tapestry of deceit and experience and efficiency." But that is not the way Gott does it. "Basically," says LaValliere, "what Jim is going to do is throw his 95-mile-per-hour fastball and his 89-mile-per-hour slider. We're not going to get tricky or try to fool anybody." And LaValliere doesn't worry about location. "As long as I can catch it and the hitter can reach it, that's what we're looking for. If Jim starts worrying about location, he's not going to be effective."

Still, Gott is not as, well, *random* as the relief pitcher of whom a team-mate said, "He doesn't throw to spots, he throws to continents." But Gott's "spot" is the strike zone. Gott says the hitters he least likes to face are "the Tony Gwynns of the world, the Tim Raineses, the contact hitters. With me coming straight at them, it's just a matter of timing. The big guys, the power hitters, have bigger holes in their swings." Gott is one power pitcher who has no trouble pitching inside. "They know that I like to pitch inside and that I'm not in a situation to throw at somebody because the last thing I want in short relief in a close game is to hit someone and put him on first." Gott also throws what is being called "the pitch of the Eight-ies." Baseball is a bit like New York society, which produces a "hostess of the decade" every year or so. The first "pitch of the Eighties" was the split-finger fastball. But the stately march of progress is ever onward, as is the struggle of pitchers against the fire-breathing dragon of offense. So the second "pitch of the Eighties" became—drumroll—the circle change. It is thrown with the arm motion of a fastball but is significantly slower. Fur-thermore, it tumbles out of the circle formed by thumb and forefinger, acquiring a rotation that causes it to run down and in (when thrown by a right-handed pitcher to a right-handed hitter). What Roger Craig has been to the split-finger fastball, Ray Miller is to the circle change.

Miller and Gott go together well, and they suit the city they found themselves in 1989, although each took a while in baseball to get there. Both Miller and Gott are no-frills people. They subscribe to the straight-ahead approach to their business. Like the Pirates, they are hard-core baseball.

The Pirates originally were called the Alleghenys. Imagine, a team named after some mountains that are, as mountains go, not much. (Could have been worse. The Brooklyn Dodgers once were the Bridegrooms.) Some franchises are strongly associated with particular parts of the game. When you think of the Dodgers you think of a tradition of pitching, particularly Koufax and Drysdale. When you think of the Pirates you think of hitting, from Willie Stargell and Roberto Clemente back through Ralph Kiner and the Waner brothers (Paul and Lloyd, Big Poison and Little Poison), Pie Traynor and Arky Vaughan and, most of all, the man Branch Rickey and some others say was the best player ever, Honus Wagner.

Pittsburgh's hard-core baseball tradition is best seen far from Pittsburgh, in the Florida town where the Pirates train. A sign on the left-field fence says Bradenton is "the friendly city" and, for good measure, "a little bit of paradise." Perhaps. But the best part of Spring Training in Bradenton is that it still has some of the scruffiness associated with life in what used to be baseball's slow lane. More and more communities have cottoned on to the fact that Spring Training can be big business and have lured teams with posh training "complexes." Crowds are so big in some places that there are ticket scalpers. Oh, well. All this is probably progress, but Bradenton's McKechnie Field, located in the midst of the hum of ordinary commerce and living, should be preserved for the flavor of Spring Training before it became upscale.

Alas, Pittsburgh, like so many other cities, suffered terribly at the hands of baseball vandals in the late 1960s and 1970s. Not since Cromwell's troops, their puritan sensibilities offended by beauty, went around smashing decorative art in churches has there been an act of folly comparable to the abandonment and destruction of Forbes Field, the Pirates' home for generations. The outrage was made worse by the replacement of Forbes Field by Three Rivers Stadium. Forgive my intensity, but a fan remembers with special fondness the ballpark where he saw his first major league game. My first was in Forbes Field in 1950. The loudspeakers were pouring forth the pop song of the moment ("Good Night, Irene") as the 9-year-old from central Illinois entered. He left after the Pirates rang up a thumping victory over the Cardinals, one of only 57 Pirate wins that year. Forbes Field was one of those old parks that combined a sense of spaciousness with a feeling of intimacy.

Three Rivers Stadium was opened in 1970, which means it was dreamed up in the 1960s, which is no excuse but explains a lot. Almost everything about the 1960s, from politics to popular music to neckties, was marked by wretched excess. It was, of course, a decade in love with professional football. It is to baseball's credit that when the times were out of joint, baseball was out of step. As Bill Veeck said, "The Sixties was a time for grunts and screams. . . . The sports that fitted the time were football, hockey and mugging." Three Rivers Stadium was built to accommodate both football and baseball. Big mistake. And speaking of mistakes (there are so many to speak of), there were those Pirates uniforms. From 1977 through 1979 the Pirates pioneered new forms of gaucherie in their three uniforms (one yellow, one black, one white with pinstripes) and two styles of hats. Could there be a more complete contrast with the sedate, unchanging vestments of the Dodgers? In many ways Gott offers a complete contrast with Hershiser. Hershiser is intergalactically famous. Gott is not. No Bob Hope specials for him. Hershiser works in one of the nation's two biggest media markets. Gott worked in one of the smallest of the 26 major league markets. Los Angeles is synonymous with glitter. It should not be. It is as much the home of gang war as of Hollywood. (Gott, by the way, was born in Hollywood.) Pittsburgh is synonymous with sweat and soot. It should not be. The image of Pittsburgh as the Steel City is more than a generation out of date. No steel is made within the city limits. There is only one producing steel mill in the metropolitan area. The city's largest employer is the University of Pittsburgh. But the biggest contrast between Hershiser and Gott is in what they do. Hershiser has a star's job: starting pitcher. Gott's job is to prevent disasters and sometimes tidy up messes that other pitchers have made. Hershiser has the glamour of a surgeon. Gott is one of those harried doctors you see—and are mighty glad to see—coping with crises in busy emergency rooms. When major league managers reach for the dugout phone to call the bull pen they should dial 911. The Book of Job—the relief pitcher's handbook—got it right: Man is born unto trouble as the sparks fly upward.

You do not have to be a bit touched in the head to want to earn a living as a reliever, but many relievers seem to be. There is a tendency for relief pitchers to seem a bit mad—mad meaning angry (Goose Gossage), mad meaning crazed (Sparky Lyle), or both angry and crazed (Al Hrabosky). Moe Drabowsky collected the phone numbers of bull pens all over the major leagues and enjoyed lightening the burden of boredom by calling bull pens in other cities. Imitating the voices of various coaches, he would order relievers hundreds of miles away to start warming up.

Gott, too, tends toward the manic, another complete contrast with cool-hand Hershiser. "My father was a very hard worker, came from nothing and made a lot of money. You don't listen to parents when you are growing up, so my dad found other people for us to listen to." Gott's brother went to golf camps and twice won the California state high school golf championship. Gott went to baseball camps. As a junior in high school he went out for football for the first time. He did it on a dare. Someone challenged him to prove that he was tough enough to play. He could play.

As a senior he was all-conference. UCLA recruited him as a defensive end and middle linebacker. But his father had been a baseball prospect who injured his arm just at the time he was about to make the transition from amateur to professional ball and he wanted one of his children to be a ball player. "My brother," says Gott, "is an introvert and went into golf." Gott is not an introvert. For a while during his, shall we say, vigorously lived youth, which extended well into his twenties, Gott was, he admits, "the classic million-dollar arm with the ten-cent brain." He will be 30 on Opening Day, 1990, and he is still not your typical sight when he arrives at the mound.

It is one of the oldest sayings in baseball. It is what innumerable coaches and managers have said (or are to have said) to innumerable pitchers having problems: "Babe Ruth is dead—throw strikes." It is said that Art Fowler, Billy Martin's Sancho Panza and pitching coach at various stops in Martin's career, was once approached before a game by a young pitcher who said: "In the late innings I seem to lose my control. I'm doing something wrong—opening my shoulder or otherwise developing a flaw in my mechanics. Watch me closely tonight and see if you can spot the problem." Around the seventh inning the young pitcher did indeed lose his control and walked three people. Fowler came to the mound and the young pitcher asked anxiously, "What am I doing wrong?" Fowler, drawing upon years of experience, said, "You're walking people and Billy's pissed."

Fans are forever wondering what gets said to a relief pitcher when he comes to the mound in a difficult situation. With Gott, says LaValliere, "I just try to stop him from snorting. He comes in like a horse, running in from the bull pen. He's huffing and puffing, so the first thing I want to do before I go back to warm him up is let him catch his breath a little bit." Doesn't that surge of adrenaline make it hard for him to keep his mechanics stable? "That is one reason why he has to throw from a stretch even when he is starting an inning. He gets so excited he really couldn't keep all the body parts going in the same direction enough to throw strikes." Steve Carlton used to go into a semi-trance of concentration before a game. But Carlton was a silent, solitary, withdrawn man most of the time. Gott is the soul of sociability, up to a point. "You can talk to him in the bull pen until up around the seventh inning," says LaValliere. "Then he goes into a kind of trance. When he finally gets the phone call, he works himself up. He has to be in fourth gear when he comes in." Gott says, "We're little kids playing a little kid's game. Why shouldn't we show emotion?"

There is an answer to that question. Showing emotion is just *not done* because baseball is such a humbling game. The exultation of success is going to be followed in short order by the cold slap of failure. Any team's success. Anyone's success. So why get high when a low is just around the corner? Baseball is a life best lived in an emotionally temperate zone. Still, relief pitchers and especially closers can be forgiven for being different. Gott sure is.

◆   ◆   ◆

BARRY BONDS

From 1990 to 1992, Pittsburgh collected three Eastern Division titles, two National League's Manager of the Year Awards for Jim Leyland, a National League's Cy Young Award for Doug Drabek, and two National League's Most Valuable Player titles for the team's best player, Barry Bonds. But for all their regular-season successes and awards, the Pirates lost the National League Championship Series three straight years and never advanced to the World Series. By the 1993 season the team had also lost Bobby Bonilla, Doug Drabek, and Barry Bonds to free agency. No player was more of a lightning rod in the early 1990s for the frustrations of fans and the press than Barry Bonds. Bob Smizik's "Give Him a Break: Don't Boo Bonds" is an unusual appeal to fans to overlook Bond's boorish behavior in a much publicized spring-training incident with Jim Leyland and to cheer Bonds at the Pirate home opener.

Give Him a Break: Don't Boo Bonds

BOB SMIZIK

When he takes the field tomorrow night before the Pirates' opener, it will have been 180 days since Barry Bonds last walked across the Three Rivers Stadium turf. That's about six months since Pittsburgh fans have seen him in the flesh in a Pirates uniform. That's half a year since they have had a chance to let Bonds know what they think of him.

When Bonds last walked across the turf of Three Rivers it was after a Pirates' 3-2 victory against the Cincinnati Reds in the fifth game of the National League Championship Series. He was seven weeks away from winning the Most Valuable Player award and was the Pirate most responsible for the team's 1990 success.

He also was minutes away from the start of a series of irrational outbursts that has eroded his popularity, threatened to curtail his career in Pittsburgh and nationally made him the embodiment of the spoiled baseball player.

In defeating the Reds on that night of Oct. 10, the Pirates had extended the championship series to a sixth game. Theirs was a happy club house. But Bonds found a way to sour the victory. He astonished his teammates, the media and the public by suggesting third baseman Jeff King was a malingerer for not being in the lineup that night.

The reaction, understandably, was, "What kind of jerk is this guy?" The answer was months in coming.

After maintaining a low profile for most of the winter—not even the Pirates had his telephone number—Bonds popped off on ESPN about never signing a long term contract with the Pirates. In February he predicted a victory for himself in arbitration, only to lose. In the process, he managed to convey the impression that although he was a 26-year-old man who would be making in excess of $2 million, the public should feel sorry for him.

In early March, Bonds destroyed any kind of image he had of being a decent fellow. It started at Pirate City with a shouting match with Jim Lachimia, the director of media relations, evolved into a confrontation with special instructor Bill Virdon and ended with Manager Jim Leyland screaming in his face. It was recorded on tape and shown repeatedly on local and national television.

In response to the question of what kind of jerk is this guy the public had an answer: A big one.

And now he's back home. The columnists, letter writers and talk-show callers have had their day with Bonds and most have not been kind. And now it's the paying customers' turn. How should tomorrow night's sellout crowd deal with Bonds?

Gently, folks, gently. Give him a break. Does he deserve it? Probably not. But the Pirates do. He is their most important player. This is no time for vengeance; it's a time for compassion. Why start the season on a sour note just because Bonds ended the last one that way.

To boo Bonds, and it certainly is the fans' right, is to mess with his mind. That not only affects Bonds, it affects the Pirates.

Players don't often admit booing affects them, but it does.

"Of course, booing bothers a player," Andy Van Slyke said. "How would you like to be standing out there in front of 50,000 people and have them booing you?"

Beyond the sake of the Pirates, there's another reason to relax about Bonds. Maybe you haven't noticed, but he has shut up for more than a month. Maybe his mouth will get in the way of his playing any day now, but by all indications he's trying. It's as if he realizes he has gone too far.

Bobby Bonilla, Bonds' best friend on the Pirates, preaches understanding for his pal.

"People have to have a lot of patience with Barry. They forget that Barry has done all his growing up in the big leagues and we tend to be a little spoiled up here."

Yeah, he's spoiled. The son of Bobby Bonds, the godson of Willie Mays, he has had life easier than most. He grew up in a big-league clubhouse. He was special. He is having to learn about life as he goes along.

Maybe he's getting better at it. Or maybe his recent behavior is an aberration. But he has earned a reprieve.

"I hope there's total appreciation for Barry Bonds' effort because he has given us nothing but his best since he has been here," Leyland said. "I would hope there's nothing but total applause for him."

"I also want to say if someone is booing Barry Bonds because of the incident we had, then that's not right. I've had screaming matches with four or five players since I've been here. That should not dictate somebody being booed. I think that would be totally unfair. If I were a fan I'd cheer Barry Bonds."

It's up to the fans. Maybe some have been waiting for months to have their say about this troubled athlete. But let compassion rule the night. If Bonds' later actions reveal he hasn't earned this reprieve, there will be other nights.

◆   ◆   ◆

THE LAST BASEBALL GAME IN PITTSBURGH?

By the end of the 1995 season, the loose-knit, private and public Pirate ownership group, the Pittsburgh Baseball Associates, had lost more than twenty-two million dollars and, after ten years of mounting debt, was ready to sell the franchise. With the lowest attendance in major-league baseball and with no clear option to keep the team in Pittsburgh, the Pirates were on the verge of moving to another city. When the team played its last home game of the season at Three Rivers Stadium, many people believed that, after 109 years of National League baseball in Pittsburgh, the team had played its final game in Barney Dreyfuss's first-division city.

Saying Goodbye Would Be Hard

PAUL MEYER

If that really was the Pirates' last home game—ever—last night . . .

"I would be devastated," said Sally O'Leary, scheduled to retire next May after 32 years in the Pirates front office. "I would be very hurt to think baseball would not be in Pittsburgh. It's been part of the scene for 109 years. It doesn't seem right it wouldn't be here anymore."

But the possibility the Pirates will leave does exist and has existed for some time.

"One day you're up. The next day you're down," O'Leary said. "It's been like a roller coaster—because my future is affected, too. I'm still going to be involved in the Pirates Alumni. But if there isn't a Pirates team, what happens to the Pirates Alumni? It wouldn't carry as much weight. That would make me unhappy.

"We have good traditions here. We have a good bunch of former players who still live here and who still help us in a lot of ways."

Blass Hopeful

"I would be devastated," said former Pirates pitcher Steve Blass, now one of the team's broadcasters. "To me, it's always the 'Pittsburgh Pirates.' It's not the 'anything else Pirates.' Most of my baseball life has been in this park. I know everybody from the guy who takes your parking ticket to the president of the ball club. And, really, it's not just a ball park. It's a place where a lot of people have grown up."

Blass isn't convinced the Pirates will move.

"Because I don't want us to," he said. "I will freely admit I have my head in the sand. I hope intelligent people will get something done. To me, it's impossible that the Pirates won't be here. Therefore, it won't happen. It's insane to think there won't be anymore Pittsburgh Pirates. It's a joke that this club would leave this city.

"The more I think about it—and I try not to think about it—the angrier I get."

Gwynn Doubtful

San Diego outfielder Tony Gwynn scored the winning run for the National League in last year's All-Star game at Three Rivers Stadium.

"It was unbelievable," he said of the crowd. "That's the most enthusiastic and most into-the-game-of-baseball fans that I've seen in all my years in the big leagues. It was just unbelievable. People were hyped up for that game. They were excited. But I haven't seen it like that here since. Or before, either.

"It doesn't really concern me if the Pirates leave. That's how I look at it. The Pirates have been around for a long time. They've got a nice history, a nice tradition. They've had great players. But economically, I don't think it can survive here, to tell you the truth. They've had great players and great teams, but it's still a tough sale."

Working Hard

"I'd be extremely disappointed," said broadcaster Lanny Frattare, finishing his 20th season behind the Pirates' mike, "because I sincerely believe a lot of people have worked very hard on behalf of this organization for a long time."

Frattare said he hadn't thought much about the prospect of last night being the Pirates' final home game.

"And only because people have been talking about it so much," he said. "Do I believe it's our last home game? No I don't. There are still a large number of people who are committed to working hard to ensure the future of our ball club in Pittsburgh."

A Good Town

Bobby Del Greco also grew up in Pittsburgh and played for the Pirates in the 1950s after being signed by Pie Traynor, the former Pirates manager and Hall of Fame third baseman.

"I'd feel very, very bad about it," Del Greco said of the possibility of the Pirates leaving. "After a hundred years or so, it would be really tough for the town if they lose it.

"I used to go to Pirate games when I was a kid. I never dreamed I'd wind up playing for them. It would be terrible if they left. This is a good baseball town. We're having our problems now, but if we keep the team here, it will come around."

Great Rivalries

Phillies broadcaster Harry Kalas remembers Three Rivers Stadium as the place where Danny Ozark failed arithmetic.

It was here one season after the Phillies lost to the Pirates that Ozark told his players, "Don't give up."

One problem, though. The Phillies had fallen 6½ games off the lead—with only six games left.

"I'd feel very badly if the Pirates left," Kalas said. "You're talking about great tradition here. And the Phillies and the Pirates always had a great rivalry. Great games. The Pirates clinched championships against us here. And, we clinched against them here too."

Would Hurt City

John Candelaria, who pitched the only no-hitter by a Pirate in Three Rivers Stadium, dropped by the stadium the other day.

"I wouldn't like it at all if the Pirates left," he said. "You think about all the great players who have come through here. I think it would hurt the city. There are a lot of good people who would lose jobs. And I don't think Pittsburgh would ever get major-league baseball back. That would be a shame."

Kids' Nightmare

John Wehner grew up in Pittsburgh as a Pirates' fan and now plays for the Pirates.

"It would just be a shame if we left," Wehner said. "I don't think people realize what losing the Pirates would mean. I think of my dream of growing up to be a Pirate. There have to be hundreds, if not thousands of kids who have the same dream. If we're not here, what's their dream going to be—growing up to be a Cleveland Indian?

"I don't think we're going to leave, but I'd say the chances are like a coin flip. Heads we stay, tails we leave. It's that close. And that's pretty scary."

Long Memories

"I will not bring myself to believe it's the last home game," broadcaster Greg Brown said.

"My father took me to my first game here in 1970 when I was nine years old. That memory, along with a handful of others, is as vivid as any I've ever had.

"We used to drive over from Mechanicsburg, about a four hour drive. We'd stay at the visiting team's hotel, and I'd get autographs. In my whole life, my greatest memories are of this team and this park.

"It may not be realistic, but I just can't bring myself to think the powers that be—whoever they may be—will allow this club to leave."

A Sad Day

To former Pirates pitcher Bob Walk, last night was reminiscent of his last game with the Pirates in 1993.

"In the back of my mind, I thought that it could be my last game as a Pirate," Walk said of his start against Philadelphia. "But I didn't know for sure. That was better. I wasn't all emotional.

"I would feel a lot different if I knew that last night was the last game. It would be a very sad day for me. But I don't know that, so I don't feel that bad. I went in with the attitude that we'll be back. If we're not, then it was an awful sad last day here."

Not the Same Place

"I don't think the city would feel poorly about this team leaving anymore," former Pirate Gary Varsho said recently. "It's just not the same baseball city it used to be.

"Don't get me wrong—I loved it here. I had some of the best times of my career here. But they can't get the fan base . . . All Jimmy [Leyland] and the Pirates have ever done is try to put as good a team as the Pirates could afford on the field.

"Your diehard Pirates baseball fans will miss them. But how many of them are left?"

It's a Tradition

Kent Tekulve, who grew up near Cincinnati and now lives in Pittsburgh, definitely would miss the Pirates.

"It would be the first time in 48 years I didn't have a local major-league team to watch," Tekulve said. "That would be a radical change of lifestyle for me.

"If it all dried up and went away, I'd be disappointed on two fronts. One, I played here for ten years. To have the team move, it's like your past history is now dissolved. It would be the same players, but not the same team.

"And, two, I still live here. I know what it was like to grow up with a major-league baseball team in Cincinnati. I hope my kid will have a chance to grow up and have a major-league team to watch—and I have a team to watch in my golden years."

Petty Piracy

Last night Walk planned a bit of petty piracy.

"Just in case," he said, "I want to collect a little dirt from the pitcher's mound, put it in a jar and take it home and put it in the attic. That's where all my baseball stuff is.

"Then, if we're back next April, I'll bring the jar to the stadium and put the dirt back out there on the mound."

That would be a ceremony almost everybody at the stadium last night would have attended.

◆   ◆   ◆

KEVIN MCCLATCHY

On the brink of losing its National League franchise for the second time in ten years, the Pirates needed a savior, or, at the least, a hero; someone willing to buy the team and keep it in Pittsburgh despite mounting debt, a diminishing fan base, and an uncertain future in a stadium best suited for football. The city found its hero on February 14, 1996, when Sacramento-based Kevin McClatchy forged a limited partnership at the last hour and became the owner of the Pittsburgh Pirates.

"The Education of Kevin McClatchy" by columnist Sam Edelmann and baseball historian Rob Ruck highlights the early controversies surrounding McClatchy, including the criticism that he was an intellectual and business lightweight and the contradictory suspicion that he really bought the Pirates to make money by moving the team to another city. But, more than anything else, the article focuses on the growing importance of building a new ballpark to the future of the Pirates in Pittsburgh.

The Education of Kevin McClatchy

SAM EDELMANN and ROB RUCK

When the Pirates take to the field on opening day, the most recognizable face connected to the club will belong to its CEO and managing partner, Kevin Soerensen McClatchy. Hailed as a savior when he gained control of the team on Valentine's Day 1996, the 34-year-old scion of a California newspaper family has since been savaged by sportswriters and fans incensed over the departure of Jim Leyland et al., and fearful that the Bucs are not long for this town.

McClatchy's motives have been impugned and his intelligence questioned. *Post-Gazette* columnist Bruce Keidan, certainly one of the best-connected sportswriters in Pittsburgh, wrote of McClatchy last fall that "you could put his business acumen in a thimble and have plenty of room left over for your thumb."

In early August, general partner Frank Fuhrer pulled out his $5 mil-

From *Pittsburgh Magazine*, April 1997. Reprinted with permission of Sam Edelmann and Rob Ruck.

lion investment, claiming that McClatchy's financial projections were wildly inaccurate. A week later, general partner Kenneth Pollock announced that he would follow suit. Both felt McClatchy had pulled a fast one, promising them more of a role in running the club than they actually got. Since then, says one source, "The corporate lockerroom talk about him is that he might be in over his head. There's a 50-50 chance he won't be here in a year."

McClatchy now reflects about the tumult of the past year. "I didn't feel it was a lot of fun at the time," he says wryly. "Couple of days in a row, I woke up and asked myself, 'Why am I trying to save this baseball team?'"

Why indeed? Why risk about half of your personal worth of roughly $20 million, subject yourself to denunciation in the papers and on the air, and surrender your privacy for once and for all?

"If I wanted to make money, there are much easier ways to do it," McClatchy acknowledges. "I'm not in this to get rich. I am in it to turn a baseball team around and to make something that folks say won't work, work. But I don't want it to sound like I'm a martyr, because the simple fact is that, for the most part, I love what I do."

Despite a lifetime spent around the news media, McClatchy was unprepared for the skepticism he encountered. "I read newspaper columns on how I should get back on the plane and go back" because a deal to buy the club was considered unmakeable. "I thought it was strange how I had already gone to the judge and the guillotine had flown before we really had time to get anything established."

That McClatchy was young, a multimillionaire and from California raised eyebrows in a city whose elite only recently opened itself up to more than a tightly knit Scots-Irish Presbyterian cohort. Of course, if McClatchy had been born here, he would have been a member of the club.

His father was the late Charles McClatchy, the progressive editor of the *Sacramento Bee*, which James McClatchy, Kevin's great-great-grandfather, founded in 1857. His mother is Grace Kennan Warnecke, a former photographer and editor who runs a consulting firm for companies involved in the former Soviet Union. Her father and Kevin's grandfather is George Kennan, a foreign-service legend and the preeminent expert on Soviet–U.S. affairs since the 1930s.

Though he had a morning paper route in the fifth grade and later worked for the *Miami Herald*, Kevin was always more interested in sports than journalism and foreign affairs. "I'm a little different from people in my family," he laughs. When he was 14, Kevin attended Trinity Pawling High School in New York City because of the school's program for students with dyslexia, with which he had been diagnosed in fifth grade. There, Kevin roomed with Dan Rooney Jr. and played basketball, football and tennis. He played cornerback at the University of California at Santa Barbara, where in 1983 he helped revive a football program that had been discontinued in 1971.

After college, McClatchy worked as a reporter and in sales and marketing in the newspaper business. In 1994, he bought a piece of the Modesto A's, a minor league ball club, but failed in a later bid to gain control of the Oakland A's.

McClatchy arrived in Pittsburgh in June 1995, after an offer to buy the team from John Rigas was rejected by Major League Baseball because of insufficient capitalization. Dismissed as a lightweight who, if he bought the team, would move it, McClatchy gradually overcame both Pittsburgh mayor Tom Murphy's resistance and that of the ownership coalition.

In addition to his own $8 million investment, McClatchy convinced about 30 individuals and businesses, including Heinz CEO Anthony O'Reilly, Indy car team owner Chip Ganassi and Fuhrer, to throw in another $38.5 million. He then persuaded most of the club's owners to keep their investment in the Pirates and stay on as limited partners. That greatly reduced the amount of money McClatchy had to raise to meet the league's requirements. And though his actual investment represented only about 13 percent of the total, McClatchy wound up as CEO and managing partner—and the youngest owner in the majors.

Not too shabby for a guy dismissed as a business nebbish.

The Pirates have not had an easily recognizable owner who resided in the city in half a century. Believing it vital for fans to have someone they could identify as the owner, McClatchy threw himself into a whirlwind of public appearances. He also took up residence in a dugout-level seat right behind home plate and figured front and center in advertising campaigns.

Last August, however, McClatchy reversed his strategy of gradually increasing the payroll and, instead, traded off his major-league assets for minor-league prospects. When Jim Leyland was allowed to leave a few weeks later, McClatchy was vilified. Most fans believed he was slashing the payroll not to save baseball but to guarantee its failure so that he could move elsewhere.

"If I wanted this thing to fail," McClatchy said this winter, "I could do it from California. I wouldn't be making 140 speaking engagements a year. By saying I'm going to move the club, they're essentially calling me a liar. It's tough to deal with that."

But the boy who overcame dyslexia and the young man who persisted in his efforts to buy the team when few thought it possible is dealing with it. "Tenacity," Malcolm Prine says with respect. "You've got to give him that."

Prine, president of the franchise after its purchase in 1986, points out that the sudden overhaul of the club and concerns about its financial stability have undermined McClatchy. He, like others interviewed for this story, believes that McClatchy needs to articulate a stronger case for the club and the new ballfield.

McClatchy agrees. But it has taken him time to figure out Pittsburgh. Over the winter, he observed that the region had internalized a sense of decline. "I always hear how we can't be successful," he reflects. "That has to change, because if you truly want to bring companies into this area, you can't do it with your tail between your legs."

A new ballpark, he argues, would "show the rest of the country that Pittsburgh is moving forward."

McClatchy has been roughed up, but he's learned from the bruising. He realizes the Allegheny corridor project provides the ballclub with its best—and maybe last—chance of making it in Pittsburgh.

He also wants to clear up two misconceptions. The first is that he's so rich that this investment is only a small risk. "I've got a lot of my money sunk into this," he protests. "The truth is that I'm not Disney, I'm not Ted Turner." If he fails, he says, "I will also be taking a pretty big hit."

The second misconception is that this is a hobby for him. "This is what I do 16 hours a day," McClatchy stresses. "I live and breathe this stuff. And it's a dream at the same time."

McClatchy still hears that his real goal is to make money by moving the club or selling it to a Sunbelt city. If financing for the new ballpark is not in place by 1998 and the facility complete for the 2001 season, McClatchy could do either. The city, however, would have nine months to find a local buyer, with the sales price determined by arbitrators judging the franchise's fair market value in Pittsburgh—which would be substantially less than the club could fetch on the open market. Any debts the current owners incur would be their own responsibility. These terms seriously constrain the owners' potential to make a profit on selling the club—if that is truly their motive.

McClatchy denies that he and his mostly Pittsburgh-based partners have any intention of moving the club. "I am very driven," he reflects, "but not necessarily driven to make more money than anyone else." His challenge is to pull off the biggest turnaround in recent baseball history.

But if the drive to build a new ballpark fails and his losses mount, McClatchy admits he would eventually be forced to sell the team. But, he swears, he is not entertaining offers. "I won't be doing the moving. I've put too much into this in the last year and a half, basically shutting my life down."

For McClatchy to make the Pirates a success, he'll need public backing for a new ballpark. But with such public financing comes enormous civic responsibility. The coalition of corporations, individuals and the Heinz Endowments that bought the team in 1986 did not do so to make a profit or appreciate its capital. They did so to keep the team from leaving for the Sunbelt. They brought the club back from three last-place finishes in a row, then tripled attendance and won three consecutive division titles. But ownership fell behind the curve and was unable to forestall the Pirates collapse, which began in 1993.

One bright spot has been the team's efforts of the past decade to better connect with the region's African-American community. Al Gordon, director of community services, has become a familiar figure in the black community. The club has also championed the RBI (Reviving Baseball in the Inner City) program.

The team's front office has tried hard to make baseball work in Pittsburgh, despite the double whammy of a protracted labor dispute and an 18-month-long search for new ownership. They are an earnest lot, as is McClatchy, who continues to learn the landscape here.

But that's not a new scenario. The Pirates have been bought by out-of-towners twice before. In 1900, the savior was Barney Dreyfuss, a 35-year-old German Jew who got a piece of the club as compensation for his Louisville team's losing its league franchise. Dreyfuss brought Honus Wagner and Deacon Phillippe with him and turned the Pirates into a National League powerhouse. In 1909, he built Forbes Field in Oakland—which most people at the time saw as a leap of faith—and brought the region its first World Series Championship the same year.

Like Dreyfuss, John Galbreath built a new ballpark and won the World Series. Galbreath emerged as the principal owner after a four-man syndicate bought the club from Dreyfuss' daughter and son-in-law in 1946. Though he never relocated from Columbus, Galbreath oversaw the 1960 championship, the move to Three Rivers Stadium in 1970, and the 1971 and 1979 titles.

Can McClatchy make it three owners in a row who arrive from afar, build a new ballpark and bring home the flag? Is he building the Pirates of the next millennium or writing the last chapter on major league baseball in Pittsburgh?

THE PIRATE FAN

The fan book has become one of baseball writing's most popular genres. From James T. Farrell's My Baseball Diary *and Arnold Hano's* A Day in the Bleachers, *two classics from the 1950s, to the more recent Doris Kearns Goodwin's* Wait Till Next Year *and Scott Simon's* Home and Away, *the best fan memoirs have given baseball readers a great deal of insight into both the psychology and mythology of being a fan.*

Laurie Graham, a longtime editor at Scribners, grew up a Pirate fan because of her family's Pittsburgh roots, but she didn't become a resident of the city until 1990. Since that time, she has written Singing the City, *a celebration of Pittsburgh's industrial landscape, as well as "Let's Go Bucs!" which appeared in* Pittsburgh Sports. *This segment of that essay describes her strong emotional identification with Pittsburgh and its baseball team during a period of disappointment, uncertainty, and struggle and her renewed hope for the city and the Pirates at the end of the decade and the century.*

Let's Go Bucs!

LAURIE GRAHAM

The year 1990 marks a dividing line in my life as a fan. Until then I had lived in other cities. But shortly after that playoff game against the Reds, I found an apartment in Pittsburgh, on a bluff overlooking the confluence of the rivers, Three Rivers Stadium, the skyscrapers of downtown. It was a difficult time for me. My husband had died several years before, and I knew I didn't want to start again in New York without him. The playoff games against the Reds had brought me home. For the first time in my life the Pirates would be literally my home team.

I couldn't have articulated it when I was a child, what it was that made Pittsburgh home. I'm not even sure I was conscious of it at the time. Pittsburgh then meant simply family. But when I came back to the city in 1990 I realized that it was something more. Looking out over the city one afternoon shortly after my return, I felt what I am convinced is a genetic link to the place where generations of my family had lived and worked before me. I felt at one with the hills, the converging rivers, their towboats and their bridges, the freight trains passing below me along the Monongahela,

From "Let's Go Bucs," in *Pittsburgh Sports: Stories from the Steel City*, edited by Randy Roberts (Pittsburgh: University of Pittsburgh Press, 2000).

even the new glittering skyscrapers that had not existed in my youth. I remember feeling the city almost literally inside of me. The Pirates, too, were part of the city's identity. Not only did they link me to my family and to a place. They were, in the deepest sense, a part of me.

The Pirates would win no more games in 1990. They lost the final playoff game, in Cincinnati, by a score of 2-1, giving the championship series to the Reds, four games to two. For three years running, the Pirates would reach the playoffs only to fall short: to the Reds in 1990 and to the Braves in '91 and '92. Andy Van Slyke. Bobby Bonilla. Barry Bonds. Were they simply not good enough? I don't know. But certainly, in 1990 and 1991, the bats died. I remember the chill, dark night of game 7 in 1991, as Pirate pitcher John Smiley gave up three runs in the top of the first. I think we knew even then that the game was lost. In 1992, well, the reader might expect me to say something about Francisco Cabrera's game-winning hit for Atlanta in game 7. But in this respect I resemble the renowned evolutionary biologist and Yankee fan Stephen Jay Gould, who refuses even now to discuss Mazeroski's 1960 Series-winning home run. If you want to hear about Francisco Cabrera, you'll have to ask somebody else.

For me, the playoffs of '90, '91, and '92 underscored the city's consciousness of loss. During the 1970s and 1980s much of Pittsburgh's industrial base was shattered. In the 1980s alone 130,000 jobs were lost; 176,000 people left. In the steel industry, an entire multigenerational way of life—and the sense of identity that went with it—largely disappeared. I remember reading the paper after the final playoff game of 1991. Some Pirate fans sitting in the upper deck had offered congratulations to a clutch of Braves fans before the game was even over. I didn't like that graciousness in losing, the anticipation and acceptance of loss. The acceptance of that creeping suspicion that, as a city, we might not be good enough to win. I didn't want to see that Pittsburgh inferiority complex, born of years of being identified as a smoky city. I wanted us to be proud. Much of the work of Pittsburgh has been hard. Much of it has taken courage. But Pittsburghers have gotten it done. We are part of the nation's bedrock.

For much of the 1990s Pirate fans have had another possible loss to contemplate, a loss more devastating than that of any single game. For much of the 1990s we have faced the possible loss of the franchise itself. It wasn't the first time we had had to face such a possibility. We had pulled back from the brink less than a decade before. In the mid-1980s, drug scandals and what were perceived as overpaid, lackadaisical players had soured the team's image. In 1985 the Pirates finished last in the National League East, 43½ games behind the division-winning Cardinals. Attendance for the season was 735,900. The team was bleeding red ink. Eager to sell, Dan Galbreath, whose family had owned the Pirates for nearly forty years, was ready to put the team into bankruptcy if a buyer could not be found. He could no longer promise to sell only to a group dedicated to keeping the team in Pittsburgh. It was only in the nick of time that a consortium of private individuals and local corporations, with an additional loan from the city's Urban Redevelopment Authority, saved the franchise for Pittsburgh.

The tenuousness of the franchise remained a subtext, though muted, even during the playoff years of the 1990s. National sportscasters cackled if a playoff game did not completely sell out, refusing to acknowledge the economic hit the city had suffered in the 1980s. Many fans were saving discretionary income for the Series—though of course we never got that far. I found myself monitoring attendance, and as the stars of the early 1990s—Bonilla, Bonds, Drabek, Smiley—left for other teams, somehow trying to save the team on my own, seldom missing a game, feeling that somehow my presence at the stadium was connected with the team's survival here. I was seldom seen without a Pirates T-shirt—I had them in every design, and some brought better results on the field than others. Finding a way to win games—even by wearing the right T-shirt—was crucial to a franchise at risk. A loss could mean lower attendance at subsequent games; lower attendance could mean the loss of the franchise itself. But they also served two related purposes. In my T-shirt I was a walking advertisement in support of the team, and part of the T-shirt's purchase price would be a small contribution to the team's coffers. It was a heavy responsibility, that superstitious self-identification with the team's destiny (and I write about it in the full knowledge that the reader may think I've gone over the edge). It took several years for my subconscious to realize that I was not a talisman, that I couldn't do it on my own. Still, even today, an unease lingers, tells me that I must not let up, that I must earn the privilege of keeping the Pirates here.

In 1994, saddled with some $60 million in debt, the consortium of Pirate owners that had saved the team in 1985 triggered their option to sell. The city had 180 days to find a buyer who would keep the team in Pittsburgh. The sharks started to circle, super-rich men from other cities determined to snag a franchise for their own hometowns. I remember after the final home game of the '95 season, as 11,000 fans stood silent in the rain, not wanting to leave, sensing that they had just seen the last game ever to be played in Pittsburgh. The scoreboard screen read something like "Opening Day. Pirates vs. Phillies. April 8, 1996. See you next year!" But few thought that promise could be kept.

On April 8, 1996, the Pirates played that home opener at Three Rivers against the Phillies. The team had been bought less than two months before, on Valentine's Day. The group of investors was headed by a 33-year-old member of a California newspaper family named Kevin McClatchy, who had vowed to keep the team in Pittsburgh on the condition that a new stadium be built to give the team the revenue streams it needed to survive. Some fans, and many in the local media, distrusted him, fearing that he had bought the team only to move it to Sacramento. But he has kept his promises to Pittsburgh, winning a number of hearts in the process. He lives in Pittsburgh now and seldom misses a game, sitting in the front row of the stands behind home plate.

I have never expressed my own gratitude to Kevin McClatchy. I've had ample opportunity, as he is very accessible to Pirate fans. But each time I've been around him, I've been seized by an attack of shyness and backed away. So perhaps this is my opportunity to say what I had in mind to say to him on the night of the groundbreaking for PNC Park: "Thank you, Kevin, for sticking it out."

As Kevin McClatchy became the Pirates' future, Jim Leyland, the team's manager for eleven seasons, became the Pirates' past. Leyland hadn't the stomach for the further dismantling and slow rebuilding that McClatchy saw as essential to creating a winning team in Pittsburgh. The team couldn't afford to buy a passel of high-priced free agents. Leyland had come to the Pirates in November 1985, a virtual unknown, after eighteen years of "scuffling" in the minors and four years of coaching with the White Sox under Tony LaRussa. The Pirates lost 98 games in his first season as manager. (At least that was better than the 104 games they lost the year before.) By 1990, he had led them to the first of three consecutive Eastern Division championships. In 1991, season attendance reached an all-time high: 2,065,302. Regarded as one of the best managers in baseball, he wanted a World Series ring before he retired. He no longer had the time or the patience to do it with a young team.

For a moment it seemed the ultimate betrayal. With the loss of many of its stars, Leyland had become the face of the team, the one constant holding things together. As a person he was the embodiment of how we, as a city, envisioned ourselves: unpretentious, straightforward, self-deprecating, tough when he needed to be, a family man, a believer in work. He was proud of his players, proud of their effort. I think back in particular to a rainy, cold afternoon in April 1991. It was the last game of a four-game series against the Cubs. After the top of the eighth, the Cubs had a 7-2 lead. Only a smattering of fans remained in the stands, in ponchos, or huddled under umbrellas. Then in the bottom of the eighth the Pirates scored four runs to make the score 7-6. In the bottom of the ninth, they scored again to tie the game. The fans were jubilant. But in the top of the eleventh Doug Dascenzo's RBI single and right fielder Andre Dawson's second grand slam of the series put the Cubs up 12-7. The crowd fell silent. Surely the game was over. I remember the crush of disappointment. But in the bottom of the eleventh the Pirates chipped away at the lead, two runs and then another and another, until, with the score 12-11 and the bases loaded, catcher Don Slaught sent a drive over the centerfielder's head. They had come back twice from five-run deficits to win the game. "They showed why they're professionals," Leyland said through tears in the interview after the game. He could hardly look at the camera. "Nobody gave up. . . . They always give their best. I'm proud of that."

He wore his heart on his sleeve. "Do you think I'm proud that the whole country sees me with tears rolling down my face?" he asked in his goodbye to the fans of Pittsburgh. "Let me try to explain something to you. My dad was one of 16 children. He was raised in a family that got very emotional when one of its members accomplished something. That's the same way he raised us. He always preached family to us. And he always challenged us to make something of ourselves. I think that's why I'm like I am. It's like I worked hard all my life to make my dad proud. That's all I ever wanted to do." When Leyland was introduced at the All-Star game at Three Rivers Stadium in 1994, Pirate fans gave him a thunderous standing ovation. I remember the sweet look of congratulation on Giants' manager Dusty Baker's face. Leyland got his World Series ring in 1997, with a Florida team that had far deeper pockets than the Pirates. But I'm not sure that by then it was all that much fun anymore.

For the Pirates 1997 was a year of joyful overachievement. The team had a cumulative payroll of $9,100,000, less than the White Sox were paying their surly slugger Albert Belle. Predicted to finish last, they were the kind of scrambling, hustling team that Pirate fans love. And they were in contention for a division title (in an admittedly weak National League Central Division) the entire year. On July 12, in perhaps the season's greatest moment, a sellout crowd of 44,119 saw two Mexican pitchers, Francisco Cordova and Ricardo Rincon, pitch the first combined extra-inning no-hitter in major league history.

Watching a no-hitter may be baseball's most exquisite tension. Each batter, each pitch, inning after inning bears such a burden, the possibility of that slight mistake that will mean the end. Cordova pitched nine hitless innings that night. The Pirates were playing the first-place Houston Astros.

In second place, only one game out, they would be tied for first with a win. By the fifth, the stands buzzed with the awareness of a possible no-hitter. I can still see the image of a disgusted Jeff Bagwell, slamming down his bat after popping to right for the final out of Houston's ninth. But the Pirates had yet to score, and didn't score in the bottom of the ninth. Cordova's night was over. Manager Gene Lamont sent in Rincon to pitch the top of the tenth. He gave up a walk, but no hits. In the bottom of the tenth, with two on and two outs, journeyman outfielder Mark Smith came off the bench and sent an 0-1 fastball from John Hudek high into the left-field stands. Forty-four thousand voices roared their delight. "The best baseball game I ever saw," said owner Kevin McClatchy. "It was like something out of a movie." There was a sense that these young, overachieving, low-salaried (in major league baseball terms) players were playing for the pure love of the game. Just before the All-Star break, Pirate right-hander Jon Lieber had struck out the mighty Albert Belle in all four at-bats in the first game of a three-game sweep of the White Sox. (It was the first year of interleague play.) They were, in the words of left-fielder Al Martin, "a blue-collar team in a blue-collar city." The '97 Pirates were Pittsburgh's and baseball's darlings.

After nearly two years of rancorous debate, public and private funding is in place to build a new ballpark for the Pirates, as well as a new stadium for the Steelers, and the structures are now going up on their respective sites. The odds of keeping the Pirates in Pittsburgh long-term look better than they have for some time. I understand the arguments against using public funds to build professional sports stadiums. Too many people struggle here to hold life together on minimum wage. Why should their tax money be used to support a sport whose economics are barely under control? In an era when a pitcher can command a seven-year contract at $15,000,000 a year, when too many teams are owned by fabulously wealthy media conglomerates, how can a small-market team like the Pirates survive? I understand all this. But there is a realistic hope of increased revenue-sharing to narrow the gap between the "haves" and the "have-nots." Pittsburgh is building for a new high-tech future now. We can't afford to lose any more of our assets. The Pirates have been Pittsburgh's team for 113 years. I have to wonder how we could ever let them go.

I think back on the 1998 season. On the whole, it was disappointing. They had lost the magic of 1997. But still there was much to remember. Catcher Jason Kendall's aerial corkscrew slide to avoid the tag at home. Jose Guillen's strike from right field to nail the runner at third. The elegant line of first baseman Kevin Young's torso as he completed a home-run swing. Backup outfielder Turner Ward crashing through the wall to catch a fly ball, disappearing completely as the wall panel closed behind him like a door. And then, there was nineteen-year-old rookie Aramis Ramirez and his first major-league hit. Ramirez was 0 for 24 in major-league at-bats. The Pirates were holding on in the seventh to a 1-0 lead against the Mets. With two outs and the bases loaded, Ramirez headed toward the plate. The crowd rose in a standing ovation. A vote of confidence and encouragement. But also a lot of pressure to put on a rookie. The first pitch was a called strike one. Still the crowd cheered and applauded. On the next pitch Ramirez lined a double into left field. The crowd roared. "The people were real happy," Ramirez said after the game, "like me. I wanted to smile, but this is the big leagues. I acted real serious, but I was real happy."

"A great baseball moment," said former pitcher and Pirate color commentator Bob Walk.

"I don't think I've ever seen that," said manager Gene Lamont. "It gave you chills. I think the fans wanted to show him they like young, hungry players, which he is. The kid surely had to like it. I know I did."

It was a moment that confirmed all that is right and beautiful in baseball, the gift of hope and possibility, the sense, even if just for a moment, that the world is good. Baseball is a game of new beginnings. Each game, each inning, each at-bat brings new opportunity, a clean slate, another chance. You begin again.

The 1999 season was a season of promise unfulfilled. What could have been closer to a contending team was decimated by injuries, including the horrific season-ending ankle injury to All-Star catcher Jason Kendall. "It was like there was a death in here," Al Martin said of the clubhouse atmosphere after the game in which Kendall was hurt. Kendall's drive and gutsy play had made him "the heart and soul of the team." And even before his injury, for much of the first half of the season, increased offense could not always compensate for faltering starting pitching. Still, the nucleus of the future contender is in place in such players as Kendall (whose ankle, as of spring training 2000, appears to have healed), Kevin Young, Brian Giles, 1999 rookie pitcher Kris Benson, among others—the dream of a new ballpark and a winning team in the year 2001.

I may seem to idealize baseball. But I am acutely aware of its problems: often hostile labor relations, wildly escalating salaries, too many owners and players (and umpires!) who lose sight of the greater good of the game. But that isn't baseball. I think of what the Pirates have meant to generations of my family. I think of Al Martin's fluid grace as he jogged toward his position in left field. I think of his grace off the field as he came to terms with a disappointing season in 1998, and followed with a near career year in 1999. I think of my step-granddaughter Caitlin, whose first word, after "book," was "Bucs." Overriding all the negatives is the simple fact that, in baseball, we find a focus and a context for our capacity to love. How indeed, I ask myself, could we ever let that go?

◆　◆　◆

A LAST AND LASTING TRIBUTE TO POPS

Shortly after midnight on April 9, 2001, with the historic opening of PNC Park just hours away, Willie Stargell, Pittsburgh's respected and beloved "Pops," passed away at the age of sixty-one after a long bout with declining health. Two days before his death, the Pirates had unveiled a bronze statue in honor of Stargell. With the dedication of his statue, Stargell joined Honus Wagner and Roberto Clemente as the only Pirates so honored in the history of the ball club.

Ron Cook's "Blass Delivers a Final Pitch to Stargell" unites the unassuming hero of the 1971 World Series with the legendary hero of the 1979 World Series.

Blass Delivers a Final Pitch to Stargell

RON COOK

What a shame they didn't ask Steve Blass to speak at Willie Stargell's funeral yesterday.

What a story he could have told.

It goes back to 1974, Blass' final spring training with the Pirates. In 1971, he had been a World Series hero, pitching complete-game victories against the Baltimore Orioles in Games 3 and 7. Now, mysteriously, he couldn't throw a strike. He couldn't come close, actually.

"No one wanted to take batting practice against me," Blass said. "I could see the fear in their eyes. No one wanted to be hit in batting practice. It wasn't comfortable for me. It wasn't fun.

"But Willie never hesitated. When it was my turn to pitch, he'd always say, 'I'll be first.' He did it every time. And he would go into the cage without a batting helmet. That was his way of saying he still was with me, that

I meant something to him. It was like he was saying, 'Go ahead. Hit me in the shoulder. Hit me in the ribs. It doesn't matter. Our relationship is stronger than that.'"

You think there was any way Blass was going to miss the chance to say goodbye to Stargell yesterday?

He dreaded the service—"Life is so short," he said, sadly, the night before—but it turned out to be therapeutic for him. He delivered the eulogy at Roberto Clemente's funeral in Puerto Rico early in 1973 and was such a big part of that service that the significance of the loss of his friend didn't hit him until later. But yesterday, he could sit in a far back corner of St. Paul's Episcopal Church and laugh a little and cry a little as Pirates owner Kevin McClatchy and Hall of Famers Hank Aaron and Joe Morgan, among others, paid their tribute to Stargell.

It brought back such memories for Blass.

"I guess Willie and I go back to 1961 at spring training in Jacksonville. I remember getting on the bus with the white players and driving over to Colored Town to pick up Willie and the black players. I was just learning about racism at that time. But I really learned a lot about Willie. That stuff didn't jade him. It didn't ruin him."

The memories of 1971, obviously, are a lot more pleasant.

"People talk about what Clemente and I did in that Series, but we never would have gotten the chance if it hadn't been for Willie," Blass said. "He hit 48 home runs and drove in 125 runs that season."

It's largely forgotten now that Stargell was horrible in the 1971 postseason, worse than Barry Bonds ever was. He went 0 for 14 with six strikeouts against the San Francisco Giants in the playoffs. Then he went 5 for 24 with nine strikeouts and just one RBI against the Orioles.

"That's why I was so happy when Willie got that second chance in '79," Blass said.

Stargell hit .455 with two home runs in the three-game sweep of the Cincinnati Reds in the playoffs that season. He hit .400 with three home runs and seven RBIs against the Orioles in the World Series and won Game 7 with a sixth-inning homer.

Stargell always was a bigger-than-life hitter to the other players in the game. Morgan talked Friday night of how uncomfortable he was playing second base when Stargell was at the plate.

"He hit some rockets at me. I remember one that he especially smoked. I dove for it and just missed it. He gets to first base and says to me, 'You know, Joe, if you had gotten your glove on that ball, it would have dragged you to death.'"

But it was Stargell's performance in that 1979 season that made him a bigger-than-life figure to baseball fans everywhere. He was 39, the patriarch of the Pirates. "Pops," everyone called him. In that magical summer, he and his team made "We Are Family" a national hit.

"Whenever that song was played, everyone in America thought of Willie Stargell and the Pittsburgh Pirates," Dale Petroskey, president of the National League Hall of Fame, said during his portion of the eulogy yesterday. "It was their anthem. They showed everyone that it's possible to work together and have fun together and, if you believe in yourself, win together.

"That was vintage Stargell. He was a leader. He was a unifier. He excelled. And he did it all with great joy and a big smile."

The summer of '79 also assured that a statue of Stargell would be built one day in Pittsburgh. McClatchy approached him with the idea in 1999 during one of Stargell's all-too-frequent hospital stays.

"I took a bunch of pictures with me when I went to see him," McClatchy said. "He picked out the one we based the statue on. I can still hear him saying, 'I want them to show me hitting the stuffing out of the ball.'"

Stargell cried at the news conference announcing plans for the statue Sept. 29. That Friday night, before the Pirates played the first of their final three games in Three Rivers Stadium, he was introduced to the crowd of 40,128. It's a wonder the old stadium didn't implode then, the ovation was so thunderous.

Blass was the emcee for that pregame ceremony.

"They gave me a script to read, and I asked if I could add something to it. They said I could so, after I read what I was supposed to read, I said, 'On a personal note, I'd just like to say that when I was going through my problems late in my career, no one ever stood taller for me than Willie Stargell . . . Willie, I'll never forget that.'

"I'm so glad I said that now."

Stargell and Blass embraced that night on the turf near home plate.

"What a hug," Blass said. "Of course, there were no small hugs from Willie Stargell."

As Blass left the church yesterday, it was clear he would have given just about anything for just one more.

◆ ◆ ◆

BUILDING A FUTURE AND HONORING THE PAST

In 2001, one hundred years after Pittsburgh celebrated its first National League pennant, Pirate fans, after several seasons of turmoil and uncertainty, received two wonderful gifts. The first, the opening of PNC Park, contained the promise of a secure future for baseball in Pittsburgh and the hope for a return to the team's winning tradition. The ballpark itself, with its echoes of Forbes Field and its picturesque view of the city's landscape, drew instant praise as the most beautiful of baseball's new parks. The second gift, Bill Mazeroski's election to the Baseball Hall of Fame, after decades of unnecessary delay, was an emotional reminder of the Pirates' glorious past and the greatness of one of Pittsburgh's most popular heroes.

Fans Will See a Different Brand of Baseball

ROBERT DVORCHAK

PLAYERS FACE NEW CHALLENGES AT PNC PARK

It's like meeting a new heartthrob. There is an instant physical attraction, and you can't wait to discover more about this charming personality. But as with any new love interest, you'll need more time to find out what she's really like.

Introducing PNC Park and its grass field, short foul lines and intriguing proximity to the Allegheny River. Its spacious outfield likely will produce more triples and will require fielders to be fleet of foot. The distances from home plate to the outfield fences seem fair but beg the question of how much of a factor the wind will be. Foul territory is sparse and the pretty limestone wall behind home plate could send wild pitches careening every which way.

No more symmetrical, generic layout like Three Rivers Stadium. This is a one-of-a-kind diamond with idiosyncrasies waiting to be discovered, a real baseball park that looks small—certainly less spacious than Forbes Field—but one that should provide a real showcase for baseball.

One of the universal charms of baseball is that the field has a part in the way the game unfolds. Hockey rinks and football fields have set dimensions; real baseball parks have individual personalities and play a role in how the games turn out.

From the *Pittsburgh Post-Gazette*, April 15, 2001. Copyright/*Pittsburgh Post-Gazette*, 2002. All rights reserved. Reprinted with permission.

The first time the players toured the construction site in November, when the grass carpet had been laid but had not yet taken root, center fielder Adrian Brown heard it from his teammates: "A. B., you'd better be in shape to run down some balls."

Standing in a concrete shell that is now the Pirates dugout on the third base side, Brown gazed out to the gaps with the look of a kid staring into a candy store window.

"There's a lot of room out there," Brown said. "Time will tell, but it looks like a lot of ground to cover."

PNC is 325 feet down the left field line, which swings out quickly to 389 feet in the gap. There's a cranny in left center that forms the deepest part of the ballpark at 410 feet, and a ball hit there could do a lot of tricks. Straight-away center field is 399 feet, which cozies back in to a 375-foot power alley in right center and then back to 320 feet down the right field line.

It has fences that don't confine because the city skyline is the outfield backdrop. Conversely, a person looking at the park from Stanwix Street and Fort Duquesne Boulevard, Downtown, might feel like he's inside the park. The left field fence is six-feet high, which will make for some interesting interplay with the fans. In center, the wall is 10 feet. And in right, it's 21—a tribute to Roberto Clemente, whose name adorns the bridge leading to the ballpark's front door on Federal Street.

"The gaps are so big, I think you're going to see a lot more triples," left fielder Brian Giles said after getting his first impression. "The detail work is unbelievable. When all is said and done, I think it's going to be exciting."

A ball will have to carry more than 450 feet to clear the right field wall and the Riverwalk behind the stands to splash into the Allegheny River. Will there be boaters racing to retrieve balls, a la McCovey Cove outside of Pacific Bell Park in San Francisco?

"That's a long way. To hit one out there (in the water), you'd have to hit a bomb," said Giles, who maybe hit three or four of his 35 home runs that far last year.

The ballpark has elements of Wrigley Field and Camden Yards, but it was designed specifically for the Pirates. Major input came from General Manager Cam Bonifay, who is partial to the National League game that requires foot speed, arm strength and athleticism over the American League power game played out in hitters' parks.

"It's not a banger's box, so to speak," Bonifay said. "You're going to have to have somebody who can run the ball down. I gave our hitters a little sweetener down the corners. If you really turned on it, you've got a short corner, but you still have to hit the ball out in the gaps. I didn't want to make it too unfair for our pitching staff."

But don't think for a moment the pitchers haven't checked out those foul line dimensions while imagining Mark McGwire, Sammy Sosa and Ken Griffey Jr. digging into the clay of the batter's box.

"You don't want to let anybody pull the ball," said pitcher Todd Ritchie.

Nobody's going to know until the weather warms in May how the ball will carry, especially with the wind an unknown factor in an open setting, but finding out about the corner porches won't be a mystery for long.

"Early in the season, you have to pitch inside," said reliever Jose Silva.

"It maybe can go either way on whether it's going to be a hitter's ballpark or a pitcher's park. The big thing that will tell the story is how the wind blows. We're going to have to learn as we go along. But I think it's going to be true," pitcher Jason Schmidt said.

The Pirates commissioned a wind study in 1999 that determined that prevailing winds blow up the Allegheny River from behind the ballpark in the direction of Downtown. On the compass, the playing field is oriented the same as the old one at Three Rivers Stadium, but the enclosed bowl caught the winds out of the northwest and blew them back toward the plate, so there never was much of a jet stream heading out.

"I think you're going to see a lot more carry," said outfielder John Vander Wal. "But we won't know until we take batting practice a few times."

It's true that the ballpark has been shoehorned onto its site, borrowing a bit from the river and from the old General Robinson Street right of way. The snugness makes it seems tight, but nobody expects it to become Ten Run, uh, Enron Field in Houston.

"It looks pretty short," said first base coach Tommy Sandt. "The people in Houston didn't think Enron would play that short either."

The closeness of the stands to the field is another concern for pitchers. There won't be a lot of room to catch foul balls, certainly not as much room as in, say, Dodger Stadium. Pirates batters estimate it could mean as many as 10 fewer outs per season for them.

"I like foul territory," said Schmidt.

Closer Mike Williams likes a generous foul territory but said it will be the same for both sides.

"They've got to play in it too. I'm not going to pitch any different," Williams said.

Starter Kris Benson likes the tight design because it will make him feel like he's right on top of the hitters, but stingy foul lines might mean pitchers will throw an extra five or six pitches a game.

The biggest change for the players and the fans will be the playing surface of Kentucky sports grasses. For the pitchers, the switch from the artificial surface of Three Rivers to the real turf of PNC Park will be a plus.

"We're all sinker-ball pitchers, so we get a lot of ground balls," Benson said. "Balls that scooted through last year will be scooped up."

Manager Lloyd McClendon said the Pirates will have some input to give to groundskeeper Luke Yoder on how high the grass should be cut.

"I think grass makes us a better defensive club," he said. "It slows the game down. I wish we would have had a slower infield last year. It's hard to play on Astroturf. It's built for speed. We don't have blazing speed. I'm just happy to be on that type of surface. Physically, it should help players like Kevin Young, Pat Meares and Mike Benjamin, who likes to dive and throw his body around."

First baseman Kevin Young says he's glad to be on natural turf.

"That's 81 games off artificial turf. It'll be good for my knees," he said. "Turf is not good for the body. Baseball is meant to be played in a park, not a stadium."

Bill Mazeroski played at Forbes Field and moved to Three Rivers. He never cared for artificial grass.

"I hated turf," Maz said.

Mike Benjamin said there will be fewer base hits on grass, but he likes the natural stuff too. "Guys with bad knees and bad backs hate turf."

He also said it would help aesthetically. PNC Park is built strictly for baseball, so there won't be any of those unsightly outlines of the yard lines and numbers painted on the turf for football.

One of the unique features of the park could be how the ball bounces behind home plate.

While Wrigley Field's signature sight is the smooth-faced red brick wall as a backdrop, the area behind home plate is mortared with the same yellow Minnesota limestone that graces PNC Park's exterior. But the limestone isn't smooth. It has all kinds of angles on its face, which is the first thing Jason Kendall noticed after he signed his contract extension. When a round ball strikes an irregular surface, it could create chaos.

"If the ball gets by me, it'll be like pinball. I'll have to use my video game skills back there," Kendall said. "I don't know whose idea it was. We'll have to figure out a way to use it to our advantage."

The idea came from the mind of Steve Greenberg, the Pirates vice president of new ballpark development who is always looking for ways to jazz up the game with entertainment. When someone suggested smoothing out the face of the backdrop, Greenberg said: "Over my dead body."

All of the quirks and idiosyncracies are what's part of the home-field advantage because the Pirates will get to know the place more intimately than anybody else. And it's the players who are taking ownership of the place, at least in a competitive sense.

"It's going to be our house, we don't have to share it with the Steelers," said Rich Loiselle. "We don't want people coming in here and embarrassing us."

Which brings up an element that can't be known by looking at blueprints or an empty arena. This is the most intimate major league ballpark ever built. It puts the fans right on top of the action and will make them part of the game, which McClendon hopes to use to his advantage.

The first time he led his troops onto the battlefield, back on a dreary November day, McClendon gathered them in the outfield and gazed back at a seating bowl that was just naked concrete. While baseball is at its purest when there's hardly anybody around on a sandlot, it is meant to be played in front of a packed house on the major league level.

"Take a look around. It's going to be a full house every night," he told them, creating an image that is the antithesis of too many charmless, empty days at Three Rivers.

And just like he motivates his players, McClendon has a message for the partisans.

"We can't do this without our fans. I'm hoping they'll be our 10th man, so to speak," McClendon said.

"I want our fans to be alive, to be relentless, to really be on top of the other team. There's nothing I'd like more for the other team to say, 'Damn, we have to come to Pittsburgh in front of all those screaming fans.' That could be the biggest factor of all."

The Reluctant Hero

JOHN PERROTTO

Late on the night of August 10, Bill Mazeroski could finally exhale.

The life of the Pittsburgh Pirate all-time great second baseman had finally settled down. At last, the quiet man from tiny Tiltonsville, OH could get away from the hoopla that had surrounded him since way back in March and try to become a normal person again.

From *On Deck*, September 2001. Reprinted by permission of John Perrotto.

"Boy, this has been a little tough," Mazeroski said with a smile. "I'm just not used to people making a fuss over me. It has all been great, but I don't know how to take it."

Mazeroski's wild ride began on the morning of March 6 when he was elected to the National Baseball Hall of Fame by the Veterans Committee. Serving as a special infielder instructor for the Pirates at their spring training camp in Bradenton, Fla., Mazeroski was whisked away for an hour-long drive to Tampa for a press conference.

That began five whirlwind months. Mazeroski did countless interviews and made numerous public appearances leading up to his induction and even had the chance in May to go to Cooperstown, N.Y., for a tour of baseball's Hall of Fame and Museum.

Everything then culminated for Mazeroski in the first 10 days of August.

On August 5, he was officially inducted into the Hall of Fame in a moving ceremony outside the Clark Sports Center in Cooperstown. Five days later, the Pirates honored Mazeroski with "Maz Night" at PNC Park and the city of Pittsburgh renamed a street after him outside the first-year ballpark.

During that time he went from an old player best known for hitting a home run in the bottom of the ninth inning of Game Seven that gave the Pirates an upset of the New York Yankees in the 1960 World Series to a national celebrity. The eight-time Gold Glove winner and 10-time All-Star Game participant struck a chord with baseball fans around the country during the induction as he became so emotional that he was forced to abandon his 12-page speech and end his talk after just two and a half minutes.

"There's a different feeling now than I've ever had before in my life," Mazeroski said after his night at PNC Park. "People are looking at me in a different way. People are making it out like I'm bigger than I actually am."

Mazeroski paused and laughed as he pointed to his mid-section.

"I don't mean bigger that way, though I am bigger there than I used to be," he said. "But they look at me like I'm some kind of big deal and that surprises me. I don't consider myself a big deal. But now that I'm a Hall of Famer, it's something to see the way people look at me."

Much of that has to do with becoming one of only 253 men to be enshrined in Cooperstown. More of it undoubtedly has to do with the way Mazeroski showed his emotions while being honored. His tear-filled exit from the podium drew a large ovation from the large crowd at the induction and was replayed countless times on television in the days that followed.

"I don't think anybody who was in Cooperstown that day will ever forget Maz," said current Pirates broadcaster and former pitcher Steve Blass, who was a teammate of Mazeroski. "I was fortunate enough to be the winning pitcher in Game Seven of (the 1971) World Series and seeing Maz at the podium and showing the kind of emotion he showed was just as memorable as winning that game in Baltimore."

Those in attendance at Cooperstown on a 91-degree day knew Mazeroski's speech was going to be different from the time he stepped to the podium moments after Hall of Fame Chairman Jane Forbes Clark unveiled his plaque and Commissioner Bud Selig read its inscription.

"I've got 12 pages of speech written here," Mazeroski began. "I probably won't need half of it. I probably won't get through the whole thing."

With that, Mazeroski began his speech, pointing to the fact he was elected on the strength of his fielding excellence and all-time record 1,706 double plays rather than his .260 life-time average and 138 homers with the Pirates in 17 seasons from 1956 to 1972.

"I think defense belongs in the Hall of Fame," Mazeroski said. "Defense deserves as much credit as pitching and hitting. I'm proud to go in on the defensive side. I feel special."

At that point, the tears started flowing as Mazeroski dabbed at them with a handkerchief.

"This is going to be hard," Mazeroski said before another pause. "I thought that when the Pirates retired my number (9 in 1987) that would be the greatest thing that ever happened to me. But it's hard to top this."

Mazeroski stopped again and it became very obvious at that point he wasn't going to win this battle with his emotions.

"You can kiss these 12 pages down the drain," he said. "I want to thank all of my family and friends for making the long trek up here to hear this crap. That's it. That's enough."

With that, Mazeroski turned around and walked back to his seat as the estimated crowd of 23,000, including seven busloads from the tri-state area, gave him a thunderous ovation. The 40 returning Hall of Famers in attendance also gave Mazeroski an unprecedented standing ovation and several of his contemporaries such as Ernie Banks, Frank Robinson and Tom Seaver moved forward on the stage to embrace him.

Kirby Puckett and Dave Winfield, who were also in the Hall's Class of 2001 with late Negro League pitching star Hilton Smith, were also touched by Maz's speech. Sunglasses hid the tears of Puckett, whose voice never cracked during his 10-minute speech later in the ceremonies.

"How could you not cry?" Puckett said. "To see a guy start crying before he even begins his speech . . . well, it was very moving. I couldn't help but cry when I saw that. It was a very special and emotional moment that really sums up how special getting into the Hall of Fame really is."

That enabled Mazeroski to steal the show on a day that was supposed to belong to Puckett and Winfield, the more contemporary superstars.

"It wasn't my plan to steal anyone's thunder," Mazeroski said. "But I think the emotion I showed had a lot to do with the people's reaction. I was kind of embarrassed, but more mad at myself for not being able to go on.

"That's why I finished my speech with that line about thanking my family and friends for coming there to listen to that crap. That wasn't planned by any means. It just came out that way."

Mazeroski admits he is having a hard time getting used to all the attention. He is an unassuming man and younger fans would likely never guess the 64-year-old with white hair and a much bigger waistline than his playing days is a Hall of Famer.

"It's funny how many people recognize me again," Mazeroski said. "I remember when we first moved to Greensburg, people made it a big deal for a while that I was living in town. After about a year, everyone got used to having me around and it was no longer a big deal. I was just like everyone else.

"Even after I hit the home run to win the World Series, people didn't make this big of a deal. After a day or two, it was just like any other home run that won a ballgame and it didn't get real big until after I retired.

"Hopefully, after a year or so, it will settle down again. I hope it does. I'm not used to all this attention. When people start cheering me I get emotional. I knew I was going to break down in Cooperstown as soon as I was introduced and received such a great ovation."

He elicited another large roar at PNC Park after receiving nine special gifts that included a home theater system, a diamond ring for his wife, Milene, and a baseball signed by President George W. Bush that included a personal inscription congratulating Mazeroski for making the Hall of Fame.

Mazeroski received a prolonged ovation when he was driven around the warning track in a 1960 convertible and another when he threw out the ceremonial first pitch with the presidential baseball. Earlier in the day, the former Avenue of the Pirates, located on the west side of PNC Park adjacent to the Honus Wagner statue, was renamed Mazeroski Way.

Mazeroski addressed the crowd briefly during the on-field ceremony before the game against the San Diego Padres. He touched primarily on how much he enjoyed spending his career with the Pirates and joked he could indeed get through a speech without crying.

However, the 12-page speech he never got through in Cooperstown remained on the shelf.

"I even had that speech all memorized," Mazeroski said with a laugh. "I've still got the speech somewhere or other. I just wanted to thank a lot of people and I feel bad I wasn't able to get those words out.

"Who knows? Maybe I'll print the speech some time and let everyone know what I was going to say."

Touched by Magic

In the fall of 1999, more than 14,000 Pirate fans cast ballots in the Pittsburgh Post-Gazette *for the Pirates' Team of the Century. The five top vote-getters, not surprisingly, played on Pittsburgh's five World Series championship teams. They included Honus Wagner, who outdueled Ty Cobb in the 1909 World Series, and Pie Traynor, who led the Pirates to their incredible comeback victory against the Washington Senators in 1925. Also near the top of the list were Roberto Clemente, who turned the 1971 World Series into his personal showcase, and Willie Stargell, who became the Most Valuable Player in the Pirates' comeback in the 1979 World Series. But the top vote-getter, outdistancing Wagner, Traynor, Clemente, and Stargell, was Bill Mazeroski, the hero of the 1960 World Series. The votes cast for Mazeroski and the selection of nine players from the 1960 Pirate team for the twenty-four first- and second-place positions on the Team of the Century clearly illustrate the powerful emotional pull of the 1960 World Series on Pirate fans, decades after Mazeroski's home run.*

Bang for the Bucs

WILLIAM NACK

> Sport as much as steel has cast the image of Pittsburgh to the world.
> Pittsburghers have used sport to tell a story about who they are both to them-
> selves and to others. It's about tough, hard-working, gritty people who struggle
> and win and lose and win. The 1960 World Series was that story.
> —Robert Ruck, Lecturer in Sports and Urban History, University of Pittsburgh

Toward the end of that autumn afternoon at old Forbes Field, near the close of a record-breaking World Series that had already emerged as the weirdest, wildest, most improbable ever played, Pittsburgh Pirates second baseman William Stanley Mazeroski, the 24-year-old son of an Ohio coal miner, sensed that he had been through all this before, felt he'd already lived and seen it. Sensed it as he stepped off the field and inhaled the moment's bitter, ascending air of gloom. *How did this happen?* he thought. *How is it they always come back?*

It was 3:30 P.M. on Thursday, Oct. 13, 1960, 40 years ago last week, and the last half of the ninth inning of the Series' seventh game was beginning. The Pirates and the New York Yankees were locked in a 9-9 tie. Less than 30 minutes earlier Pittsburgh had scored five runs in the eighth inning, coming from three runs down to take a 9-7 lead. All the Bucs had needed to win it all, to exorcise those roistering ghosts from the '27 World Series—when Ruth and Gehrig, Lazzeri and Combs had swept them in their last go at a world championship—was one more peaceful inning, three more painless outs. But, as Mazeroski knew, these were the 3M Yankees of Mickey Mantle, Roger Maris and Moose Skowron, the Yankees who had won eight pennants and six of 10 World Series in the 1950s, who had won their last 15 regular-season games while running their home run total for the year to an American League record 193, three more than their old mark, set in '56. New York had won its three Series games against the Pirates by the scores of 16-3, 10-0, and 12-0, setting a passel of club and individual World Series hitting records. Sure enough, in the ninth, just as Mazeroski had feared, the deathless Yankees had struck again.

After Mantle singled in a run, driving second baseman Bobby Richardson home as he raised his batting average in this Series to .400, he kept New York alive by pulling off the strangest act of baserunning in the Series. With one out and Mantle on first, and third baseman Gil McDougald representing the tying run on third, Yankees left-fielder Yogi Berra pulled a hard, one-hop smash down the line that Pittsburgh first baseman Rocky Nelson snatched deftly. After stepping on the bag to get Berra at first, Nelson moved toward second base to throw out Mantle. But Mantle, instead of racing for second, dove back toward first and crawled like a lizard to the bag, slipping under the surprised first baseman's reach as McDougald scored.

Many saw what Mantle did as dumb. All he had to do, to ensure that McDougald would score and tie the game, was dash for second and force a rundown. Had Nelson tagged out Mantle, the Pirates would have been world champions. So why did Mantle scramble back to first? Nelson says Mantle later told him that he thought Nelson had caught Berra's drive on the fly and that, since he had not tagged up, the only way to save himself and McDougald was to scramble safely back to first.

In any event, after Skowron, the Yankees first baseman, hit a grounder that forced Mantle at second to end the top half of the ninth, the game was tied 9-9. The Yankees had new life. Recalls Richardson, "We thought, *Boy, we got 'em now!*"

Stunned by the turn of events, Mazeroski went down the stairs into the Pittsburgh dugout, sat on a bench and stared vacantly across the ancient playing field—toward the vines that climbed the outfield fence, past the silent thousands shifting uneasily in their seats, beyond all those damned Yankees grinning as they took the field and waited for pitcher Ralph Terry to finish warming up.

Mazeroski lapsed into a kind of trance, as though peering into his backwoods past, into the days when he was growing up in a little wooden house with no electricity or running water, on a glade known as Skunk Hollow, on the banks of the Ohio River near Rush Run. The sun lit his days, kerosene his nights, and on many summer afternoons he listened to his battery-operated radio tell stories of the distant suffering of his beloved Cleveland Indians. In the dugout, Mazeroski remembers, "all I could think of was how the Yankees used to beat up on Cleveland for years and years, and how the Yankees would come back and how, just now, they'd come back on us with all that hitting. I felt so bad; we all did. I was staring out of the dugout and thinking about this when. . . ."

"Maz, you're up!" he heard a voice call out from down the pine.

So absorbed had he been in memory, Mazeroski hadn't realized he was leading off. He rose from the bench, picked up his helmet and bat and walked to the batter's box. For weeks preceding the Series, Yankee scouts had tracked the Pirates from city to city, and their report on Pittsburgh had been unambiguous: "They're high fastball hitters. Give them low, breaking stuff all the time."

So Mazeroski, who'd been seeing a steady diet of curves, was expecting another. He was a notoriously dangerous clutch hitter, and all he could think of, as he stood facing Terry, was getting on base, giving the Pirates a chance to end the game before New York had another go in the 10th. He thought, *Just hit the ball someplace. Get on base. Hit the ball hard. Line drive! Line drive!* When Terry fired a fastball high and inside, a surprised Mazeroski took it for a ball, and Yankees catcher Johnny Blanchard stepped forward and hollered to Terry, "Get it down! Get it down! This guy's a high fastball hitter."

Terry peered in at Blanchard. It was 3:36 P.M. Terry wound up and fired his second pitch. It was lower than the first but still up in the zone and looking as fat as a melon to Mazeroski as it whistled toward the plate—a high hummer just where he wanted it. He swung and struck the ball flush, sending it in a rising white arc to left centerfield. Mazeroski was racing toward first base when he saw what everyone else saw, what Pirates Bill Virdon and Bob Skinner saw from the first base dugout, what Skowron saw from first and Richardson from second, what all those millions saw who were watching from the stands and on national TV: Berra, the unmistakable squat figure in left, crabbing back to the 406-foot mark, to the warning track, his back turned to the infield diamond as he faced the wall and looked up, his rounded figure looking like the 8 ball he was now behind. "Soon as you saw Yogi's back, his number 8, you knew dang well that ball had a chance," says former Pittsburgh pitcher Vern Law, who won two games in the Series. "A dream come true!"

"I didn't think the ball was going out," Berra recalls. "A lot of people thought I turned around to see how far it would go. I thought it was going to hit the wall. I turned around because I was going to play the carom."

The bespectacled Virdon, along with Skinner and every other Pirate, leaped off the bench the instant Mazeroski swung. "We knew he hit it good," recalls Virdon, "but we didn't know if it was going out. We all looked at leftfield, and we saw that Yogi was not going to catch it, so we started rooting for it to go."

Maz had no idea what he'd wrought. All he knew was that he had hit a fastball solidly and that it had whizzed over short and was climbing for the fence. He felt a rush as he sprinted around first, hoping to stretch the hit into a triple. "I knew Yogi wasn't going to catch it," says Mazeroski. "When he turned, I knew it was over his head, and I thought maybe it was going to be off the wall. I'd hit it hard, but it was 406 feet out there, and the wall was 12 feet high. I was thinking, *If Yogi misplays it coming off the wall, then I could be on third base with no one out, and I can score a hundred ways from third base, and we win!* Then I round first and I hear the fans going crazy."

Helpless, Berra watched the ball sail over his head and clear the wall. "It grazed the vines as it went over the fence," he says.

Galloping toward second base, Mazeroski glanced over short and saw the left-field umpire, Stan Landes, make the call: "He was holding up his hand and giving it this little circle thing, and I knew it had gone out. From the time I hit second base, I don't think I touched the ground the rest of the way home."

He pulled the helmet off his head, held it high and screamed to himself, *We beat the Yankees! We beat the Yankees! We beat the Yankees!* Fans raced onto the field and pounded his back as he turned on third and headed for the plate. Pandemonium shook the rust and coal dust from the girders of the 51-year-old ballpark. A man later dug up home plate with a shovel as policemen watched. Mantle sat by his locker and wept. Blanchard sobbed into his hands. A red-eyed Skowron, who had tied a World Series record with 12 hits, joined them in wordless mourning.

All over Pittsburgh, for the next 12 hours, reigned a state of merriment unprecedented in the city's 202-year history. Confetti rained on the just and the unjust alike. Office workers emptied whole file cabinets into the streets, covering the trolley tracks with so much paper that the trolleys stalled. It was bigger than V-E day, bigger even than V-J day. So many thousands of revelers descended on the town from outlying cities, from places like Youngstown, Ohio, and Erie, Pa., that the cops closed off the bridges and tunnels leading into the city. Unable to get home, many commuters slept in hotel lobbies. By midnight, all the downtown bars had run out of glasses—two-fisted drinkers were wandering the streets with them—and to buy a drink you had to bring your own tumbler. Except for the Pittsburgh Crawfords and the Homestead Grays, both of the old Negro leagues, the city had not had a championship team since 1925, when the Pirates beat Walter Johnson and the Washington Senators 9-7 in the seventh game of the World Series. The Steelers, as beloved as they were, had had an undetectable pulse for decades, and the familiar greeting of long-suffering Steelers fans was SOS, for Same Old Steelers.

"It had been a long time," says Robert Ruck, the Pitt historian. "There were two generations in Pittsburgh who had known nothing but defeat."

Never had there been a World Series like this one, and no sooner had the last stragglers left town than press-box wags were calling it the Weird Series. Frederick G. Lieb, the estimable baseball writer for *The Sporting News*, who had seen all but three of the previous 51 world championships, said this one was the "wackiest ever." For 50 years, since the 1910 World Series, when a young team of Philadelphia Athletics teed off on a cork-centered baseball, beating the Chicago Cubs in five games, their team batting average of .316 had survived as the highest in Series history—higher than that of any of those vaunted Yankees clubs that followed. Then came 1960, New York, hitting a phenomenal .338, eclipsed the record by 22 percentage points and outhit Pittsburgh by 82 points.

And lost. The Yankees had 31 more hits than the Pirates (91 to 60), outscored them by more than 2 to 1 (55 runs to 27), had six more home runs (10 to 4), 28 more runs batted in (54 to 26) and the three liveliest bats in the Series: Mantle's, Richardson's and Skowron's.

Richardson, a singles-hitting schnauzer at 5'9", had hit only one home run all season, on April 30, so no one was more surprised than he was when, in Game 3 of the Series, he punched a grand slam over the Yankee Stadium fence in left—for four of his six RBIs that day, a single-game Series record. That was far more than pitcher Whitey Ford needed, and he went on to win the game 10-0. By the end of Game 6, in which Richardson had two triples, he had knocked in 12 runs, a World Series record that still stands. Lieb crunched the numbers and quietly asked, "Who ever would have fancied, even in his wildest dream, that a club launching such an offensive could lose a Series?"

As if credulity had not been strained enough, the whole unlikely megillah came to the most dramatic finish possible—no other Series in the Classic's 97-year history has ended with a homer in the last inning of the seventh game—and only after the lead had changed hands twice. No matter what the Yankees did, no matter how hard and how far they hit the ball, the Pirates were ultimately favored by the baseball gods to prevail. Tilting at windmills had become as much a part of Pittsburgh's drill as shagging flies and watching Ralph Kiner hit boomers in BP, but at the start of the '60 season, after a disappointing fourth-place finish the year before, no one except family and friends had expected the Bucs to be in the chase for the pennant, much less the world title.

Only eight years earlier, in 1952, the Pirates had finished last in the league, with a record of 42-112, and had been proclaimed to be among the worst teams in baseball history. They also came in last in the next three years under general manager Branch Rickey, but by the time the Mahatma was fired in the fall of '55—the franchise had been hemorrhaging financially for years—he had assembled the core of the '60 team, including pitchers Law, Bob Friend and Elroy Face; shortstop Dick Groat, an All-America basketball player whom Rickey had signed out of Duke in '52; Mazeroski and rightfielder Roberto Clemente.

Rickey left his fingerprints all over the franchise. In early '54, at a pre-spring-training camp for young players, Mazeroski was one of seven shortstops doing fielding drills when he took a turn at second base to pivot on the double play. Rickey saw that Mazeroski was a natural second baseman, quick and agile, who could throw without cocking his arm, and told the coaches, "Don't move him. He stays at second."

It was the sea-change moment of Mazeroski's life. He taught himself how to turn the double play, how to catch the ball and release it so quickly that it seemed to enter one end of a bent stovepipe and exit the other. He taught himself not to catch the ball in the pit of his glove and then dig it out to throw—that took too much time—but rather to deflect the ball off the heel of the glove into his throwing hand and, in the same moment, toss it to first.

That spring of '54 was propitious for the Pirates. Rickey told Face that he would need more than a fastball and a curve to stick in the big leagues, even with the last-place Bucs. "You don't have a changeup, and you need an off-speed pitch," Rickey said. At the Pirates' camp in Fort Pierce, Fla., former Yankees reliever Joe Page was trying to come back, and Face saw him throw his storied forkball, for which he fit the ball deep between the first two fingers of his throwing hand and fired with the same speed and motion he used on his other pitches. Today that pitch is known as the split-finger fastball. Thrown well, it looks like a fastball but, at the plate, falls off the world. Rickey's decision to ship Face to Double A New Orleans for a year to work on the off-speed pitch was the turning point in Face's career.

But nothing Rickey ever did for the Pirates quite matched the way they picked the Brooklyn Dodgers' pocket. Rickey, a former Dodgers general manager, knew that Brooklyn was hiding a gifted Puerto Rican outfielder on its Montreal farm team. So he drafted Clemente for Pittsburgh. Clemente was a rookie in 1955 and five years later a .314-hitting All-Star with a Springfield rifle for an arm and racehorse speed.

Those were the players Joe Brown inherited when he took over as Pittsburgh G.M. in '55. By the 1960 season he had subtracted one catcher and added three more, including lefthanded-hitting Smoky Burgess and righty Hal Smith; acquired a fiery third baseman, Don Hoak; and added the wiry, chain-smoking spot starter Harvey Haddix, a lefty nicknamed the Kitten because as a rookie with the St. Louis Cardinals in '52 he had studied at the paw of aging lefty Harry (the Cat) Brecheen. Brown, who would win two championships in Pittsburgh, in '60 and '71, traded with St. Louis for the sweet-fielding outfielder Virdon in '56, the year after Virdon had been voted National League Rookie of the Year. Brown also added utility outfielder Gino Cimoli—a cheerful butt-slapper in the clubhouse—and dug around the minor leagues in search of missing links.

Because of his zeal, Brown took some ribbing from his colleagues. Before the 1958 draft he asked one of his scouts to name the best lefthanded hitter available. "Rocky Nelson," said the scout, referring to a first baseman with Triple A Toronto, but he warned that Nelson had been up and down and never stuck in the majors. At the draft Brown was sitting in front of his longtime friend Chub Feeney, G.M. of the San Francisco Giants, and when it was Pittsburgh's turn to pick, Brown said, "The Pirates draft Rocky Nelson from Toronto."

The Adventures of Ozzie and Harriet, the TV show starring the Nelsons and their sons, David and Ricky, was all the buzz in those days, and in a loud voice—to much alpha-male laughter—Feeney intoned, "Don't you mean *Ricky* Nelson?" Brown tells that story in a flat, humorless voice, as though the remark still bites him. "A lot of people thought Rocky was a joke, but he was not," says Brown. "He served us admirably." Indeed, in the most crucial game of 1960, Brown was the man still laughing.

No one knows why such things occur, whether it's the alignment of the planets or the karma of the clubhouse, but every now and then a team begins to play as though it has been touched by magic. Unexpectedly, the 1960 Pirates started to win, and before long they believed they would win every time they played. The city folk started believing the same thing, and they came to games flashing their BEAT 'EM, BUCS signs. All the while the team's tobacco-chewing manager, beagle-faced Danny Murtaugh, thought the world was his spittoon, and he sat there spitting on everybody's shoes. "I started chewin' so I could spit back on his," says Mazeroski.

Before you could say Pie Traynor, the Pirates had won 95 games and the pennant, losing only 59. Groat hit .325 to win the National League batting title. Nelson hit .300 in 200 at bats. Law won 20 games and Friend, 18, while Face forkballed his way to 24 saves. Mazeroski led major league second basemen in putouts (413), assists (449), double plays (127) and fielding average (.989).

By that year, his fourth full season in the major leagues, Mazeroski had asserted himself as the finest second baseman in the game, a nonpareil turner of the double play and a student of the position who had brought his own aesthetic to playing defense. "Nobody ever played second base like he did," says Virdon, "and I've been in it for 50 years. One thing I know for sure: Many second basemen could make the double play if they got good throws. Maz did not have to have a good throw to complete the DP. He worked on it constantly, every day."

Groat would play seven years at short with Maz at second base, and together they would turn hundreds of double plays. Groat came to view his teammate as an artist. "Mazeroski's release on the double play was phenomenal," he says. "Bill *made* himself a great defensive second base-man. And let me tell you something: You and me, we couldn't catch a ball with the glove he used, it was so small. But he had the most marvelous hands in the world."

In fact, says Brown, Mazeroski's hands were so fluid and smooth that no one talked much about his quick, nimble feet, perhaps the most impor-tant element of his genius as a fielder. "Danny Murtaugh always said that no one mentioned what great feet Mazeroski had," recalls Brown. "He had that blocky build, but he was so graceful. He made everything he did look easy. So quick with his feet, his body was always standing and facing the right place to make the catch and the throw. Guys would slide into him, into those powerful legs, and they'd just stop and drip off him."

Talented as they were, however, the Pirates would be hard-pressed to beat the Yankees, and they nearly squandered what chances they had in the World Series on Sept. 25, the day they clinched the pennant despite losing to the Braves in Milwaukee. On the Pittsburgh team bus a rowdy gang of players, tearing off one another's shirts, grabbed Law—a non-drinking deacon in the Mormon church—and wrestled him down. At the bottom of the pile, someone grabbed and twisted Law's right foot, trying to pull off his shoe, and sprained it. That was the pitcher's push-off foot, the one that helped generate his power, but he insisted on playing through the Series.

The bookmakers made the Pirates underdogs against New York, but these Yanks were not Ruppert's Rifles, the Ruth-led team in the '20s, nor the Bombers of Gehrig and DiMaggio and King Kong Keller in the late '30s and '40s, nor even the Yankees of the '50s, with Hank Bauer and the young Berra and Mantle and all that pitching. In a paragraph almost eerie in its foresight, New York *Herald-Tribune* columnist Red Smith wrote before the first game of the '60 Series, "Chances are the importance of the manager's role is exaggerated oftener than it is underestimated, but in a series of seven games or fewer it can be the deciding factor. There may not be time to repair the damage caused by a single error in judgment."

Casey Stengel's first error was surely his worst. He picked Art Ditmar (15-9), who had no decisions in World Series play, to start the first game over the vastly more seasoned Ford (12-9), the Chairman of the Board, who had a Series record of 5-4 and was the ace of the Yankees' staff. "Ford was our big pitcher," says Richardson, "and in any big game he would be the one to start. Stengel said that Forbes Field was a small park and Ditmar throws a sinker, and he was saving Whitey for New York—double-talk like that. Stengel was always playing hunches, but that didn't make any sense. I remember Mantle saying, 'How can you not start your best pitcher?' It was a topic among the players."

It was an even bigger topic when Ditmar was lifted in the first after facing only five batters, getting one out and giving up three runs. Pittsburgh went on to win 6-4, with Law getting the victory and Face the save. Mazeroski's Game 7 home run would be so stunning that it would relegate his other decisive swing of the Series to the precincts of half-forgotten trivia: In the fourth inning of Game 1, with one out, Hoak on first and the Pirates leading 3-2, Maz crushed an 0-2 fastball from Jim Coates that flew over the scoreboard in dead left and gave Pittsburgh a 5-2 lead. "I was on cloud nine," Mazeroski says. "A home run in the World Series! I thought it was the greatest thing that had ever happened to me. It relaxed me for the rest of the Series."

New York won the second game 16-3, and all the Pirates could talk about was Mantle's second homer of the day. Struck from the right side of the plate, it was a 450-foot blast that sailed over the iron gate in right centerfield and was still carrying as it left the park. Groat was whirlpooling an injured wrist at the end of the game when Virdon dashed into the clubhouse and blurted to him, "Roomie, you missed the granddaddy of them all! I never in my life saw a ball hit as hard as Mantle just hit it. So help me, it went over the iron gate, and it was still going straight!"

Those first two games set the tempo for the next four. The Yankees won in blowouts, the Pirates in tight games. In Game 3 in New York, Ford pitched a nearly spotless 10-0 shutout, deepening suspicions that Stengel had blundered in Game 1, but Law came back and won Game 4 for the Pirates 3-2, with Face again getting the save. The Series was even, 2-2. Matters only got worse for Stengel. He went with Ditmar over Bill Stafford in Game 5 and came under even greater fire when Ditmar gave up three runs and was chased in the second inning. Stafford pitched five scoreless innings as a middle reliever, but the Pirates won 5-2. Haddix got the victory, and Face threw 2⅔ hitless innings in relief for his third save.

Face was a carpenter and lumberjack from upstate New York, and like his fellow backwoodsmen Law (an Idahoan who once worked as a deliveryman for a creamery) and Mazeroski, he was seen in blue-collar Pittsburgh as a hardscrabble working stiff. Nothing buoyed his teammates or the home crowds more than the sight of Face coming in from the bullpen, all 5' 8" and 155 pounds of him. "He had that swagger," says Maz, "a little guy walking in there with that cockiness. He threw strikes and feared nobody."

All the Pirates had to do was win one more game at Forbes, and they would be world champs. The celebration would have to wait, however. Ford was back in Game 6, and he threw a seven-hit shutout, and New York won 12-0. In the New York clubhouse after that third slaughter of the Series, Berra muttered to Joe Reichler of the AP, "I dunno. This game is getting funnier and funnier. We do everything but punch 'em in the nose, and here we are all tied up. . . . How do you figure that?"

That was the question of the day. From the Pirates side, Red Smith reported, "Immediately on reaching the safety of the clubhouse, Pittsburgh's well-read leader, Danny Murtaugh, thumbed through the rule book and gleefully announced a discovery: 'The series will be decided', he said, 'on games won, not total runs scored.'"

All of which made the prospect of the seventh game as delicious to contemplate as any in World Series history. Would the Pirates, starting Law, win another squeaker? Or would the Yankees, going with their Game 2 starter, Bullet Bob Turley, end it all with thunder?

The game went neither way. In fact, the whole script was rewritten at the outset. By the end of the second inning, it was the Pittsburgh bats that had been heard. In the first, after Skinner, the leftfielder, had walked, the butt of Chub Feeney's little joke, Rocky Nelson, pulled a Turley fastball into the lower rightfield stands to put the Pirates ahead 2-0. In the second, with Hoak on third and Mazeroski on second, Virdon stroked a long single to center, scoring both runners, and the inning ended with the Bucs ahead 4-0.

Just as it looked like a rout by the wrong team, little Bobby Shantz—

at 5'6", even shorter than Face—came in to start the third inning for the Yankees. Shantz could tease hitters into madness. Throwing a whole farmers' market of sinking pitches, the lefty had the Pirates hammering balls like stakes into the ground: Over the next five innings Shantz gave up just one base hit, a single to catcher Burgess that would prove to have unforeseeable consequences. Murtaugh lifted Burgess for a pinch runner, Joe Christopher, and brought Hal Smith in to catch in the eighth.

Aside from allowing Skowron's solo homer in the fifth, which made the score 4-1 Law had frozen the Yankees' bats. Unable to push off on his injured foot, he had to draw on his arm as his only source of power. "I'd more or less fall toward the plate and make up the difference with my arm," Law says. "In doing that, I learned later, I tore my rotator cuff."

Murtaugh came to the mound in the sixth, after Law had given up a single to Richardson and had walked shortstop Tony Kubek on a full count. Murtaugh was ready to bring in Face, but Law didn't want to leave the game. "Skip, I feel O.K.," he said. But Murtaugh just shook his head. Hoak came in from third as Law, his head down, stood on the mound waiting.

"Look here, Deacon," said Hoak. "You walk off this mound, you hold your head up! You've done a good job."

Face's fourth Series appearance came at the end of a season in which he had pitched in a National League—leading 68 games, and he was tired and not at his sharpest. After Mantle rolled a single through the box, scoring Richardson, Berra golfed a towering shot down the foul line toward the upper deck in rightfield. It looked to Berra as if the ball might hook foul. As it flew past the pole, a three-run homer, Richardson saw the stoical Berra do something he'd never seen him do. "Halfway between home and first, he was jumping up and down, Richardson recalls. "Boy, was he happy to hit that ball!"

The Yankees mobbed him. Now they were ahead 5-4, and they finally had the measure of Elroy Face. When they scored twice more off Face in the eighth, the Yankees led 7-4 and were looking like winners yet again.

Then came the most bizarre half-inning of the Series. Cimoli led off by clipping Shantz for a dinky single to short right. Skowron and Cimoli had played on the same all-star team when they were teenagers, and as Cimoli stood on first base, Skowron needled him about the dinker: "Jeez, Gino, did you eat any breakfast today? Hit the ball!" The next batter, Virdon, slashed a low grounder toward the rocky Forbes infield at short. It was heading right at Kubek for an easy double play, and Virdon shouted, "Oh, s—!" But when the ball struck the dirt, it rose suddenly like a high-kicking tennis serve and struck Kubek in the Adam's apple. Kubek fell backward, holding his throat. Cimoli stopped at second, and time was called. Stengel ran over to Kubek and tried to break up the crowd gathering around him. "Stand back!" he yelled. "Give him room. He'll be all right."

Cimoli drifted over. "He started to choke; he was gasping for air," he says of Kubek.

Skowron watched the shortstop gag. "He was coughing up blood," he says.

Richardson heard Kubek gasp, "get me to the hospital. I can't breathe." When Kubek was taken off the field, the crowd gave him a standing O. It was not much consolation to the Yankees. Instead of two outs and nobody on, the Pirates had two on and nobody out. Then, after Groat had lined a single to left, scoring Cimoli, Stengel made another fateful move. With no one out, men on first and second and New York leading 7-5, the situation called for the batter, Skinner, to bunt. But Stengel had another hunch, and though Shantz could field anything—"Bobby was probably the greatest fielding pitcher in the history of baseball," says Brown—the manager lifted him for Coates.

The Pirates were euphoric. "Bobby Shantz had dazzled us," Groat says.

Skinner's sacrifice bunt was fielded cleanly by Clete Boyer, but it moved Virdon to third, Groat to second. After Nelson flied out to Maris, with Virdon holding at third, Clemente came to bat with two outs. What happened next is now a part of 1960 World Series lore. Clemente hit a slow chopper toward first. Skowron backhanded it and looked to throw to Coates covering first, but Coates was not there. It is the Series moment that Richardson remembers best. "Routine play!" he says. "Any ball to the right side of the infield, the pitcher covers first."

The inning should have been over, the score still 7-5, Yankees. Instead, Virdon scored from third, making it 7-6. Groat was on third and Clemente on first as catcher Hal Smith walked to the plate. In the stands, Virdon's wife, Shirley, was sitting next to Smith's wife, also named Shirley, when Coates fired a fastball. Smith swung and missed. Coates threw a second heater to the same spot, and Smith launched it on a 420-foot flight over the leftfield wall. All of Forbes went up in a roar. Shirley Smith threw her camera high into the air, and Shirley Virdon reached out to catch it.

Smith was rounding second before it dawned on him what he had done. "I looked over, and people were dancing on the dugout," he recalls. "They were dancing in the stands and screaming and hugging and jumping up and down all over the ballpark. I remember thinking, *Boy, this is something!*"

Groat and Clemente met Smith at the plate, and both yelled to him above the din, "You won the game! You won the game!"

Pittsburgh's euphoria disappeared, of course, when New York roared back in the ninth to tie the score. As the Pirates sat in the dugout, waiting for Maz to hit, a saddened Smith said to Skinner, "Bob, I guess I wasn't destined to be a hero."

Forty years have come and gone since Mazeroski hit the Home Run, and it has remained a part of Pittsburgh's mythology, as big and vivid now as when it happened. It left its imprint on many lives. Stengel did not survive it as Yankees skipper. Many sportswriters speculated during the Series that the 70-year-old Stengel would retire after the last game, but he wanted to stay after suffering the bitterest loss of his career. At his final press conference, five days later, he said, "They have paid me off in full and told me my services are not desired any longer by this club."

Ralph Houk took his place and led the Yankees to two world titles, in '61 and '62. Seeing Mazeroski years later, Houk kidded him, "If it weren't for you, I might not have got that job."

Some of Maz's former teammates think that, in a perverse way, the Home Run has prevented him from gaining induction into the Hall of Fame. "That's all people remember about him," says Groat.

There is considerably more to remember about Mazeroski as a player. Bill James, the guru of baseball statistics, has developed a numerical system for judging fielders, and his conclusion is unequivocal: "I have no doubt that Mazeroski is the premier defensive second baseman in the history of baseball, and I would list him among the five best defensive players of all time." James puts him in the company of Ozzie Smith, Honus Wagner and Johnny Bench. Mazeroski was a .260 lifetime hitter, but he had 2,016 hits over 17 seasons, and no doubt he prevented more runs with his glove than most major leaguers have scored. Like many of his teammates and many fans who saw him play, Mazeroski hopes the Veterans Committee will vote him into the Hall.

Mazeroski is sitting in the living room of his house in Panama City, Fla., which he shares with his wife, Milene, whom he met through Murtaugh and married in 1958. The old second baseman spends his days fishing for striped bass and playing golf. A shy, humble man, protective of his privacy, he is not one for indulging in nostalgia.

Every year since 1985, on the anniversary of the Home Run, several hundred people have congregated on the Pitt campus at the site where Forbes Field stood until 1970 and where a part of the centerfield wall remains. At 1 P.M., the time Game 7 began, they start listening to a tape of the game's radio broadcast. At 3:36 P.M., sure enough, the announcer calls the Home Run.

Where the wall in left center used to be, a bronze plaque embedded in a sidewalk marks the spot where the ball sailed out to win the World Series. Mazeroski has never attended the ritual rebroadcast of the game. He has trouble fathoming all the fuss. He shifts in his chair at home. "Forty years ago!" he says. "I never dreamed when it happened that people would still be talking about it 40 years later. It has seemed to grow and grow and grow. Amazing, really amazing."

What he appreciates is that he was blessed to live the oldest of youthful dreams. As a boy in Skunk Hollow, he would go down to the highway with an empty bucket, fill it with stones and trudge back up the hill. He would then spend hours whacking the stones with broken broom handles.

"That is so clear in my mind, throwing those stones up and hitting them," he says. "All summer long. I didn't have anybody to play with. I'd hit it so far for a single, so far for a double, so far for a home run. I was Babe Ruth. Always. You always got in a situation when it was the seventh game of the World Series, everybody's counting on you. Then you hit the home run. I was no different from any other boy doing that."

Just one difference, really. He nods his white-thatched head.

"I got to do it in real life," he says.

ACKNOWLEDGMENTS

The best time that I had in editing *The Pirates Reader* was at the beginning, when I visited *The Sporting News* archives, the National Baseball Hall of Fame Library, and the research room at PNC Park. A good part of the fun was seeing old friends again and making new friends. I would now like to thank them personally for all their practical help and good counsel.

I'm grateful to Steve Gietshier and Jim Meier of the Historical Records office at *The Sporting News;* to Tim Wiles and Rachael Kepner of the Hall of Fame Library; and to Jim Trdinich, Mike McNally, and Dan Hart of the Pittsburgh Baseball Club. I would also like to thank, for their long-distance help, Marilyn Holt of the Pennsylvania Room in the Carnegie Library; Brian Butko, editor of the *Western Pennsylvania History* magazine; Tom White of the Western Pennsylvania Historical Society; and Dennis DeValeria and Jim Haller of the Forbes Field chapter of the Society of American Baseball Research.

My special gratitude goes to David Welky and Randy Roberts, editors of *The Steelers Reader*, for sharing their experiences and their invaluable sources; to Niels Aaboe, my editor at the University of Pittsburgh Press, for his constant good cheer and steady guidance, and to his intern, James J. Stitt for coming through in the pinch. Thanks also to Deborah Meade of the Press for the care she took in editing the text. I also owe an immense debt to Sally O'Leary of the Pittsburgh Pirates Alumni Association for making it possible for me to contact former Pirate players, who were always gracious and generous in responding to my requests.

I wish to give my deepest gratitude to Eileen Glass for her remarkable skill and dedication in preparing the manuscript and for her warm friendship in listening to my concerns and getting me through the process in spite of myself.

And, finally, I would like to give my loving gratitude to my wife, Anita, who went with me on all the trips, listened to all my baseball stories along the way, and still managed to hold on to her sanity.